1993

This volume presents the most recent trends in Mendelssohn research, examining three broad categories – reception history, historical and critical essays, and case studies of particular compositions. Much of the book depends on a wealth of primary nineteenth-century documents, including little-known autograph manuscripts, letters, and sketches of the composer.

Four studies consider various facets of Mendelssohn reception in the nineteenth and twentieth centuries. Friedhelm Krummacher considers the abiding popularity of Mendelssohn's music in England, while Peter Ward Jones reviews Mendelssohn's business dealings with English publishers; Donald Mintz examines the composer's posthumous reputation from the perspective of the revolutionary agenda of mid-nineteenth-century Germany; and Lawrence Kramer considers dynamic multiple layers of meaning in the *Calm Sea and Prosperous Voyage* Overture and *The First Walpurgisnight*. Four essays, by Judith Silber Ballan, J. Rigbie Turner, Wm. A. Little, and David Brodbeck, treat Mendelssohn's relationships with A. B. Marx, E. Devrient, Franz Liszt, and Frederick William IV. Finally, two studies by R. Larry Todd and Christa Jost focus on two major piano works, the Preludes and Fugues op. 35 and the *Variations sérieuses* op. 54.

Mendelssohn Studies

Mendelssohn Studies

Edited by

R. LARRY TODD

CAMBRIDGE
UNIVERSITY PRESS

Published by the Press Syndicate of the University of Cambridge
The Pitt Building, Trumpington Street, Cambridge CB2 1RP
40 West 20th Street, New York, NY 10011–4211, USA
10 Stamford Road, Oakleigh, Victoria 3166, Australia

First published 1992

Printed in Great Britain at the University Press, Cambridge

A catalogue record for this book is available from the British Library

Library of Congress cataloguing in publication data

Mendelssohn studies / edited by R. Larry Todd.
    p.   cm.
  ISBN 0–521–41776–7 (hardback)
   1. Mendelssohn-Bartholdy, Felix. 1809–1847. I. Todd, R. Larry.
ML410.M5M63 1992
780'.92 – dc20 91–34370 CIP MN

ISBN 0 521 41776 7 hardback

Contents

List of illustrations	*page*	viii
Preface		xi
Acknowledgments		xiii
1	A winter of discontent: Mendelssohn and the *Berliner Domchor*	1
	DAVID BRODBECK	
2	In mutual reflection: historical, biographical, and structural aspects of Mendelssohn's *Variations sérieuses*	33
	CHRISTA JOST	
3	*Felix culpa*: Goethe and the image of Mendelssohn	64
	LAWRENCE KRAMER	
4	Composition as accommodation? On Mendelssohn's music in relation to England	80
	FRIEDHELM KRUMMACHER	
5	Mendelssohn and Liszt	106
	WM. A. LITTLE	
6	1848, anti-Semitism, and the Mendelssohn reception	126
	DONALD MINTZ	
7	Marxian programmatic music: a stage in Mendelssohn's musical development	149
	JUDITH SILBER BALLAN	
8	*Me voilà perruqué*: Mendelssohn's Six Preludes and Fugues op. 35 reconsidered	162
	R. LARRY TODD	
9	Mendelssohn's letters to Eduard Devrient: filling in some gaps	200
	J. RIGBIE TURNER	
10	Mendelssohn and his English publishers	240
	PETER WARD JONES	
Index		256

Illustrations

1.1.   Exemplar of the Prussian *Agende*, revised for Berlin   *pages* 12–13
        Cathedral, 1843; Oxford, Bodleian Library, M. Deneke
        Mendelssohn, c. 21, item 76; reprinted with permission.

1.2.   Harmonization of Psalm 24 (melody copied from *Die*   14
        Psalmen Davids, nach Frantzösischer Melodey in Teutsche
        Reymen gebracht durch D. Ambrosium Lobwasser [Amsterdam,
        1696]). From vol. 38^2 of the *Mendelssohn Nachlass*
        autographs in Kraków, Biblioteca Jagiellońska; reprinted
        with permission.

2.1.   *Album-Beethoven* (Vienna: Pietro Mechetti, 1841), title page;   36
        Berlin, Stiftung Preussischer Kulturbesitz.

2.2.   Mendelssohn, *Variations sérieuses*, op. 54, autograph;   48
        Kraków, Biblioteca Jagiellońska, *Mendelssohn Nachlass*,
        vol. 35, pagina 1 (23/25).

2.3.   Mendelssohn, *Variations sérieuses* op. 54, autograph;   50–53
        Kraków, Biblioteca Jagiellońska, *Mendelssohn Nachlass*, vol.
        35: (a) pagina 2, with pasteover removed; (b) pag. 2, with
        pasteover; (c) pag. 3, with pasteover removed; and (d)
        pag. 3, with pasteover.

2.4.   Mendelssohn, *Variations sérieuses* op. 54, autograph;   55
        Kraków, Biblioteca Jagiellońska, *Mendelssohn Nachlass*, vol.
        35, p. 33, with deleted Variation 14.

8.1.   Carl Czerny, *Die Schule des Fugenspiels* (Vienna: Ant.   181
        Diabelli, 1836); Chicago, The Newberry Library.

8.2.   Carl Czerny, Autograph letter to Mendelssohn, Vienna, 8   183
        April 1836; M. Deneke Mendelssohn Collection, Green
        Books V, No. 63, Bodleian Library, Oxford.

8.3. Mendelssohn, Autograph first page of "Etude" version of   189
      the Prelude in E minor op. 35 no. 1; Tokyo, Musashino
      Academia Musicae.
9.1. Letter from Mendelssohn to Eduard Devrient, 5 January   211
      1832, The Pierpont Morgan Library, New York

Preface

Continuing the Cambridge series of volumes devoted to individual composers, *Mendelssohn Studies* is intended to offer a sampling of present trends in research about Felix Mendelssohn Bartholdy, whose life and music are currently enjoying a healthy resurgence of interest in the scholarly literature. Arranged alphabetically by author, the ten studies divide into three basic groups, organized according to *Rezeptionsgeschichte*, historical/critical essays, and case studies. Much of the volume depends fundamentally on the truly remarkable wealth – by no means yet fully catalogued or investigated – of surviving primary sources, including the composer's manuscripts, sketches, correspondence, and many other materials. Throughout his short career Mendelssohn endeavored to collect systematically his manuscripts and correspondence, much of which he had bound in volumes, almost as if he intended to preserve for future historians a careful record of his life's work. The survival of these precious materials has facilitated a critical revaluation of Mendelssohn and has opened up new avenues of inquiry about his music and central role in the European concert life of the 1830s and 1840s.

Probably no major composer of the nineteenth century has had as unpredictable and mercurial a posthumous reception as Mendelssohn. Lionized and subjected to a kind of cult worship after his death in 1847, he soon fell victim to Wagner's mid-century critique, *Das Judenthum in der Musik*. What is more, Mendelssohn's music, characterized in part by classicist/historicist tendencies, by an emphasis on symmetry, and, in general, by an avoidance of dramatic modes of composition, was measured against Wagnerian criteria, and inevitably suffered in the comparison. During the twentieth century, of course, Mendelssohn's statue in Leipzig was destroyed and his music banned by the Nazis. The post-war era now has seen continuing attempts to reconstruct Mendelssohn's work. The eventual outcome of this process remains unclear, though the essential significance of Mendelssohn's influence on the development of nineteenth-century music cannot be denied.

Four studies consider various facets of Mendelssohn's reception. Donald Mintz examines the posthumous reputation of the composer from the perspective of the revolutionary agenda of mid-century Germany. Friedhelm Krummacher considers the popularity of Mendelssohn's music in England, while in a related article Peter Ward Jones reviews Mendelssohn's dealings with English publishers. Lawrence Kramer, endeavoring to strip away encrusted layers of the Mendelssohn reception, proposes that in two works inspired by Goethe, the *Calm Sea and Prosperous Voyage* Overture and the cantata *The First Walpurgisnight*, Mendelssohn's stylistic approach was a dynamic, not static, one, and that these works offer multiple layers of interpretation.

A second group of four essays examines Mendelssohn's circle by focussing on his relationships with Adolf Bernhard Marx, Eduard Devrient, Franz Liszt, and the court of Frederick William IV. Judith Silber Ballan examines the influence of the theorist Marx on Mendelssohn's work of the later 1820s, and demonstrates that the *Midsummer Night's Dream* Overture, *Calm Sea and Prosperous Voyage* Overture, and "Reformation" Symphony in part were an attempt to respond to Marx's views of programmatic music propounded in the *Berliner Allgemeine musikalische Zeitung*. J. Rigbie Turner, noting that early on Mendelssohn was ill served by his editors, reconsiders the Mendelssohn-Devrient *Briefwechsel*, and restores important passages deliberately omitted by Devrient when the letters first appeared in the nineteenth century. Wm. A. Little reviews in detail for the first time Mendelssohn's relationship with Franz Liszt. And, through a careful archival study, David Brodbeck examines Mendelssohn's expectations and frustrations at the Berlin court of Frederick William IV, where Mendelssohn was appointed Generalmusikdirektor in 1842 and where he composed several sacred works for use in the liturgy of Berlin Cathedral.

Finally, two case studies are devoted to two major piano works of Mendelssohn. R. Larry Todd reconstructs the genesis of the Preludes and Fugues op. 35 and considers the stylistic ramifications of the first prelude and fugue, in E minor. Christa Jost studies the composing score of the *Variations sérieuses* op. 54 and reviews its complex historical resonances.

As familiar as Mendelssohn's music was during the nineteenth century, the various contexts in which it was created have become, with time, increasingly unfamiliar. *Mendelssohn Studies* seeks to elucidate only a few critical aspects of Mendelssohn's life and work, thereby to stimulate further the twentieth-century Mendelssohn revival.

Durham, N.C.

June 1991

R.L.T.

Acknowledgments

Several individuals have contributed to seeing *Mendelssohn Studies* through the press, and the editor is deeply indebted to them: at the Press, Penny Souster, for continuing editorial advice, and Ann Lewis and Caroline Murray, for the copyediting and production; J. Michael Cooper and J. Bradford Robinson, for undertaking the translations of the essays by Friedhelm Krummacher and Christa Jost; J. Michael Cooper and Anna Harwell, for preparing the index and attending to a host of editorial details; and to Donna Lynn and Tatsuhiko Itoh for assistance of various kinds. Several papers were originally presented at a Mendelssohn Symposium held at Amherst College on 2 December 1989, made possible by the John Tennant and Elizabeth Collins Adams Fund. The editor wishes to thank Dr. Marian Zwiercan of the Biblioteca Jagiellońska, Kraków, and Professors Naotaka Fukui and Takayasu Furusho of the Musashino Academia Musicae, Tokyo, for assistance in preparing facsimiles of Mendelssohn's autographs. Several institutions contributed illustrations for this volume, and their permission to reproduce them is gratefully acknowledged here: Berlin, Stiftung Preussischer Kulturbesitz; Chicago, Newberry Library; Kraków, Biblioteca Jagiellońska; Oxford, Bodleian Library; and Tokyo, Musashino Academia Musicae.

1 A winter of discontent: Mendelssohn and the *Berliner Domchor*

DAVID BRODBECK

In his monograph *The Music of the Nineteenth Century and its Culture* (1855), the critic and theorist Adolph Bernhard Marx lamented the current state of church music in Protestant Germany:

> In the Protestant places of worship, grand orchestral and choral performances become every day more rare. As regards, in particular, the liturgy of the united Evangelical church of Prussia, it is impossible, if considered from a musical point of view, to look upon it otherwise than as a most meagre and, in fact, unartistic and artistically inefficient substitute for that which the music of the Lutheran church once was. The only new institution of any importance in this sphere of art is the Berlin cathedral choir, [which] has been instrumental in the production of a series of compositions written specially for it, as well as in the revival of works of a more ancient date, particularly those of the middle ages, by Palestrina and others. On the whole, it must therefore be acknowledged that church music – as a matter of course – is both less in extent and intrinsic power than it was in the preceding period.[1]

Coming in the midst of a mostly gloomy report, Marx's positive remarks about the Berlin cathedral choir are all the more worthy of note. This ensemble had in effect been created especially for Felix Mendelssohn, in connection with his appointment in 1842 as *Generalmusikdirektor* to the court of King Frederick William IV. In the monarch's own words, the choir was to be an "instrument" upon which Mendelssohn was to make music.[2] We shall

The research for this essay was made possible through generous grants from the National Endowment for the Humanities, the American Philosophical Society, and both the Faculty of Arts and Sciences and Central Research Development Fund, University of Pittsburgh.

1 Adolph Bernhard Marx, *The Music of the Nineteenth Century and its Culture*, trans. August Heinrich Wehrhan and C. Natalia Macfarren (London, 1855), p. 55 (*Die Musik des neunzehnten Jahrhunderts und ihre Pflege* [Leipzig, 1855]).

2 See Mendelssohn's letter of 23 November 1842 to Karl Klingemann, in *Letters of Felix Mendelssohn Bartholdy from 1833 to 1847* [hereafter cited as *Letters from 1833 to 1847*], ed. Paul and Carl Mendelssohn Bartholdy, trans. Lady Wallace (London, 1863), p. 277.

1

examine the compositions that Mendelssohn made for this group in due course; first, we must consider the liturgical and aesthetic constraints under which he worked.

I

One of Frederick William's first decisions after his coronation in June 1840 was to draw to his court all the leading figures in German arts and letters. For advice in these matters, he relied on his friend Christian Karl Josias von Bunsen, a noted diplomat and scholar, who in October proposed an ambitious musical plan:

> It is a matter of reintroducing the most beautiful and noble music into life – not only into the general life of the people, but also into the social life of the higher and highest classes of the most musical people in the world. It seems to me that this can come about if three aims that are now entirely unfulfilled can be realized:
> 1. An outstanding educational institution for all music ...
> 2. Performance of really appropriate music for the Divine Service ...
> 3. Performance of great old and new oratorios ...
>
> Is that not enough for one man and master? I rather think it would be too much for anyone but Felix Mendelssohn.[3]

The king soon acted on Bunsen's advice. In November 1840 the Under Secretary for the Royal Household, Ludwig von Massow, invited Mendelssohn to assume the directorship of the musical class at the Academy of Arts, which was to be developed into a genuine conservatory, and to lead each year several concerts of oratorios and symphonies. Doubting the court's will to form a conservatory, Mendelssohn hesitated to accept the offer. In May 1841 Massow proposed a compromise calling for the composer merely to agree to a one-year trial residency in Berlin while plans for the founding of the school were laid. Still, negotiations dragged on over the particulars of the appointment, and in August it was an exasperated composer who came at last to Berlin, having as yet received no salary and still without announcement of title or duties but presumably wishing to commence his one-year term as soon as possible – that is, to get it behind him. Only in September was Mendelssohn made a Kapellmeister and charged with presenting several concerts in the forthcoming season.[4]

3 Letter of 30 October 1840 from Bunsen to Frederick William IV, in *Bunsen aus seinen Briefen*, vol. II, pp. 142–3; quoted in Eric Werner, *Mendelssohn: a New Image of the Composer and His Age*, trans. Dika Newlin (London, 1963), p. 371. See also Bunsen's letter of 31 October 1840 to Alexander von Humboldt, *Briefen*, vol. II, pp. 143–4, partially trans. in Werner, p. 371.

4 Cabinet order of 8 September 1841 to the Minister for Religious Affairs, Health, and Education J. A. F. Eichhorn: "Nach den Anträgen in Ihrem Bericht vom 27. d. M. will Ich 1.

As Mendelssohn had suspected, little progress was made during the ensuing months toward the founding of a conservatory. Indeed, by June 1842 Frederick William had placed his plans for a comprehensive music school in abeyance and instead taken up Bunsen's call to employ Mendelssohn in the task of providing "really appropriate music" for the church. "My intention," the king declared in a cabinet order to his Minister for Religious Affairs, Health, and Education, J. A. F. Eichhorn:

> is directed primarily at the revival and advancement of singing in the Evangelical Church, and here would be offered the broad and adequate field of activity that Mendelssohn desires, as I intend to place him in charge of all Evangelical Church music in the monarchy. It will be a question of rescuing the past, to some extent, the traditional, from oblivion, and making it suitable for the needs of the present. . . . I therefore want first of all to begin only with the founding in Berlin of a school of singing, which is to be placed under the chief leadership of Mendelssohn. From this school then is to be formed a choir, which would be used for singing in the cathedral. . . . The main thing is to interest Kapellmeister Mendelssohn in this idea and to solicit his suggestions concerning the means suitable to its realization.[5]

In the event, Mendelssohn had no interest in such a position. It was not merely because he had little desire, as he put it to Massow, to supervise the work of "all the present organists, choristers, schoolmasters, etc.," or because he doubted whether appropriate regulations could be enacted and adequate resources found to ensure a proper training of the various cathedral choirs.[6] No, Mendelssohn must have resisted also because he considered himself

---

den Komponisten Dr. Felix Mendelssohn zum Kapellmeister ernennen und die Zahlung des ihm bewilligten Gehaltes vom 1. Mai d. J. ab genehmigen. Der beabsichtigten Veranstaltung akademischer Konzerte schenke ich Beifall und gestatte 2. dass dazu ein Königlicher Konzertsaal benutzt, 3. in demselben ein Orgel zum Gebrauch bei den Konzerten aufgestellt und 4. Meine Kapelle und die Solisten des Theater-Gesang-Personals zur Mitwirkung herangezogen werden" (quoted in Wilhelm Altmann, "Zur Geschichte der Königlichen Preussischen Hofkapelle," *Die Musik* 3/21 [1903/4], 212–13).

5 "Meine Intention ist hauptsächlich auf Belebung und Förderung des evangelischen Kirchengesanges gerichtet, und hier dürfte sich für die von dem Mendelssohn gewünschte Wirksamkeit ein weites und hinreichendes Feld eröffnen lassen, indem Ich ihn an die Spitze aller evangelischen Kirchen-Musik der Monarchie zu stellen beabsichtige. Es wird darauf ankommen, das Alte, zum Theil Traditionelle der Vergessenheit zu entreißen und es dem gegenwärtigen Bedürfniß anzupassen; . . . Von diesen Ansichten ausgehend will Ich daher zunächst nur mit der Errichtung einer Gesangschule in Berlin beginnen, und solche unter der Ober-Leitung Mendelssohns gestellt wißen. Aus dieser Gesangschule wird dann ein Chor zu bilden sein, welcher bei dem Kirchengesang im Dom . . . Es kommt nun darauf an, den Kapellmeister Mendelssohn für diese Idee zu interessieren und seine Vorschläge über die geeigneten Mittel zu deren Verwicklichung zu vernehmen." Quoted in Georg Schünemann, "Zur Geschichte des Berliner Domchors: Ein vergessenes Jubiläum," *Die Musikpflege* 6 (1935/6), 382.

6 Letter of 23 October 1842, in *Letters from 1833 to 1847*, p. 271.

ill-suited to the task. Whereas the king, like his friend Bunsen, believed he knew what constituted "appropriate" music for the church – above all, choral works in the style of Palestrina and other *altklassische* Italian composers – Mendelssohn was less certain, troubled by the conflicting demands of functionality and artistic expression. As he had put it some years earlier in a letter to Albert Bauer, a Lutheran pastor in Belzig:

> Real church music, that is, for the evangelical Divine Service, which could have its place within the ecclesiastical ceremony, seems to me impossible, not merely because I am not at all able to see where music is to be introduced during the service, but because I am unable to conceive of this place. . . . As yet – even forgetting the Prussian liturgy, which cuts off everything of the kind and will probably not be permanent or far-reaching – I have been unable to understand how for us music may be made to become an integrated part of the service and not merely a concert which, to a more or less degree, stimulates piety.[7]

Thus, far from welcoming the offer to be placed at the head of Evangelical music, Mendelssohn determined to meet with the king and to take leave of his duties in Berlin altogether.[8]

The desired interview took place on 26 October 1842 but did not have the intended consequences. "The King must have been in an especially good humor," the composer wrote to his friend Karl Klingemann:

> for, instead of finding him angry with me, I had never seen him so amiable and really confidential. To my farewell speech he replied: he could not, to be sure, compel me to remain but that he wanted to tell me that it would cause him heartfelt regret if I left him; that, by doing so, all the plans which he had formed from my presence in Berlin would be frustrated, and that I should make a tear which he could never again mend.[9]

The king then spelled out his intention to establish at the cathedral, under Mendelssohn's leadership, a select choir and small orchestra. Against his better judgment, the composer accepted this position, provided that he be permitted

---

7 "Eine wirkliche Kirchenmusik, d.h. für den evangelischen Gottesdienst, die während der kirchlichen Feier ihren Platz fände, scheint mir unmöglich, und zwar nicht blos, weil ich durchaus nicht sehe, an welcher Stelle des Gottesdienstes die Musik eingreifen sollte, sondern weil ich mir überhaupt diese Stelle gar nicht denken kann. . . . Bis jetzt weiß ich nicht – auch wenn ich von der Preussischen Liturgie absehe, die alles Derartige abschneidet, und wohl nicht bleibend, oder gar weitergehend sein wird – wie es zu machen sein sollte, daß bei uns die Musik ein integrierender Theil des Gottesdienstes, und nicht blos ein Concert werde, das mehr oder weniger zur Andacht anrege" (letter of 12 January 1835; translation after *Letters from 1833 to 1847*, p. 62).

8 Mendelssohn requested Massow's aid in obtaining the meeting in a letter of 23 October 1842 (*Letters from 1833 to 1847*, pp. 271–3).

9 Letter of 23 November 1842; translation after *Letters from 1833 to 1847*, p. 276.

to remain in Leipzig until the Music Institute of the Court and Cathedral Church, as the establishment was to be named, had been founded.[10]

Three weeks after this extraordinary interview, Frederick William named Mendelssohn *Generalmusikdirektor* for church music and instructed his advisors Massow and Count Wilhelm von Redern, the Intendant-General of Court Music, to proceed with the formation of the Institute.[11] The instrumental ensemble was to consist simply of twenty-four to thirty musicians selected from the court orchestra. The choir, by contrast, had to be established. In the ensuing months, under the leadership of Major J. D. C. Einbeck, a noted developer of military vocal ensembles who was assigned to assist Mendelssohn, Massow, and Redern, a choir of eighteen boy sopranos (plus five reserves), eighteen boy altos (plus another five reserves), nine tenors, and fifteen basses was formed and placed under the direction of August Neithardt (conductor of the existing cathedral choir) and Eduard Grell (cathedral organist and conductor of the choir of the Royal Chapel).[12]

This flurry of activity generated considerable excitement in the court, and led to Massow's announcement to Mendelssohn in March 1843 that the choir would be ready by the following winter.[13] The composer received this report with skepticism and expressed his reservations about giving up a productive musical life in Leipzig for a potentially unproductive one in Berlin. Einbeck had in fact told him that the choir might need a full year to attain maturity. Furthermore – what was probably more disturbing – nothing had yet been settled about the participation of the instrumentalists from the court orchestra.[14] Accordingly, though the Institute officially came into its existence on 1

10 Mendelssohn's lengthy account of the interview is described in *ibid.*, pp. 275–9; see also his letter of 28 October 1842 to the king (*Letters from 1833 to 1847*, pp. 273–5).

11 Cabinet order of 22 November 1842; Mendelssohn's copy is preserved as item 127 in volume XVI of the so-called Green Books (GB), in which Mendelssohn collected his correspondence; all twenty-seven volumes are preserved in the Bodleian Library, Oxford, as a part of the M. Deneke Mendelssohn collection of Mendelssohniana. The author wishes to thank Dr. Hans-Joachim Schulze (Leipzig) and Dr. Peter Ward Jones (Oxford) for their kind assistance in transcribing a number of documents from this collection. The king also wrote directly to the composer of his nomination; this letter is preserved in GB XVI, item 126, and quoted in Mendelssohn's letter of 5 December 1842 to his brother Paul (*Letters from 1833 to 1847*, p. 283).

12 On the establishment of the choir, see especially A. Richard Scheumann, "Major Einbeck: Der Organisator der Militär-Kirchenchöre unter Friedrich Wilhelm III. und des Königlichen Hof- und Domchores zu Berlin," *Die Musik* 7 (1907/8), 323–34; and Max Thomas, "Heinrich August Neithardt" (diss., Berlin, 1959), pp. 75–8.

13 Unpublished letter of 27 March 1843 (GB XVII, item 161).

14 Letter to Massow of 31 March 1843, quoted in Richard Scheumann, "Briefe berühmter Komponisten aus dem Archiv des Königlichen Hof- und Domchores zu Berlin," *Die Musik* 8 (1908/9), 259; a copy is preserved in the Bodleian Library, Oxford (M. Deneke Mendelssohn c. 18, item 5).

May, and the choir was able to perform the choral liturgy for the first time the following Sunday,[15] much remained to be settled.

Mendelssohn must have suffered an unpleasant experience of *déjà vu*. Just as negotiations for his original position at the court had dragged on for months into the summer of 1841, so now did negotiations concerning his relationship to the royal orchestra continue through the summer of 1843. Mendelssohn's encounters with the orchestra in the preceding two seasons had been strained, and the composer did not, as he put it to Massow in June, relish the idea of having to deal with "reluctantly obeying and contradicting subordinates."[16] At the same time, the composer was apprehensive about his prospective relationship with the Kapellmeisters Carl Henning and Wilhelm Taubert, who had only recently initiated a series of subscription concerts and now would have to give way.[17] At a parley held on 10 July it was agreed that Mendelssohn would each year lead the court orchestra in several "Symphonic Soirées" and in performances of two oratorios, and that on high holidays thirty-six members of the group would be assigned to accompany the congregational singing at the cathedral. The bureaucracy dragged its feet, however, and not until 2 September did the king confirm these arrangements in a cabinet order.[18]

It was necessary to establish not only the Institute but also the role of music within the liturgy. As we have seen, the king's intention was to "revive" and "advance" the singing in the church by reclaiming the musical practices of the past and making them "suitable for the needs of the present." This program required, first of all, liturgical revisions that would allow a richer musical treatment than was possible under the rubrics of the so-called Prussian Agende of 1829, which limited congregational participation to the singing of a few chorales and permitted only *a cappella* choral settings of the prescribed texts

---

15 According to a report by Redern to the Cathedral Ministerium on 1 May 1843; quoted from the Berliner Dom-Akten, D 5, 185, 2, in Thomas, "Neithardt," p. 79.

16 Letter of 23 June 1843; quoted from the Brandenburg-preußisches Haus-Archiv 509 in Thomas, "Neithardt," p. 80. The letter continues: "Ich möchte mich nicht an die Spitze von Leuten gestellt sehen, die mich nicht an ihrer Spitze wünschen."

17 See Altmann, "Geschichte der Hofkapelle," pp. 223–4.

18 This "*zehntausendjährige* affair," as Mendelssohn described it, in an ironic reference to the celebration in August of the 1000-year anniversary of the founding of the German Reich (at which he had been requested to make his début with the Domchor as conductor and composer), may be followed in Massow's letters of 1, 16, and 24 July (GB XVIII, items 1, 22, and 34) and in Mendelssohn's reports of 21 and 26 July to his brother Paul (*Letters from 1833 to 1847*, pp. 304, 306–7). Mendelssohn's copy of the cabinet order is preserved in GB XVIII, item 88; it was sent by Massow in his letter of 7 September 1843 (GB XVIII, item 97).

(see Table 1.1). To understand the nature of the king's reforms, a short digression to review the musical practices in the Agende may be helpful.[19]

During the Enlightenment, the rich worship patterns of "high" Orthodox Lutheranism – whose classic expression may be seen in the liturgical practices of J. S. Bach's Leipzig – gave way to informal services comprising little more than unembellished hymns, moralistic prayers, and preaching. Stirrings of reform could be felt among musicians in the first years of the nineteenth century, when, for example, Carl Friedrich Zelter, director of the Berlin Singakademie, called for an enriched style of music and liturgy for the Holy Communion. A dissatisfaction with current circumstances was shared by no less a figure than Frederick William III, who, having been impressed by the ritual and music of the Russian Orthodox Church, established two commissions to consider liturgical reforms. At first work was hampered by the demands of the Napoleonic Wars; but shortly after the Congress of Vienna the king undertook two major religious initiatives: in 1816 he drafted a formal liturgy for the use in the *Hof- und Domkirche* in Berlin and the garrison churches of Berlin and Potsdam, and in the following year, during the tercentenary of Luther's posting of the Ninety-Five Theses, he called for a unification of the Lutheran and Reformed (or Calvinist) congregations within his realm into a single Evangelical Church of the Union.

Frederick William revised his liturgy a number of times during the ensuing years. The texts and rather modest musical demands of the first versions showed the influence of Reformed practices, which is not surprising since the Hohenzollern dynasty had traditionally professed Calvinism. A dramatic change in the king's perspective is evidenced by a new order of worship introduced at the Berlin garrison church in October 1821. This liturgy was the first to be ordered according to historical Lutheran practices, and it formed the basis of both the *Kirchenagende für die Königlich-Preußische Armee* (published in December 1821) and the closely related *Kirchenagende für die Hof- und Domkirche in Berlin* (which appeared in print a few months later). The *Musik-Anhang* that was issued with these liturgies consisted of a hodgepodge of simple four-part *a cappella* arrangements, by a variety of Berlin musicians, of psalm tones, a Kyrie adapted from Luther's German Mass of 1526, a Swedish Agnus Dei, several Russian melodies, and even a Gregorian Offertory. The king was especially fond of Russian liturgical music and in 1824 requested a setting of the liturgy from Dmitri Bortniansky, Director of the Imperial

---

19 The best introduction to the music of the Agende is Ulrich Leupold, *Die liturgischen Gesänge der evangelischen Kirche im Zeitalter der Aufklärung und der Romantik* (Kassel, 1933), pp. 110–55.

Table 1.1. *The Prussian Agende*

Role (1829)	1829 Edition	Role (1843)	1843 Revision
		Chor:	Psalm (Introit) Lesser Doxology (Gloria patri)
	Chorale		**Chorale**
Geistliche[a]:	Opening Prayers and Confession of Sins	Geistliche:	Opening Prayers and Confession of Sins
Chor[b]:	*Amen*	Gemeinde[c] und Chor:	Kyrie
Geistliche:	Absolution	Geistliche:	Absolution
Chor:	Lesser Doxology (Gloria patri)	Gemeinde und Chor:	*Amen*
Geistliche:	*Herr, sey uns gnädig.*	Geistliche:	*Ehre sei Gott in der Höhe.*
Chor:	Kyrie	Chor:	*Und Friede auf Erden, und den Menschen ein Wohlgefallen. Amen, Amen, Amen.* [On festivals: Great Doxology]
Geistliche:	*Ehre sei Gott in der Höhe.*	Gemeinde:	"Allein Gott in der Höh'"
Chor:	*Und Friede auf Erden und den Menschen ein Wohlgefallen. Amen, Amen, Amen.* [On festivals: Great Doxology]	Geistliche:	*Der Herr sei mit euch.*
Geistliche:	*Der Herr sei mit euch!*	Gemeinde und Chor:	*Und mit deinem Geiste.*
Chor:	*Und mit deinem Geiste.*	Geistliche:	Prayer before the Epistle (Collect)
Geistliche:	Prayer before the Epistle (Collect)	Gemeinde und Chor:	*Amen*
Chor:	*Amen*	Geistliche:	Epistle
Geistliche:	Epistle	Chor:	Verse (Gradual) – Alleluia
Geistliche:	Verse (Gradual)	Geistliche:	Gospel
Chor:	Alleluia	Gemeinde und Chor:	*Ehre sei Dir, Herr.*
Geistliche:	Gospel	Geistliche:	Creed
Chor:	*Ehre sei Dir, Herr.*		
Geistliche:	Creed		

Table 1.1. (Cont.)

1829 Edition		1843 Revision	
Chor:	*Amen, Amen, Amen.*	Gemeinde und Chor:	*Amen, Amen, Amen.*
	Chorale		**Chorale**
	Sermon		**Sermon**
	Chorale		**Chorale**
Geistliche:	Verse (Offertory)	Geistliche:	Verse (Offertory)
Geistliche:	*Erhebet eure Herzen.*		*Erhebet eure Herzen.*
Chor:	*Wir erheben sie zum Herrn.*	Gemeinde und Chor:	*Wir erheben sie zum Herrn.*
Geistliche:	*Lasset uns danken dem Herrn unserm Gotte.*	Geistliche:	*Lasset uns danken dem Herrn, unserm Gotte.*
Chor:	*Recht und würdig ist es.*	Gemeinde und Chor:	*Recht und würdig ist es.*
Geistliche:	Preface	Geistliche:	Preface
Chor:	Heilig (Sanctus)	Gemeinde und Chor:	Heilig (Sanctus)
Geistliche:	General Prayer	Geistliche:	General Prayer
Chor:	*Amen.*	Gemeinde und Chor:	*Amen.*
Geistliche:	Our Father	Geistliche:	Our Father
		Gemeinde und Chor:	*Amen, Amen, Amen.*
			[On festivals: "Herr Gott, dich loben wir"]
Geistliche:	Blessing	Geistliche:	Blessing
Chor:	*Amen, Amen, Amen.*	Gemeinde und Chor:	*Amen, Amen, Amen.*
	Chorale		

[a] Minister [b] Choir [c] Congregation

Chapel in St. Petersburg, who, before his death in 1825, supplied some but not all of the pieces. For the *Agende für die evangelische Kirche in den Königlich-Preußischen Landen*, which, after much acrimony, was gradually introduced throughout the state church beginning in 1829, Zelter was commissioned to produce a new musical supplement. The composer, who later described the Agende as "liturgical bunglings" (*liturgische Pfuschereien*), borrowed several responses from the *Musik-Anhang* of 1821–2, included Bortniansky's setting of the so-called Great Doxology, and throughout adopted the popular and devotional chordal style favored by the king. The same style was maintained in the revision of the *Anhang* for men's choir made in 1830 by Zelter's assistant Eduard Grell, which included some additional Russian melodies but otherwise broke no new ground. Thus the disparaging remarks about the Prussian liturgy quoted earlier from Marx's commentary on nineteenth-century Protestant church music and Mendelssohn's letter to Pastor Bauer.

In January 1843, the Cathedral Ministerium met to deliberate on the matter of a new liturgy and by the summer had drafted their revision.[20] The first change affecting the choir consisted in the introduction of an Introit Psalm at the beginning of the service; another, in the singing of the Verse before the Alleluia. At the same time, the congregation gained in importance; whereas the old Agende had reserved all the responses for the choir, these might now be shared with the congregation, which, on certain high festivals, was even called upon to sing the German *Te deum* (Luther's chorale paraphrase "Herr Gott, dich loben wir").

The king especially encouraged the congregation's role in the new liturgy. For example, in a meeting held in July with Eichhorn and the cathedral clerics Ehrenberg and Strauss, he proposed congregational participation in the singing of the Introit and determined that, for this purpose, Mendelssohn ought to resuscitate the cantus firmi of the old Reformed metrical psalters of the sixteenth and seventeenth centuries. In his report of this meeting, Massow

20 See Thomas, "Neithardt," p. 79, and Massow's letter to Mendelssohn (GB XVII, item 32). Massow enclosed his copy of the draft of the liturgy in his letter to Mendelssohn of 1 July 1843; it is preserved in the Bodleian Library, Oxford (M. Deneke Mendelssohn c. 49, item 14). These changes betray the influence of the king and his advisor Bunsen. In a long and extraordinary letter of March 1840 that drew inspiration from the so-called Anglo-Catholic movement emanating from Oxford, Frederick William had revealed to Bunsen what he described as a "Midsummer Night's Dream" of a Prussian "high church" (see Leopold von Ranke, *Aus dem Briefwechsel Friedrich Wilhelms IV. mit Bunsen* [Leipzig, 1873], pp. 46–75). Although Bunsen could not agree with all the particulars of the monarch's plans (*ibid.*, pp. 75–6), he must have been excited by the prospect that the Prussian Agende might now, as he had long advocated, be reformed along the lines of the Book of Common Prayer. Indeed the revised order evinces an English influence, above all in its inclusion of both a complete psalm and the *Te deum*, which are characteristic neither of the Lutheran nor Roman Masses, the natural ancestors of the Agende, but of the Anglican service of Morning Prayer, with its origins in the Roman Office of Matins.

sent Mendelssohn an exemplar of the revised liturgy, whose annotations in the king's hand make vivid the royal preference for an antiphonal performance of the psalm divided between choir and congregation (see Plate 1.1).[21] Frederick William likewise sought to ensure the foundation of an "ecclesiastically proper" instrumental accompaniment for the congregational singing. Again, the exemplar of the liturgy is telling; the annotations respecting the Lied "Allein Gott in der Höh' sei Ehr'" and the "Gesang der Gemeinde" hint at what the king later made explicit: "In order to avoid misunderstanding," he declared in his cabinet order of 2 September, "I determine that in the church music no wind instruments (except trombones etc.) are to be used."[22]

Mendelssohn spent the autumn of 1843 commuting between Berlin, preparing for the first performances of the incidental music to *A Midsummer Night's Dream*, and Leipzig, where he was now winding down his work at the Gewandhaus. In October he obtained from Ehrenberg a list of the psalms for the period from the First Sunday of Advent through Palm Sunday, but in his busy schedule could find little time to devote to his forthcoming work with the Domchor. Thus when Mendelssohn finally moved to Berlin, on 24 November, his portfolio of liturgical works contained nothing more than harmonizations, made in accordance with the king's directive of the previous summer, of seven French melodies that he had copied from a late seventeenth-century monophonic edition of the psalter and which could be used during the first seasons of the church year.[23]

The revised liturgy was celebrated for the first time at the cathedral on 10 December. One witness to this event wrote mockingly in his diary: "Not only without authority, but without rhyme or reason, it is begun. ... The Protestant Church will become utterly depraved! ... Music and singing, divided between the clergy and the laity, many 'Kirie eleisons' and 'Amens.'

---

21 Letter of 12 July 1843 from Massow to Mendelssohn (GB XVIII, item 293); the exemplar is preserved in the Bodleian Library, Oxford (M. Deneke Mendelssohn c. 21, item 76).

22 "Um Mißverständnißen vorzubeugen, bestimme Ich ferner wiederholt, daß bei der unter 1. gedachten Kirchen-Musik keine Blasinstrumente (außer Posaunen etc.) verwendet werden" (GB XVIII, item 88).

23 Ehrenberg enclosed the catalogue in his letter of 17 October 1843 (GB XVIII, item 146). The list itself, with checks next to the psalms for the First Sunday of Advent (no. 24), the First Day of Christmas (no. 2), the Sunday after Christmas (no. 93), New Year's Day (no. 98), the First Sunday after Epiphany (no. 100), Quinquagesima Sunday (no. 31), and Invocavit Sunday (no. 91), is preserved in the Bodleian Library, Oxford (M. Deneke Mendelssohn c. 49, item 14). Mendelssohn's unpublished autograph of the harmonizations, which is dated "Leipzig, d. 13 Nov. 1843" and contained in volume 38² of his *Nachlass* autographs (formerly housed in the Deutsche Staatsbibliothek, Berlin, now found in the Biblioteca Jagiellońska, Kraków [pp. 181–3], comprises settings of each of the checked psalms in Lobwasser's translation of the French psalter (*Die Psalmen Davids, nach Frantzösischer Melodey in Teutsche Reymen gebracht durch D. Ambrosium Lobwasser* [Amsterdam, 1696]).

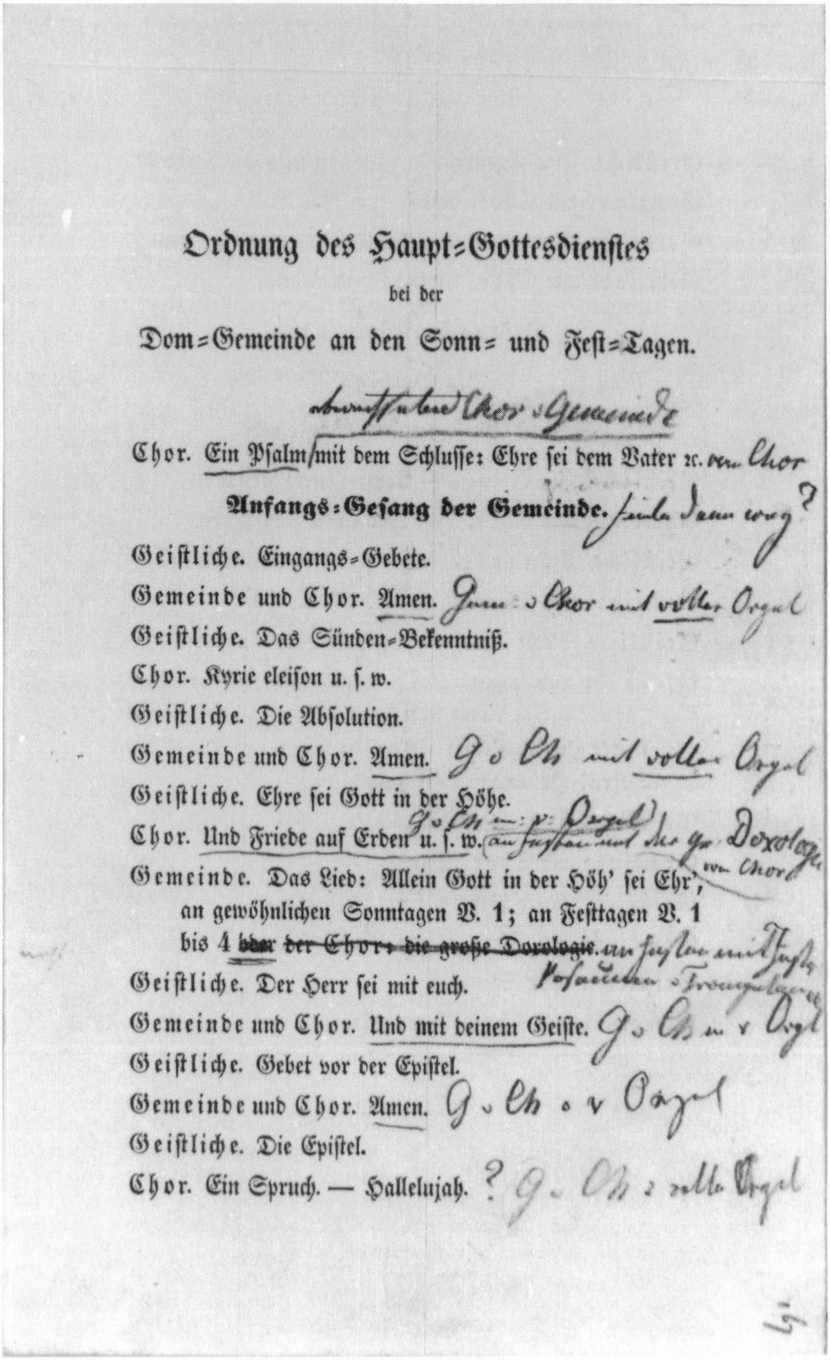

Ordnung des Haupt=Gottesdienstes

bei der

Dom=Gemeinde an den Sonn= und Fest=Tagen.

[handwritten annotation]

Chor. Ein Psalm/mit dem Schlusse: Ehre sei dem Vater rc. *[handwritten: von Chor]*

Anfangs=Gesang der Gemeinde. *[handwritten]*

Geistliche. Eingangs=Gebete.

Gemeinde und Chor. Amen. *[handwritten: Gem. u Chor mit voller Orgel]*

Geistliche. Das Sünden=Bekenntniß.

Chor. Kyrie eleison u. s. w.

Geistliche. Die Absolution.

Gemeinde und Chor. Amen. *[handwritten: G. Ch. mit voller Orgel]*

Geistliche. Ehre sei Gott in der Höhe.

Chor. Und Friede auf Erden u. s. w. *[handwritten]* Doxologie *[von Chor]*

Gemeinde. Das Lied: Allein Gott in der Höh' sei Ehr',
an gewöhnlichen Sonntagen V. 1; an Festtagen V. 1
bis 4 ~~oder der Chor die große Doxologie.~~ *[handwritten]*

Geistliche. Der Herr sei mit euch.

Gemeinde und Chor. Und mit deinem Geiste. *[handwritten: G. Ch. u. Orgel]*

Geistliche. Gebet vor der Epistel.

Gemeinde und Chor. Amen. *[handwritten: G. Ch. u. Orgel]*

Geistliche. Die Epistel.

Chor. Ein Spruch. — Hallelujah. *[handwritten: ? G. Ch. z voller Orgel]*

Geistliche. Das Evangelium. – Gelobet seiest du, o Christe!

Gemeinde und Chor. Amen.

Geistliche. Der Glaube.

Gemeinde und Chor. Amen. Amen. Amen.

Gesang der Gemeinde.

Die Predigt.

Schluß-Gesang der Gemeinde.

Geistliche. Ein Spruch. — Erhebet euere Herzen!

Gemeinde und Chor. Wir erheben sie zum Herrn.

Geistliche. Lasset uns danken dem Herrn unserm Gott!

Gemeinde und Chor. Recht und würdig ist es.

Geistliche. Recht ist es und wahrhaft würdig u. s. w.

Gemeinde und Chor. Heilig, heilig, heilig ist der Herr
Zebaoth! Alle Lande sind seiner Ehre voll. — Hosianna
in der Höh'! Gelobt sei der da kommt im Namen des
Herrn! Hosianna in der Höh'!

Geistliche. Das allgemeine Gebet.

Gemeinde und Chor. Amen.

Geistliche. Unser Vater u. s. w.

Gemeinde und Chor. Amen. Amen. Amen.

Geistliche. Der Segen.

Gemeinde und Chor. Amen. Amen. Amen.

1.1. Exemplar of the Prussian *Agende*, revised for Berlin Cathedral, 1843; Oxford, Bodleian Library, M. Deneke Mendelssohn, c. 21, item 76.

1.2. Harmonization of Psalm 24 (melody copied from *Die Psalmen Davids, nach Frantzös-ischer Melodey in Teutsche Reymen gebracht durch D. Ambrosium Lobwasser* [Amsterdam, 1696]). From vol. 38[2] of the *Mendelssohn Nachlass* autographs in Kraków, Biblioteca Jagiellońska.

The people were completely dumbstruck."[24] The only music that Mendelssohn had yet composed that might have been used during this service was his harmonization of the Advent Introit, Psalm 24 (see Plate 1.2).[25] The composer soon took up his pen in earnest, however, and on 19 December reported to his friend Ferdinand David:

> Next Sunday for the first time we shall have grand church music, which, however, will consist of small things, namely an eight-voice Psalm without orchestra by me (composed expressly for this occasion), a chorus from Handel's

24 See *Tagebücher von K. A. Varnhagen von Ense* (Leipzig, 1861; rpt. Berne, 1972), vol. II, p. 238 (entry for 12 December 1843).

25 The congregational responses and the Verse before the Alleluia probably were Grell's, and in all likelihood the German Gloria was sung in the popular setting by Bortniansky found in the *Musik-Anhang* to the old Agende. The autograph of Grell's setting of the Advent Verse "Lasset uns frohlocken" is dated 28 November 1843; the organist's manuscript of his setting of the congregational responses is inscribed "Gilt in der Dom Gemeinde zu Berlin seit dem 28sten April 1844." Both sources are preserved in the Deutsche Staatsbibliothek, Berlin (Mus. ms. E. Grell 397 and 71, respectively). The responses were published in the *Liturgische Andachten der Königlichen Hof- und Dom-Kirche für die Feste des Kirchenjahres*, ed. Friedrich Adolph Strauss, 3rd. edn. (Berlin, 1857), where we find evidence that they might date from 1843: "Die nachfolgenden Responsorien für die Gemeinde (mit Ausnahme des Heilig &c.), componirt vom Organisten der Hof- und Domkirche, Musikdirektor E. Grell, sind, sowie die gesammte beifolgende Ordnung des Haupt-Gottesdienstes bei der Domgemeinde seit 1843 ... eingeführt" (p. 156). Bortniansky's Gloria was taken into the Domchor's repertoire and published in *Sammlung religiöser Gesänge älterer und neuester Zeit zum bestimmten Gebrauch für den Königl. Berliner Domchor*, Musica sacra, V, ed. August Neithardt (Berlin, [1853]).

Messiah, and three chorales "with trombones, etc." Such is the king's rule, over which there had earlier been so much distress; since etc. there can now be wind instruments of every kind, so I have made the instrumentation after my own taste and will keep to the oboes, etc. We have managed to get thus far with great difficulties ... and at last the great, much-heralded "grand" church music will have shrunk to a single piece before the beginning of the service.[26]

So began Mendelssohn's activity with the Domchor – with muted enthusiasm. To the works he created for the ensemble – and the controversy they touched off – we now turn.

II

Table 1.2 provides information about Mendelssohn's first efforts at the cathedral, for the festivals of the First Day of Christmas and New Year's Day.[27] The Christmas liturgy called for choral settings of Psalm 2 and the Verse before the Alleluia, "Frohlocket, ihr Völker," as well as orchestrally accompanied settings of "Vom Himmel hoch" (the chorale *de tempore*), "Allein Gott in der Höh'" (the chorale paraphase of the Gloria), and the opening stanza of the German *Te deum* ("Herr Gott, dich loben wir"). For the *Te deum* Mendelssohn seems to have reused the initial stanza of his setting of the previous July, which the king had commissioned for a special cathedral service on 6 August commemorating the 1000th anniversary of the founding of the German Reich. Mendelssohn scored this piece, in the officially sanctioned manner, for trombones, organ, and strings.[28] By contrast, the Psalm (written for

26 "Nächsten Sonntag ist nun zum erstenmale große Kirchenmusik, die aber aus kleinen Sachen besteht, nämlich aus einem 8stimmigen Psalm von mir ohne Orchester (*composed expressly for this occasion*)[,] einem Chor aus den *Händel*schen Messias, und 3 Chorälen mit 'Posaunen etc.' Gerade so lautet die Bestimmung des Königs, über die früher so viel Noth war; da nun etc. alle möglichen Blasinstrumente sein können, so habe ichs mir nach meiner Weise instrumentirt, und es wird nun auch wohl bei Hoboen etc. bleiben. So kommt man hier mit großen Schwierigkeiten endlich so weit, ... und am Ende wird sich die große, vielbesprochene Kirchenmusik dahin verkleinern, daß sie zu einem Musikstück vor Anfang des Gottesdienstes zusammenschrumpft" (Felix Mendelssohn-Bartholdy, *Briefe aus Leipziger Archiven*, ed. Hans-Joachim Rothe and Reinhard Szeskus [Leipzig, 1972], p. 189).

27 Printed orders of worship for these services are preserved in the Bodleian Library, Oxford (M. Deneke Mendelssohn c. 49, item 14). The Christmas service was noted in leading musical journals, including the *Allgemeine musikalische Zeitung* 46 (1844), col. 79; and the *Allgemeine Wiener Musik-Zeitung* 4 (1844), 4.

28 Massow delivered the king's commission, to be fulfilled "so schnell als möglich," in a letter of 14 July (GB XVIII, item 20); the unpublished manuscript, contained within volume 38² of the *Mendelssohn Nachlass* (Biblioteca Jagiellońska, Kraków), is headed "Zur Feier des tausendjährigen Bestehens von Deutschland" and dated "Leipzig den 16ᵗᵉⁿ July 1843." Coming in the midst of the protracted negotiations concerning his relationship to the court orchestra, this request clearly irked the composer, who, in a letter of 21 July to his brother Paul, described the piece as "the longest chorale and most tiresome work which I [have] ever attempted" (*Letters from 1833 to 1847*, p. 304).

soloists, double choir, and organ) and the Verse (for double choir *a cappella*) were completed by around the middle of December, as were the first two chorales, in which Mendelssohn made use, as he put it to David, of the "oboes etc."[29]

Similarly, the festive liturgy for New Year's Day required settings of Psalm 98 and the Verse "Herr Gott, du bist unsre Zuflucht," the chorale *de tempore*, "Wachet auf," and, again, the "Allein Gott in der Höh'" and "Herr Gott, dich loben wir." The Psalm (for soloists, double choir, and orchestra) and the Verse (for double choir *a cappella*), are dated 27 and 25 December, respectively.[30] Arrangements of two of the chorales were, of course, already at hand; and so too was an orchestrally accompanied version of "Wachet auf," which was sung, apparently at Frederick William's command, in Mendelssohn's setting from the oratorio *St Paul* of 1836.[31] Mendelssohn's other contributions to the music of these liturgies came not in the form of original works but from his decision in both instances to replace the *Gloria patri*, which normally followed the Psalm, with familiar choruses from Handel's *Messiah* – on Christmas, "Denn uns ist ein Kind geboren," and on New Year's Day, the great "Hallelujah Chorus."[32]

During the rest of the winter Mendelssohn composed music for only two other liturgies, Passion Sunday and Good Friday (see Table 1.3). All these pieces are in eight parts and were meant to be sung *a cappella*. First to be set was Psalm 43, which was completed on 3 January. Two weeks later the composer finished the *Gloria Patri* ("Ehre sei dem Vater"). The two required Verses – "Herr, gedenke nicht unsrer Übeltaten" and "Um unsrer Sünden" – were

---

29 These works are found in volume 38^2 of the *Mendelssohn Nachlass*, where they are collectively headed "Psalm und Gesänge zur Feier des ersten Weihnachtstages in der Domkirche zu Berlin"; the setting of "Vom Himmel hoch" carries the date "Berlin d. 15ten Dec. 1843."

30 These works are found in volume 38^2 of the *Mendelssohn Nachlass*; the title page reads "Psalm und Spruch zur Feyer des Neujahrstages in der Domkirche zu Berlin 1844, d. 27 Dec. 1843." A new critical edition of Psalm 98 has appeared in the Carus-Verlag Mendelssohn series (ed. R. Larry Todd [Stuttgart, 1990]).

31 See Mendelssohn's unpublished letter of 10 December 1843 to Conrad Schleinitz: "Ich hörte gestern, daß der König sich an dem Tage [Neujahr 1844] ein Stück aus meinem Paulus für den Dom bestellt" (preserved in the Staatsbibliothek Preußischer Kulturbesitz Berlin, Handschriftenabteilung; quoted in Wolfgang Dinglinger, "Ein neues Lied: Der preußische Generalmusikdirektor und eine königliche Auftragskomposition," *Mendelssohn-Studien* [Berlin, 1982], vol. V, p. 104). "Wachet auf" is the only number in the oratorio having a place in the liturgy for New Year's Day; that the king requested this setting, which includes oboes, clarinets, bassoons, and horns, suggests that Mendelssohn had dissuaded the king from his earlier prohibition of the woodwinds.

32 Mendelssohn's organ parts for these choruses are preserved in volume 38^2 of the *Nachlass* autographs (Biblioteca Jagiellońska).

Table 1.2. *Music for Christmas and New Year's Day*

First Day of Christmas	Original Version[a]	Revised Version[a]	First Edition
1. Psalm 2 (Introit) "Warum toben die Heiden" (solo vv., dbl. ch., org.)	Berlin, Dec 1843 38^2/219–28 (vv.) 38^2/233–4 (org.)	Frankfurt, March 1845 40/25–34[b]	op. 78/1 (1848)[c]
2. Chorus from *Messiah* (organ part) "Denn uns ist ein Kind geboren" (ch., orch., org.)	Berlin, Dec 1843 38^2/235–6	–	–
3. "Vom Himmel hoch" harmonization (obs., cls., bsns., trps., trbns., timp., str.)	Berlin, 15 Dec 1843 38^2/232	–	Carus (1982)
4. "Allein Gott in der Höh'" harmonization (obs., cls., bsns., trps., trbns., str.)	Berlin, Dec 1843 38^2/229	–	Carus (1982)
5. Verse (Gradual) "Frohlocket, ihr Völker" (dbl. ch.)	Berlin, Dec 1843 38^2/229–31	Frankfurt, March 1845 40/25–34	op. 79/1 (1848)[c]
6. "Herr Gott, dich loben wir" harmonization (trbns., org., str.)	Leipzig, 16 July 1843 38^2/199–216	–	–
New Year's Day			
1. Psalm 98 (Introit) "Singet dem Herrn" (solo vv., dbl. ch., orch.)	Berlin, 27 Dec 1843 38^2/241–67	–	op. 91 (1851)
2. Chorus from *Messiah* (organ part) "Hallelujah" (ch., orch., org.)	Berlin, Dec 1843 38^2/237	–	–
3. Chorale harmonization from *St. Paul* "Wachet auf" (obs., cls., bsns., hrns., trps., trbns., str.)	18 April 1836?	–	op. 36 (1836)

Table 1.2. (*Cont.*)

4. "Allein Gott in der Höh'"	d	
5. Verse (Gradual)	Berlin, 25 Dec 1843	Op. 79/2 (1848)
"Herr Gott, du bist unsre Zuflucht" (solo vv., dbl. ch.)	38²/269–71	—
6. "Herr Gott, dich loben wir"	d	

[a] Cited by place and date of completion, and vol. no./inclusive pages in the *Mendelssohn Nachlass* autographs (Biblioteca Jagiellońska, Kraków).
[b] Concludes, on p. 34, with a setting of the "Ehre sei dem Vater." Draft of the same on p. 24 (dated Frankfurt, 2 March 1845); working copy on p. 50 (dated Frankfurt, 5 March 1845).
[c] Based on the revised version.
[d] As for Christmas.

Table 1.3. *Music for Passion Sunday (Judica) and Good Friday*

Passion Sunday (Judica)	Original Version[a]	Revised Version[a]	First Edition
1. Psalm 43 (Introit) "Richtet mich Gott" (dbl. ch.)	Berlin, 3 Jan 1844 39/47–52	Frankfurt, March 1845 40/39–44	op. 78/2 (1848)[b]
2. Lesser Doxology (Gloria patri) "Ehre sei dem Vater" (dbl. ch.)	Berlin, 17 Jan 1844 40/45–6	Frankfurt, March 1845 40/45–46[c]	part of op. 69/2 (1848)[d]
3. Verse (Gradual) "Herr, gedenke nicht unsrer Übeltaten" (dbl. ch.)	Berlin, 14 Feb 1844 39/52–3	Frankfurt, March 1845 40/47–9	op. 79/4 (1848)[e]
Good Friday			
1. Psalm 22 (Introit) "Mein Gott, warum hast du mich verlassen?" (solo vv., dbl. ch.)	Berlin, Feb 1844 39/55–65	–	op. 78/3 (1848)
2. Lesser Doxology (Gloria patri) "Ehre sei dem Vater" (dbl. ch.)	[f]	–	
3. Verse (Gradual) "Um unsrer Sünden" (dbl. ch.)	Berlin, 18 Feb 1844 39/66–7		op. 79/6 (1848)

[a] Cited by place and date of completion, and vol. no./inclusive pages in the *Mendelssohn Nachlass* autographs (Biblioteca Jagiellońska, Kraków).

[b] Based on *original* version.

[c] Revision of the setting of the text "Amen" written over the original version.

[d] German edition only.

[e] Based on revised version.

[f] Presumably as for Psalm 43, perhaps transposed to E (cf. the "Ehre sei dem Vater," in the *Deutsche Liturgie* [41/105–6]).

written in rapid succession, on 14 and 18 February, respectively; and, at about the same time, the setting of Psalm 22 was composed.[33]

This impressive body of music was created under trying circumstances. Fanny Hensel described her brother's position at the cathedral as "so-so," adding that he found it impossible to get along with the cathedral cleric Friedrich Adolph Strauss.[34] The composer's dissatisfaction with the church authorities was even circulated in the press, as we read in the pages of the *Signale für die musikalische Welt*:

> Mendelssohn Bartholdy can admirably subdue every orchestra and knows how to control the most intractable and unruly of musicians, but with the clergy even the son of Jupiter and Alcmene [i.e., Hercules], who ... led [with] a ... club, instead of a conducting baton, would not [yet] be finished.[35]

Scholars have traditionally assumed that the bone of contention between composer and clergy concerned Mendelssohn's lack of sympathy for the *a cappella* ideal of church music. According to this view, the introduction of the orchestra in the Psalm for New Year's Day brought to a head a conflict that had been simmering since before Christmas, when, in Fanny's words, her brother, who "prefer[red] composing with orchestra," had first gotten in "the thin end of the wedge by introducing Handel's choruses after those *a cappella*."[36] This reasoning is sound, as far as it goes, but it cannot tell the entire story. Actually, the controversy was fiercest, not around Christmas and New Year's Day, two of the handful of holidays when members of the orchestra were available, but rather during the ensuing seasons of Epiphany and Lent,

---

33 With the exception of the Lesser Doxology, all these pieces are contained within volume 39 of the *Nachlass* autographs (Biblioteca Jagiellońska); the Doxology is found in volume 40. The only undated work is Psalm 22. This piece could not have been begun before 13 February, when Mendelssohn received word of the assigned psalms for the period beginning with Good Friday (see below, p. 23), and it must have been finished by 18 February, when the composer used a leaf containing a part of the psalm for the first measures of "Um unsrer Sünden."

34 Letter of 30 January 1844 to Rebecka Dirichlet, quoted in Sebastian Hensel, *The Mendelssohn Family (1729–1847), from Letters and Journals*, 2nd rev. edn., trans. Karl Klingemann, 2 vols. (1882; rpt. New York, 1969), vol. II, p. 252.

35 "Mendelssohn Bartholdy weiß jedes Orchester trefflich zu bändigen und die unlenksamsten und widerspänstigsten Musici zu zähmen, aber mit den Geistlichen würde selbst der Sohn Jupiters und Alkmenens nicht fertig werden, der bekanntlich statt des Tactstabes einen anständigen Prügel, Keule genannt, führte" (*Signale für die musikalische Welt* 2 [1844], 106; quoted in Susanna Großmann-Vendrey, *Felix Mendelssohn Bartholdy und die Musik der Vergangenheit* [Regensburg, 1969], p. 176).

36 Letter of 26 December 1843 to Rebecka Dirichlet, quoted in *The Mendelssohn Family*, vol. II, p. 244. See also Dinglinger, "Ein neues Lied," p. 107. E. Werner, *Mendelssohn: a New Image*, pp. 416–47, and Rudolf Werner, "Felix Mendelssohn als Kirchenmusiker" (diss., Frankfurt am Main, 1930), p. 89, both argued Mendelssohn's use of the harp created the problem, citing "profane" connotations of the instrument.

when no instrumentalists were assigned to the Music Institute. On 8 February, in an ironic note to his brother Paul, the composer made reference to a certain difficulty with the "psalmody" in the cathedral;[37] one week later, writing to his sister Rebecka, he mentioned that he had been quarrelling with the clergy "on principle."[38] These remarks suggest that the matter at stake was not merely a narrow one concerning instrumentation but a broader one embracing the whole practice of presenting the psalms during worship.

Why *did* Mendelssohn's first psalms for the cathedral raise hackles? Emil Naumann, writing in the mid-1850s, recalled complaints about their supposed "novelties" and the damage they purportedly inflicted on the "essential simplicity" of the Evangelical service.[39] In truth, these pieces do have much in common with the sprawling "psalm cantatas" of earlier years, which were written for soloists, chorus, and orchestra, and intended not for the church but for the concert hall. Like the great settings of Psalm 42 (op. 42, dating from 1837) and Psalm 95 (op. 46, first begun in 1838), Psalms 2 and 98 fall into four diverse movements and unfold according to the large-scale tonal plan I–VI–IV–I. Psalm 98 (op. 91), as we have seen, actually draws upon the resources of the orchestra, which enters in the third movement, at the moment when the text invites the people to praise the Lord with harps, trumpets, and horns. Even the comparatively short *a cappella* setting of Psalm 43 recalls the earlier "psalm cantatas"; in setting its last verse, Mendelssohn quoted the final chorus of Psalm 42, whose text is echoed almost exactly.

Notwithstanding these allusions, the greatest concern to the clergy may well have been Mendelssohn's approach to text setting. Psalms 2 and 98 especially show a distinctly non–liturgical approach, wherein textual clarity is sacrificed for the sake of musical or dramatic expression. The authorities, who understandably wanted the biblical texts to be fully accessible to the congregation, desired choral "recitatives," so to speak. Mendelssohn, by contrast, favored the dramatic "ensemble" (see Table 1.4). He frequently resorted to word repetition, as in the third movement of Psalm 2 (whose forty measures present a single verse), and occasionally even presented two lines of text at

37 Unpublished letter in the New York Public Library: "Da dich die Nachricht vom Psalmodiren im Dom neulich so verdrossen hat, so wird es dich vielleicht vergnügen zu erfehren [sic] daß heut über die ganze ausführliche Order wieder eine Contra-Order gekommen ist, wonach es nun vorlaüfig wieder beim Alten bleibt. Laß dies unter uns."

38 Hensel, *The Mendelssohn Family*, vol. II, p. 253.

39 Preface to *Psalmen auf alle Sonn- und Festtage des evangelischen Kirchenjahres, auf Allerhöchsten Befehl Sr. Majestät des Königs Friedrich Wilhelm IV. von Preussen componirt von Engel, Eduard Grell, Ferdinand Hiller, Kästner, Felix Mendelssohn-Bartholdy, Giacomo Meyerbeer, Emil Naumann, Neithardt, Otto Nicolai, Reinthaler, C. C. Reissinger, Richter, Schulz, Stahlknecht, Taubert, und zum Gebrauch des Königl. Domchores so wie aller evangelischen Kirchenchöre*, Musica sacra, VIII–X (Berlin, *c.* 1855), vol. VIII [p. ix].

Table 1.4. *Psalm II op. 78/1 (Original Version)*

	Moderato (g)	1. *Warum toben die Heiden, und die Leute reden so vergeblich?*
		2. Die Könige im Lande lehnen sich auf, und die Herr'n rathschlagen mit einander wider den HErrn und seinen Gesalbten:
		3. "Lasset uns zerreissen ihre Bande, und von uns werfen ihre Seile!"
		4. *Aber der im Himmel wohnet, lachet ihrer, und der HErr spottet ihrer.*
		5. *Er wird einst mit ihnen reden in seinem Zorn, und mit seinem Grimm wird er sie schrecken.*
40	Andante (E♭)	6. Aber ich habe meinen König eingesetzt, auf meinem heiligen Berge Zion.
		7. Ich will von einer solchen Weise predigen, daß der HErr zu mir gesagt hat: "Du bist mein Sohn, heute hab' Ich dich gezeuget;
		8. Heische von mir, so will ich dir die Heiden zum Erbe geben, und der Welt Ende zum Eigenthum.
63	Con moto (c)	9. *Du sollst sie mit eisernem Scepter zerschlagen, wie Töpfe sollst du sie zerbrechen.*"
103	Andante	10. So lasset euch nun weisen, ihr Könige, und lasset euch züchtigen, ihr Richter auf Erden!
		11. Dienet dem HErrn mit Furcht und freuet euch mit Zittern!
	(G)	12. *Küsset den Sohn, daß er nicht zürne, und ihr umkommet auf dem Wege; denn sein Zorn wird bald anbrennen. Aber wohl allen, die auf ihn trauen!* (142)

NOTE: Italics indicate phrases of text that are repeated.

once, as in the final movement of the same composition (see Ex. 1.1), in which the dark warning about the Lord's anger intoned repeatedly by the two choirs ("denn sein Zorn wird bald anbrennen") yields only at the end to the soloists' hopeful message of a happiness that awaits those who trust in Him ("Aber wohl allen, die auf ihn trauen").

This comparatively free approach to text setting is perhaps best understood as a symptom of Mendelssohn's underlying orientation toward *geistliche* rather than *kirchliche Musik*, toward "artistic" settings of sacred texts rather than "liturgical music" in the strict sense. Under that circumstance, conflict with the clergy was inevitable. Mendelssohn's response was to take the path of least resistance, first to compromise and then to flee. On 14 February 1844, after receiving from Ehrenberg a catalogue of the introits for the period from Good Friday through the Fifth Sunday after Pentecost,[40] he wrote to Redern, formally requesting, in the most diplomatic of terms, that the task of setting these psalms be shared with other composers:

> It is not laziness or a lack of zeal that prompts this request. . . . The composition of the psalms in a worthy, genuinely ecclesiastical manner is a task that is too difficult for a single individual; the perfect solution certainly can only be expected from a collaboration of various powers. . . .
>
> In regard to musical matters it would be well only to remark: that the setting of the psalm should be to Luther's translation without any instrumental accompaniment (*a cappella*),
>
> [and] that the destination of this composition for the Divine Service makes desirable a setting in a declamatory manner, thus with the least possible amount of word repetition and with the slightest possible figuration, so that the meaning of the words is understandable to the listeners.[41]

The psalms for the holidays beginning with Easter, he suggested, should be commissioned from August Neithardt, Moritz Hauptmann, Ludwig Spohr, Carl Loewe, and a Danzig organist named Granzin. "All these men,"

---

40 Enclosed in a letter of 13 February 1844 (GB XIX, item 101).

41 "Es ist nicht Untätigkeit oder Mangel an Eifer, was mich zu dieser Bitte veranlaßt. . . . Zudem ist eine würdige, echt kirchliche Komposition der Psalmen eine Aufgabe, die für einen Einzelnen zu schwer ist, deren vollkommene Lösung gewiß nur durch ein Zusammenwirken verschiedener Kräfte zu erwarten steht. . . . In musikalischer Hinsicht wäre dabei wohl nur zu bemerken: daß die Komposition des Psalmes nach der Lutherschen Übersetzung ohne alle Instrumental-Begleitung (a capella) erforderlich sei, daß die Bestimmung dieser Komposition für den Gottesdienst es wünschenswert mache, daß sie deklamatorisch, also mit möglichst geringer Wiederholung der Worte und mit möglichst geringer Figurierung gehalten werde, so daß der Sinn der Worte den Zuhörern verständlich . . . werde" (quoted in Scheumann, "Briefe berühmter Komponisten," p. 261).

DAVID BRODBECK

24

Ex. 1.1: Felix Mendelssohn Bartholdy, Psalm 2 op. 78 no. 1, conclusion (original version, 1843)

Mendelssohn continued, "are to be requested to take into consideration the above-indicated musical restrictions."[42]

Mendelssohn set to work on the Psalm for Good Friday, No. 22. Significantly, in this composition he broke with his own past practice and imposed on himself the same restrictions he was now urging on others. The setting is *a cappella*, of course. Moreover, several passages are marked "recitativo," others present stylized intonations, and, in keeping with one of the oldest traditions of psalmody, much of the setting is responsorial by the half verse, with one or more soloists answered by the choir. As shown in Table 1.5, word repetition is kept to a minimum in this austere work, occurring only briefly in the music for verses 8, 15, and 18, wherein the textual imagery – the mocking outburst of the people, and the dry tongue and casting of lots described in the dramatic narrative – seems to draw it out. Indeed, Mendelssohn rewrote the only passage in which his treatment of the text might have seemed overly interpretive (see Ex. 1.2a). Originally the Andante con moto, which, in verses 19–22, ends in hopeful supplication, was linked to the laudatory Animato that follows by a recurrence of the first half of verse 23 ("Rühmet den Herrn, die ihr ihn fürchtet"); then, as the upper parts continued the verse (beginning "es ehre ihn aller Same Jacobs"), the basses added an admonitory gloss, reminiscent of the intonations at the end of Psalm 2, reading "fürchtet den Herrn." Eventually Mendelssohn settled on a more

---

42 "Sämtliche dieser Herren sind unter Berücksichtigung der oben angedeuteten musikalischen Bedingungen aufzufordern" (*ibid.*, p. 262).

25

Table 1.5. *Psalm XXII op. 78/3*

Andante	1.	Mein GOtt, mein GOtt, warum hast du mich verlassen? Ich heule, aber meine Hülfe ist fern.
	2.	Mein GOtt, des Tages rufe ich, so antwortest du nicht; und des Nachts schweige ich auch nicht.
	3.	Aber du bist heilig, der du wohnest unter dem Lobe Israels.
	4.	Unsre Väter hofften auf dich, und da sie hofften, halfest du ihnen aus.
	5.	Zu dir schrieen sie, und wurden errettet; sie hofften auf dich, and wurden nicht zu Schanden.
	6.	Ich aber bin ein Wurm und kein Mensch; ein Spott der Leute, und Verachtung des Volks.
	7.	Alle, die mich sehen, spotten meiner, sperren das Maul auf, und schütteln den Kopf:
	8.	*Er klage es dem HERRn, der helfe ihm aus,* *und errette ihn, hat er Lust zu ihm.*
~~Andante~~	9.	~~Denn du hast mich aus Mutterleibe gezogen,~~ ~~du warest meine Zuversicht, da ich noch an meiner Mutter Brüsten lag.~~
	11.	~~Sey nicht ferne von mir, denn Angst ist nahe;~~ ~~denn es ist hier kein Helfer.~~
~~Lento~~ ·	14.	~~Ich bin ausgeschüttet wie Wasser, alle meine Gebeine haben sich getrennt;~~
58 Andante con moto	14.	Ich bin ausgeschüttet wie Wasser, alle meine Gebeine haben sich getrennt; mein Herz ist in meinem Leibe wie zerschmolzenes Wachs.
	15.	Meine Kräfte sind vertrocknet wie eine Scherbe, *und meine Zunge klebet an meinem Gaumen*; und du legst mich in des Todes Staub.
	16.	Denn Hunde haben mich umgeben, und der Bösen Rotte hat sich um mich gemacht; sie haben meine Hände und Füße durchgraben.
	18.	Sie theilen meine Kleider unter sich, *und werfen das Loos um mein Gewand.*
	19.	Aber du, HERR, sei nicht ferne; meine Stärke, eile mir zu helfen.
	20.	Errette meine Seele vom Schwert, meine Einsame von den Hunden.
	21.	Hilf mir aus dem Rachen der Löwen, und errette mich von den Einhörnern.
	22.	Ich will deinen Namen predigen meinen Brüdern, ich will dich in der Gemeinde rühmen.
	23.	Rühmet den HERRn, die ihr ihn fürchtet;
~~Animato~~		*~~Rühmet den HERRn, die ihr ihn fürchtet;~~* ~~es ehre ihn aller Same Jakobs,~~ ~~und vor ihm scheue sich aller Same Israels.~~
	24.	~~Denn er hat nicht verachtet, noch verschmäht das Elend des Armen,~~ ~~und sein Antlitz vor ihm nicht verborgen,~~ ~~und da er zu ihm schrie, hörte er es.~~

		25.	~~Dich will ich preisen in der großen Gemeinde;~~
			~~ich will meine Gelübde bezahlen vor denen, die ihn fürchten.~~
103	Assai animato		es ehre ihn aller Same Jakobs,
			und vor ihm scheue sich aller Same Israels.
		24.	Denn er hat nicht verachtet, noch verschmäht das Elend des Armen,
			und sein Antlitz vor ihm nicht verborgen,
			und da er zu ihm schrie, hörte er es.
		25.	Dich will ich preisen in der großen Gemeinde;
			ich will meine Gelübde bezahlen vor denen, die ihn fürchten.
127	(Tempo I)	26.	Die Elenden sollen essen, daß sie satt werden;
			und die nach dem HERRn fragen, werden ihn preisen;
			euer Herz soll ewiglich leben.
		27.	Es werde gedacht aller Welt Ende,
			daß sie sich zum HERRn bekehren,
			und vor ihm anbeten alle Geschlechter der Heiden.
		28.	Denn der HERR hat ein Reich, und er herrscht unter den Heiden.
			(150)

NOTE: Italics indicate phrases of text that are repeated; text with strike-overs was set in the manuscript but later crossed out.

straightforward version, omitting both the repetition and the gloss (see Ex. 1.2b).[43]

III

Mendelssohn introduced Psalm 22 at the cathedral on Good Friday (29 March 1844). Having relegated to others the task of providing music for the next several holidays, the composer was able to depart Berlin at the beginning of April. After visiting Leipzig and Frankfurt he arrived several weeks later in England, where he happily passed the first months of the summer, leading a busy professional life and a social life, as he described it, of "the wildest sort."[44] Yet there seemed to be no escape from the irritations of the preceding winter of discontent. In several letters Bunsen importuned Mendelssohn to attend to the king's wishes, and in another, of 2 June, to Bunsen's wife, in London, he spoke of the need to encourage the composer in his task at the cathedral, mentioning

43 That the responsorial and declamatory text setting employed in this work represents a fundamentally changed approach and is not simply owing to the imagery and length of the text is suggested by the two Verses before the Alleluia that date from the same time. Whereas the Verses for Christmas and New Year's Day echo the comparatively free handling of text seen in Psalms 2 and 98, those for Passiontide and Good Friday conform to the new restrictions. The similarity in tempo and tonality between "Herr Gott, du bist unsre Zuflucht," for New Year's Day, and "Herr, gedenke nicht unsrer Übeltaten," for the First Passion Sunday, only throw into relief their contrasting treatment of text – the one, with its points of imitation and large-scale text repetition; the other, with its solo declamations answered in choral homophony.

44 Quoted in Werner, *Mendelssohn: a New Image*, p. 394.

(a)

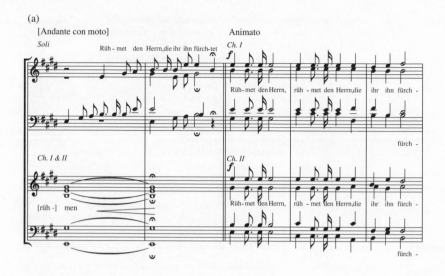

(b)

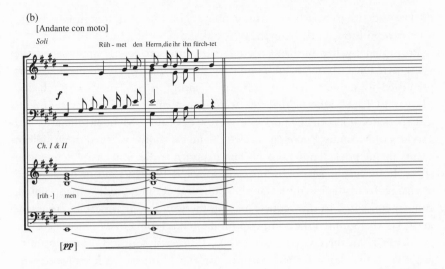

Ex. 1.2: Felix Mendelssohn Bartholdy, Psalm 22 op. 78 no. 3, mm. 101ff: (a) first version, (b) revised version

the king's desire to hear "excellent, genuine choral singing, that is, Gregorian, with compositions in the church style, old and new."[45]

Prompted by her husband's letter, Mrs. Bunsen herself approached the composer. On 11 June, in a note inviting the German visitor to breakfast, she presumed to suggest that he hear the chanting at St. Peter's Church and Margaret Chapel, where "that fine accompaniment to Divine Service [might be experienced] in pristine purity."[46] A few days after, Mendelssohn attended a service of Morning Prayer at St. Peter's and carefully inscribed the Anglican chants in his pocket notebook.[47] The experience did not have its intended effect, however, as Mendelssohn soon solicited Bunsen's aid in obtaining a discharge from all his duties at the cathedral. Undoubtedly disappointed, Bunsen consented to this request, paving the way for an amicable settlement in the fall that granted the composer his desired release. On 27 June, in answer to a letter from the composer, now lost, Bunsen announced his intention to propose to the king certain changes for the Domchor; six days later he reported that he would shortly be arriving in London, bearing news about the choir that he hoped would meet with Mendelssohn's approval.[48]

Subsequent events at the court suggest that this news might have concerned a possible successor. Having been disappointed by Mendelssohn, Bunsen now

45 "The king has expressed to me his 'wish' that I might remain here until Mendelssohn returns (18 August), so that I might persuade him to execute the king's idea with regard to the cathedral choir. The king has named him Director-General of church music in the monarchy and desires to hear in the cathedral excellent, genuine choral singing, that is, Gregorian, with compositions in the church style, old and new. Mendelssohn doesn't know what to do and is unable to deal with the officials. 'He should not,' says the king, 'be misled by the Berlin gossip of catholicizing, which is to be despised.'" ([Frances Bunsen], *Christian Carl Josias von Bunsen: Aus seinen Briefen und nach eigener Erinnerung geschildert von seiner Witwe*, ed. Friedrich Nippold, 3 vols. [Leipzig, 1869–71], vol. II, p. 266).

46 The note reads: "I wish so much to have the pleasure of seeing you before I set out on my journey to Berlin (hoping to take good accounts to your Lady, & very ready to take charge of any packet you may wish to send to her) – that I am induced to ask if your many engagements will allow of your breakfasting with me on *Friday morning* at 1/2 past 9 o'clock. I shall be in town on business, the business of packing & getting ready for embarking on the 18th, & I should be sorry that you should call by chance, when I might be out. I supposed last week that my husband was on the point of returning, but before the week had elapsed, he announced that what His Majesty had desired him to do would detain him over July, & thus there would be time for me to bring my invalid daughter to consult Schönlein. Will you forgive my presumption in proposing to you to hear the *channting* [sic] of the Psalms & other portions of Divine Service in *St. Peter's Church, Wilton Place* (near Belgrave Sq.) & in *Margaret Chapel, Margaret St. Regent St.* supposing you have not heard it *in those places*. The channting in our Cathedrals is generally so indevout, so hurried over, so spoilt, that one seldom hears there anything like what it ought to be. These churches, & that at *the Seminary, Stanley Grove, Chelsea*, have somewhat reinstated that fine accompaniment to Divine Service in pristine purity. – This is a very abrupt suggestion, if I could see you, I could explain why I have just thought of making it. I believe you will not find the subject unworthy of your attention" (GB XIX, item 296).

47 Bodleian Library, Oxford (M. Deneke Mendelssohn g. 9).

48 Unpublished letters of 27 June 1844 and 3 July 1844 (GB XIX, item 60 and XX, item 10).

placed his hopes on Otto Nicolai, whom he had known since the time when Nicolai served as organist at the chapel of the Prussian embassy in Rome, and whom he now sought to entice from Vienna.[49] When, in July, Nicolai passed through Berlin, he was introduced to Minister Eichhorn and, through Bunsen, granted an audience with the king, who commissioned from him a setting of the complete liturgy and commanded him to lead the Domchor in a private concert consisting of his own *Pater noster* as well as some Roman psalmody. A few weeks later, Nicolai encountered Frederick William again, this time at the tercentenary celebration of the founding of the university in Königsberg, where he was asked to direct, of all pieces, the première of Mendelssohn's *a cappella* chorus "Denn er hat seinen Engeln befohlen." In a diary entry pertaining to this affair, Nicolai recorded that the king had spoken of naming him Domkapellmeister. Indeed, after Mendelssohn had been discharged from all duties in the capital, Redern made Nicolai a formal offer of the post. Showing a wariness of "the difficult situation that [he] might discover between the wishes of the king, those of the clergy, those of influential and esteemed men and [his] own" – a situation that Mendelssohn knew all too well – Nicolai refused this offer.[50] Three years passed before Nicolai was persuaded to take up the post, and this only after he had been granted also the directorship of the court opera and orchestra.

Meanwhile, on two occasions, Mendelssohn considered publishing the works of his one season with the Domchor; in both instances he came to think the better of it. The music for Christmas and Passion Sunday was revised in 1845, and a selection offered to the Berlin publishers Bote & Bock; yet the scores ultimately were withheld.[51] In the following year, after fulfilling a royal commission to compose additional Verses before the Alleluia, Mendelssohn offered a set of six to the same publisher; but in the eleventh hour, after the scores had been sent, this project too was scuttled.[52] Perhaps Mendels-

49 See Wilhelm Altmann, *Otto Nicolais Tagebücher* (Regensburg, 1937), pp. 227, 231–2; and Georg Richard Kruse, *Otto Nicolai: ein Künstlerleben* (Berlin, 1911), pp. 166–7, 172–3.

50 See his letter to Redern of 3 November 1844, quoted in Wilhelm Altmann, "Zur Biographie Otto Nicolais und Wilhelm Tauberts," *Neue Zeitschrift für Musik* 70 (1903), 572.

51 The psalms for these occasions, together with that for Good Friday, were first published posthumously, in 1848, as op. 78. Although the published text of the Christmas psalm (op. 78 no. 1) was based on the revised version of 1845, the psalm for Passion Sunday (op. 78 no. 2) was published in its original version of the previous year. For the first edition of Mendelssohn's subsequent revision of this piece, which shows a different tonal plan and a freer approach to text setting than the original, see my edition of all three op. 78 psalms (Stuttgart: Carus-Verlag, forthcoming).

52 Mendelssohn went so far as to enter this set of Verses in his personal catalogue of published compositions (Bodleian Library, Oxford [M. Deneke Mendelssohn c. 49, item 16]). The original layer of writing for one of the last entries in this listing reads: "[op.] 69 Sechs Sprüche für 8-stimmigen Chor beim Gottesdienst zu singen[,] Bote & Bock." Subsequently, after the Verses had been withdrawn and their opus number assigned finally to the three pieces of Anglican

sohn's reluctance stemmed from a sense that in these works his own stylistic inclinations had been too "compromised" – by the demands of the king, the clergy, and influential men like Bunsen. Yet these remarkable and beautiful compositions were in fact the most solitary of accomplishments, for as Moritz Hauptmann observed in 1850:

> Mendelssohn had no one to copy from. He took the Psalm itself, and nothing but the Psalm; he never thought of Bach, Handel, Palestrina, nor anyone else, nor did he adapt it to any particular style; consequently, his music is neither old-fashioned nor new-fangled, it is simply a fine setting of the Psalm. Three thousand years have not made the words sound strange to us, and I think time will not affect the music either.[53]

Nearly a century and a half later, Hauptmann's prediction still rings true.

church music that Mendelssohn composed in 1847, the composer emended his catalogue entry by means of cross-overs and other changes to read simply "[op.] 69 Chöre beim Gottesdienst zu singen[,] Breitkopf & Härtel."

53 *Letters of a Leipzig Cantor*, ed. Alfred Schöne and Ferdinand Hiller, trans. A. D. Coleridge, 2 vols. (1888; rpt. edn., New York, 1972), vol. II, p. 74.

2   In mutual reflection: historical, biographical, and structural aspects of Mendelssohn's *Variations sérieuses*[1]

CHRISTA JOST

translated by J. Bradford Robinson

DEDICATED TO LUDWIG FINSCHER

"I've had enough of the didactic vein; I must go back and play Beethoven again."[2] Thus the young Mendelssohn, writing from London in 1829 before taking the solo part in the "Emperor" Concerto. His words parody the Study Scene of Goethe's *Faust*, where they are spoken by Mephistopheles, playing the learned sage in place of the absent Faust. Tragedy turns into satyr play.[3] By projecting himself and Beethoven into this literary context Mendelssohn draws attention to two different states of affairs. First, he clearly casts the performer as the composer's double.[4] But more than this, by demonizing Beethoven in this way he also implies that composers after Beethoven had to write their music under almost "Faustian" conditions.

In 1841 Pietro Mechetti invited the leading composers of his day to contribute to an anthology, the proceeds of which were to be used to erect a monument to Beethoven in Bonn. At first, Mendelssohn declined the Viennese publisher's invitation. Later, however, Mechetti asked the music critic Karl Kunt to intercede on his behalf. Kunt was able to persuade the composer to take part. In Mendelssohn's mind this pledge was linked with lofty artistic demands. As he wrote to Kunt on 25 May 1841: "I have nought that, in my opinion, might suit an album bearing such a name; but I shall try to finish something new for it by the end of June, and only hope that I shall succeed as I

---

1 This is a revised version of a paper read at the Nineteenth-Century Conference held in Oxford on 9 July 1988.

2 Felix Mendelssohn Bartholdy, *Briefe*, ed. Rudolf Elvers (Frankfurt am Main, 1984), p. 74.

3 "Ich bin des trocknen Tons nun satt, Muß wieder recht den Teufel spielen." Johann Wolfgang von Goethe, *Faust, erster Teil, Studierzimmer*, ed. Erich Trunz, 11th edn. (Munich, 1981), p. 65, lines 2019–20 (*Hamburger Ausgabe, Dramen I*, vol. III).

4 René Leibowitz later referred to the performer as the "double" of the composer. See René Leibowitz, *Le compositeur et son double: Essais sur l'interprétation musicale* (n.p., 1971).

would like."[5] At the same time he asked about the stipulations for the entries and the overall conception of the volume. "May I write somewhat at length? How long? Perhaps you could tell me something about the rest of the project – whether it contains just instrumental music or vocal music as well, how much of the former, how much of the latter? &c. &c. If he does not need a long instrumental piece (such as a fantasy), would a short lied be in order? In short, I would like to know more about it, and if I happen to write something decent by that time, something I need not be too ashamed to put in an album of this sort, I will send it to him."[6] Mendelssohn's response to this challenge was his *Variations sérieuses* in D minor op. 54.

Two holograph manuscripts of the work have survived. The fair copy, containing a small number of corrections, presumably served for the engraving.[7] The composing manuscript is found in volume 35 of the *Mendelssohn Nachlass*.[8] Its date – "Leipzig, the 4th of June 1841" – is placed, strictly speaking, beneath a continuous draft of only fifteen variations. Not until he had completed this draft did Mendelssohn write the *maggiore* variation (the eventual No. 14). Variations 12 and 13, which return to the tempo of the theme (and to the theme itself), are the result of renewed reflection on the work's overall design. In the holograph, the piece is made up of eighteen variations. At no point in the work's genesis, however, was the coda ever referred to as a variation. Instead, as an additional link in this chain, the holograph contains a sixteenth variation, the bass line of which takes up the harshly dissonant Variation 15 verbatim.

It was probably in this form that Mendelssohn, on 15 July 1841, described the work to Karl Klingemann: "Do you know what I have been doing so passionately for the last few weeks? – variations for piano. Eighteen of them at one go, on a theme in D minor; and they gave me such divine pleasure that I immediately wrote a new set on a theme in E flat major [op. 82], and am now working on a third on a theme in B flat [op. 83]. I almost feel as if I have to make amends for not having written variations before. The first ones, in D minor, are very dear to me so far, and will appear in a Viennese album for the benefit of the Beethoven monument in Bonn. Moscheles has also included a piece of his; you will probably be seeing and hearing them in short order."[9] Mendelssohn apparently took special pleasure in the dramatic structure of his

5 Felix Mendelssohn Bartholdy, *Briefe an deutsche Verleger*, ed. Rudolf Elvers (Berlin, 1968), p. 294 (No. 348).

6 *Ibid.*   7 British Library, Additional MS. 47860, ff. 37–42.

8 Vol. 35, pp. 23/5–[36], Biblioteca Jagiellońska in Kraków, Poland. I am grateful to Dr. Marian Zwiercan for granting permission to examine the manuscript.

9 Letter from Leipzig of 15 July 1841 in *Felix Mendelssohn Bartholdys Briefwechsel mit Legationsrat Karl Klingemann*, ed. Karl Klingemann (Essen, 1909), p. 265.

cycle. In any event, it was on this aspect that he focussed his corrections. On 16 August 1841 he sent the manuscript of the *Variations sérieuses* to the publisher.[10] A letter from Mechetti, dated 8 November of the same year, confirms that Mendelssohn had finished the first stage of proofreading with "an extraordinarily large number of changes in the plates"[11] and, having read the second proofs, complained on 12 October of "many corrections not being carried out."[12]

As has recently been emphasized by Imogen Fellinger,[13] the circumstances surrounding the publication of the *Variations sérieuses* played an important part in the work's genesis. The "Beethoven Album" appeared on the market in an edition of 500 copies.[14] Its marketing area was limited to Germany so as not to violate foreign property rights.[15] It was first advertised on 19 January 1842 in the *Wiener Zeitung*.[16] The complete title of the anthology reads as follows: *ALBUM-BEETHOVEN. / DIX / Morceaux brillants / pour le / PIANO / composés par Messieurs / Chopin, Czerny, Döhler, Henselt, Kalkbrenner, / Liszt, Mendelssohn Bartholdy, Moscheles, / TAUBERT et THALBERG, / et publiés par / L'EDITEUR P. MECHETTI / pour contribuer aux Frais du Monument / de / Louis van Beethoven / à / Bonn.*[17] (See Plate 2.1.) The front cover of the binding is adorned with a bit of kitsch from the Biedermeier period – a pen-and-ink drawing by J. N. Geiger which imparts Mediterranean traits to a statue of Beethoven enthroned on a pedestal like Orpheus with his lyre. Surrounding the composer are two allegorical female figures whose emblems, a torch and lyre, proclaim them to be Eos and Terpsichore, and two male

10 *Briefe an deutsche Verleger*, p. 297 (No. 352).   11 *Ibid.*   12 *Ibid.*
13 Imogen Fellinger, "Mendelssohn und seine Zeit." Paper read on 21 June 1990 at a lecture series organized by Dr. Eva Renate Wutta at the Stadtbibliothek am Gasteig, Munich. I am greatly indebted to Dr. Fellinger for supplying valuable information by letter.
14 Dr. Helmut Hell, the head of the Music Department at the Staatsbibliothek Preussischer Kulturbesitz, Berlin, has pointed out that this was an unusually large issue. The importance of this undertaking is also evinced by the large number of foreign publishers listed on the title pages as involved in distributing the copies: R. Cocks & Co., Cramer, Addison & Beale, J. J. Ewer & Co. in London; Lucca in Milan; Simon Richault, Maurice Schlesinger, E. Troupenas in Paris; and à l'Odéon, Depot de Musique in St. Petersburg.
15 *Briefe an deutsche Verleger*, p. 293n.
16 *Verlagsverzeichnis Pietro Mechetti quondam Carlo*, ed. Alexander Weinmann (Vienna, 1966), in *Beiträge zur Geschichte des Alt-Wiener Musikverlages*, Series 2, vol. x, pp. 95–6. The Beethoven Album thus appeared between 1841 and 1842. According to Rudolf Elvers, Mendelssohn received an author's copy of the album with an undated letter (29 or 30 December 1841); see *Briefe an deutsche Verleger*, p. 298n. See also announcements in *Allgemeine musikalische Zeitung* 44 (2 Feb 1842), col. 101 ("Verzeichniss neuerschienener Musikalien und auf Musik bezüglicher Werke. Eingegangen vom 26. Januar bis 1. Februar d.J.") and 16 February, col. 151, and the *Intelligenzblatt zur Neuen Zeitschrift für Musik* 16 (February 1842).
17 Copies of the Beethoven Album can be found in, among other places, the Music Department of the Staatsbibliothek Preussischer Kulturbesitz in Berlin, the Beethoven Archive in Bonn, and the Music Collection of the Austrian National Library in Vienna.

2.1.   *Album-Beethoven* (Vienna: Pietro Mechetti, 1841), title page; Berlin, Stiftung Preussischer Kulturbesitz.

figures recognizable as shepherds on the strength of their syrinx, bagpipes, and crook. Books and paper scrolls, decorously opened, offer a selection from the composer's *oeuvre* under various captions: *Simphonies héroique et pastorale* (not the Ninth as in Gustav Klimt's Beethoven frieze from half a century later), *Sonate pathétique*, *Marcia funèbre*, the early lied *Adelaide*, the famous *Septuour*, *Prométhée*, *Egmont*, *Fidelio*, and *Coriolan*. Generic headings without specific titles alert the reader to concertos, church music, and chamber music.

The Metternich restoration period had a special fondness for joint publishing ventures. A comparable project, the Mozart Album of 1842 (for the benefit of the Mozart monument), also included compositions for voice.[18] Mechetti's anthology, however, consisted entirely of works for Beethoven's principal instrument, the piano. It opens with what might be called a "tombeau de Beethoven" – a "partition de piano" by Franz Liszt from the "Eroica" Symphony entitled *Marche funèbre de la Symphonie héroique*. This is followed by the other composers in alphabetical order: *Prélude* in C sharp minor op. 45 by Frédéric Chopin; *Nocturne* in E flat major op. 647 by Carl Czerny; *Deux Impromptus fugitifs*, no. 1 in G major, no. 2 (Tarantella) in G minor op. 39 by Theodor Döhler; *Wiegenlied* in G flat major op. 13 no. 1 by Adolf Henselt; *L'echo! Scherzo brillant* in A minor by Frédéric Kalkbrenner; *17 Variations sérieuses* in D minor op. 54 by Felix Mendelssohn Bartholdy; *Deux Études*, no. 1 in F major, no. 2 in D minor op. 105 by Ignaz Moscheles; and *Fantaisie* in B flat major op. 54 by Wilhelm Taubert. Concluding the volume is a *Romance sans paroles* in G minor op. 41 no. 1, by the piano virtuoso Sigismund Thalberg, which Mechetti also issued separately together with a piece of the same title for piano four-hands. As one reviewer curtly remarked: "Thalberg's romance makes a grand effect but is not exactly novel in invention."[19] The author of the original Songs without Words, who here abandoned the field to Liszt's pianistic rival, may likewise have been thoroughly critical in his reaction.[20] It is striking that Mendelssohn chose precisely this occasion to come to grips with an established musical genre. By

---

18 *Das Mozart-Album (zum Besten des Mozart-Denkmals)*, ed. August Pott (Brunswick: J. P. Spehr, [1842]). This anthology had been in preparation since 1839. It falls into three sections: original part songs, songs for voice and piano accompaniment, and pieces for piano. Mendelssohn was represented not with an original work, but with a piano arrangement by Carl Czerny of his lied "The Garland" on a text by Thomas Moore: *Der Blumenkranz. LIED OHNE WORTE. / COMP. VON MENDELSSOHN-BARTHOLDY. / übertragen von Charles Czerny*, pp. 124–5. A complete copy of the Mozart Album is located in the Music Department of the Staatsbibliothek Preussischer Kulturbesitz, Berlin. The author wishes to thank Dr. Joachim Jaenecke for kindly supplying this information.

19 *Allgemeine musikalische Zeitung* 44/22 (1 June 1842), col. 447.

20 Mendelssohn's fears that his Songs without Words were all too prone to shallow imitation proved well founded. See the chapter "Nachklänge" in Christa Jost, *Mendelssohns Lieder ohne Worte* (Tutzing, 1988), pp. 20–24.

so doing he also reenacted his own variation of an earlier incident which has become a legend of music history.

The alphabetical arrangement of the Beethoven Album recalls an anthology of twenty years earlier which had also appeared in Vienna. Anton Diabelli's "patriotic enterprise" was virtually an "alphabetical lexicon of all those names [of its day] which had either long been celebrated or held out much promise for the future."[21] It is made up of "variations for piano on a given theme, composed by the most distinguished musicians of Vienna and the Royal Imperial Austrian states."[22] The malleability of the given waltz theme sheds light on the state of compositional technique during this particular period of music history. Of the authors in our Beethoven Album, Czerny, Kalkbrenner, Liszt, and Moscheles had also been involved in this earlier project. Beethoven's fruitful "act of presumption" in this context is well known. Part I of the 1824 publication, we may recall, is made up of his *33 Variations on a Waltz by Diabelli* op. 120, followed in a second volume by the variations of all the other participants. "This is perfectly correct from the viewpoint of music history, but for its day it was fairly unusual, indeed even monstrous, to make Beethoven equal in significance to 'all the remaining composers combined.'"[23] Thus, for an anthology in which Beethoven's successors were meant to stand out against the backdrop of his *oeuvre*, it is not entirely fortuitous that Mendelssohn should choose to contribute to a genre rightly seen by Adolf Bernhard Marx as "one of the mainsprings of Beethoven's historical impact."

Even contemporary critics emphasized the special position of Mendelssohn's piece in this gathering of "original compositions." The *Allgemeine musikalische Zeitung*, for instance, found that "perhaps the most carefully wrought piece in the album is Mendelssohn Bartholdy's *Variations sérieuses*. We recommend a study of this work to pianists of any school; their industry will be repaid."[24] The *Neue Zeitschrift für Musik* likewise singled out Mendelssohn's piece: "If the entrepreneur merits praise for his idea, even more so do the composers who altruistically helped his idea to fruition. And here again we must give pride of place to F. Mendelssohn Bartholdy who, with a complete set of variations of no mean achievement, has contributed an opus worthy both of himself and of the project. It is not our aim to persuade anyone of contrary taste that his piece is also the most significant one from a musical

21 Heinrich Rietsch, "Fünfundachtzig Variationen über Diabellis Walzer," *Beethoven-Jahrbuch* 1 (Munich and Leipzig, 1908), pp. 28–50.
22 Thus reads the introductory title of the anthology.
23 Günter Brosche in *Anton Diabellis Vaterländischer Künstlerverein, Zweite Abteilung* (Vienna, 1824), published by Günter Brosche (Graz, 1983), p. vii (*Denkmäler der Tonkunst in Österreich*).
24 *Allgemeine musikalische Zeitung* 44 (1842), col. 447.

standpoint; it seems so to us."[25] None the less, the reviewer found fault with the "Frankish" title of the album and its use of the word "brillant," which Kalkbrenner also appropriated for the subtitle of his own composition.[26] Given these circumstances, the advisability of Mendelssohn's epithet "sérieuses" to characterize his variations can hardly be questioned. To readers of the Beethoven Album the genre of "variations brillants" would almost immediately have sprung to mind. We need only add "faciles et sur un thème connu" to describe further the many products that flooded the market at this time.

For Mendelssohn, as we know from the famous account of his musical aesthetics to Marc André Souchay, the richness of verbal expression had a negative aspect. Compared to music, the composer found words "ambiguous, imprecise, susceptible to misunderstanding."[27] In the same way, intrinsically we might say, a variety of meanings lurk in the epithet "sérieuses." An exploration of these meanings can open up new perspectives for analysis. R. Larry Todd, for example, finds in this term an allusion to the label "serioso" in Beethoven's music.[28] By way of evidence he points out several connections between Variation 10 in the manuscript version and the contrapuntal intermezzo in the Allegretto ma non troppo of Beethoven's F minor String Quartet op. 95. Besides the heading "Quartetto serioso" given to this work in the autograph, the term also crops up in the heading to the scherzo-like third movement, "Allegro assai vivace, ma serioso." Another occurrence of the term, otherwise an unusual one for Beethoven, is in the tempo mark "Allegro ma non troppo e serioso" in the sixth of the Diabelli Variations op. 120. Kurt von Fischer, who elaborated these connections in his essay "Never to be Performed in Public," considers the term "serioso" to be largely an instruction to the performer, being "the opposite of *scherzoso* and

25 *Neue Zeitschrift für Musik* 16/15 (18 Feb 1842), 57.

26 Kalkbrenner appears on the title page resplendent with awards and honors (*Officier de la Légion d'Honneur, Chevalier de l'Aigle Rouge de Prusse 3me Classe, de l'ordre de Belgique &tc.*), thereby attesting to his self-esteem. This latter was maliciously scrutinized by Heine who, in *Lutetia*, describes how Kalkbrenner's contemporaries envy the composer "for his elegant outward bearing, his polished, dapper nature, his smoothness and sugariness, for his entire marzipanesque appearance, which to a quiet observer, however, has a slight admixture of tawdriness thanks to many an involuntary Berlinism of the basest origins, so that Koreff is no less witty than accurate in remarking of the man: 'He looks like a *bonbon* fallen in the mud.'" *Lutetia*. *Berichte über Politik, Kunst und Volksleben*, LVI (Paris, 26 March 1843). Reprinted in Heinrich Heine, *Sämtliche Schriften in zwölf Bänden*, ed. Klaus Briegleb (Frankfurt, 1981), vol. ix, p. 440.

27 Letter of 15 October 1842 from Berlin, in *Briefe aus den Jahren 1830–1847 von Felix Mendelssohn Bartholdy*, ed. Paul and Carl Mendelssohn Bartholdy, 6th edn. (Leipzig, 1889), vol. II, pp. 221–2.

28 R. Larry Todd, "Piano music reformed: the case of Felix Mendelssohn Bartholdy," *Nineteenth-Century Piano Music*, ed. R. L. Todd (New York, 1990), pp. 204–07.

hence a warning not to render the music all too lightly and playfully."[29] In this context the heading of Mendelssohn's A major Fugue, the fifth of the Seven Character Pieces op. 7, is also worthy of mention: *Ernst, und mit steigender Lebhaftigkeit* ("Serious and with increasing vitality"). The same applies to its expression mark "sempre legato." While the second fugue from this opus – no. 3 in D major, marked *kräftig und feurig* ("with strength and passion") – draws on Handel's example, the A major Fugue is a musical obeisance to Johann Sebastian Bach.

According to the *Geschichte der Gewandhausconcerte zu Leipzig*, the première performance of the *Variations sérieuses* took place on 27 November 1841.[30] Having removed to Berlin at the end of July 1841, Mendelssohn visited Leipzig in November and played there in, among other events, the First Musical Soirée. Here, after giving his Piano Trio in D minor op. 49, with the violinist Ferdinand David and the cellist Franz Carl Wittmann, Mendelssohn – as our chronicler specifically informs us – played his *Variations sérieuses* from manuscript "as a novelty." His final documented performance of the work took place in private surroundings. One evening in the summer of 1846 Mendelssohn played the set to visiting house guests, among them Richard Wagner and Louis Spohr. In *Mein Leben* Wagner reports that he heard Spohr play the violin part in one of his quartets.[31] Spohr's autobiography also records that Mendelssohn appeared in the dual capacity of composer and performer: "He played a fearsomely difficult and highly idiosyncratic composition of his own, 'seventeen serious variations,' with monstrous bravura, followed by two quartets by Spohr, including his most recent one (no. 30), during which Mendelssohn and Wagner read along in the score with delighted expressions."[32]

With his *Variations sérieuses* Mendelssohn thus stood his ground even against a representative of the younger generation. Wagner, with his spectacular performance of Beethoven's Ninth during the Dresden Palm Sunday Concerts (5 April 1846), had set the foundations of a performance tradition that survived far into our own century. Whether contrary views on the interpretation of Beethoven[33] were discussed during the composers' long and exhilarating conversation remains a matter of conjecture. Wagner's personal attitude toward

29 Kurt von Fischer, "'Never to be performed in public.' Zu Beethovens Streichquartett op. 95," *Beethoven-Jahrbuch 1973–77*, ed. Hans Schmidt and Martin Staehelin (Bonn, 1977), pp. 87–96.

30 *Geschichte der Gewandhausconcerte zu Leipzig vom 25. November 1781 bis 25. November 1881. Im Auftrage der Concert-Direction verfasst von Alfred Dörffel* (Leipzig, 1884), pp. 99, 120, 122.

31 Richard Wagner, *Mein Leben: erste authentische Veröffentlichung*, ed. Martin Gregor-Dellin (Munich, 1963), p. 395.

32 Louis Spohr, *Selbstbiographie* (Kassel and Göttingen, 1861), vol. II, pp. 306–7.

33 See the document section of Richard Wagner's reduction for piano two-hands of Beethoven's Ninth Symphony, WWV 9, with an account of Wagner's encounter with this work as an arranger and conductor, in *Sämtliche Werke*, vol. xx/1, ed. Christa Jost (Mainz, 1989).

Mendelssohn was – as the investigations of Jacob Katz have shown[34] – not marked by anti-Semitic misgivings during the composer's lifetime. Since, unlike Mendelssohn, he could no longer feel rooted in a "classical" dual existence as a composer-performer, Wagner was all the more aware that certain musical genres would forever remain closed to him. When he later stated that the *sine qua non* for writing variations in the nineteenth century lay in an ability to improvise he referred specifically to the *Diabelli* Variations – and hence to a mental image of Beethoven as an improvising musician.[35]

This polarity between composition and improvisation also left its mark on the program of a soirée held at the London residence of Karl Klingemann on 9 July 1844. The performers – Mendelssohn and Moscheles – were faced with the task of playing a joint improvisation, the *Duo concertant en variations brillantes sur la Marche Bohémienne tirée du mélodrame "Preciosa" de C. M. Weber*, in contrast to the elaborately written-out *Variations sérieuses*. The *Preciosa* Variations arose in 1833 in the space of two days, and were only set down beforehand in outline. Mendelssohn undertook to play the introduction and the first two variations, Moscheles the third and fourth (with connecting *tutti*); the finale was taken by both. Thus, the execution of details was left to the spur of the moment. As Moscheles remarked after the first public rendition with orchestral accompaniment: "No one noticed that the entire thing had only been hastily sketched out and that each of us was permitted to improvise his solos until he reencountered his fellow harmonically at certain prearranged points in the score."[36] Fanny Hensel roundly criticized the published edition for piano four-hands which appeared in 1834: "Moscheles' redaction of your gypsy variations will, I venture to say, not please you. It is clumsily done and has precious little that I can attribute to you, the additions such as the introduction being very drab. I feel that, for the published version, he should have brought out the extempore character a bit."[37]

34 Jacob Katz, *Richard Wagner: Vorbote des Antisemitismus* (Königstein im Taunus, 1985), pp. 51–2.

35 "Beethoven loved this form and did himself proud in the thirty-three variations; he, Richard, could not; I said he could if he wished, at which R.: 'No, to do that one needs something at one's command, namely, an ability to improvise on the instrument.'" – From Cosima Wagner's diaries, ed. M. Gregos-Dellin and D. Mack vol. II (1878–83), entry of 11 November 1878 (Munich and Zurich, 1977), p. 226. See also the summation of the brilliant passage of 10 September 1865 regarding Franz Liszt: "I am simply too stupid for such things: I can't even vary a theme once!" Richard Wagner, *Das braune Buch: Tagebuchaufzeichnungen 1865 bis 1882*, ed. Joachim Bergfeld (Zurich and Freiburg, 1975), pp. 84–5.

36 *Aus Moscheles' Leben: Nach Briefen und Tagebüchern*, ed. Charlotte Moscheles (Leipzig, 1872), vol. I, pp. 266–7.

37 Letter from Berlin of 18 February 1834 in *The Letters of Fanny Hensel to Felix Mendelssohn*, ed. and trans. Marcia J. Citron (Stuyvesant, 1987), p. 454 (No. 51). [Translation adapted for this article.]

By and large, the *Preciosa* Variations give evidence of Mendelssohn's and Moscheles' powers of improvisation, the effect of which cannot be captured on paper. The printed text reveals how much was patched over by the "unreduplicatability" of the moment. The internal coherence of a written-out musical argument cannot simply be imposed *ex post facto* on what was merely meant to be a play of imagination. Indeed, any attempt to impart the character of an art-work to improvised music after the fact generally proves to be precarious. Thus, in so far as it applies to a set of variations, the term "sérieuses" probably also harbors a plea to adhere strictly to the printed text.[38]

Thoughts on the relation between key and musical character can easily end in barren speculations. Nevertheless, Mendelssohn once made a remark in this regard which directs us precisely to this topic. In a letter to his sister Rebecka he wrote: "The variations go from D minor and are irksome."[39] In musicological writings the key of D minor is quite often linked with melancholy.[40] "Melancholy femininity that breeds phantasms and vapors" was how Schubart once characterized the key of D minor.[41] Overlooking the masculine smugness detectable between these lines, we note that D minor is accorded an urge toward the speculative. Mendelssohn's compositions in D minor are marked by quite contrasting characters. Yet a certain inclination toward a

38 The clarity with which Mendelssohn in particular used to distinguish between improvisation on the one hand, and interpretation and composition on the other, is revealed by his violent reaction to the improvisatory playing of Franz Liszt. His outrage found expression in a letter to David: "Not even Liszt can give me half as much pleasure here as elsewhere, and he sacrificed a large part of my esteem by the foolish antics he plays not just with his audience (there is no harm in that) but with the music itself as well. He played Beethoven, Bach, Handel, and Weber with such wretched shortcomings, so untidily and ignorantly, that I had much rather have heard them played by mediocre pianists. Here he added six measures, there he omitted seven; here he took the wrong harmonies and then set them aright by playing more wrong ones to boot, there he turned the quietest passages into an ugly *fortissimo* – and who knows what other sad nonsense besides. No doubt it's good enough for the audience, but not for me, and that it was good enough for Liszt is what cost him a large part of my esteem. And yet – my esteem was so great that a good deal of it still remains." – Letter of 5 February 1842 from Berlin to Ferdinand David in Felix Mendelssohn Bartholdy, *Briefe aus Leipziger Archiven*, ed. Hans-Joachim Rothe and Reinhard Szeskus (Leipzig, 1972), p. 174 (No. 108). Mendelssohn's view, that musical performance should seek the most authentic rendition of a work, proved after the event to be the more modern of the two. His profound respect for Bach's music, however, did not prevent him from making an arrangement for violin and piano of the Chaconne from the D minor Partita.

39 Letter to Rebecka Dirlichet, quoted in Eric Werner, *Mendelssohn: Leben und Werk in neuer Sicht* (Zurich, 1980), p. 392.

40 The notions of "grave and death" and the "frozen stoniness of the crypt" which Hermann Beckh associated with the key of D minor are obviously derived from Mozart's *Don Giovanni*; see Hermann Beckh, *Die Sprache der Tonart in der Musik von Bach bis Bruckner* (Stuttgart, 1941), p. 110. Regarding Schumann's characterization of D minor see Reinhard Kapp, *Studien zum Spätwerk Robert Schumanns* (Tutzing, 1984), pp. 152–5.

41 Christian Friedrich Daniel Schubart, *Ideen zu einer Aesthetik der Tonkunst*, ed. Ludwig Schubart (Vienna, 1806), p. 377.

more serious vein is unmistakable. The D minor opening of *Elijah*, from the prophet's curse to the cry of the Israelites against the overwhelming affliction of drought in Chorus No. 1 ("Herr, willst du uns vernichten"), deals with the vulnerability of life. In the incidental music to Sophocles' *Oedipus in Colonos*, death appears as the backdrop against which life takes on meaning. The second number ("Grausam ist es, O Freund"), in D minor, discloses the ominous fate that awaits the blind hero. In the "Reformation" Symphony op. 107, elements from Protestant church music are incorporated into the symphonic tradition. The Allegro con fuoco, in D minor, is linked thematically with the slow major introduction, at the end of which, as at the beginning of the recapitulation, Mendelssohn quotes the "Dresden Amen." Though the composer later withdrew this composition of 1830, he continued to accord great importance to its overall design. Similarly impressive is the Organ Sonata op. 65 no. 6, a set of variations with a fugue on the theme "Vater unser im Himmelreich." Minor lyric pieces in D minor, on the other hand, are rare. His only D minor lied for voice and piano – "Seemanns Scheidelied," on a poem by Hoffmann von Fallersleben[42] – is a peripheral work. The "irksome" mood, which reaches a low-point in the refrain "ach hätt ich dich doch nie geliebt" ("ah! if only I had ne'er loved thee!"), was apparently not enough to inspire the composer musically. The meaning of D minor for Mendelssohn, however, goes beyond a mere *lamento* character. The composer explored less "serious" realms of expression in, for example, his Second Piano Concerto op. 40, the most prominent counter-example to our foregoing remarks. At all events, in light of this work we can hardly claim that for Mendelssohn the "psyche" of D minor automatically conjured up sorrow and death.

Mendelssohn's contemporaries held his op. 54 in high regard as a major set of variations. Moscheles mentions them in one breath with the Songs without Words: "It refreshes both mind and heart that I have the task of correcting the fourth volume of 'Songs without Words'. I play them and the *Variations sérieuses* again and again, enjoying their beauties anew at every turn."[43] Robert Schumann, on the other hand, saw a qualitative difference between the two genres. As he wrote to Franz Brendel on 18 September 1849: "What a capital work are Mendelssohn's D minor Variations – yet ask whether they are one-quarter as well known as, say, the Songs without Words."[44] The critic of the *Allgemeine musikalische Zeitung* emphasized the work's proximity to Bach: "Admittedly no one will fail to notice the influence of Sebastian Bach;

---

42 The two remaining lieder in D minor – *Das Heimweh* op. 8 no. 2 (after Friederike Robert) and *Verlust* op. 9 no. 10 (after Heinrich Heine) – were written by Fanny Mendelssohn.
43 *Aus Moscheles' Leben: Nach Briefen und Tagebüchern*, vol. II, pp. 80–81.
44 *Robert Schumanns Briefe, neue Folge*, ed. T. G. Jansen, 2nd edn. (Leipzig, 1904), p. 312.

the theme, already in a legato style, betrays not an inkling of what is about to be gleaned from it by a master contrapuntist."[45] Its relation to Beethoven was remarked upon in 1971 by Charles Rosen, who saw its forebear in the C minor Variations for Piano, WoO 80.[46] Eric Werner contested this thesis in a footnote only to confirm it by remarking that "the Beethoven of the C minor Variations" had, among other things, "stood godfather" to the work.[47] Beethoven's piece, published in 1807, took recourse in Baroque techniques.

In this connection we might note the sets of variations for piano two-hands that Mendelssohn performed during his tenure at the Leipzig Gewandhaus. On 21 January 1841, in the first of the Historic Concerts, devoted to Bach and Handel, he played a "theme with variations (in E major) by Handel (from the *Lessons for the Harpsichord*, first published in the year 1720)"; on 27 November of the same year the *Variations sérieuses*, as mentioned above; and on 12 February 1846 Beethoven's C minor Variations.[48] Yet even if the *Variations sérieuses* allude to Beethoven's methods, they are not patterned after an earlier model but, instead, follow their own internal logic. Mendelssohn's compositions, as Carl Dahlhaus put forth in an analysis of the *Die erste Walpurgisnacht*, "cannot be described in categories abstracted from Beethoven's works without doing them a grave disservice."[49]

The manuscript of the *Variations sérieuses*, written in ink, is located in volume 35 on pp. 23/25 to [36], and encompasses ten pages. Page numbers have been added by the librarian, with pasted pages being treated as ordinary pages. This pagination is referred to below with the abbreviations "p." or "pp." Mendelssohn also supplied his own pagination from 1 to 8 (referred to below as "pag."), thereby skipping the deleted Variations 10 to 14 on pp. [32]–3. Mendelssohn's thoughts on the ultimate order of the variations can be reconstructed from his many insertions, regroupings, and deletions. Since he renumbered some of the variations many times the changes can be retraced with some degree of accuracy. The following analysis attempts to shed light on Mendelssohn's train of thought as documented in the holograph. Table 2.1 lists the renumberings, insertions and original tempo marks of the source. Deleted numbers are indicated by horizontal strokes. Numbers in parentheses refer to the pagination prior to revision. Remarks enclosed in angle brackets were added in pencil at a later date to clarify the process of composition. They are possibly not by Mendelssohn.

45 *Allgemeine musikalische Zeitung* 44 (1842), col. 447.
46 Charles Rosen, *The Classical Style: Haydn, Mozart, Beethoven* (London, 1971), p. 401.
47 Werner, *Mendelssohn: Leben und Werk*, p. 394.
48 Alfred Dörffel, *Geschichte der Gewandhausconcerte*, pp. 122–3.
49 Carl Dahlhaus, "'Hoch symbolisch intentioniert': Zu Mendelssohns 'Erster Walpurgisnacht,'" *Österreichische Musikzeitung* 36 (1981), 290–97.

Table 2.1. *Mendelssohn, Variations sérieuses op. 54. Overview of the composing manuscript (Kraków, Biblioteca Jagiellońska, Mendelssohn Nachlass, 35).*

Page	Pag.	System	op. 54	MS	Revision	Insertion	Tempo mark
23/25	1	1–2	Theme	II.		*⟨Var 1 pag.4⟩	Andante sostenuto
		2–5	Var.2	III.			Un poco più animato
		5–7	Var.3		(2.)		Presto
		7–8	Var.16	17	~~14.15.~~	Var.4,5 und 6 vide pag.4	
	2[a]	1–2	Var.16 [cont.]				
		2–4	Var.17	18			
		5–8	–	[Var. w/o no.]			
	[b]	1–2	Var.16 [cont.]	18	16(15)	vi= ⟨pag.3 Mitte⟩	
		2–8	Var.17	18 [theme over dominant pedal point, Coda]			
27/29	3[a]	1–3	Var.8			Var.10. ⟨pag.5⟩	Allegro vivace
		3–5	Var.9			= de	
		6–8	[theme over dominant pedal point, Coda]			⟨hier folgt die pag 6 in der Mitte⟩	
	[b/c]	1–3	Var.8	8			
		3–5	Var.9	9		vi=	
		6–8	[coda]				

Table 2.1. (*Cont.*)

4	1–2	Var.1	1		★⟨Var.2 pag.1⟩	
	blank					
	3–5	Var.4	4			Legato ed espressivo
	5–7	Var.5	5			Più Presto
	7	Var.6	6			
31 5	1	Var.6 [cont.]			⟨folgt pag.5⟩	
	1–4	Var.7	7		Var.8 vide pag.3	
	4–6	Var.10	10	(8)		Più Moderato
	6–8	Var.11	11	(9)	Var./12. vide pag.7.	
	1–2	Var.15	10			
	2–4	—	11			
—	4–7	—	12			
	7–8	—	13			
33	1–3	—	13 [cont.]			
—	3–6	—	14 [?]			
6	1–2	Var.15	15		Var.17 ±5 vide pag.1	
	2–4	—	16	13(12)		Poco a poco cre[sc]
				14(13)		ed accelerando
						f sempre più Presto
	5–8	Coda			= de	
35 7	1–2	Coda			⟨hier folgt pag.7⟩	
	blank				Leipzig d. 4ten Juni 1841.	
	3–4	Var.14	14	~~12~~	~~Dur~~ Variation	Adagio ~~Mod~~to
					Var.15(13) vide pag.6.	
	5–7	Var.12	12		Volti subi[to]	
					Var.13. pag.8.	
8	1–5	Var.13	13		Var.14. vide pag.7.	Tempo del Tema

Table 2.2. *Mendelssohn*, Variations sérieuses *op. 54. Final order of variations*

Theme	Andante sostenuto
Var. 1	
Var. 2	Un poco più animato
Var. 3	Più animato
Var. 4	
Var. 5	Agitato
Var. 6	A tempo
Var. 7	
Var. 8	Allegro vivace
Var. 9	
Var. 10	Moderato
Var. 11	
Var. 12	Tempo del Tema
Var. 13	
Var. 14	Adagio
Var. 15	Poco a poco più agitato
Var. 16	Allegro vivace
Var. 17	
	Presto

Mendelssohn's efforts with the work, however, did not end with his revision of the draft. Even the engraver's copy seemed to him to stand in need of revision, as is shown by the aforementioned changes he made to the engraved plates. Table 2.2, for purposes of comparison, contains the final sequence of the variations and their tempo relations. What strikes us at first glance is that early on the holograph presents the material ultimately used in the finale (see Plate 2.2). The sixteen-measure four-voice theme, marked "Andante sostenuto," is followed for the moment by only two variations, numbered II and III, in the tempo of the theme. In the printed version, the legato Variation 2 already has the tempo mark "un poco più animato" which Mendelssohn applied to the staccato Variation III in the holograph. In the manuscript this is immediately followed by Variations 16 and 17, here marked "Presto." The finale section on pag. 2 extends to the return of the theme over a dominant pedal point. The beginnings of a coda, differing radically from that of the printed version, are elaborated on pag. 3. Alongside the finale we also find Variations 8 and 9 on pag. 3, from systems 1 to 5. These embody the first climax of the set. In the printed version Variations 8 and 16 have the same tempo mark, "Allegro vivace," suggesting that they share a similar virtuoso

2.2.   Mendelssohn, *Variations sérieuses*, op. 54, autograph; Kraków, Biblioteca Jagiellońska, *Mendelssohn Nachlass*, vol. 35, pagina 1 (23/25).

gesture. The three different pastings of systems 4 to 8 on pag. 2, systems 6 to 8 on pag. 3 and system 5 on pag. 3 (from measure 3ff.) have each come undone on one side, revealing the first fair copy intact beneath them. This originally foresaw Variation 9 and the later final variation as a self-contained sixteen-measure entity (see Plate 2.3). To summarize, following a complex made up of early versions of Variations 2, 3, 16, and 17, the composer elaborates a new, unnumbered variation up to the return of the theme over a dominant pedal point, after which he turns to the stretto of the coda. At this stage the repeated chords begin with the right hand instead of the left, as in the printed version. Quite obviously, then, Mendelssohn first sketched the overall shape of the work and only then considered in detail how to manipulate his theme.

In elaborating the piece from pag. 4 Mendelssohn now set up the sequence of variations systematically. Variation 1 departs from the theme by introducing a constant sixteenth-note motion in the middle voice. The blank line after the first two systems doubtless signifies that Variations 2 and 3, which had already been written down on pag. 1, were to be inserted between Variation 1 and Variation 4, the latter being a two-part canon. While retaining the same meter and roughly the same length, the variations nevertheless point in different directions with regard to their compositional technique. Here Mendelssohn has combined contrasting characters in mutual interaction. The canonic texture of Variation 4, for instance, is offset by chordal writing in the *agitato* Variation 5. Following Variation 10, a fugato, the next variation stands out by adopting the tone of a lyric piano piece. Mendelssohn's insertion of Variations 8 and 9 from pag. 3 proves to have been an afterthought. The fugato, originally marked "Var. 8," thus had to be renumbered, as did all the subsequent variations up to the coda. In the work's final form Variation 10, marked "Moderato," slows down the increase in tempo and dynamics, thereby turning Variation 9 with its virtuoso figurations into a temporary climax. These two variations depart from the regular sixteen-measure pattern, being respectively twenty and eighteen measures long.

A continuous 2/4 meter was not necessarily one of the work's axioms. Among the variations from the deleted complex on pp. [32]–3, nos. 12 and 13 are in 6/8 meter. The last of the deleted variations, no. 14, then returns to 2/4. The metric relations Mendelssohn had in view can be found in the E major variation movement of his String Quartet op. 81 no. 1 (1847), which was published posthumously in 1850. Another possible example, from Beethoven's *oeuvre*, is the *Eroica* Variations. In the sketches for his later Variations in E flat major op. 82, located on pages 15 to 17 of volume 35, Mendelssohn likewise considered the possibility of changing from 2/4 to 6/8 meter. Here, too, he breaks off his piece with the change of meter and tempo

2.3. Mendelssohn, *Variations sérieuses* op. 54, autograph; Kraków, Biblioteca Jagiellońska, *Mendelssohn Nachlass*, vol. 35; (a) pagina 2, with pasteover removed; (b) pag. 2, with pasteover; (c) pag. 3, with pasteover removed; and (d) pag. 3, with pasteover.

(*a*)

(b)

(c)
2.3 (cont.)

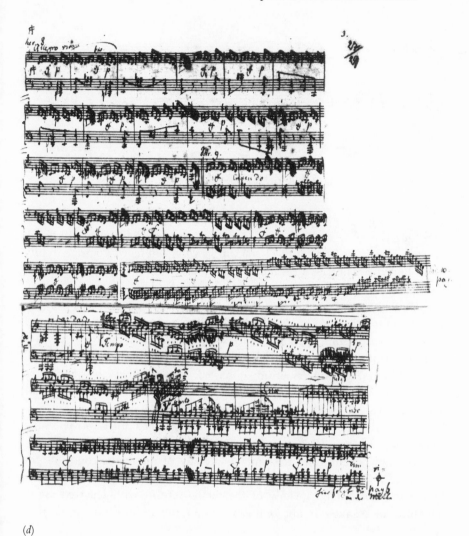

(d)

Ex. 2.1:   Beethoven, *An die ferne Geliebte* op. 98, mm. 301ff

(Allegro vivace / L'istesso tempo) in Variation 5 after writing down the theme and four variations in 2/4 meter. Thus, the complete draft on pp. 19 to 22, located directly in front of the *Variations sérieuses* and dated Leipzig, 25 July 1841, likewise maintains a 2/4 meter throughout.

Before discarding Variations 10 to 14 wholesale Mendelssohn first deleted no. 12. This variation, like nos. 13 and 14, allowed greater license in the number of measures. As his deletions called for a stricter handling of form, the variation process shifted from the surface of the composition to a less visible stratum. At the same time Mendelssohn also jettisoned several direct allusions to Beethoven. As Todd has already observed,[50] the chromatic bass line in the deleted Variation 13, though derivable from the theme, recalls in its shape the chaconne bass of Beethoven's C minor Variations. Furthermore, the suppressed Variation 11 contains a phrase from the final lied of Beethoven's song cycle *An die ferne Geliebte* (see Exx. 2.1 and 2.2). A clear indication that distance and proximity to the soprano melody of the theme constitute the backbone of the cycle can be seen in the deleted Variation 14 (see Plate 2.4). At this point the soprano melody of the theme returns with renewed vigor. Doubled in octaves, it not only appears in the right hand but is then

Ex. 2.2:   Mendelssohn, *Variations sérieuses* op. 54, suppressed Variation 12 (*Mendelssohn Nachlass*, vol. 35, p. 32)

50 Todd, "Piano music reformed: the case of Felix Mendelssohn Bartholdy," p. 206.

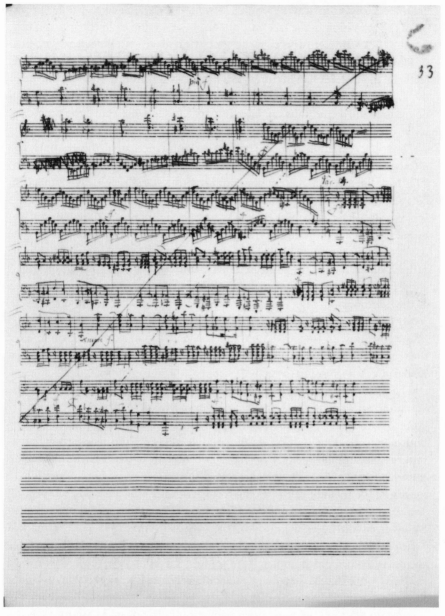

2.4.   Mendelssohn, *Variations sérieuses* op. 54, autograph; Kraków, Biblioteca Jagiellońska, *Mendelssohn Nachlass*, vol. 35, p. 33, with deleted Variation 14.

hammered out in the lower register as well. This march-like opening breaks off at the repetition of the second eight-measure section of the theme. On pag. 7 and 8 the composer turns to more sophisticated structural devices. The final system on the discarded p. 33 contains an idea which only entered the coda after the manuscript had been revised. Here the concluding *gruppetto* figure in the soprano part of the theme (measures 14–16) seems extracted from the span of a minor third, and thus can later impart a cadential effect to the preceding scalar descent (measures 12–14).

The only variation which retained its substance after this section was discarded is Variation 10, which figures in the printed version as Variation 15. The bass line, opening with descending tritones and originally doubled in octaves, forms the basis for Variation 16 which follows in the manuscript but was cut at a later stage (pag. 6). The octave doubling in Variation 15 was deleted as early as the autograph stage; isolated instances were deleted at a later date. Mendelssohn concluded his piece by expanding the variation of the finale written out at the fourth position in his manuscript. As the pastings on pag. 2 and 3 reveal, he thereby retained the essence of the discarded complex as well as the additions on pag. 7 and 8 which, rather than alluding to Beethoven, return in a highly sophisticated manner to the opening theme. The conclusion of the coda now follows on pag. 6 and 7. Mendelssohn's original plan to have the truncated dominant-seventh arpeggio played *ad libitum* and the restrained final cadence *a tempo* was already rejected at the autograph stage.

The first addition on pag. 7 completes the set by adding the *maggiore* variation, lacking till now. Its original tempo mark, "Moderato," was later corrected to read "Adagio." While Variation 1 starts the variation process with sixteenth-note motion in the middle register, the *maggiore* variation restores the soprano melody of the theme. The next two variations develop this idea further. As early as the repeated thirty-second notes of Variation 12 on pag. 7 the melody of the theme recurs complete. In Variation 13 (pag. 8), surrounded by thirty-second-note figuration in the soprano and underpinned by even eighth notes in the bass, the "melody for piano alone" (marked "sempre marcato e cantabile" in the holograph) quotes the soprano line of the theme verbatim and dominates the texture. So seamlessly does this inward shift take place that Martin Friedland could reproach the work at this point for "clinging sensuously to the theme."[51] In any event, it negates the change of texture no less than the movement's function in the overall design.

Also relevant in this context is a compositional design invented by E. T. A. Hoffmann in the opening number of his *Kreisleriana*. Here Kapellmeister

51 Martin Friedland, *Zeitstil und Persönlichkeitsstil in den Variationswerken der musikalischen Romantik* (Leipzig, 1930), p. 71.

Johannes Kreisler chooses not to end his rendition of the Goldberg Variations with a *da capo* of the Aria. Instead, he improvises his own flamboyant variations on the subject of Bach. Notes, keys, fingertips, and ideas are interwoven in the dying flicker of the candlelight to form ever-new grotesqueries. Kinesis culminates in ecstasy. The boundaries of reality and dream begin to blur in this scene, for Kreisler's compositions are nothing more than phantasms of his brain. Hoffmann unites a real performance of a set of variations with the literary fiction of a final apotheosis. This scene outlines an idea which, though deriving from Bach, recalls Beethoven's handling of form. As Stefan Kunze has remarked, it is this sense of finality, of a "formal design deducible from its conclusion," that forms the crucial criterion of the "truly and completely new manner" in Beethoven's *Eroica* Variations.[52]

It is probably no coincidence, then, that in confronting his *Variations sérieuses* Mendelssohn should have started the compositional process with their final climactic gesture. The *maggiore* variation with its tempo mark "Adagio" (seldom encountered in Mendelssohn's music) signals the beginning of a new section which ends with the final climax of the coda and casts all of the preceding musical events in a new light, not only with regard to their mode and tempo relations (from *adagio* to *presto*), but also regarding the work's structure. In contrast, Variations 12 and 13 conclude a circular process in which the increasing tempo of the first part is restored to the "tempo del tema." The arch extending from the four-voice texture of the theme to the texture of a Song without Words in Variation 13 recalls one of Mendelssohn's improvisations as described by Ferdinand Hiller: "He had to return to the piano and improvise by weaving a Bach motif in the most ingenious fashion into the first of his well-known Songs without Words, uniting past and present [*Sonst und Jetzt*] into something new and virtually unnameable."[53] Evolution is no longer teleological. The past is embodied in a Bach quotation, Mendelssohn's own music in a Song without Words. Distance and proximity overlap. Improvising, the composer reflects on the past as the condition of the future in order to develop from it something entirely new.[54]

---

52 Stefan Kunze, "Die 'wirklich gantz neue Manier' in Beethovens Eroica-Variationen op. 35," *Archiv für Musikwissenschaft* 29 (1972), 124–49.

53 Ferdinand Hiller, *Felix Mendelssohn Bartholdy: Briefe und Erinnerungen* (Cologne, 1874), p. 144.

54 It should also be mentioned that the title "Sonst und Jetzt" also heads Spohr's Concertino for Violin and Orchestra, which was premièred in Kassel during the winter season of 1838–9 and repeated at the request of the Prince Elector during a Beethoven celebration in spring of 1839 (see Spohr's autobiography, p. 227). An even more deliberate allusion to the vicissitudes of time is found in Spohr's "Historical Symphony in the Style and Taste of Four Different Eras." Here music history becomes the subject of a composition. In the final movement Spohr gives vent to his estrangement from the music of his contemporaries. The periods of Bach and Handel (first

Ex. 2.3: Handel, Suite No. III, Air, mm. 1–4

If Mendelssohn worked out the overall shape of his piece in various stages, by the time he wrote down the main theme it had already assumed, by and large, its final form. True, he continued to make corrections to the part writing in manuscript, but they are relatively insignificant. On closer observation Mendelssohn's original theme proves to be highly complex. Following a detailed analysis of its harmony Peter Rummenhöller could refer to the four-part texture as "one of the most sophisticated Mendelssohnian hybrids of sentimentality and patina."[55] He also stresses the merging of past and present, albeit with a somewhat irreverent undertone. One indication that Mendelssohn, like Beethoven in his C minor Variations, found his bearings in Handel is provided by the fifth movement of the latter's Keyboard Suite No. 3 in D minor (see Ex. 2.3). The sixteen-measure theme of the *Variations sérieuses* reveals clear similarities with Handel's twelve-measure "Air" in common meter.[56] Leaving aside the notes in small type, measures 3 and 4 of Handel's piece contain a scalar progression, $f''-e''-d''-c\sharp''-d''-e''-a'$, which recurs intact in Variation 5, measures 82 to 84, of Mendelssohn's piece (apart from a final $c\sharp$ in lieu of a). A variant of this figure inscribes a similar arc in the stretto of the coda (measures 339–41). In Mendelssohn's theme itself, on the other hand, the scalar descent in measures 2 to 4 leads from f'' to a' by way of c'', the fifth scale degree of the relative major. Certain details in the harmony coincide as well. In

movement), Haydn and Mozart (Adagio) and Beethoven (Scherzo) repudiate the "most recent" period of 1840 (Finale), which Spohr refuses to take seriously. Mendelssohn criticized this stance in his report of the Leipzig Gewandhaus performance on 7 January 1841: "In the last piece I began to feel that the most recent time, for the very reason that you are its musical expression, should have been presented differently and with more grandeur; I thought it might crown the entire piece to have the earlier simple movements in contrasting styles followed earnestly and portentously by a final movement in your own manner that would in itself sum up the underlying idea of your symphony." See Spohr, *Selbstbiographie*, p. 232.

55 Peter Rummenhöller, *Romantik in der Musik* (Kassel, 1989), pp. 178–81.

56 This similarity was kindly pointed out to me by Dr. Ernst-Günter Heinemann of Munich.

both pieces the aforementioned scalar figure ends at measure 4 on the dominant, and both pieces cadence in the relative major after eight measures. In measure 9 of Handel's work, and from the latter half of measure 8 to measure 9 in Mendelssohn's, the section following the double bar opens with an F major chord in root position with the bass displaced one octave higher, the difference being that whereas Handel has the soprano on the third degree of the scale Mendelssohn has it on the fifth. Further points of similarity can be found in the composers' technique of variation. To thicken the texture of his D minor Suite Handel shifts the even sixteenth-note motion of the soprano part (Double 1) first to the bass (Double 2) and then to the middle voice (Double 3). Double 4, in 12/8 meter, intensifies the flow of the music by adding three-note figures in parallel motion. In this respect Doubles 3 and 4 resemble Mendelssohn's initial complex of Variations 1 and 2.

Another movement from Mendelssohn's *oeuvre* merits consideration in this context: the Andante con Variazioni from his Sonata in C minor for Viola and Piano, written between 23 November 1823 and 14 February 1824. The slow movement, in C minor, opens with a long theme of eighteen measures in 2/4 meter, starting on the upbeat. Its opening two-note figure, marked by appoggiaturas, is followed by a descending scalar figure leading through the subdominant and ending at $b'\natural$, the leading tone, on the dominant (see Ex. 2.4). The crucial difference between these themes, for all their melodic similarity, lies in the harmony. The former, an inspired piece of Mendelssohn juvenilia, decisively establishes the key of C minor by opening with the progression tonic–dominant seventh–tonic–subdominant–dominant. The theme of the *Variations sérieuses*, on the other hand, opens with the clearly articulated if disconcerting progression D minor–E major seventh–G minor–A major seventh, thereby obscuring the main harmonic functions (see Ex. 2.5). This may be seen as another connection to Beethoven. Beethoven's use of harmonic progressions whose tonal centers are not stated *a priori*, but emerge only in the

Ex. 2.4: Mendelssohn, Sonata in C minor for viola and piano, Andante con variazioni, mm. 1–8

Ex. 2.5:   Mendelssohn, *Variations sérieuses* op. 54, Theme, mm. 1–8

course of the music, has been studied by Peter Cahn and linked to Arnold Schönberg's concept of "fluctuating tonality."[57]

Looking at the thematic "germ-cell" *a'–g♯'–d"–c♯"* we can see how, in the *Variations sérieuses*, melody takes precedence over harmony. This initial melodic strain is typical of Mendelssohn. Figures of this sort have (in the words of Lars Ulrich Abraham) "leaps occurring in lieu of singable steps" and are hence "angular, unusual and, we might add, especially memorable."[58] The opening configuration of two half-steps separated by a tritone is counterbalanced in measures 4 to 6 by a descending chromatic line *a'–g♯'–g♮'–f♯'*. The descending scale had already been anticipated at the opening in the middle voices, following the chromatic cells in the soprano. In measures 8–9 and 10–11 the half-steps come to rest on the lower note, which increases in intensity by being sounded four times, like a *Bebung* on the clavichord, before the interval is inverted. Finally, hovering between leading tone and tonic, the melody inscribes a *gruppetto* within the interval of a minor third, from *c♯"* to *e"*.

Variation 1 alters the phrasing. The appoggiaturas on *a'* and *d"* now appear *sforzato* in the soprano while the bass, shortened to eighth notes, is made at once more striking and transparent by the octave doubling and *marcato* wedges. Even the viola-like sixteenth-note motion interpolated in the middle register is made to stand out against the upper voice by its own phrase mark. In Variation 2 the appoggiaturas dissolve into sextuplets as early as the second sixteenth note, bringing the more active figuration of the middle voices into the soprano melody and adding a soaring upward motion to the falling lines. These two legato variations are then followed by another two in staccato. We

57 Cahn, however, also draws attention to similar phenomena in slow introductions by Haydn and Mozart and to related traditions existing "ever since the Baroque period for free forms such as the fantasy." Peter Cahn, "Zum Problem der 'schwebenden Tonalität' bei Beethoven," *Studien zur Instrumentalmusik: Lothar Hoffmann-Erbrecht zum 60. Geburtstag*, ed. Anke Bingmann, Klaus Hortschansky, and Winfried Kirsch (Tutzing, 1988), p. 291.

58 Lars Ulrich Abraham, "Mendelssohns Chorlieder und ihre musikgeschichtliche Stellung," *Das Problem Mendelssohn*, ed. Carl Dahlhaus (Regensburg, 1974), pp. 79–87.

recall that, in the theme, the two chords of the final cadence are written as staccato sixteenths (measures 15–16). Variation 3 takes up the *gruppetto* motif that immediately precedes this cadence. Embedded in these spiralling figures, the half-steps now change direction, from $g\sharp'$ to a' and from $c\sharp''$ to d''. This subdivision and imitative compression of the chromatic germ-cells culminate in the canonic Variation 4. Here, starting with the first note of each beat, the melody unfolds in an even sixteenth-note motion. Taking the lead, the right hand varies the configuration $a'\!-\!g\sharp'\!-\!d''\!-\!c\sharp''$ of the antecedent (measures 64–6) while the left hand, in turn, takes up the chromatic descent of the consequent, $a\!-\!g\sharp\!-\!g'\!-\!f\sharp'$, this time with octave displacement (measures 68–70). The first four variations are interlinked by fluent transitions. Not until the eighth-note rest in measure 80 does the piece come to a temporary halt.

Variation 5 again approaches the melody of the theme. The heading "agitato," allowing greater liberties in tempo, and the expression mark "legato ed espressivo" focus attention on the sonority, now thickened by chordal repetition. The intervening tritone of the theme is expanded to form a perfect fifth by the addition of a minor second, from $g\sharp'$ to $g\natural'$. In Variation 6 the soprano melody spans two octaves, beginning with the sequence $a''\!-\!a'\!-\!g\sharp'\!-\!g\sharp''$ (measures 96–7) and gradually widening its ambitus. Equally irregular is the progression $d''''\!-\!d''\!-\!g'\!-\!g\sharp''$ in measures 97 and 98. The dynamic level expands in range from *pp* to *ff* in Variation 6. The sixteenth-note arpeggio of its final measure moves seamlessly into the next variation, marked "con fuoco." Here the structure is dominated by chords, either broken or simultaneous, with the upper notes of the latter bearing the chromatic germ-cells of the theme. These cells then dissolve in the fast virtuoso triplets of Variations 8 and 9. Chromatic tension is generated by the opening notes of the triplet figures on either side of the bar lines, whether in measures 128–31 ($a'\!-\!g\sharp'$) and 132–4 ($d''\!-\!c\sharp''$) or, in Variation 9, in measures 144–5 and 146–7.

In Variation 10 the melodic particles appear for the first time in a low register. The descending half-step $a\!-\!g\sharp$ (measures 164–5) ushers in the first entrance of a fugato, which is then answered one fourth higher by the second entrance on $d'\!-\!c\sharp'$ (measures 166–7). The texture of Variation 11 evokes a character piece. Its unreal, dream-like atmosphere results from a new harmonization. The whole step $a'\!-\!g'$ in measures 182–3 begins a five-note figure rising under a phrase mark to a'' in measure 184. In place of the D minor–E major seventh progression we now have a D major seventh chord leading to the subdominant and dominant, stabilizing the harmony and at the same time slowing down the harmonic rhythm. This lyric episode is made up of a

61

soprano part marked "cantabile," regular eighth notes in the bass and a rhythmically displaced chordal accompaniment in the middle register. In Variation 12 the soprano melody of the theme is already discernible in the repeated thirty-second notes taken alternately by the right and left hands. Variation 13 presents the theme *da capo* as a cantilena. This phase of recognition comes to an end with the fermata placed over the eighth-note rest in measure 234.

In the *adagio* variation the thematic "inner voice" again recedes against the luminescence of the added soprano melody. Variation 15 then draws attention to the "empty" space between the two half-steps. This middle interval in the $a'-g\sharp'-d''-c\sharp''$ figure, a tritone, is put center stage in inversion in measures 250 to 252 ($d-G\sharp$ and $g-c\sharp$) while the basic germ-cell is divided between different registers. In Variations 16 and 17 the appoggiatura note is separated from its resolution by interpolated slurs. Finally, from measure 323, falling lines in the upper voices are concentrated over a tremolando pedal point on the dominant.

Mendelssohn, then, does not manipulate the bass of his theme but rather the cantilena. Having broken down its structure in Variations 1 to 4, he then explores and juxtaposes its different characters in Variations 5 to 13. The final section elaborates the double meaning of the "variation motif." Not even in the brilliance of the coda does he depart from his rigorous musical conception. At most, its underlying gesture recalls an improvisation. Subtle variants are now chiselled out in staccato chords, relentlessly repeated. The concluding Presto once again presents the figure $a-g-d'-c\sharp'$ in the melody (measures 337–9) with the descending whole step now harmonized by a progression from tonic to supertonic seventh in third inversion. The background tritone comes to the fore in the figure $a'-g\sharp'-d''-g\sharp'$ (measures 346–9). The "floating tonality" of the thematic complex is now complemented by dramatic shifts between major and minor, culminating in a diminished-seventh chord spanning the tonal ambitus from $B\flat$ to e'''' in *fortissimo*. Finally, the resolution of the leading tone ushers in the concluding chords, *piano*.

The four-note germ-cell of this analysis is less a matter of expression than a constructive device. Whether integrated into a canonic texture, broken up into wide-ranging virtuoso figurations or varied melodically, it never loses its identity. The defining features of the theme, presented to us at the very outset, reappear in the concluding Presto as if enlarged under a microscope. Even here, despite its improvisatory flourish, the music maintains its rigorous level of workmanship. The compositional devices that link each variation with the theme clearly identify the *Variations sérieuses* as a forerunner of modern music.

Thus, once we leave the "didactic vein" to "go back and play Mendelssohn again," we must pay heed to background tonal relations and devote special care to the dramatic structure of the music. In their final form, the *Variations sérieuses* develop a life of their own by placing different eras of history side by side in mutual reflection. In this way Mendelssohn marked out a place of his own *vis-à-vis* the classical tradition.

3 *Felix culpa*: Goethe and the image of Mendelssohn

LAWRENCE KRAMER

> There is *no* such thing as an excess of emotion; what goes under that name is in fact a lack of it.
>
> Felix Mendelssohn

> The scherzo [to *A Midsummer Night's Dream*] ends with an astonishing *tour de force* for the flute. Listeners who wish to appreciate what this involves may be recommended to pronounce two hundred and forty intelligible syllables at the uniform rate of nine to a second without taking breath.
>
> D. F. Tovey[1]

In a recent essay, the literary critic Michael André Bernstein turns a cold eye on what he sees as a historical tendency to celebrate in art the violent emotions and extreme mental states that would generally bring discomfiture in life. "Already in the Renaissance," he writes,

> in Shakespeare's magical land of Illyria, there is no one, on stage or in the stalls, to side with Malvolio ... although [his antagonists'] jokes are singularly unfunny and their characters ignoble. . . . At times one has the feeling that were Malvolio to read Dostoyevski, he, too, would refuse to recognize where his real kinship of mind and temperament lies and begin to cheer for the success of a mob of frenzied anarchists.[2]

Art, Bernstein suggests, is too often or at least too unreflectively assigned the role of challenging the "normative quotidian rationality" that grounds the dominant social order. Ironically, he adds, such rationality might be said to

---

1 Mendelssohn, letter to Rev. Albert Bauer, 4 March 1833; quoted in *Music and Aesthetics in the Eighteenth and Early-Nineteenth Centuries*, ed. Peter le Huray and James Day (Cambridge, 1988), p. 310; D. F. Tovey, *Essays in Musical Analysis: Symphonies and Other Orchestral Works* (1935–9; new edn. London, 1981), p. 411.

2 "'These children that come at you with knives': *ressentiment*, mass culture, and the saturnalia," *Critical Inquiry* 17 (1991), 358–85; the passage cited appears on pp. 360–61.

have wielded all too little influence on a modern history shot through with the deplorable results of extremist and utopian thinking (pp. 362–3).

The critical reputation of Felix Mendelssohn has been both made and marred by the association of art with irrationalism. Since his music generally lacks the rhetorical extremity typical, say, of Beethoven's, which he of course took as a model, or of Robert Schumann's, which he consistently championed, Mendelssohn has been damned with faint praise as the most classical of Romantic composers. Suspected of harboring too much technical perfection, his music is regarded as just not transgressive enough. So entrenched is Mendelssohn's reputation as a prig of genius that rhetorical extremity can hardly be heard in his work when it does appear, and the pieces marked most signally by it – notably the F minor String Quartet op. 80 and C minor Piano Trio op. 66 – have trouble finding their way into the canonical repertoire. Mendelssohn remains the composer of a "fairy music," the real implications of which are never thought out, and of a popular violin concerto squashed between the "greater," more serious behemoths of Beethoven and Brahms.

Thus fabricated, Mendelssohn's classicism, understood as a form of defensiveness or timidity, is linked with a number of unpleasant traits. These include sentimentalism (too many Songs without Words), respectability (no one admired by Victoria and Albert can be all good), and middle-class philistinism (George Bernard Shaw said that the "Scottish" Symphony "would be great if it were not so confoundedly genteel").[3] At the same time, and rather oddly, Mendelssohn's classicism is allotted a formidable model in the famous classicism of the elder Goethe, who from 1821 until his death in 1832 served the young Mendelssohn as a mentor.[4]

The oddity I speak of has two sides. First, there is Goethe's classicism itself, which no one ever spoke of as confoundedly genteel; love of Goethe was popularly supposed to save one from bourgeois tepidness, not damn one to it. Second, there are the compositions that Mendelssohn actually based on works by Goethe, a surprisingly small group given the resonant effect of Goethe's mentorship, which is not in doubt. These works, the Overture *Calm Sea and Prosperous Voyage* op. 27 (*Meeresstille und glückliche Fahrt*, 1828), the cantata *The First Walpurgisnight* op. 60 (1831–2, 1842), and a handful of songs, do not advertise self-restraint or court a defensive formalism. They form, instead, explicit assertions of exuberance, heterodoxy, and passion.

I do not mean to suggest by this that Mendelssohn's reputation can or

---

3 George Bernard Shaw, *The Great Composers: Reviews and Bombardments*, ed. Louis Crompton (Berkeley and Los Angeles, 1978), p. xvi.

4 On Goethe and Mendelssohn, see George R. Marek, *Gentle Genius: the Story of Felix Mendelssohn* (New York, 1972), pp. 107–45, 170–72.

should be recuperated by showing that the supposed Victorian gentleman is really a wild man in disguise, a Captain Sir Richard Francis Burton in Prince Albert's clothing. That would be merely to repeat the sentimentalization of wildness, that genuinely bourgeois trait, which underwrites the ruling critical paradigm. What is distinctive about Mendelssohn's assertive energy is that it is revisionary without being adversarial or aggressive. It represents a liberatory dynamism that is not automatically at odds with what Bernstein calls "prudential, rational, and antiapocalyptic modes of cognition" (p. 362). And that dynamism does, indeed, find a model in Goethe, both in Goethe's philosophical aesthetics and in the popular figure of Goethe as an ideal type, the personification of (German) cultural achievement.

A major source of Goethe's cultural authority was the perception, among his contemporaries, that his work embraced the restless self-consciousness but not the attendant alienation of modernity. If, in August Schlegel's memorable phrase, "the contemplation of the infinite [had] destroyed the finite" for the modern West, Goethe approached matters infinite with a cosmopolitanism, an energetic worldliness, that continually rehabilitated finitude. For Novalis, he was "altogether a practical poet" who "accomplished in German literature what Wedgwood did in the world of the English arts." This practicality, downright enough to resemble the material production of the Wedgwood workshop, was the key to Goethe's supremacy. "He abstracts," Novalis continues, "with a rare precision but never without at the same time constructing the object to which the abstraction corresponds." Similarly, if less dauntingly, Wilhelm von Humboldt found in Goethe's work the prototype of an art that combines the "highest ideas" with "the simplicity of what is natural." Goethe led the way in showing that "there is absolutely nothing so extraordinary that it cannot be brought into association with the relationships and conditions proper to the human character." Goethe himself characterized the dynamism that intertwines objects and abstractions, natural experience and high ideas, with a metaphor that locates sacred truth in the pulsing of secular life: "the external systole and diastole . . . the breathing in and out of the world in which we live, move, and have our being."[5]

Mendelssohn's music, with its combination of formal clarity and restless, at times even hectic, melodic vitality, takes this Goethean ambience as its own. A reconsideration of Mendelssohn, accordingly, might well begin with a look at his major Goethe-inspired pieces, which can be taken as musical credos or

5 August Schlegel, "Lectures on dramatic art and literature," Lecture 1; Novalis (Friedrich von Hardenberg), "Teplitz Fragments," no. 455; Wilhelm von Humboldt, "On the imagination," *German Romantic Criticism*, ed. A. Leslie Willson (New York, 1982), pp. 183, 75–6, and 160 respectively. Goethe's statement is quoted in Thomas McFarland, *Romanticism and the Forms of Ruin* (Princeton, 1981), p. 303.

manifestoes that articulate Mendelssohn's brand of dynamism against the originary background of Goethe's. In the remainder of this essay, I will offer a fairly intensive reading of the ideology of dynamism in *Calm Sea and Prosperous Voyage*, and a necessarily more generalized reading of the less compact *First Walpurgisnight*.

Before we proceed, however, it is important to recognize that Mendelssohn's antiapocalyptic dynamism supplies the impetus not for these pieces alone, but for most of his chamber and orchestral compositions. (The relative glibness of the lyrical piano pieces and choral religious works, the venues of sentiment and piety, can be conceded.) Mendelssohn's dynamism declares itself most directly in the melodic impetuosity of his up-tempo writing: the strong rhythmic and registral profiling, the agitated or repercussive counter-melodies and accompaniments, the love of sheer high velocity. Attracted to static slow music as a counterweight, this impetuosity famously outdoes itself in mercurial scherzos and propulsive finales where melody is articulated at a breakneck pace over long musical spans, recurrently dancing on the border that separates melody as such from figuration.

At certain cardinal moments, moreover, Mendelssohn's dynamism declares itself reflectively. It becomes dialectical when scampering melody is polarized against the braying of Bottom and the groaning of the ophicleide in the Overture to *A Midsummer Night's Dream*. It mythifies itself as bardic and archaic in the main theme of the *Hebrides* Overture, the instability of which – the downswing of the melodic phrase to the fifth scale degree – not only ordains its own haunted restlessness but also reverberates from within the halcyon lyricism of the second theme. And it allegorizes its own genesis, this dynamism, in the first movements of both Piano Trios (opp. 49 and 66), the development sections of which, with little precedent, begin with an entropic gesture that they proceed by reversing. (Perhaps the pattern of Goethe's *Calm Sea and Prosperous Voyage* acts as an implicit paradigm here.) Rushing precipitously to a statement of the second theme in which motion and energy drop almost to zero, each develop-ment unfolds by gradually recovering an intense animation that has earlier impelled the exposition. This structural rhythm of de- and reanimation then proceeds to shape the course of the recapitulation and extended coda.

Mendelssohn's dynamism, then, may not be aggressive, but neither does it represent the prattle of a repressive tolerance. Like Fingal's Cave to nine-teenth-century travelers, it signifies a problematical crossing of the natural and the magical, the socialized and the legendary. It is not, in any sense, to be denied: not by sentimental criticism masquerading as unorthodoxy, and not by performances that – a little too slow, a little wanting in crispness – prettify Mendelssohn's music.

Turning to *Calm Sea and Prosperous Voyage*, we can begin with Goethe's texts, the seeming simplicity of which masks a sophisticated blend of description and allegory:

Tiefe Stille herrscht im Wasser,
Ohne Regung ruht das Meer,
Und bekümmert sieht der Schiffer
Glatte Fläche rings umher.
Keine Luft von keiner Seite!
Todesstille fürchterlich!
In der ungeheuren Weite
Reget keine Welle sich.

[Deep stillness rules the waters, / Without motion rests the sea, / And aggrieved the steersman sees / A flat plane everywhere. / No wind from any quarter, / Fearsome death-stillness! / In the monstrous waste / Not one wave stirs.]

Die Nebel zerreisen,
Der Himmel ist helle
Und Äeolus löset
Das ängstliche Band.
Es säuseln die Winde,
Es rührt sich der Schiffer.
Geschwinde! Geschwinde!
Es teilt sich die Welle,
Es naht sich die Ferne;
Schon seh' ich das Land!

[The mists tear asunder, / The heaven is bright / And Aeolus unties / The eager band. / The winds rustle, / The steersman rouses. / Quickly! quickly! / The waves part, / The distance nears, / Already I see land!]

First published in a literary almanac edited by Schiller, these texts can most effectively be read in relation to Schiller's famous essay of 1795, "On Naive and Sentimental Poetry" ("Über naive und sentimentalische Dichtung"). The essay develops a contrast between the unreflective unity with nature evident in classical poetry (the naive) and the self-conscious alienation from nature evident in modern poetry (the sentimental or romantic). As Goethe tells it:

I had in poetry the maxim of objective procedure and would tolerate no other. But Schiller, who in his work was wholly subjective, thought his way the right one and wrote his essay in order to uphold himself against me.... He proved to me that I was romantic against my will.[6]

6 J. P. Eckermann, *Conversations with Goethe*, ed. Hans Kohn, trans. Gisela O'Brien (New York, 1964), p. 162.

"Calm Sea" and "Prosperous Voyage," also written in 1795, form a case in point. The poems are sentimental (i.e., reflective) because they perceptibly seek the naive. More exactly, they artfully disguise the sentimental as the naive in the hope of endowing modern experience with the aura of unselfconscious ideality that late eighteenth-century German classicism found in classical Greece.[7]

The poems achieve this mimicry of unselfconsciousness by tacitly confusing literal and figurative, descriptive and allegorical meanings. The exclamation "Todesstille fürchterlich!" may figure the becalmed sea as an allegory of engulfing death – "Tiefe Stille" collapsing rhetorically and phonetically to "Todesstille" – or it may merely add panic to the immediately preceding statement that in every quarter the wind is still: "Keine Luft von keiner Seite!" The statement that the waves are parting – "Es teilt sich die Welle" – may merely state a fact, or it may allude to the biblical account of the parting of the waters on the second day of Creation, and thereby trace parallel allegorical paths from death to life and chaos to cosmos. The remark that Aeolus is untying the winds may be a fancy bit of eighteenth-century rhetoric, or it may place what could be an eighteenth-century voyage in ancient Greece, playfully reversing, perhaps, Odysseus' mishap with the Aeolian winds and the unprosperous voyage that ensued. In sum, without actually committing the reader to a reflective interpretation, Goethe makes a range of such interpretations tacitly available within the process of reading. Exiled from nature by modernity, he tries to cast what he writes as a second nature: to "[give] his work such a content and form that it will seem at once natural and above nature."[8]

Goethe understands such "spiritual-organic" (*Geistig-organisches*) form as the outcome of what he calls *Steigerung*: ascent or increase, enhancement, evolutionary process. *Steigerung* is a dynamic principle that characteristically seeks to repeat originary conditions at higher levels of development.[9] "Calm Sea" and "Prosperous Voyage" can be taken not only to presuppose this principle as a cause, but also to celebrate it. The semi-allegorical movement from the stasis of the first poem to the eager motion of the second is inclusive enough to suggest an ascent from paralytic self-consciousness to the liberatory energy of *Steigerung*. This reading is concretized most strikingly in phonetic

7 On the naive and sentimental, see M. H. Abrams, *Natural Supernaturalism: Tradition and Innovation in Romantic Literature* (New York, 1971), pp. 213–17, and Tilottama Rajan, *Dark Interpreter: the Discourse of Romanticism* (Ithaca and London, 1980), pp. 30–41.

8 "On truth and appearance in the artwork," quoted by M. H. Abrams, *The Mirror and the Lamp: Romantic Theory and the Critical Tradition* (New York, 1958), p. 206.

9 Abrams, *Natural Supernaturalism*, p. 184. Thomas McFarland links the concept of *Steigerung* to a network of late eighteenth-century ideas linking the Kantian subject–object polarity with scientific studies of material, especially magnetic, attraction and repulsion. See *Romanticism and the Forms of Ruin*, pp. 289–341, esp. pp. 297–313.

terms. Given the content of "Calm Sea," the tight rhyme scheme of the poem (abab cdcd) presents itself as the embodiment of an involuted and mechanical energy. "Prosperous Voyage" limbers this energy up, throwing off rhymes in an intricate, irregular pattern (abcd ef ebgd) that seems both vital and spontaneous.

Both *Steigerung* and indirect reflection figure largely in Mendelssohn's overture, but in terms that differ significantly from Goethe's. More than either Beethoven, in his miniature cantata "Calm Sea and Prosperous Voyage" (*Meeresstille und glückliche Fahrt* op. 112), or Schubert, in his song "Calm Sea," (*Meeres Stille* D. 216), Mendelssohn takes the loose suggestiveness of Goethe's allegory as a model rather than as an interpretive provocation.[10] Although he assumes Goethe's aesthetic as a premise, he alters its focal points. Where Goethe's paired poems are redemptory, Mendelssohn's overture is progressive; where Goethe's *Steigerung* is housed within the dialectics of subject and object, Mendelssohn's is intersubjective, a vehicle for the enhancement of social energy.

The overture falls into three parts, the first and third of which freely exceed or contradict the poetry. There is an Adagio for the calm sea, an Allegro Molto e vivace for the prosperous voyage, and an Allegro maestoso epilogue. The Adagio portrays a sea that is more halcyon than becalmed. Although Mendelssohn follows Beethoven in painting the motionlessness of the waves with pedal points, he combines the pedals with slow, steady melodic motion to create a dominant impression of motion in embryo, motion impending. A homogeneous texture heightens the effect; both the motion and the stillness are primarily etched by the strings, with minimal echoes and underlinings from the other choirs. (The string texture is also borrowed from Beethoven, who, however, uses it entirely to create a sense of strangulation.) The Allegro molto, which is closest to Goethe in feeling, forms the main body of the overture and combines the tone-painting of the Adagio with the interplay of three animated melodies. The Allegro maestoso, another piece of painting, is exuberantly ceremonial, suggestive of a great public festivity. Where Goethe's text closes with an act of individuation – the speaker first says "I" in his last line, "Schon seh' ich das Land!" – Mendelssohn's overture closes with an act of collectivization.

The three sections of the overture are all impelled by a single, strongly profiled melodic process. The music finds a memorable primary motif and continually enhances it and evolves from it. This musical *Steigerung* is what

---

10 For an analysis of Schubert's song, with a brief nod at Beethoven, see my "The Schubert Lied: romantic form and romantic consciousness," *Schubert: Critical and Analytical Studies*, ed. Walter Frisch (Lincoln, Nebraska, 1986), pp. 210–15.

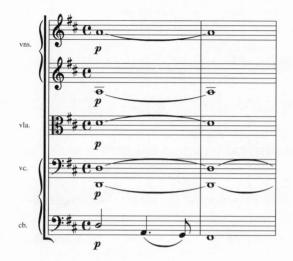

Ex. 3.1: Mendelssohn, *Calm Sea and Prosperous Voyage Overture* op. 27, opening on primary motif

transforms the indeterminate potential energy of the Adagio through the articulate dynamism of the Allegro into the triumphant sociability of the Maestoso. All of this, it is important to add, happens with consummately "naive" clarity, in broad daylight. Like Goethe, Mendelssohn is only esoteric in his studied avoidance of esotericism.

The Adagio begins with a perfect image of embryonic motion as solo basses state the primary motif under the veil of a static D major chord (mm. 1–2; see Ex. 3.1). The motif can be divided into a signature rhythm, ♩♩·♪|o, and a signature melody, a lightly embellished descending triad. These signatures, separately or in combination, form the kernel of virtually every melodic gesture in the overture. In saying this, however, I am explicitly *not* saying that the signatures are a source of unity or serve an ideal of unity. Rather the opposite: the signatures are the means by which the overture can diversify itself prolifically but intelligibly within the almost inescapable unity imposed by classical tonic–dominant harmony.

Before that diversification can take place, however, the primary motif must establish itself as the vehicle of an originary impulse, the dynamic core of all motion to follow. This it does by exfoliating across the otherwise neutral texture, detaching itself for solo statements, at successively higher pitch levels, on clarinet, cellos, violas, and first violins (mm. 10–26). The opening image then undergoes an expansion that is also a mirror reversal (mm. 29–37). The

71

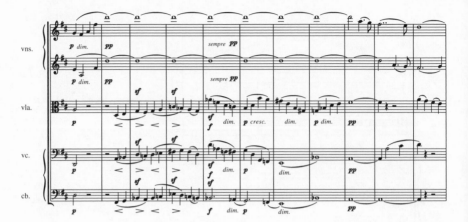

Ex. 3.2: Mendelssohn, *Calm Sea and Prosperous Voyage Overture* op. 27, Adagio, upper pedal and primary motif

first and second violins start an upper pedal that becomes the longest in the Adagio while the lower strings trace wave patterns in quarter notes. The incipient dynamism proves decisive, and even as the lower strings fail to sustain it the first violins renew it by resolving the pedal into the primary motif (see Ex. 3.2). A moment later, the opening image returns in its original form, but enhanced by a strong feeling of liminality, of something, as they say, in the wind.

Very much in the wind. The signal for the beginning of the Allegro is a vivid tone picture of a fluttering breeze: a dipping and rising phrase on the solo flute sounded and repeated *perdendosi* over a dominant pedal. The phrase, however, also marks an important moment of indirect reflection. It sounds something like a bird call. And the call of a bird over tranquil waters has allusive resonance: it could suggest either the stirring of the mythical halcyon, ready to release the seas from enchantment and depart from its floating nest, or the dove returning to Noah with the olive branch in her mouth. Or the phrase might not mimic a bird call at all. In sum, without actually committing the listener to a reflective interpretation, Mendelssohn makes a range of such interpretations tacitly available within the process of listening.

The Allegro that follows carries out the prolific, multi-faceted *Steigerung* of the primary motif. The signature rhythm animates the first and third Allegro themes and generates a great abundance of subsidiary figures. The signature melody fills wide registral spaces with diatonic energy, extending itself through multiple triadic descents in the first and second themes and con-

Primary motif

First Allegro theme (mm. 99-102)

Second Allegro theme (mm. 149-156)

Third Allegro theme (mm. 185-186)

Subsidiary idea (mm. 137-183)

Ex. 3.3: Mendelssohn, *Calm Sea and Prosperous Voyage Overture* op. 27, primary motif and selected derivatives

Subsidiary idea (mm. 235-236)

Subsidiary idea (mm. 239-246)

Subsidiary idea (mm. 255-259)

Subsidiary idea (mm. 457-460)

picc., fl. 1 + 2

Ex. 3.3   *continued*

tinually varying the number and position of its embellishing notes. The work of both signatures is selectively illustrated in Ex. 3.3.

This flourishing foreground dynamism also extends to the next highest level of melodic structure. The cardinal element here is the third Allegro theme, the only one subjected to any sonata-style development. The theme is a narrow-gauge version of the primary motif; it repeats the signature rhythm but contracts the triadic motion of the signature melody to the descent of a third. In its defining statements, however, the theme unfolds through a three-part sequence in which the missing triadic motion is structurally articulated in ascending form (see Ex. 3.4). This triadic articulation is missing from the

74

Ex. 3.4: Mendelssohn, *Calm Sea and Prosperous Voyage Overture* op. 27, final statement of third Allegro theme (mm. 379–384)

developmental episodes based on the third theme (mm. 271–83, 335–75), and its absence sets up a diffuse structural tension which is resolved when the theme makes its last appearance (mm. 379–96). The resolution is many-sided. As last heard, the theme not only restores the extended triad, but also replaces the extended dominant triad of its finst version with a tonic triad, and, for good measure, projects that tonic triad as a sixth chord, the form it takes in the primary motif (see Ex. 3.4). For yet a further measure, the instrument that does all this is the solo clarinet, enhancing – this is pure *Steigerung* – the work of the solo clarinet in the Adagio which gives the primary motif its first separate, unveiled statement and impels its ascent through the string choir.

The Maestoso epilogue is introduced by a timpani crescendo that efficiently upstages the rest of the orchestra and evolves into an unaccompanied solo (starting *ff* and getting louder) on one note. The drumbeats concretize the prolific musical energy of the Allegro in a material form, felt as much as heard, a form directly linked to bodily vigor and pleasure. The one-note passage, on the tonic rather than the dominant, is fulfilling, not expectant. The timpanist should regard the whole episode as a written-out cadenza – better still, a solo break before its time – and play every note to the hilt. The idea is to jubilate.

The Maestoso proper begins by building up a *tutti* as various groups of instruments join in successively with the timpani. A last antiphonal flurry of wind-and-wave motion then ushers in an invitation to festivity: a fanfare for three unaccompanied trumpets. First joined by the timpani in gala trumpet-and-drum style, the fanfare becomes the core of another *tutti* built up from successive blocks of sound, this one animated by the signature rhythm. Moving at its Allegro pace, but at half the Allegro tempo, the rhythmic motif is now expansive rather than propulsive. Enhancing its rise to prominence in the Adagio, it fans out confidently throughout the entire orchestral texture: here proclaiming itself in one instrumental group, there overlapping from one group to another, and finally abbreviating itself to parade to a close through the tones of the tonic triad.

The festive hullabaloo of this epilogue offers an important new object for indirect reflection. As portrayed by the Allegro, the prosperous voyage of the overture fully retains the mythic-heroic aura that belongs to it by tradition. The public celebration of the Maestoso, however, adds a connotation not usually thought of as auratic, namely the idea of mercantile adventure, the modern (that is: capitalist) heroism of voyaging for wealth. The suggestion is heightened by the deliberate archaism of the epilogue, the atmosphere of which is more suggestive of a Renaissance city-state (easy to idealize) than of a nineteenth-century harbor (impossible to idealize). By appropriating both the heroic-mythic and the heroic-mercantile, and appropriating them with willed naivete, Mendelssohn offers the listener a chance to celebrate the historical power of Enlightenment-style bourgeois idealism, with its cross-cultivation of cultural, social, and economic productivity.

Potentially disenchanting, this offer is not made to disenchant. The three final measures, which Donald Tovey called "a poetic surprise of a high order," seem specifically designed to sustain the possibility of enchantment.[11] The surprise is a grateful reminiscence of the calm sea of the opening: a sudden decrescendo into a simple plagal cadence. There could be no clearer suggestion that the dynamic process traced by the overture is cyclical and self-renewing, that the multiple forms of dynamism represented in the overture are interconvertible. If there is also a hint of rest after labor, a touch of sabbath feeling underlined by the plagal progression, so much the better.

The cantata (or ballad) *The First Walpurgisnight* involves a sabbath of another sort. Not a more dynamic piece than *Calm Sea and Prosperous Voyage*, it is certainly a more rambunctious one. Its text traces the origin of the Walpurgisnacht, the mythical Witches' Sabbath celebrated on the Brocken over May eve, to a raucous masquerade staged by a group of medieval pagans to frighten off their Christian oppressors. (The trick worked.) Goethe, who had long wanted his treatment of this subject set to music, greeted Mendelssohn's plan for a cantata with warm encouragement – and interpretive advice:

> In a true sense the poem is highly symbolic in intention. For in world-history it must continually be repeated that something old, established, proven, reassuring is pressed, shifted, displaced by emerging innovations, and, where not wiped out, none the less penned up in the narrowest space. The medieval era, where hatred still can and may produce countereffects, is here impressively enough represented, and a joyous indestructible enthusiasm blazes up once more in radiance and clarity.[12]

11 Tovey, *Essays in Musical Analysis: Symphonies and Other Orchestral Works*, p. 402.
12 Letter of 9 September 1831, my translation from *Goethe's Briefe*, ed. Karl Robert Mandelkow (Hamburg, 1967), vol. IV, p. 447.

Mendelssohn placed this statement at the head of the score that he published in 1843. Clearly, he was sympathetic to Goethe's sketch of a historical process that counters blind hostility with dialectical subversion and answers destructive hatred with creative mockery.

In representing that process, Mendelssohn's *The First Walpurgisnight* nominates the pre-modern social energy of Goethe's pagans as an ideal for the modern age. The pagans have not yet separated the terms – self and society, nature and culture, secular pleasure and spiritual elevation – that the civilization of modern Europe is famous for wanting to reunite. Unbeset by internal divisions, the pagans can even embrace Saturnalian extremes without fetishizing the frenzy of antagonism. As Mendelssohn stages it, working from mere hints in Goethe's text, the Witches' Sabbath embraces more than just the *Schadenfreude* enjoyed by the pagans as they triumphantly flyte the Christians. Irradiated by its closeness to traditional festive practices, the Sabbath evolves into a vehicle of pleasure and self-renewal for both its imaginary celebrants and its real audience. Without ever losing its aggressive edge, it becomes above all an interlude of uninhibited collective play in which social and bodily energies merge and circulate.

The music imparts this character to the revelry in the most straightforward of ways. The Sabbath begins with *moderato* march rhythms as a male chorus summons the people and the orchestra gradually catches fire. The march, however, is only a prelude to the revelry itself, which begins as the orchestra ups the tempo drastically and whirls forth in 6/8 triplets. What follows is like a wild song–and–dance routine. In form, it is something like a gigantic stretto; in feeling, it is something like a fertility rite. The male chorus starts things off with an extended turn, the women's chorus answers in kind, and then the two unite. Thereafter this pattern is repeated irregularly with ever-increasing animation. The interplay of choruses is condensed into a hurly-burly of short phrases, bursts of antiphony imploding into massed singing which reexplodes to renew the antiphony. The male and female voices seem to hurl the music back and forth before rushing together, a process that ends, like a ritualized consummation, when the choirs enter successively, basses to sopranos, to build up a final extended turn for full chorus. It is worth adding that the most persistent choral device in this music is the conclusion of a rising soprano phrase on a high note, sometimes a sustained high note. The effect, heightened by the fast tempo and busy texture, is to combine a cry of pleasure with a cry of triumph.[13]

---

13 This treatment of the sopranos also suggests an effort to imagine an empowered position for women within a stringently patriarchal text. I cannot develop this idea here; suffice it to say

Like *Calm Sea and Prosperous Voyage*, *The First Walpurgisnight* seeks to be simultaneously many-sided, spontaneous, and lucid. Drawing on multiple dynamisms, it interrelates them in ways that, though uninhibited, never become alienated from normal quotidian rationality. Many of Mendelssohn's contemporaries admired this in the work. Berlioz, most famously, praised the score for achieving "perfect clarity" despite its textural complexity. "Vocal and instrumental effects," he wrote, "are constantly intermingling, running in opposite directions, even colliding, with an apparent disorder which is the very summit of art."[14] The compliment is the more telling because Berlioz's own Saturnalian movements, the Witches' Sabbath from the *Fantastic Symphony* and the Brigands' orgy from *Harold in Italy*, neither have nor, perhaps, seek such clarity; they are more orthodox in their Romantic unorthodoxy.

The mention of orthodoxy starts a related issue that deserves more attention than I can give it here. It is odd to find the devout Mendelssohn writing an anti-Christian piece, even if the Christians in question are safely Catholic – *dumpfen Pfaffenchristen*, as the text calls them. Not that the music is seriously anti-Catholic; it is just pro-pagan. The oddity diminishes when we recognize that the music of Mendelssohn's Druids is distinctly Christian in its rhetoric, especially the concluding C major hymn to light, with its prominent ecclesiastical trombones. The pagans actually seem to personify a certain type of progressive bourgeois Christian, bred of the Enlightenment; this suggestion is heightened by another rhetorical affinity of the concluding hymn, which is reminiscent of Sarastro's ceremonial music in *The Magic Flute*. So the object of Mendelssohn's carnivalesque flyting is not (of course) Christianity, but Phariseeism, the narrow, dogmatic, anti-cosmopolitan cast of mind that Robert Schumann identified with the Philistines.

Perhaps the issue of cosmopolitanism should take pride of place here. Mendelssohn uses the bass drum and cymbals to punctuate the Witches' Sabbath, and even adds a transitional postlude that strikes a clear-cut Janissary note. His pagans would seem to have ties to the non-Christian East, ties that not only intimate the long history of European conflict with the Islamic world, but that may also intimate something closer to (Mendelssohn's) home. Anti-Semitic rhetoric in the early nineteenth century tirelessly insisted that the Jews were aliens in Europe, "oriental" figures, figures from the

that the persistent high-note endings revalue an object of traditional masculine repulsion, the shrieking of "hysterical" women that elides into the sound of the castrated voice.

14 Quoted by Richard Dyer in his liner notes to a 1985 Arabesque recording of *The First Walpurgisnight*. A somewhat different version appears in *The Memoirs of Hector Berlioz*, trans. and ed. David Cairns (New York, 1975), p. 294.

East.[15] In a work protesting the oppression of a minority by Christians, the stylish use of Turkish music would form a conveniently indirect way to bite back at anti-Semitism. Mendelssohn, it is true, was normally a tight-lipped assimilationist, but that fact does not necessarily betoken indifference. Perhaps the voice of the pagans in *The First Walpurgisnight* is the voice of the Mendelssohn who refused, defying his father, to call himself Bartholdy, and who, in the flush of triumph, exclaimed to his collaborator in the revival of the *St. Matthew Passion*, the actor Edward Devrient: "To think that it should be an actor and a Jew that gave back to the people of Europe the greatest of Christian works!"[16]

If the large Goethe-based pieces are any index (and the composer himself thought of them as milestones), then Mendelssohn's music demands a thoroughgoing re-thinking that cuts through encrusted habits of reception and takes seriously the far-from-extramusical factors of cosmopolitanism, literacy, and sociability. The familiar music needs to be defamiliarized, so that my local classical-music radio station stops making aural wallpaper of the "Italian" Symphony an average of once a week; the less familiar works need to become familiar; criticism must stop making neo-Wagnerian noises about Mendelssohn's unadventurous harmony and start paying attention to how his music behaves; and (with apologies to the biographers) the Gentle Genius whose Song without Words rises On Wings of Song can decently retire to the attic.

15 For a survey of anti-Semitic discourse in early nineteenth-century Germany, see Leon Poliakov, *The History of Anti-Semitism: Volume 3, From Voltaire to Wagner*, trans. Miriam Kochan (New York, 1975), pp. 380–429.
16 Reported in Devrient's memoirs; quoted by Jack Werner, *Mendelssohn's "Elijah"* (London, 1965), p. 85.

4 Composition as accommodation? On Mendelssohn's music in relation to England

FRIEDHELM KRUMMACHER

translated by John Michael Cooper

That Felix Mendelssohn was too successful in England has clearly not reflected well on his own reputation or that of English music. None the less, the idea persists if we compare contemporary judgments of his achievements with subsequent evaluations by historians. One apparent explanation may be that Mendelssohn's English fame was possible only because of the generally regressive state of English music at the time, or, conversely, that England's capitalist music industry exacted a serious toll on the works of its composers. On the other hand, the thought occurs that Mendelssohn's music may have actually contributed to the stagnation of English music, or rather, that his continuing influence may be explained only by the Victorian era's tendency toward regressiveness. However one considers the problem, negative associations are hard to ignore if Mendelssohn's name is linked with nineteenth-century English music, and if the memory of his public successes is set aside. What remains is to consider whether Mendelssohn or English music was more adversely affected by their mutual association.[1]

But there is no longer reason enough to accept unquestioningly the nineteenth century's judgments and prejudices. The recent interest in the nineteenth century, surely not just a passing trend, owes its existence to more than an increasing temporal separation from the century. Rather, the distinct caesura of modern, twentieth-century music has also demarcated changes

Originally published in *Musik ohne Grenzen*, vol. I: *Deutsch-englische Musikbeziehungen*, ed. Wulf Konold (Munich, 1985), pp. 132–56.

1 To be rebuffed here are not only the critical views of G. B. Shaw or Wilfrid Mellers (see notes 6 and 12). A growing skepticism about Mendelssohn may be observed in English literature since the turn of the century, for example in S. S. Stratton, *Mendelssohn* (London, 1901; 2nd edn., 1934); A. Brent Smith, "The workmanship of Mendelssohn," *Music and Letters* 4 (1923), 18–25; or Philip Radcliffe, *Mendelssohn* (London, 1954; 3rd edn., 1967). This skepticism is all the more apparent in comparison, for example, with H. F. Chorley, *Modern German Music*, vols. I and II (London, 1854); F. G. Edwards, *The History of Mendelssohn's "Elijah"* (London and New York, 1896); or C. W. Pearce, *Mendelssohn's Organ Sonatas* (London, 1902).

which have left traditional appraisals undisturbed. Our critical evaluations of the nineteenth century, notwithstanding the extent to which they have been received as "history," clearly demand further scrutiny. And if we are to revise our evaluation of Mendelssohn's worth as a composer, then the relationship of his music to the English tradition must be explored anew. Such an attempt is all the more justified if it brings into focus some typical difficulties encountered in historical interpretations.[2]

However important it may be to adduce new sources that clarify Mendelssohn's ties to England, there exist numerous, equally important documents which, though long accessible, have yet to be exploited for their full critical worth. These must be examined first to answer questions that can only be sketched here, and the basis for these answers must be established facts: Mendelssohn's trips to England, his concerts and correspondence, and his contacts with friends, colleagues, and pupils.[3] First, initial assumptions will be reviewed to determine the strength of Mendelssohn's influence in England, as well as its later course. Second, some consequences and problems for Mendelssohn's approach to composition will be sketched. And finally, some examples bearing on our understanding of Mendelssohn's music will be presented.

I

That Mendelssohn attained a significantly greater success in England than in France seems to be a burden primarily for the historian who views Paris, not London, as the unequivocal center of progressiveness in music. And if one considers Mendelssohn's reserve toward Berlioz, it may seem particularly regressive that a composer of the 1830s should seek his audience in England, not in France.[4] It is also true, of course, that our image of Paris as a

2 Along with the increasingly frequent performances and recordings of his works, three volumes of essays reflect a new interest in Mendelssohn: *Das Problem Mendelssohn*, ed. C. Dahlhaus, Studien zur Musikgeschichte des 19. Jahrhunderts No. 41 (Regensburg, 1974); *Felix Mendelssohn Bartholdy*, ed. H.-K. Metzger and R. Riehn, Musik-Konzepte No. 14/15 (Munich, 1980) [includes a select discography by Wulf Konold (pp. 153–9) and select bibliography by R. Riehn (pp. 160–76)]; and *Felix Mendelssohn Bartholdy*, ed. G. Schuhmacher, Wege der Forschung No. 194 (Darmstadt, 1982).

3 See P. Ranft's biographical overview, *Felix Mendelssohn Bartholdy: Eine Lebenschronik* (Leipzig, 1972). For a detailed account, see E. Werner, *Mendelssohn: a New Image of the Composer and His Age* (London, 1963; rev. German edn., Zürich and Freiburg i. B., 1980). Other important sources include *Briefe aus den Jahren 1833 bis 1847* ed. P. and C. Mendelssohn Bartholdy (Leipzig, 1863); *Felix Mendelssohn-Bartholdys Briefwechsel mit Legationsrat Karl Klingemann in London*, ed. K. Klingemann (Essen, 1909); *Briefe von Felix Mendelssohn Bartholdy an Ignaz und Charlotte Moscheles*, ed. F. Moscheles (Leipzig, 1888); and S. Hensel, *Die Familie Mendelssohn 1729–1847*, 2 vols. (Berlin, 1879).

4 For his evaluation of Berlioz, see *Briefe an Moscheles*, pp. 85 and 185; F. Hiller, *Felix Mendelssohn-Bartholdy, Briefe und Erinnerungen* (Cologne, 2nd edn., 1878), p. 36. For Mendels-

representative of modernity during Mendelssohn's time is biased; otherwise, Berlioz surely would not have encountered difficulties in attaining success there. None the less, we must also add that Mendelssohn's music later enjoyed no less a success in France than it had earlier in England (this may be demonstrated not only in written accounts, but also in certain works of Gounod and Saint-Saëns). On the other hand, England's native musical tradition – unlike that of France – appears to have been inextricably tied to certain genres of sacred music. The greater the skepticism with which one regards the aesthetic legitimacy of the oratorio, the more awkward the situation that Mendelssohn's English ties were strongest in that genre, or, more broadly, in sacred music. For if the oratorio was the genre most closely associated with Mendelssohn's English success, the notion then arises that such success could only have been the result of a conscious accommodation on Mendelssohn's part. Certainly one might object that sacred works and oratorios were also composed elsewhere – in France, for example – and indeed, by such musicians as Liszt and Berlioz, and that the English oratorio tradition was in no way represented by Mendelssohn alone, but also by such acknowledged masters as Handel and Haydn. But such observations, although true enough, do not fully vitiate the skepticism that has been focussed upon Mendelssohn's influence on English music. For one thing, oratorios like those by Berlioz and Liszt hardly attained a following comparable to that of Mendelssohn's. For another, Mendelssohn's oratorios became the enduring standard by which the English oratorio was defined – even though that tradition existed well before their time.[5] From the English perspective, however, such objections only reinforced the conclusion that Mendelssohn's oratorios had effected an unfortunate influence. Since he prevented the emergence of a truly indigenous English musical style, Mendelssohn's success came to represent an accommodation to the aesthetic and moral norms of the Victorian era.

Nowhere was this conviction more succinctly expressed than in the music criticism of George Bernard Shaw, who may be accused of prejudice, but never of incompetence. Shaw appreciated that Mendelssohn "expressed himself in music with touching tenderness and refinement," but added: "and sometimes with a nobility and pure fire that makes us forget all his kid glove gentility, his conventional sentimentality, and his despicable oratorio monger-

sohn's impressions of Paris, see *Reisebriefe aus den Jahren 1830 bis 1832*, ed. P. Mendelssohn Bartholdy (Leipzig, 1861; 3rd edn., 1869), pp. 300–56. One should remember, of course, that the decisiveness with which Mendelssohn expressed his own evaluations was related to his tolerance for contrary opinions.

5 See A. Schering, *Geschichte des Oratoriums* (Leipzig, 1911); E. Walker, *A History of Music in England* (Oxford, 3rd edn., 1952); J. A. Westrup, "Oratorium," §G: "Das englische Oratorium," in *Die Musik in Geschichte und Gegenwart*, ed. F. Blume, vol. X (Kassel, 1962), cols. 158ff.

ing."[6] The criticism was thus turned against the oratorios, even though the subject of the review was a string quartet. In Mendelssohn's instrumental works, Shaw noted primarily suggestions of intimacy, tenderness, nobility, and fire – though these qualities, too, were marred by an irritating regularity. The "Scottish" Symphony, perhaps, was "a work which would be great if it were not so confoundedly genteel." And concerning the *Midsummer Night's Dream* music: "How different this music is from the oratorio music! how original, how exquisitely happy, how radiant with pure light, absolutely without shadow."[7] The quartet, however, required a critic "who is not only devoid of superstition for Mendelssohn, but also for the sacredness of sonata form." Shaw's objections were to "the twaddling passages" between the themes, "the superfluous repeat," the "idiotic working out," and "the tiresome recapitulation." But the instrumental works did have one thing in common with the oratorios: "Their deadliness kills Mendelssohn's *St. Paul* and the 'regular' movements in his symphonic and chamber music."[8]

This jab at the "sacred" sonata-form movement reveals the extent to which instrumental forms, with their techniques of varied repetition and transition, proved problematic for the reviewer. But Shaw harbored the same reservations about the fugue and, as its chief exponent, Bach. Thus he did not hesitate to assert: "The fugue form is as dead as the sonata form; and the sonata form is as dead as Beethoven himself." Thus, the skepticism for Mendelssohn was based primarily on the rejection of the genres which he represented; for Shaw, their time had passed. But the skepticism was also motivated by Shaw's conviction that the history of music was one of progress, in which instrumental music had been superseded by the music drama. The perception of Mendelssohn as "a master yielding to none in the highest qualification" had perhaps been permissible earlier, "long ago, when Mendelssohn's power was at its height"; but such an evaluation had become "out of date by this time."

This ambivalent motivation becomes all the more striking when we consider those qualities of Mendelssohn's music to which Shaw *was* receptive. In general, he no way misjudged its artificial characteristics and aesthetic charm. Shaw's emphasis fell upon the composer's faculties for musical expression, to which qualities such as fire, tenderness, and aesthetic sensibility – qualities aroused in the listener – correspond. Behind this emphasis lies an aesthetic of feeling born of a confidence in the spontaneous power of music.

6 G. B. Shaw, *London Music in 1888–1889 as Heard by Corno di Bassetto (Later Known as Bernard Shaw) with Some Further Autobiographical Particulars* (London, 1937; 3rd edn., 1950), pp. 68ff. Cf. also G. B. Shaw, *Musikfeuilletons des Corno di Bassetto*, ed. E. Klemm (Leipzig, 1972), pp. 44ff. Still, Shaw based his choice of pseudonym on Mozart's and Mendelssohn's use of the basset horn.

7 Shaw, *London Music*, pp. 312, 287.

8 *Ibid.*, p. 69 (also for the following quotations).

Music's ability to affect emotionally presupposes an ability in the critic to pass immediate judgment. This conviction – like the "progressive" interpretation of history – displaces the problem of an aesthetic that had sought to determine the artistic worth of a composition precisely by its power to withstand the test of time. To put it differently: dispassionate historical and aesthetic reflection is suppressed by the immediate emotion, which in turn does not feel threatened by its transient nature, if it self-consciously acknowledges its demise in history. However progressive an image of himself Shaw may have wished to project, his argument remains dependent on conventional aesthetics. This is to some extent understandable. Since the categories of corresponding aesthetic approaches were hardly reliable, there remained precious little room for different interpretations of classical instrumental music.

All these considerations had to exert their first real influence on the understanding of Mendelssohn's music. The stronger the orientation toward emotional effect, the paler his music appeared (at least with regard to new effects) – and thus the less problematic its evaluation. And the more clamorous its previous success, the sharper became the objections of the critic who perceived himself to be an advocate of modernity. This applies in particular to the sacred music and the oratorios, in which one immediately encountered Mendelssohn's tremendous influence. For one thing, these works consisted in part of compositions written with English texts for English occasions; and for another, these works became threatened by a process of secularization which, by Shaw's time, was rendering them increasingly questionable and unconvincing. In opposition to the "expressive and vigourous choruses of Handel," Mendelssohn's choruses represented, for Shaw, "that dreary fugue manufacture, with its Sunday-school sentimentalities and its Music-school ornamentalities."[9] In sum, the harsh criticism was directed at the otherwise prudent composer's failure "to serve up the chopping to pieces of the prophets of the grove with his richest musical spice to suit the compound of sanctimonious cruelty and base materialism which his patrons, the British Pharisees, called their religion."[10]

This criticism of the British bourgeoisie here became mingled with criticisms of art and religion – or music and morality – and offered a polemic in which Mendelssohn was an easy target. But as clear as the tone of the argument may seem, the greater the caution with which one must read the text in order to distinguish the actual criticism from its motivations. Strikingly ambiguous is the comparison with Handel, in whose choruses Shaw finds "expressive" power in contrast to Mendelssohn's "sentiment." This not

9 *Ibid.*, p. 221.   10 *Ibid.*, p. 251.

only raises the question of whether enduring emotional effects have become a more important basis of comparison than inherent musical qualities; it also leads one to ask, in retrospect, whether Handel's pomp is really any more respectable than Mendelssohn's sentiment.

But if the distant past is played out against a more recent time, the comparison remains one between traditions which can only be evaluated in contrary ways. The references leave open to question why one type of music should fade before the other (though the references are based on evaluative criteria which fail to produce legitimate arguments). Now a different matter entirely is Shaw's verdict concerning a passage in *Elijah* important to the plot but not emphasised in the music: in truth, the "hacking to pieces" (*Zerhacken*) of the Priests of Baal signifies the triumph of God over Baal, even though the text is taken directly from the Bible, right up to the word "slaughter." If need be, the composer might be accused of sticking too closely to the biblical text without softening its drastic tone. Whoever advances this argument obviously feels deprived of the moral of the ancient biblical account. For if one grasps the biblical context, the symbolic meaning of the heinous act emerges as a prophecy of holy triumph through Christ. Thus, if Shaw was repulsed by this – which he perceived as a concession to the Victorian "Pharisees" – he fell victim to the very moral norms which he himself attacked so strongly.

Shaw evidently also failed to perceive how painstaking the passage in question was for the composer himself. Mendelssohn's music in no way grants to the slaughter of the priests the status of its own movement; rather, it relegates the event to a recitative (the close of No. 16), which is taken up in turn by the chorus in stark unison ("Greift die Propheten Baals, daß ihrer keiner entrinne"). And the addition "and slaughters them there" ("und schlachtet sie daselbst") describes in the Bible an act committed by Elijah's very own hands (cf. I Kings 18:40). In the oratorio, on the other hand, this act appears only as a request of the prophet, and this request is not repeated by the people.[11]

Still more striking is Shaw's emphasis on the "richest musical spices" with which Mendelssohn is supposed to depict the macabre scene. The wording not only suggests a hidden respect for the composer's capabilities; more importantly, it applies to a part of the work which is accomplished in a decidedly quick, efficient manner that in no way belongs to an "advanced" school of composition. Shaw's assertion that tribute is paid here to Victorian moral conventions might be demonstrated more convincingly in the reserve with

11 The German and English texts differ here, however. The choral version, "daß ihrer keiner entrinne," with the repetition of the words "keiner entrinne" is translated as "and let not one of them escape you," after which the words of Elijah, "let them be slain" are taken up.

which Mendelssohn handles the episode, failing to grant to it the full weight it receives in the Bible. Shaw's criticism, however, requires a distortion of its object in order to render its assessment: to detect any signs of accommodation to the morals of the "Pharisees," the critic – almost unwillingly – has to find in the movement characteristics which are simply not there. Only in this way does the music become so distasteful that it is overwhelmed by a moral verdict that, for its part, relies on those very norms which Shaw so vehemently attacks.

To be sure, as one might well object, Shaw is not an impartial witness to the influence of Mendelssohn's music in England, and his reviews reflect a late era of mixed reception of Mendelssohn, rather than the earlier era of unanimous acclaim. But it would be much simpler if reasons for Mendelssohn's success could be given that applied equally well to his music and to our suppositions about English musical life; moreover, to limit the historian's efforts to the reconstruction of the original context in which the music first found its resonance would be extremely one-sided. That the question is one of art, not of fashion, becomes clear only when we consider that these works, after all, have survived a continually changing process of reception. If we are to describe their relationship to contemporary reception, then we must take into account changing perceptions of the two in the course of history; for they are as two sides of an artistic entity that respond to the demands of the present and of the past.

Drawing on Shaw's criticism, Wilfrid Mellers re-summarized the English reception of Mendelssohn in his study of music and society in the nineteenth century. Neither the assumptions of this book nor its problematic method-ology are the subject of the present discussion. Mellers' style of argument is similar to Shaw's, whose texts Mellers cites with complete approval.[12] The belief in a progress that is thrown off-course by music such as Mendelssohn's is joined with a faith in emotional characteristics which are judged without formality. Initially, Mellers' critical procedure delineates no specifically English reaction to Mendelssohn, but rather a general viewpoint which had long been dominant. The "conservatism of his nature," "homage to tradi-tion," "mechanical manipulation" of "pseudo-classical material," "rendering bourgeoisie," and "sentimentality" of the melody – these quotes appear everywhere.[13] But in Mellers they are coupled with a sociological interpreta-tion which appears so irrefutable as not to require further explanation.

---

12 W. Mellers, *The Sonata Principle: Romanticism and the Twentieth Century* (London, 1957); trans. T. M. Höpfner as *Musik und Gesellschaft*, vol. II: *Die Romantik und das 20. Jahrhundert* (Frankfurt am Main, 1965), pp. 37f.

13 *Ibid.*, pp. 32, 34.

Mendelssohn relied "upon the fact that he was close enough to the classical tradition for its conventions to be still acceptable to a middle-class public that then, as now, feared change."[14] The conclusion from this sociological analogy is evident: since the composer risked no innovations in his musical material, he accommodated a bourgeoisie that feared revolution – in art as in commerce and politics. If this is particularly true for England, the judgment especially applies to the oratorios.

Mendelssohn's attempt "to create a nineteenth-century version of Handelian oratorio and Bachian cantata," therefore, "was doomed to failure." And so "Gounod's sweetness seems preferable to Mendelssohn's solemnity" and "pietistic morality."[15] Thus, Mendelssohn "reached the pinnacle of his fame in a rapidly and recently industrialized England. Our native musical tradition being moribund, we were the more prepared to accept a consciously archaistic style: and to welcome in musical convention a spurious religiosity which reflected the element of unconscious humbug in our morality and beliefs." All the "sadder" is "Mendelssohn's case", for "he prostituted his gifts wilfully." The relationship is clear: false religiosity and an inauthentic archaism in Mendelssohn's music correspond to the hypocritical morality and moribund musical culture of England. And, there is a perfect two-fold correlation: just as false faith and lifeless music interact in England, so do religious and musical deficiencies coalesce in the case of Mendelssohn. In combination the two express a reciprocal affinity. And the analogies are directed in such a way that the question scarcely arises how their validity may be demonstrated so that they become more than personal opinions: the facts, in short, are already established.

II

Despite their differences, Shaw and Mellers share a mistrust of religious morality as well as an antipathy toward Mendelssohn's religious music. Indeed, they display certain prejudices of their time, although the language of their criticism defends those prejudices. Both express boredom in their reaction to Mendelssohn's achievements, and, characteristic of the later nineteenth century, both turn themselves against a particular situation. On the other hand, in order to demonstrate Mendelssohn's earlier appeal, they allow citations of a long series of favorable, if not enthusiastic, opinions from the middle of the century. Clearly, it was precisely the praise of Mendelssohn's proponents that provoked the protests of his critics. In short, these critical

14 *Ibid.*, p. 36; English version, p. 30.
15 *Ibid.*, p. 37; English version, p. 31 (also for the following quotes).

positions point to a single fact: Mendelssohn's detractors, like his followers, are still aroused because his music found its success in England.

Shaw and Mellers give the impression that the displeasure caused by the stubborn popularity of Mendelssohn's music stems from the time of its first performances in England. According to this argument, the early reception of Mendelssohn was already based upon an inherent mediocrity shared by Mendelssohn's style and contemporary English musical conditions. But the sociological implications of such an analogy – and indeed, their very foundations – are delicate.

The overwhelming wealth of possibilities which English musical life offered continental musicians around 1830 was by no means taken for granted at the time. England's attractiveness certainly rested upon an economic base; and to be sure, the coupling of art and commerce in London was far more advanced than in Leipzig or Berlin. Yet this was the negative side of a progress that doubtless generally benefitted music. When Mendelssohn first came to England in 1829, the failed expectations that followed the Wars of Liberation and the Congress of Vienna were making their effects felt upon the Continent. England, on the other hand, was the country in which the emancipation of the middle class had initially taken hold. English musical life, which offered inconceivable opportunities, had not yet become encrusted; rather, it appeared to redeem the revolution's ideals of civic opportunity and community participation. Therefore, that more persons could participate in music in England than elsewhere, as William Weber has shown in his studies about the social structure of concert life, is not at all surprising.[16] And to dismiss this aspect of English musical life as mendacious commercialism would be historically short-sighted, for in rural areas, too, there were choruses whose musical capabilities were only rarely matched in Germany (principally at music festivals). In England, then, was found real potential: to bridge, perhaps for the last time, the gap between art and its public by means of active community participation, and thereby to salvage a bit of revolutionary Utopia.

Clearly, contradictory trends also manifested themselves in English musical life. The trend toward commercialization, the concessions to the general taste, the dominance of publishers and agents, the cautious and conventional programming of concerts, the entrenched cult of stardom – all these are conditions which asserted themselves just as demonstrably (although not yet so strongly) on the Continent. If the appearance of these factors resulted naturally from the business of middle-class concerts, their appearance earlier in

16 William Weber, *Music and the Middle Class* (London, 1975).

England than elsewhere was inevitable.[17] To stress these factors out of context would be an oversimplification, for they also represent the conditions essential to the development of contemporary musical life. Undeniably great art-music found its success in England only slowly after the classic era. But this situation was not much different in Germany, where success was limited to those works which proved influential precisely because they initially encountered impediments to their acceptance. That German music of the classic era was able to gain a foothold in England was a decisive moment, an achievement that should not be underestimated.[18]

Equally problematic is the assertion of a relationship in England between music and religion (or morality); the notion that the situation was substantially different in Protestant Germany is not at all tenable. The relatively early appearing signs of secularization in England were a direct consequence of the middle-class revolution. What eventually became distorted during the Victorian period into that image of false religiosity – the image that so irritated Shaw and Mellers – was not necessarily so distorted earlier in the century. To impugn insincere motives to all the supporters of the oratorio tradition would be not only inhuman; such a criticism would fail to recognize the inherent artistic problems posed by the dignity of sacred themes in the nineteenth century. For the sake of argument one might ask Shaw whether the mysticism of the Grail in *Parsifal* is really any more tasteful or authentic than the Old Testament prophecy in *Elijah*. Not only in England did religious themes proceed from certain traditions, even from those which were not accepted without question; and if the attempt to confront this difficulty was necessarily insincere, then one would have to reject a good amount of the nineteenth-century's creative output. Also, the performance of religious music outside the church in England, in large-scale gatherings in music halls and concert rooms, merely reflected a trend – a trend, to be sure, encouraged by the nature of the English tradition – that elsewhere brought the *Missa Solemnis* and the B minor Mass to performance outside the church. By no means did the composition of such works have to represent a concession to England's Pharisees. The aesthetic legitimacy of a composition must be determined not on the basis of its genre or choice of text, but rather on the basis of the work itself.[19]

17 See Percy A. Scholes, *The Mirror of Music, 1844–1944* (London, 1947); J. A. Fuller Maitland, *English Music in the Nineteenth Century* (London, 1902); and J. A. Westrup in *MGG* III (1954), cols. 1401–7.

18 Also not to be underestimated are Mendelssohn's own contributions to this area, beginning with his performance of Beethoven's "Emperor" Concerto on 24 June 1829, during the first trip to England. See Hensel, *Die Familie Mendelssohn*, vol. I, p. 230, and Werner, *Mendelssohn: a New Image*, p. 149.

19 That this point is not entirely obvious has been demonstrated most recently by R. Hauser's article, "'In rührend feierlichen Tönen': Mendelssohns Kantate *Die erste Walpurgis-*

For the most part, Mendelssohn's many letters and drawings from his English sojourns betray his acknowledgement of and sense of wonder at the island's musical life. To be sure, he also laments and remains defensive about the impositions of promoters, agents, and publishers.[20] But these reservations scarcely diminish the general impression that Mendelssohn enjoyed his reception in England, particularly in London. What drew him there was the abundance of concerts, the wealth of opportunities, and the greater receptiveness of English audiences compared to German ones. Not without reason did he view London as the center of the modern musical world; nor did he fail to recognize the limitations this center could impose on the effectiveness of music. With the very sensitivity that he expressed in recording the appeal of English nature and landscapes, so too did he record the signs of industrialization. And his observations about English society may be found in letters that reveal an interest in the daily press as well as in political issues.[21] His view of England thus leans neither toward sympathy nor idealization. Still, nothing was more important to this composer than the ability of musicians and audiences to understand spontaneously, to engage themselves, and to participate in musical life.[22] He perceived this openness as part of the progress that distinguished England. Mendelssohn was in no way drawn to England by a desire to forsake reality for convention, but by just the opposite: by his fascination with England's multitude of opportunities and their accompanying risks.

nacht . . .," *Musik-Konzepte* 14/15 (Munich, 1980), 75–92. The criticism of Goethe's text is here projected onto Mendelssohn's music without any further analytical argumentation. To discredit the work's conclusion in this way is to ignore its compositional circumstances as well as the historical novelty of Mendelssohn's solution.

20 For example, see the letter of 19 June 1844 (*Briefe aus den Jahren 1833 bis 1847*, pp. 422ff); also of 27 April 1832 (*Reisebriefe aus den Jahren 1830 bis 1832*, ed. Paul Mendelssohn Bartholdy, 3rd edn. [Leipzig, 1869], pp. 357ff); as well as of 13 May 1844 (S. Hensel, *Die Familie Mendelssohn*, vol. III, pp. 150ff).

21 See for example Hensel, *Die Familie Mendelssohn*, vol. I, pp. 217ff, 224ff, 236f, 268f; also the letter of 3 November 1829 in *Ein tief gegründet Herz: Der Briefwechsel Felix Mendelssohn Bartholdys mit Johann Gustav Droysen*, ed. C. Wehmer (Heidelberg, 1959), pp. 27ff; as well as Klingemann's discussion of daily politics in his letter of 3 February 1832, in Klingemann, *Felix Mendelssohn-Bartholdys Briefwechsel*, pp. 168ff. On the other side, Mendelssohn remained more than critical of English musical life and even of the Philharmonic Society. See for example E. Devrient, *Meine Erinnerungen an Felix Mendelssohn-Bartholdy und seine Briefe an mich*, 2nd edn. (Leipzig, 1872), pp. 77–90, and especially the letters of 29 October 1829 (*ibid.*, p. 89) and 19 July 1844 (*Briefe aus den Jahren 1833 bis 1847*, p. 423). Moreover, he remained skeptical of his own successes in England; see the letters of 4 October 1837 (*ibid.*, p. 151) and 10 December 1837 in F. Hiller, *Felix Mendelssohn-Bartholdy: Briefe und Erinnerungen*, 2nd edn. (Cologne, 1878), pp. 90f.

22 This is borne out particularly by reports of the first performances of *Elijah*; cf. the letters of 26 August 1846 and 31 August 1846 (*Briefe aus den Jahren 1833 bis 1847*, pp. 467ff, 470ff). See also F. G. Edwards's study (see note 1) and Jack Werner, *Mendelssohn's "Elijah": a Historical and Analytical Guide* (London, 1965), pp. 12ff, 22ff.

If one is to speak of more than some vague affinity between Mendelssohn's music and the Victorian standards, reason dictates that one consider to what extent his works were created for England or accommodated English standards. Compositions conceived in England or in fulfillment of English commissions must be distinguished from works which were only performed there.

To the second group belong not only almost all of Mendelssohn's works, but also just as many works by other composers, from Bach and Beethoven to Schubert and Schumann. We should not forget that Mendelssohn used his position to introduce, for example, Schubert's "Great" C major Symphony and Schumann's *Paradies und die Perie*.[23] On the other hand, a work such as the String Quartet in E flat major op. 12 (1829) – which, incidentally, comes under attack from Shaw even though it contains none of the "regular" sonata forms to which he referred – was actually composed in England.[24] In these works, however, we would be hard pressed to point out any accommodations to English taste, unless we simply designate the subtle genre of the string quartet as the prototype of the English tradition. For in its blend of lyricism and experimental form, Mendelssohn's op. 12 (which distinguishes itself clearly from late Beethoven) remained widely accepted outside England during the nineteenth century.

The "Scottish" Symphony, on the other hand, is admittedly inspired by landscape and history, and, indeed, is dedicated to the Queen. But in it, as in the *Hebrides* Overture, the subject is Mendelssohn's impressions of contemporary England. What is more, both works were composed outside England, and both freed themselves from that particular geographical association in their performance and reception history. Thus, Shaw would have designated neither as "English" or even "Victorian." (Indeed, Schumann thought that the "Scottish" was "Italian" in conception – an instance of mistaken identity, but telling none the less.)[25]

Remaining for consideration are Mendelssohn's works actually composed for England: primarily the Organ Sonatas op. 65, *Elijah*, and a few smaller church pieces (of which we mention here only the anthems "Hear My

23 Concerning the introduction of Schumann's piece see the letter to Buxton (E. Werner, *Mendelssohn: a New Image*, pp. 440f); concerning the (admittedly unsuccessful) attempts on behalf of Schubert's C major Symphony, see *ibid.*, pp. 395f.

24 On the genesis of the quartet, completed, according to the autograph, in London on 24 September 1829, see Hensel, *Die Familie Mendelssohn*, vol. I, pp. 276, 279f, and Klingemann, *Felix Mendelssohn-Bartholdys Briefwechsel*, pp. 57, 60. Although op. 12 contains no "regular" sonata-form movements, it was the target of Shaw's criticism (see Shaw, *London Music*, pp. 68ff) rather than a work such as the E flat major Quartet op. 44 no. 3, which was less well known in the nineteenth century but still won the approval of Mellers (*The Sonata Principle*, pp. 35f).

25 R. Schumann, *Gesammelte Schriften über Musik und Musiker*, ed. H. Simon (Leipzig, n.d.), vol. III, pp. 145f; see also Shaw, *London Music*, pp. 35f.

Prayer," "Why, O Lord," and the chorus "To the Evening Service"). In works of a religious character Mendelssohn closely met the demands of English taste; especially striking is their congruency with those conditions targeted by Shaw and Mellers, who seek to confirm a connection between Mendelssohn's religious music and English musical life. To put it differently: the composer's *Gebrauchsmusik* was, seemingly, a response to English taste. But we must still consider the depth of this relationship, whether or not it led to compositional deficiencies in the works, and to what extent it established a type of criticism based on morals. Though we must investigate the extent to which the relevant works followed English conventions, we must also consider whether they actually marked a departure from other works of Mendelssohn.

Georg Knepler has explored the relationship between art and society in England, as well as Germany, in his *Musikgeschichte des 19. Jahrhunderts*. Although his views largely agree with those of Mellers, Knepler's evaluation of Mendelssohn differs significantly.[26] Reviewing the period of the English middle-class revolution, Knepler paints a picture of an English musical life characterized above all by a murky blend of economic interests and artistic conflicts. Without ignoring the opportunities and achievements of the musical culture, he stresses above all the fatal consequences which the domination of economic premises had for the productivity of composers in England. The emigration of musicians such as Onslow and Field is similarly explained by the English need for musical imports. The "cause of the dearth of composers" was therefore unmistakable: church and capital relied on an "erroneous circle of faulty ideas and good business"; "unfavorable conditions" hindered "the production of meaningful music."[27] Evidently, for Knepler as for Mellers, these factors explain Mendelssohn's particular reception in England. Knepler, however, paints a completely different picture of Mendelssohn – though without specifically considering his relationship to England. Only the key points of the debate may be addressed here. To his credit, Knepler establishes from the outset that Mendelssohn was anything but conservative in his political and musical convictions. The burden of a public career, which he accepted as a matter of moral obligation, was made no lighter by a chain of conflicts that pervaded the ostensibly carefree existence of the *Glückskind*. Mendelssohn's increasing resignation, too, was the result of failed hopes for the social reforms that would have been necessary to realize an aesthetic Utopia. Numerous studies since Knepler's have demonstrated too that Men-

26 Georg Knepler, *Musikgeschichte des 19. Jahrhunderts. II: Österreich – Deutschland* (Berlin, 1961), pp. 747–70; and *I: Frankreich – England* (Berlin, 1961), pp. 346ff, 354ff, 447ff.
27 Knepler, *Österreich – Deutschland*, vol. II, p. 763.

delssohn's music is in no way conventional, or conservative – even if this is the initial impression it creates (as has been hinted here on more than one occasion). The burden of the traditions handed down to Mendelssohn in turn produced neither slavish imitation nor decadence in his style, but rather a chain of productive reactions. To return to Knepler: unlike Schumann's "youthful revolts," "Mendelssohn's no less path-breaking innovations stream forth naturally, as a matter of course," because they are "so seamlessly joined to tradition that they fail to impress as innovations."[28]

The considerable changes in the evaluation of the aesthetic and historical position of Mendelssohn's art must be a primary topic of our inquiry. But beyond this assumption the relationship between his music and its reception in England must be viewed from two perspectives. In Mellers' or Shaw's view, the inferior conventions of English musical life were perfectly congruent with the conservative character of Mendelssohn's *oeuvre*. On the other hand, the success which Mendelssohn's music, with its mixture of innovation and new demands, was able to achieve in England contradicts Knepler's picture of the wretched condition of English culture. Thus, sociological attempts to find plausible explanations become all the more difficult. The analogy postulated by Mellers is itself difficult to substantiate; to put it simply, the self-contradictory relationship between a reactionary musical culture and a successful, musically progressive style could be still more difficult to substantiate. And the problems become seemingly intractable when the ambivalent position of religious music is thrown into the mix. For though religious works, despite their ties to sacred texts and models, no longer had a place in the church, their traditional purposes and idioms remained intact and posed a problem for their use in the concert hall. If contemporary aesthetic thought accepted unquestioningly the idea that all worthwhile music had some metaphysical value, then any music which sought to identify its metaphysical content through its text or musical idiom was necessarily suspect.[29] With the orientation of aesthetic criteria toward instrumental music – seemingly the purest representative of autonomous art – the artistic nature of vocal music and its ties to texts became open to question. But if the association with historical conventions and dogmatic content led to a dependency on the text, then such religious music was in real jeopardy of becoming a deficient type of art. In short, the more all music as an art came to signify a religious work, the greater the danger that specifically religious music became tautological and superfluous. In order to attain legitimacy, such

---

28 *Ibid.*
29 See Carl Dahlhaus, *Die Idee der absoluten Musik* (Kassel, 1978), pp. 91ff; and Friedhelm Krummacher, "Kunstreligion und religiöse Musik," in *Die Musikforschung* 32 (1979), 365–93.

music required compositional measures that compensated for its aesthetic deficiencies.

How religious music could achieve success, particularly in English contexts, could be more easily explained if the merits of a particular composition could be measured against a rule of mediocre standards. The relationship becomes more complex, however, if one accepts the contradiction between a work's intrinsic compositional value and the social circumstances that surrounded it. These difficulties are of consequence not only for our understanding of Mendelssohn or for our evaluation of English music, but also for the basic tasks confronting the sociology of music. Only if we refuse to consider one-sided evaluations may we find solutions. We must concede, then, that Shaw's critical survey was too widely accepted, just as Knepler's view of English musical culture has been. But if we are prepared to deal with the potentials and limitations of the English tradition, then we might detect trends in Mendelssohn's music that reflect both. That religious works had to articulate their artistic worth through special compositional measures throws into focus their aesthetic ambivalence. And contradictions of this kind explain not only the changing reception of such music, but also its tendency to provoke contrary judgments. Clearly, the very music that at first wins universal acceptance later may be praised as art or criticized as kitsch. But that the *Rezeptionsgeschichte* of such works permitted divergent opinions also reflects some of the effectiveness through which they attained their artistic identities; for the divergent opinions presumably reflected upon the works themselves and not merely the critic's personal biases. What remains to consider is which qualities accounted for the works' affinities with England and also permitted their reception abroad. Inability to find unequivocal answers should not be viewed as a failure. Not only do contradictions abound in the reception of nineteenth-century music; they may also assist analytical attempts to identify the inherent conflicts of the music in order to evaluate, in turn, the potential of the music.

III

Without providing detailed analyses, we may adduce here three examples that illustrate the difficulties posed by the changing perspectives and styles of arguments: *Elijah*, the Organ Sonatas op. 65, and the hymn "Hear my Prayer."

1. Of Mendelssohn's major works, none is more closely associated with England than *Elijah*. Indeed, this work succeeded earlier in England than in Germany, where it initially competed with *St. Paul*. Though not a commis-

sioned English work, *Elijah* was none the less clearly written to be premièred in Birmingham. The two versions were first performed in cities historically associated with the English oratorio tradition (Birmingham, 26 August 1846; London, 23 April 1847). As F. G. Edwards, Jack Werner, and (most recently) Arno Forchert have shown, Mendelssohn's plans for the work extended back to 1837.[30] If the autograph resurfaces, just how much the creation of the work proceeded from the English text will become significantly easier to determine. While composing the oratorio, Mendelssohn was in contact with the translator W. Bartholomew; the published correspondence, however, suggests that the primary text during this stage was the German one, and that this caused the difficulties which are found in the translation.[31] Further, Mellers' suggestion that Mendelssohn had already chosen his material at this time so that he could claim the British as his "chosen people" is rather unlikely; much more probable is the possibility (stressed by Eric Werner) that the choice of subject reflected the composer's Jewish heritage.[32] And finally, *Elijah* was conceived as the Old Testament part of a trilogy which was to have been completed by the unfinished oratorio *Christus*. Thus, in its musical genesis as well as its choice of texts, *Elijah* provides no evidence to support the notion of an accommodation to English taste. Such an assertion would therefore have to rest upon musical criteria.

Certainly as an oratorio *Elijah* is from the same mold as *St. Paul*, which was written for the Rhenish Music Festival and found its spectacular success primarily in Germany. We need not elaborate on the many analogies between the two works: their orchestration and scoring; their choral movements and styles of vocal writing; their musical forms and variants of those forms; their dove-tailing of recitatives and arias into song-like arioso scenes. But there are also significant differences. First, as is often observed, *St. Paul* is more clearly oriented toward Bach, whereas *Elijah* exhibits more pronounced Handelian tendencies. But such a generalization is difficult to substantiate on the basis of the musical text; even if one admits that the observation is an oversimplification, *Elijah* still differs as much stylistically from Handel as from Bach. What is more, the apparent proximity of *Elijah* to Handel may reflect primarily the dramatic mode of the work, rather than actual techniques of

30 In addition to the studies of F. G. Edwards and J. Werner cited in notes 1 and 22, see A. Forchert, "Textanlage und Darstellungsprinzipien in Mendelssohns Elias," in *Das Problem Mendelssohn*, ed. C. Dahlhaus, pp. 61–77.

31 See J. Werner, *Mendelssohn's "Elijah"*, pp. 26ff, and A. Forchert, "Textanlage," pp. 62ff, 66ff. The autograph, long believed lost but now held in Kraków (along with other manuscripts of the Deutsche Staatsbibliothek), remains to be consulted.

32 Mellers, *The Sonata Principle*, p. 37; E. Werner, *Mendelssohn: a New Image*, pp. 457–73. Concerning the choice of texts see *Briefwechsel zwischen Felix Mendelssohn Bartholdy und Julius Schubring*, ed. J. Schubring (Leipzig, 1892; rep. Wiesbaden, 1973), pp. 124–5.

composition. And even if the observation were valid, it would mean nothing more than that one historical model had been replaced by another. In fact, the aesthetic problem that has prompted this dispute is common to both *Elijah* and *St. Paul*. That *Elijah*, unlike *St. Paul*, forgoes arrangements of chorales might suggest evidence of an orientation toward Handel rather than Bach, and thus of a concession to the English public, to whom Protestant chorales would have been foreign. But the omission of chorale material in *Elijah* was due primarily to the work's Old Testament theme; further, this omission was likely Mendelssohn's response to the criticism, directed at *St. Paul*, that chorale material, as an homage to Bach, was unfitting for the genre of oratorio. As Eric Reimer has demonstrated, in the theory of oratorio, the function of the chorale belonged to those questions which Mendelssohn sought to resolve.[33] If the role of the chorale came into question in *Elijah*, the matter was thus an aesthetic one, not an accommodation to England. This is evident in the quartet "Wirf dein Anliegen auf den Herrn" ("Cast Thy Burden upon the Lord"; No. 15), which contains a hidden chorale quotation based on "O Gott, du frommer Gott" (1693).[34] That this melody is quoted amidst the appeals of the Priests of Baal is certainly not without significance. Since the movement does not readily identify itself as a chorale, however, it impresses more as a lyrical moment if the listener is not aware of its background. And if the quartet retains for the informed listener some elements of its original meaning, this can hardly be described as a facile accommodation to English conventions.

Finally, to speak of a ready compromise of standards in *Elijah* is difficult because the work is certainly no less two-sided than *St. Paul* – indeed, it is richer and more complicated in conception. We may point to the rigorous consolidation of motivic relationships and the development of scenes; to the dramatic structuring of the first half as well as to the non-schematic, free fugues; but above all to the minimal number of recitatives and to the considerably more colorful harmonic fabric. Schumann sought to explain the differences between the two works in a remarkably perceptive comparison: "Just as Beethoven wrote the *Missa Solemnis* after *Christ on the Mount of Olives*, so did the oratorio of the mature Mendelssohn follow that of his youth."[35] If this comparison is

---

33 E. Reimer, "Kritik und Apologie des Oratoriums im 19. Jahrhundert," *Religiöse Musik in nichtliturgischen Werken von Beethoven bis Reger*, ed. W. Wiora, G. Massenkeil, and K. W. Niemöller, Studien zur Musikgeschichte des 19. Jahrhunderts No. 51 (Regensburg, 1978), pp. 247–56.

34 For Mendelssohn's own thoughts concerning the employment of chorales in *Elijah* see the letter to W. Bartholomew of 30 December 1846, reproduced in Edwards, *Mendelssohn's "Elijah"*, pp. 106f. E. Werner (*Mendelssohn: a New Image*, p. 470) added that the chorus "Wer bis an das Ende beharrt" (No. 32) was perhaps based on the chorale "O Welt, ich muß dich lassen."

35 R. Schumann, *Gesammelte Schriften*, vol. II, p. 116 (in the note appended to the review of *Elijah*).

generally valid, then we must conclude that contemporary audiences perceived *Elijah* as the weightier and more mature work. It was, therefore, precisely the more demanding work that was written for England – again, hardly a sign of accommodation to mediocre tastes. All of this illustrates the ambivalence of a work which to the critics initially seemed too involved and difficult, yet at the same time won the enthusiastic acclaim of audiences. If *Elijah* was understood as the culmination of its genre, it in turn was able only to establish a tradition that ultimately led to polemicizing and its suppression, even up to the present.

2. To those works Mendelssohn specifically wrote in response to English needs belong the Organ Sonatas op. 65. According to the correspondence (see the letter of 28 August 1844), the publisher Coventry's commission, which stemmed from Mendelssohn's editions of Bach organ music, was for a set of "Voluntaries."[36] This term, which simply denoted "free" organ music, was common only in England and referred to relatively small pieces that employed no particular characteristic form or cyclic arrangement. That Mendelssohn immediately accepted and rapidly fulfilled the commission, and that the "voluntaries" achieved a lasting success in England, might be interpreted as signs of accommodation. And that Mendelssohn chose the term "sonata" due to a misreading of "voluntary" might be congruent with this interpretation. In point of fact, none of the works is a proper sonata; rather, each was assembled from a number of independent movements that had been composed earlier. Furthermore, op. 65 entered the standard repertoire of organists much earlier in England than in Germany; and serious studies of the opus were available only in English until the recent publication of an article by Susanna Großmann-Vendrey (in response to the work's increasing prominence in the repertoire).[37]

On the basis of this evidence, the only possible conclusion is that these Sonatas were pieces written for hire; whether one views the heterogeneous whole as a unique composition or the result of a smooth process of assimilation appears to be of secondary importance. But other factors must also be considered. Thus, attempts to trace direct ties to English voluntaries have been unsuccessful, partly because no specific type of voluntary exists whose connection with op. 65 is more than coincidental.[38] Such attempts have run aground

36 See S. Großmann-Vendrey, "Stilprobleme in Mendelssohns Orgelsonaten op. 65," in *Das Problem Mendelssohn*, ed. C. Dahlhaus, pp. 185–94, especially p. 186, n. 2. For a discussion of the term see Peter F. Williams, "Voluntary," *MGG*, XIV (Kassel, 1968), cols. 8–10.

37 In addition to the article mentioned in note 36, see S. Großmann-Vendrey, "Die Orgelwerke von Felix Mendelssohn Bartholdy" (diss., Univ. of Vienna, 1964); and G. Zacher, "Die riskanten Beziehungen zwischen Sonate und Kirchenlied. Mendelssohns Orgelsonaten Op. 65, Nr. 1 und 6," *Musik-Konzepte* 14/15 (Munich, 1980), pp. 34–5.

38 See Williams, in *MGG* XIV, col. 9; S. Großmann-Vendrey, in *Das Problem Mendelssohn*, p. 187; C. W. Pearce, *Mendelssohn's Organ Sonatas* (London, 1902), pp. 3ff.

also because the enthusiastic reception afforded op. 65 would be difficult to understand if the Sonatas were merely replicas of contemporary models. Moreover, op. 65 was preceded by the piano Preludes and Fugues op. 35, which, though nominally harkening back to Bach, are closely affiliated generically and structurally to the Organ Sonatas. Indeed, the Sonatas sometimes draw upon material composed or sketched earlier.[39] Thus, the rapid completion of the commission can hardly have been the result of Mendelssohn's passion for business, for he probably was not in need of money. Rather, the English publisher's request coincided with the plans of the composer, who on 10 April 1845 presented his idea for the opus to Breitkopf as the product of his "way of performing on and thinking of the organ." But if the works became "larger than I myself had earlier anticipated," they also exceeded the terms of the English commission. For this reason, the publication notice stressed that the works were written "expressly for publication in England" but represented "his own peculiar style of performance."[40] Had the connection to English voluntaries been sufficiently clear, no publisher would have hesitated to release them without further explanation.

That Mendelssohn avoided the term "voluntary" because it was a foreign term is certainly plausible. But the assertion that the term "sonata" was a makeshift one is certainly not tenable for a composer such as Mendelssohn, who had a lifelong familiarity with the sonatas of Beethoven. Indeed, the term is more helpful to the historian, since it reflects Mendelssohn's intention to write organ music as artistically demanding as the piano sonata. The Organ Sonatas, alluding to J. S. Bach's trio sonatas and the classic piano sonata, mark *de facto* the beginnings of a new genre. At the same time, their interrelationships articulate a changing response to the canon of classic piano sonatas, whose influence is always present in Mendelssohn's late instrumental works (for example, in opp. 58, 66, and 80). Through precisely this break with tradition, op. 65 shaped history, up to Rheinberger and even Reger. Today, their juxtapositioning of diverse forms and structures makes them seem heterogeneous. But these aesthetic difficulties do not necessarily betray signs of accommodation to the English public (nor does the incorporation of chorale movements); rather, they reflect discrepancies in historical perception. The

39 Concerning the compositional history of the Organ Sonatas, see S. Großmann-Vendrey, "Die Orgel-Sonaten," vol. I, pp. 109–16. The C major Fugue op. 65 no. 2 was composed in 1839, and the introduction to the A major Sonata op. 65 no. 3 was already sketched in 1829 (cf. *Briefe aus den Jahren 1832 bis 1847*, pp. 426, 428). For a new critical edition of the organ sonatas, see Felix Mendelssohn Bartholdy, *Complete Organ Works*, ed. Wm. A. Little, vols. II, III and IV (London, 1987, 1988, and 1990).

40 See Großmann-Vendrey, "Stilprobleme," p. 186. See also the letter of 10 April 1845 to Breitkopf in *Felix Mendelssohn Bartholdy: Briefe an deutsche Verleger*, ed. R. Elvers (Berlin, 1968), p. 156.

early reviews expressed no dissatisfaction with the works' internal incongruencies. In all likelihood, what was originally perceived as compelling and unified is today considered disunified primarily because of our own lack of familiarity with the music. Remarkable indeed is the situation in the case of the Organ Sonatas that a composer usually criticized for merely glossing-over and imitating inherited forms was subjected to the opposite criticism: that he had proceeded in too free and undoctrinaire a fashion.

Certainly the difficulties posed by the Organ Sonatas should in no way be underestimated. Yet to dismiss them as a fashionable collage is hardly justified; this would require further explanation of the conception of the work, which we cannot provide here.[41] The combination of diverse elements in op. 65 owes not to some improvisational practice, even if individual movements were first conceived as improvisations. If we consider how scrupulously Mendelssohn polished his works, then it seems improbable that traces of improvisation were left undetected in these sonatas. Nor is the independent genesis of the individual movements much help; since the proper number of movements in the correct keys was available when Mendelssohn received the commission, he may have had early on a cyclic conception for the opus. Nevertheless, the incongruencies are significant, and give the performer reason enough to contemplate these works. This applies, first of all, to the fugal movements and the opening movement of the C minor Sonata (no. 2), for which models have been sought in the works of Bach. We should not be content to accept superficial analogies without carefully considering significant discrepancies; for these discrepancies reflect not only Mendelssohn's simplification of the models, but also his ability to integrate them into his own stylistic idiom. And the individuality of this idiom is apparent not least of all in the reactions of those who were annoyed by it. On the other hand, it is above all the lyrical movements of the Sonatas that have been perceived as irritating appendages. None the less, these movements – all of which might be described as *Lieder ohne Worte* – are not mere additions; rather, they constitute something perhaps best described as the inner vanishing points of the Sonatas.[42] Not by chance are these movements placed last, after the connected Maestoso, Fugue, and Chorale in the A major Sonata (no. 3), and after the chain of chorale-variations in the D minor Sonata (no. 6). In both instances the ending

41 Großmann-Vendrey, "Stilprobleme," pp. 188ff.

42 Structurally, the slow movements of the Organ Sonatas distinguish themselves from the *Lieder ohne Worte* in that they do not display textures comprising a melodic upper voice with a rhythmically constant accompaniment. This is most evident in the concluding movements of Sonatas nos. 3 and 6, while the opening movements of nos. 1 and 3, as well as the slow middle movement of no. 5, are still less song-like.

marks a turn toward the inward reflection of the subject, which ultimately emerges as itself from Mendelssohn's grappling with history.

3. Among Mendelssohn's late vocal works which appeared with German and English texts is the hymn "Hear My Prayer." The surviving autograph in Kraków was not available for this study; in that source the work is titled *Sacred Solo*, and from the available letters we know that the hymn was composed to the English text, and that the German version was arranged later.[43] The piece was finished by January 1844; editions from Bote & Bock and Ewer & Co. appeared simultaneously in 1845 in Berlin and London. Composed for William Bartholomew, the hymn represented a minor occasional piece and was published without opus number (the German edition was dedicated to Wilhelm Taubert.)[44] In Germany the composition remained largely unknown, and would deserve no special consideration had it not been so successful in England. What concerns us here therefore is the success of a "paragon" which Mendelssohn may have written with the aim of accommodating the musical market in Victorian England.[45]

In its form, scoring, and compositional technique the work is not remarkable. And its character is that of a songful lyricism which has been both acclaimed as pure and introspective and derided as saccharine and sentimental. The two outer sections commence with a soprano solo, followed by the chorus; between these two outer sections stands a short solo recitative, likewise taken up by the chorus. But the first section is divided into two parts, in which the opening solo and chorus in 4/4 are followed by an intense accelerando in 3/8 time. The closing section, on the other hand, presents a rounded-off da-capo form constructed as solo – chorus – combination of the two. This form in no way accommodates English expectations; rather, quite similar forms may be found already in earlier, comparable pieces by Mendelssohn.[46] Beyond this there occurs no melodic device, no harmonic sequence, no contrapuntal technique that is particularly noteworthy. So effortlessly does the piece conclude that it poses no difficulties for either audiences or analysts.

43 R. Werner, "Felix Mendelssohn Bartholdy als Kirchenmusiker" (diss., Frankfurt am Main, 1929), p. 101; see further the catalogue of George Grove in his article "Mendelssohn," in *Grove's Dictionary of Music and Musicians*, 3rd edn. (London, 1948), vol. III, p. 433.

44 See E. Wolff, "Sechs unveröffentlichte Briefe von Felix Mendelssohn Bartholdy an Wilhelm Taubert," *Die Musik* 8/2 (1909), 165–70; and Elvers, *Briefe*, pp. 340f.

45 See E. Werner, *Mendelssohn: a New Image*, p. 101, and S. S. Stratton, *Mendelssohn*, p. 106, and P. Radcliffe, *Mendelssohn*, p. 143 (concerning the work's acceptance in England). The hymn appears in the *Gesamtausgabe* Serie XIV/3. Early in 1847 Mendelssohn completed an orchestral arrangement of the hymn for the Irish baritone Joseph Robinson. For an edition, see Felix Mendelssohn Bartholdy, *Hör mein Bitten, Orchesterfassung*, ed. R. L. Todd (Stuttgart, 1986).

46 For example, in the *Kirchenmusik* op. 23 (1830) or the *Hymn* op. 96 (1840). Mendelssohn nevertheless considered the hymn "Laß, O Herr" to be in "the tone of the English anthems." See his letter of 20 December 1840 in *Briefe an Ignaz und Charlotte Moscheles*, p. 205.

Ex. 4.1 (a) and (b):   Mendelssohn, *Hör mein Bitten*: (a) mm. 8–13; (b) mm. 34–41

But to justify an evaluation that rests on melodic characteristics rather than structural complexities is at best difficult; and to judge works which are not particularly complex is, obviously, still more difficult.

On first hearing, there is little especially striking in this hymn; what remains unclear is why it became so popular in England. One would have to conclude that its success was due either to particular English tastes or to an act of accommodation on Mendelssohn's part – really two ways of expressing the same idea. (Such simplicity may also trouble those listeners unwilling to accept it; but for these listeners, further experiences with the work will always be available.)

The opening melodic phrase suggests little of the affect expressed by the text: it remains within the circle of G major, although it fills out this area in a variety of ways. The initial pair of descending fifths is balanced by the stepwise ascending eighth notes which follow; after a simple half cadence, the line begins anew. Only after the repeat of the opening melodic arch is the compass expanded a bit, with the first modulation to the dominant (m. 10; see Ex. 4.1a). But this regular, economical pattern only serves as a foil for the subsequent disintegration that occurs in the solo part. This disintegration is signalled not only by shortened phrase-lengths, extensions, and syncopations, but also by an increased chromaticism (though the latter reflects the diction of the vocal part and produces no particular harmonic effects). The first choral entry repeats the incipit of the solo part, suggesting a da-capo-style rounding off of the form, even though this is cut short by the onset of the Allegro in 3/8 time (see Ex. 4.1b). But the contrast is at the same time reduced, for the solo voice's response to the choral incipit ("The enemy shouteth") proceeds with a variant of the chorus's expected continuation ("on the voice of your children").

Also worthy of consideration is how this section is condensed from quickly alternating responses between solo and chorus into a coupling of the two; the frugal scoring of the chorus's first entry and its subsequent elaboration; and how this is linked to the variation of a motivic cell, granting to the part of the section a certain symmetry and a sense of development that is both motivic and expressive – if one is prepared to hear these things.[47]

Although no analogous procedure is detectable in the recitative, the middle section of the work, it is further expanded in the closing section through the da-capo technique. Only three examples of this procedure may be discussed here. In its first appearance, the text "O, for the wings of a dove" is accompanied (somewhat paradoxically) by ascending triplets over a constant pedal point on the tonic, which forms the point of departure for the phrase's melodic climax (see Ex. 4.2a). Only with the repeat of the line does the modulating expansion ("in the wilderness build me a nest") occur, though this, too, retains the triplet flow. Stronger yet is the middle section, in which the chorus declaims the same text – without triplets – in repeated notes above a bass line of changing half notes, which are gradually filled out into chords (see Ex. 4.2b). Through the absorption of the solo part into the chorus, the contrast between the sections of the work is sharpened, so that the beginning of the piece is almost forgotten. The arrival of the reprise initially has the effect of a melodic repetition above a chordal texture in the chorus, which now forfeits its earlier independence. The crucial turning point, however, is marked

Ex. 4.2a: Mendelssohn, *Hör mein Bitten*, mm. 146–9

47 The unison choral parts do not just simplify difficulties in performance; while they allude, on the one hand, to liturgical practices, they also form a basis for the unfolding of the rest of the movement.

Ex. 4.2b   Mendelssohn, *Hör mein Bitten*, mm. 173–8

Ex. 4.2c: Mendelssohn, *Hör mein Bitten,* mm. 207–211

by the continuation of the solo part ("in the wilderness build me a nest"), which is simultaneously combined with the repeated notes in the chorus and the characteristic dissonant seconds of the middle section ("O, for the wings of a dove"; see Ex. 4.2c). One might well object that the combination of melodic sequences with sequentially repeated tones is none too artful. But the reprise (which structurally suggests a kind of sonata form) draws upon the inherent affinity among these themes, whose full significance derives from their very simplicity. What initially appeared to be unrelated in these themes becomes meaningfully related when they are combined. And the artistry of this combination lies not least of all in its unpretentious nature, so that it may well be overlooked initially.[48]

Reactions to such music may differ widely. To be sure, we can enjoy the sweetness of the sound – or reject it; but we then risk failing to perceive the silent art hidden behind the façade. The notion of Mendelssohn's accommodation to English standards, however, is difficult to corroborate even where it seems to exist. In the main, the debate has centered on issues determined less by scholarly criteria than by nationalistic or historical ones. That Mendelssohn's music has remained unquestionably in the repertoire in England need not be taken as proof of a reactionary taste – for this, at the extreme, would acknowledge only German standards. Rather, the fact is that in England Mendelssohn's music was not suppressed by anti-Semitism, and as a result continued to enjoy its reception there, undeterred by ignorant prejudices. That the strongest English criticism came from a free-thinker such as Shaw only after he had taken sides with Wagner seems, therefore, especially relevant. To subscribe to these views today is to preserve judgments based on anti-Semitism. And to ignore this music simply because it does not appeal to us is no scholarly argument, but merely an indulgence of taste. We should be familiar even with what we dislike. Such music might be ignored, but only by a musicology that abandons itself to the canonization of museum collections. For a musicology concerned with art in history, on the other hand, the widespread acclaim of Mendelssohn's music should remain a primary challenge. That music was differently evaluated in England than in Germany must be a cause of concern for German musicology; and Mendelssohn's music exemplifies this problem. And that his music has remained more popular in England might be understood as a challenge for tolerance in matters of aesthetics.

---

48 Certainly one might criticize the combination of a cadential melodic line in the solo part with repeated tones in the chorus as contrapuntally weak. Yet the issue is not the effectiveness of the counterpoint, but rather its integration into a song-like movement characterized by periodicity and cadential harmonies.

5 Mendelssohn and Liszt

WM. A. LITTLE

In the course of a professional career that spanned but thirty years Felix Mendelssohn came into personal contact with virtually every major European composer of his day. Born into a patrician family of bankers and financiers, the family wealth enabled frequent and extensive travel, and already in his seventh year he was taken on his first trip to Paris, where he studied piano briefly with Marie Bigot. In 1822 the whole family made an extended journey to Switzerland, and in 1823 Felix accompanied his father to Silesia, where he made a point of seeking out local musicians at every opportunity.

In 1825, at the age of sixteen, he travelled with his father, again to Paris, where he spent slightly more than a month. Ostensibly a business trip, the real purpose of this Paris sojourn was to test the waters, to determine whether the young Mendelssohn had any real potential as a professional musician. He had already made clear his desire to make music his career, a choice that caused considerable concern in the family, and in which he was chiefly opposed by his uncle Jakob.

Mendelssohn's father was well connected in Paris, and access to the leading musical circles was quickly and easily arranged. The days were filled with musical events of one kind or another, in many of which Felix took an active part as performer. There were also visits with such prominent figures as Rossini, Reicha, Moscheles, Neukomm, Kalkbrenner, Baillot, Lesueur, Rode, and numerous others. It was Cherubini, however, who, more than anyone, encouraged Mendelssohn, even going so far as to predict an auspicious future for him as a composer, "Ce garçon est riche; il fera bien; il fait même déjà bien; mais il dépense trop de son argent, il met trop d'étoffe dans son habit."[1]

Cherubini, who was not normally known for his friendly manner toward

This is a revised and expanded version of a paper read at the Mendelssohn Symposium held at Amherst College in December 1989.

[1] Letter to his mother from Paris, 6 April 1825. New York Public Library: "Felix Mendelssohn Bartholdy: Letters to his Family." A collection of 742 letters from the composer, most of which remain unpublished. Hereafter cited as NYPL.

young composers, nor for lavishing praise lightly, received Mendelssohn with exceptional graciousness and invited him to a number of closed performances. On one occasion he invited Mendelssohn to sit with him and his friends in his private box at a concert of the *Société des enfants de l'Apollon*. On this evening, as Felix wrote to his mother with unconcealed pride, he found himself sitting in the august company of Hummel, Kalkbrenner, Rode, Kreutzer, Moscheles, Meyerbeer, Rossini, and, of course, Cherubini. And it was on this occasion that Mendelssohn first heard Franz Liszt.[2]

At that time, Liszt, although two years Mendelssohn's junior, was already a seasoned performer, having toured successfully both on the Continent and in England. In Paris he was universally acclaimed, and critics vied with each other in proclaiming his genius. He was hailed as the reincarnation of Mozart, and as "the first pianist in Europe," to which the critic, one Martainville, felt obliged to add, "Moscheles himself would not feel offended by this affirmation."[3] After a particularly brilliant performance at an earlier concert at the *Enfants de l'Apollon* in 1824, Liszt had been elected to membership in the society by a spontaneous motion.[4] As Alan Walker put it, " 'le petit Litz' had become the darling of Paris."[5] Thus when Mendelssohn heard him in concert in 1825, Liszt was already a firmly established member of the Parisian musical community.

There has never been any serious doubt, among those familiar with the Mendelssohn canon, that Mendelssohn was at best a reluctant Francophile, and his letters from Paris in 1825 bear more than ample testimony to that fact. Although he was widely admired and fêted in Paris, and although he fulfilled the social amenities convincingly, below the surface he felt uncomfortable and ill at ease in the French capital, and he had few kind words to say about either his hosts or his fellow musicians. Of Rossini, "he has a tricky look, a mixture of roguishness, insipidness and boredom ... there you have the great Maestro Windbag."[6] Anton Reicha, "is feared as the 'Wild Huntsman' (always on the prowl for fifths)."[7] As for Meyerbeer, for whom Mendelssohn cherished a deep-seated and life-long antipathy that he never took any particular effort to conceal, the comments are characteristically sharp. His opinion of most of the chamber players he heard was, "dreadful," or "pathetic," or simply, "unter

---

2 *Ibid.*, No. 25 (18 April 1825).

3 A. Martainville in *Le Drapeau Blanc* (9 March [1825]). Cited by Alan Walker, *Franz Liszt: the Virtuoso Years (1811–1847)*, vol. I (New York, 1983), p. 99.

4 Walker, *Franz Liszt*, vol. I, pp. 96–7.   5 *Ibid.*, p. 98.

6 NYPL, No. 23 (6 April 1825), letter to his mother: "Der hat ein verzwicktes Gesicht. Eine Mischung von Schelmerey, Fadaise, und Überdruß ... da habt ihr den großen Maestro Windbeutel!"

7 *Ibid.*: "so ist er hier gefürchtet, wie der wilde Jäger (er geht nämlich auf die Quintenjagd)."

aller Kritik."[8] His most virulent remarks, however, were reserved for his principal Parisian benefactor, Cherubini, about whom he found it difficult to find exactly the right words of derision. In a contrived and self-conscious metaphor he likened Cherubini to a dried-up, burnt-out volcano. "He spews forth from time to time, but he is all covered with rocks and ashes."[9] Mendelssohn regarded Reicha as utterly academic and dry, but wrote that, "with all his aridity, he is like the ocean compared with land, when compared with Cherubini."[10] Given the general tone of Mendelssohn's comments here, it should come as no surprise that his appraisal of Liszt and his playing was no more generous. "Now came Liszt, who played an improvisation and variations on a theme by Czerny. He has lots of fingers but little brain. The improvisation was wretched and dull, nothing but scale passages; the variations he played were neither smooth nor pure, nor even brilliant. . . . Kalkbrenner smiled disdainfully and was very satisfied."[11]

In none of his letters home during this Parisian visit does Mendelssohn mention any personal contact with Liszt, but it is reasonable to assume that the two became acquainted at this time, since they moved in the same social and musical circles.

Despite the extravagant disdain in Mendelssohn's comments about his hosts and colleagues, it should be borne in mind, in all fairness to him, that the Paris trip was in more than one sense a difficult rite of passage, and that however controlled and poised he may have appeared, the vehemence of his remarks tempts one to recognize in them a defensive façade, behind which lurked an understandable measure of self-doubt and insecurity. Mendelssohn was, after all, only sixteen years old and under scrutiny by some of the most distinguished musical figures of his day in what was unquestionably the musical capital of the world. In his judgment of Liszt, however, there may well have been other forces at work as well.

In the first place, Mendelssohn was on someone else's turf: Paris was Liszt's terrain and had been for some two years. Secondly, and probably more galling for someone of Mendelssohn's temperament and pride, Liszt was two years younger than he was; at fourteen he already enjoyed an international reputation, as his concert tour of England the previous year had amply

8 NYPL, No. 25 (18 April 1825).

9 NYPL, No. 23: "Er sprüht noch zuweilen, aber er ist ganz mit Asche und Steinen bedeckt."

10 *Ibid.*: "obwohl er auch ein gut Theil Trockenheit abbekommen hat, ist er doch gegen Cherubini, wie Meer gegen Land."

11 NYPL, No. 25. "Nun spielte Liszt eine Improvisation und Variationen von Czerny; er hat viel Finger, aber wenig Kopf. Die Improvisation war erbärmlich und flach, lauter Tonleiter. Die Variationen spielte er, obwohl nicht glatt und rein, doch nicht brilliant. Die Nebenloge erhielt sich ruhig, Kalkbrenner lächelte spöttisch und war sehr zufrieden."

confirmed. Whereas Liszt had already established himself on the musical scene as a force to be reckoned with, Mendelssohn had been brought to Paris for the specific purpose of determining whether, in fact, he possessed enough talent to make music his career. Clearly, in these respects Mendelssohn was at a disadvantage.

At the same time, Mendelssohn had one clear advantage: he had already attracted considerable attention as a composer, as well as a performer. By early 1825 Mendelssohn was already a serious composer who had had his first work published two years earlier. When he came to Paris he brought with him a large and impressive portfolio of compositions, including the Piano Quartet in B minor op. 3, on which Cherubini pronounced so favorably. Liszt, on the other hand, at the time of Mendelssohn's visit, had yet to publish a single work. Although he had several compositions in manuscript, and his opera *Don Sanché* was soon to go into rehearsal, nothing of what he had composed so far was of a calibre approaching Mendelssohn's. Thus Mendelssohn, given the works he had in hand, certainly had some grounds for feeling superior.

After their initial meeting in 1825 a period of almost six years elapsed before they renewed their acquaintance, and again it took place in Paris. During Mendelssohn's visit to Paris in the winter of 1831–2 he refers only sporadically to Liszt in his correspondence, but those few references, plus the reminiscences of Ferdinand Hiller, who was also in Paris at the time, suggest that a relaxed camaraderie had developed between them, and that this musical triumvirate was joined by Chopin, who had recently come to Paris for the first time.

On one occasion Mendelssohn burst into his flat, where Hiller was waiting for him, and exclaimed that he had just witnessed a miracle. He and Liszt had gone off to Erard's showrooms to try some of their pianos; Mendelssohn happened to have the draft of his Piano Concerto in G minor op. 25 with him, and though the manuscript was barely legible, Liszt had sat down and played it straight through flawlessly. "He played it off at sight in the most perfect manner, better than anyone else could possibly play it."[12]

From Mendelssohn's correspondence at this time it may be gathered that he now got on well with Liszt; he refers to him as "L" and cites the same qualities of personal charm and easy manner that he would later remark on in Leipzig. Presumably, also, it was Liszt who with great tact and gentleness broke the news to Mendelssohn of the death of his close boyhood friend, Eduard Rietz.[13]

12 Ferdinand Hiller, *Mendelssohn: Letters and Recollections*, trans. M. E. von Glehn (London, 1874), pp. 26–7.
13 Felix Mendelssohn Bartholdy, *Briefe aus den Jahren 1830 bis 1847*, ed. Paul and Carl Mendelssohn Bartholdy (Leipzig, 1870), p. 242. Letter of 4 February 1832. Hereafter cited as *Briefe*.

The first three months of Mendelssohn's stay in Paris were marked by a constant round of concerts, salons, and dinner parties, all of which he faithfully described in his letters home. With the approach of spring, however, cholera broke out in Paris and rapidly became an epidemic. The daily death toll climbed from several hundred to well over a thousand, and the epidemic reached its height on 10 April; on that day alone more than two thousand people died. By mid-March the theaters had closed; dinner parties, balls, concerts and even salons were all cancelled. Most Parisians who could fled the city, but Mendelssohn remained, as did Liszt and Chopin and for a time Hiller. During this period Mendelssohn's letters home deal almost exclusively with the epidemic and with trying to dissuade his brother Paul from coming to Paris to visit him. Finally, Mendelssohn himself contracted a slight case of cholera, but recovered and left for London as soon as his health permitted, on 21 April. Although he had continued to see Liszt with some frequency during late winter and early spring, he still refers to him as "Herr Liszt," who wishes to send greetings to this or that friend in Berlin. When he left Paris in April, he would not see Liszt again for nine years.

Although Mendelssohn had been won over to Liszt as a person, by his charm and urbanity, and had come to recognize Liszt's greatness as a pianist, he firmly believed that Liszt lacked any gifts as a composer. "What you say of Liszt's harmonies is depressing," he wrote to Moscheles in the summer of 1835.[14] "If that sort of stuff is noticed and even admired, it is really outrageous. I cannot believe that impartial people can take pleasure in discords or be in any way interested in them."[15] Over and over again through the years it was Liszt's harmonies and discords that drew most of Mendelssohn's ire. (Clara Schumann, hardly an impartial judge, spoke of a "chaos of dissonances, . . . as a composer I could almost hate him."[16])

Although Mendelssohn always remained publicly discreet, the sentiments he expressed to Moscheles reflect his consistent opinion about Liszt's music – sentiments that Liszt had apparently been aware of for some time. In a letter to Marie d'Agoult, written a year before Mendelssohn's complaint to Moscheles, Liszt acknowledges the fact: "Mendelssohn's opinion was known to me, which has by no means prevented me from praising his compositions to you

14 Felix Mendelssohn Bartholdy, *Letters of Felix Mendelssohn to Ignaz and Charlotte Moscheles*, trans. and ed. Felix Moscheles (London [1888]), p. 136.

15 *Ibid.*

16 Berthold Litzmann, *Clara Schumann: Ein Künstlerleben. Nach Tagebüchern und Briefen* (Leipzig, 1907), vol. II, p. 35: "Ein Chaos von Dissonanzen, . . . als Künstler könnte ich ihn beinahe hassen."

(as well as to everyone)."[17] With characteristic good grace and equanimity Liszt took Mendelssohn's low esteem of his work in his stride. Not only did he take it in his stride, at the time he was actively engaged in promoting Mendelssohn's music. In the same year, 1834, Liszt wrote his "Großes Konzertstück über Mendelssohns *Lieder ohne Worte*" (Raabe No. 355) for two keyboards.[18] Although the work was performed in Paris in 1835, it remained unpublished at the time of his death.

In the spring of 1840 Liszt planned a concert tour which included Prague, Dresden, and Leipzig. He had not performed before in any of these cities, and so this would be a tour of major significance. After giving six concerts in eight days in Prague, Liszt arrived in Dresden on Saturday, 14 March 1840. His plan was to give three concerts in Dresden and two in Leipzig, before proceeding on to a reunion with Marie d'Agoult in Paris. It was not going to turn out quite that way. What lay ahead were two tumultuous, often bizarre weeks, which even for Liszt – in whose daily existence tumult was the accepted norm – would constitute a remarkable and unforgettable experience.

On that same Saturday, 14 March, Robert Schumann also arrived in Dresden, having come from Leipzig to meet Liszt for the first time and to review his concert the following Monday evening for the *Neue Zeitschrift für Musik*. Although their initial meetings were cordial, and although they spent much time together over the coming two weeks, they were not by nature mutually congenial personalities. In Liszt's presence Schumann seemed withdrawn and taciturn. Eleanor Perényi reports that he would "sit for hours in Liszt's hotel rooms sunk in silence, which at one point he broke to exclaim, 'There now, that's it! We've been talking now with open hearts.' Liszt thought him 'excessively reserved.'"[19]

In the course of the weekend there were numerous soirées in honor of Liszt, and at a party on Sunday, given by Gustav Lipinsky (the Dresden Konzertmeister) and attended by Schumann, Liszt pressed Lipinsky into playing a duet version of one of Beethoven's sonatas.[20] This was the first time Schumann had heard Liszt perform, and brief though it was, it gave him some hint of what to expect on Monday evening.

Liszt's first public concert in Dresden achieved everything he had hoped for; he was jubilantly received and thunderously applauded. And Schumann's

17 Marie d'Agoult, *Correspondance de Liszt et de la Comtesse d'Agoult*, ed. Daniel Ollivier, 2 vols. (Paris, 1933), vol. I, p. 111 (25 August 1834): "L'opinion de Mendelssohn m'était connue, ce qui ne m'a point empêché de vous faire (comme à tout le monde) l'éloge de ses compositions."
18 Peter Raabe, *Franz Liszt – Liszt's Schaffen*, vol. II (Tutzing, 1968), p. 292 (No. 355).
19 Eleanor Perényi, *Liszt: the Artist as Romantic Hero* (Boston and Toronto, 1974), pp. 207–8.
20 *Allgemeine musikalische Zeitung* 42 (1840), col. 263. Hereafter cited as *AmZ*.

masterly review clearly reflected popular opinion. All of which was echoed by Johannes Heitmann, who, writing for the *Allgemeine musikalische Zeitung*, proclaimed Liszt to be, "unquestionably, the foremost living pianist.... Thus the present-day *non plus ultra* in this art has been achieved by Liszt."[21]

Liszt's first Dresden concert should have boded well for his reception in Leipzig, but Dresden was not Leipzig by any means. Musically, Leipzig was one of the most arch-conservative cities in Germany, and Liszt must surely have been aware of its reputation, as well as the fact that in German musical circles it was known as "die Tante."[22] If that had been all there was to it, there would have been little problem; Liszt with his urbanity, charm, and cyclopean technique could win over even the most reluctant of audiences. The problem, however, was not simply Leipzig; it was the confluence of a variety of factors that included coincidence, bad luck, and the catastrophic mismanagement of everything by the notorious Hermann Cohen, otherwise known as "Puzzi," a twenty-year-old con man *cum* protégé whom Liszt had taken under wing several years earlier, and to whom he now entrusted the important role of tour manager. Altogether, Liszt's opening act in Leipzig represented a textbook example of Murphy's Law.

As originally planned, Liszt's first concert (Tuesday, 17 March 1840) was to have been performed with the Gewandhaus Orchestra in the Concert-Saal. It was discovered, however, at the last minute, *after* the programs had been printed and distributed, that the orchestra had been committed before-hand to play at the opera at the same time Liszt had scheduled his perform-ance. This may have been an oversight on the part of Schumann, who was apparently in charge of programming and local arrangements, but in any case, it was the first bit of bad luck, and it forced Liszt to change his program without notice. Unfortunate, but not necessarily disastrous. What was dis-astrous was "Puzzi" Cohen's handling of the financial and logistical end of things. From the time of their inception, the cost of admission to the Gewandhaus concerts had always been 16 Groschen, but now, with little or no prior notice, Cohen nearly doubled the cost of a ticket to one Taler, or two Talers, if purchased at the time of the performance. Secondly, there had never been any reserved seating sections in the Gewandhaus, but again Cohen broke with tradition: he had a large reserved section cordoned off and demanded a further 12 Groschen to the already doubled ticket price for a reserved seat. As a consequence of these abrupt and arbitrary changes, many of those who came to the concert hall found that they did not have enough

---

21 *Ibid.*, col. 264: "unbedingt der erste jetzt lebende Pianoforte-spieler.... Mit Liszt ist mithin das *Non plus ultra* in der Kunst gegenwärtig erreicht."

22 Perényi, *Liszt*, p. 209. See also Walker, *Franz Liszt*, vol. I, pp. 347–8.

money to enter.[23] Finally, and contrary to all tradition, Cohen refused to provide any complimentary tickets, even to the press.[24] Small wonder, then, that Liszt in his first Leipzig performance faced a less than friendly audience – though certainly through no deliberate fault of his own. Neither Schumann nor the anonymous reviewer in the *Allgemeine musikalische Zeitung* mentions the audience's initial response to Liszt, but the unnamed critic for the local newspaper, *Die Eisenbahn*, was less reticent: "The artist stepped out [onto the stage, but] was not greeted with applause, but rather he was booed. The hissing did not cease, however, when he looked at the audience with pride and full of indignation."[25] In the course of the concert Liszt worked his usual magic on the audience, but, "The hissing did not die out entirely, and the artist had all he could do to suppress it."[26] Clearly, the atmosphere was tense, and even Mendelssohn, in an unpublished letter to his sister, acknowledged that the mood in Leipzig toward Liszt, even before his arrival, was "atrocious" (*abscheulich*).[27] As Hiller recalled some years later, "At his first concert, as he glided along the platform of the orchestra to the piano, dressed in the most elegant style, and as lithe and slender as a tiger-cat, Mendelssohn said to me, 'There's a novel apparition, the virtuoso of the nineteenth century.'"[28]

As for Liszt's performance itself, there was little critical disagreement: to all intents and purposes he was without peer as a pianist. As for his program, however, it irked both Schumann and the reviewer for the *Allgemeine musikalische Zeitung*, that Liszt had insisted on playing his own transcription of the Scherzo and Finale of Beethoven's "Pastoral" Symphony. Leipzig audiences were accustomed to hearing Beethoven's symphonies performed in the Gewandhaus by a full orchestra, and Liszt's distillation had seemed but a stale

23 For further details on the mishaps surrounding this concert see Peter Raabe, *Franz Liszt – Liszts Leben*, vol. I (Tutzing, 1968), pp. 78–80. See also *AmZ* 42 (1840), cols. 263–5; also Friedrich Wieck, "Liszt in Leipzig," originally published in *Leipzig–Berlin–Dresdener Dampfwagen* 12 (24 March 1840), repr. in Victor Joß, *Der Musikpädagoge Friedrich Wieck und seine Familie* (Dresden, 1902), pp. 145–52. Wieck's review, intemperate at times, served as grounds for a successful law suit against Wieck by Hermann Cohen.

24 Raabe, *Liszts Leben*, pp. 78–9. Walker's account of this debacle (*Franz Liszt*, vol. I, pp. 348–9) contains minor errors: Liszt did not "snub" Wieck by refusing to send him press tickets for "his Dresden [*sic*] concert"; no complimentary tickets were given out at all to the press for the Leipzig concert. Wieck did *not* live in Dresden at the time; he did not move to Dresden until 1844. Liszt did not "take Schumann's side" in the latter's law suit against Wieck; he barely knew Schumann, having only met him two days earlier.

25 Raabe, *Liszts Leben*, p. 78: "Der Künstler trat auf, wurde nicht mit Applaus empfangen, sondern ausgezischt. Das Zischen hörte indes nicht auf, als er mit Stolz und voll Indignation das Publikum anblickte."

26 *Ibid.*: "Das Zischen unterblieb nicht ganz, und der Künstler hatte viel zu tun, um es zu unterdrücken."

27 NYPL, No. 436 (30 March 1840), to Rebecka Dirichlet (sister of the composer).

28 Hiller, *Letters and Recollections*, pp. 164–5.

and annoying imitation of the original. Taken as a whole, and despite Liszt's brilliant playing, it was an inauspicious beginning to his visit in Leipzig, as well as a humiliating experience in the presence of his friends, Mendelssohn, Schumann, and Hiller.

Liszt's second Leipzig concert was scheduled for the following evening (18 March), but about mid-afternoon on Wednesday he was stricken with a fever and chills, and consequently he cancelled the performance. During the next forty-eight hours he remained in bed, but was by no means neglected. As he wrote to Marie on Friday, "Mendelssohn, Hiller, and Schumann hardly leave my room. Mendelssohn brings me syrups, preserves, etc. ... I've been very pleased with him; he is much more straightforward than I had imagined. Besides, he is a man of remarkable talent and very cultivated mind. He sketches wonderfully, plays violin and viola, reads Homer fluently in Greek, speaks four or five languages easily."[29]

Liszt's indisposition was probably the recurrence of a condition that had afflicted him from time to time over the past several years. Schumann expressed his concern for Liszt publicly in the *Neue Zeitschrift für Musik*, as well as in a letter to Clara where he also hinted privately that though real, Liszt's illness was "eine politische Krankheit,"[30] possibly brought on psychosomatically as a reaction to his first concert.

By Friday Liszt had fully recovered, though he postponed the king's invitation to visit him in Dresden on the weekend until the following Wednesday. Despite Liszt's recovery, however, all was still not well in Leipzig. The critics had still not had done with him, not only because of the mishaps surrounding his ill-fated first concert, but also because, as Robert Schumann wrote to Clara, he insisted on playing the aristocrat in solid middle-class Leipzig: "Liszt arrived here and complained constantly about the lack of toilets, countesses, and princesses, which annoyed me."[31] Although perfectly fluent in German, Liszt also insisted on speaking French, which clearly nettled Mendelssohn, who complained to his brother that they might just as well have been "mitten in Paris."[32]

29 d'Agoult, *Correspondance*, vol. I, p. 414 (20 March 1840): "Mendelssohn, Hiller, et Schumann ne quittent presque pas ma chambre. Mendelssohn m'apporte des sirops, des confitures, etc.. ... J'ai été très content de lui; il est beaucoup plus simple que je ne me l'étais figuré. C'est d'ailleurs un homme d'un remarquable talent et d'un esprit très cultivé. Il dessine à merveille, joue du violon et de l'alto, lit couramment Homère en grec, parle quatre ou cinq langues facilement."

30 Litzmann, *Clara Schumann*, vol. I, p. 414. There is no evidence to support Walker's assertion that this story was "put about" by Schumann (*Franz Liszt*, vol. I, p. 344).

31 *Ibid.*, p. 416: "Liszt kam hier an und klagte immer über die fehlenden Toiletten und Gräfinnen und Prinzessinnen, daß es mich verdroß."

32 NYPL, No. 576 (20 March 1840), letter to Paul Mendelssohn Bartholdy (the composer's brother).

Mendelssohn was keenly sensitive to the negatively charged atmosphere, as emerges in a letter to Moscheles, written on Saturday, 21 March: "Liszt has been here for the last six days. He has given one concert and announces another for next Tuesday. It is a pity that he should be saddled with a manager and secretary, who, between them, succeeded in so thoroughly mismanaging things that the public were furious, and we had the greatest trouble to smooth matters to some extent. ... The advertisements, the prices, the program; in short, everything that Liszt did not do himself was objectionable, and consequently, even the mildest of Leipzigers were in a rage."[33]

Not surprisingly, Mendelssohn used the occasion of this letter to complain once again to Moscheles about Liszt's total lack of creative talent. Liszt the pianist was one thing; Liszt the composer, quite something different: "The only thing that he seems to me to want is true talent for composition, I mean really original ideas. The things he played to me struck me as very incomplete, even when judged from his point of view, which, to my mind is not the right one. ... I miss those genuinely original ideas that one naturally expects from a genius."[34]

The initial furor surrounding Liszt's first concert subsided somewhat, but there was still considerable ill-feeling abroad. Moreover, the situation was a particularly difficult one for Mendelssohn, who found himself squarely in the middle of the affair. As Director of the Gewandhaus, Mendelssohn was responsible in large measure for the musical climate in Leipzig, and at the same time he was ostensibly, and for all practical purposes, Liszt's host. Thus Mendelssohn saw it as his responsibility to defuse the situation as best he could and reestablish good will among the various parties involved. The solution he devised was as brilliant as it was characteristic of his generous nature. On Saturday, 21 March, the same day that he had written to Moscheles, he suddenly decided to host, entirely at his own expense, a grand musical fête in honor of Liszt on the following Monday evening. In a letter to his sister, Rebecka, he described the event:

> Then, Saturday evening I made up my mind straight off. I had 250 invitations printed and sent them around on Monday. Early Sunday morning I secured the orchestra by means of [sending about] a circular. Liszt and Cécile helped seal and address the invitations, and early Monday morning refreshments were ordered and arranged. In short, on Monday evening I gave a soirée for 350 people in the main hall of the Gewandhaus, where I invited all my local acquaintances, and where everyone was so pleased that they swore they had never spent a more enjoyable evening. I had about 200 chorus members – men and women – and in addition about 40 instrumentalists, and 130 ladies and gentlemen in the audi-

33 Moscheles, *Letters*, p. 203.   34 *Ibid.*, pp. 203–4.

ence. In the middle of the hall stood three English grand pianos, and around them sat the audience and the whole orchestra; all the women were dressed up in their finest clothes. In the intermission came Liszt, mulled wine, crêpes and other pastries, with drinks and bonbons. Graf Baudissin himself, to whom I had written the previous day to request the parts for the Bach [Triple] Concerto, marched in straight from the train with his briefcase and several companions at the beginning of the concert. We began with the Symphony by Schubert [in C major], then my Psalm, "As the Hart Pants," then the *Meeresstille* (everything without any rehearsal at all; it sounded fabulously, and everyone sang and played with tremendous enthusiasm). After the *Meeresstille* came [more] crêpes, and then – because Hiller had mislaid the parts to his oratorio [*Die Zerstörung Jerusalems*] – came three choruses from *St. Paul*, and then the Bach Concerto, played by Liszt, Hiller, and myself. Finally, Liszt alone played a few pieces, and that was it.[35]

Mendelssohn's soirée was a total success, but it was not the only celebration in honor of Liszt. At noon the next day (23 March), Hiller arranged a dinner for Liszt, which was held in the private rooms of the Äckerlein, one of Leipzig's finest hotels.[36] Altogether, it was almost too much for Liszt: to be booed and hissed on one day, and then precisely one week later to be fêted as the guest of honor in the same hall. Taken aback though he might have been, Liszt was clearly overjoyed and duly impressed. In a letter to Marie d'Agoult he wrote, "I swear that since the ball given me by the Dames of Pesth, nothing has flattered me quite so much."[37] "The concert that Mendelssohn gave for me yesterday was a grand success. ... You can see by all this what my position

35 NYPL, No. 436 (30 March 1840), letter to Rebecka Dirichlet: "Da entschloß ich Sonnabend Abend mich kurz, ließ 250 Einladungen drücken und schickte sie am Montag umher, des ganzen Orchesters hatte ich im Früh durch ein Circular versichert; Liszt und Cécile halfen siegeln und adressieren, am Montag früh wurde Erfrischungen bestellt und angeschafft, kurz am Montag Abend gab ich eine Soirée von 350 Personen im Gewandhaussaal, wo ich alle meine hiesigen Bekannten eingeladen hatte, und wo alle so vergnügt waren, daß sie schworen, sie hätten noch keinen lustigeren Abend erlebt. Ungefähr 200 Chorsänger und = sängerinnen hatte ich, dazu einige 40 Instrumentalisten, und 130 Zuhörer und Zuhörerinnen. In der Mitte des Saales standen 3 Englische Flügel, umher sassen die Hörer und das ganze Orchester, alles voll geputzter Damen in ihren besten Kleidern – in der Pause kam Bischof und Cardinal, und Pfannkuchen und Spitzkuchen, und solche Maschinen und Bonbons. Graf Baudissin, dem ich tags zuvor nach Dresden um die Stimmen des Bachschen Concerts geschrieben hatte, marschierte beim Anfang der Musik mit seiner Mappe und einigen Begleitern selbst in den Saal, frisch von der Eisenbahn gekommen – wir fingen mit der Symphonie von Schubert an, dann mein Psalm 'Wie der Hirsch schreit' (Mme. Frege sang die Solos *charmant*), dann die Meeresstille (alles ohne die geringste Probe und knallte unglaublich, die Leute spielten und sangen mit rasendem Enthusiasmus). Nach der Meeresstille kamen die Pfannkuchen, dann (weil Hiller die Stimmen zu seinem Oratorium verlegt hatte) 3 Chöre aus Paulus, dann das Bachsche Flügelconcert von Liszt, Hiller und mir, dann Liszt allein noch einige Stücke – dann war's aus."

36 Hiller, *Letters and Recollections*, p. 166. See also Litzmann, *Clara Schumann*, p. 420.

37 d'Agoult, *Correspondance*, vol. I, p. 416 (22 March 1840): "J'avoue que depuis mon bal des Dames de Pesth, rien ne m'avait autant flatté."

is here in Germany!"[38] Liszt goes on to suggest that it might do no harm for Marie to insert a few lines, describing the event in the *Journal des Débats* and the *Revue Musicale*: "... on écrit de Leipzig ...."

The omens for Liszt's second Gewandhaus concert the following evening were excellent, and when the time of the concert arrived, he took advantage of the turnabout in public opinion to demonstrate to his Leipzig audience the full range of his powers. He opened the program with Weber's *Konzertstück* op. 79 and played it with such fire and brilliance that nothing afterwards could equal it. As Schumann reported in the *Neue Zeitschrift für Musik*, such wild applause had never before been heard in Leipzig, and that "Das Concertstück war und blieb die Krone seiner Leistungen."[39] Liszt's triumph was now complete, and as a gesture of his appreciation he offered on the spot to give a third Leipzig performance, a benefit concert for the Pension Fund for sick and elderly musicians.

The next day, Wednesday (25 March), Liszt left for Dresden, and on the following Friday and Sunday he gave his second and third concerts in that city. Meanwhile, Schumann, who had kept Clara (then in Berlin) fully posted on the fast-moving events in Leipzig, urged her to come and bring her mother to Leipzig so that they might hear Liszt's final concert. Until this time Clara had had only unqualified praise for Liszt, and so she was easily persuaded to make the trip.[40]

On Monday morning (30 March) Liszt made the four-hour train trip back from Dresden and arrived in Leipzig about mid-morning. After a brief visit with Robert and Clara, he went directly into rehearsal, which lasted most of the rest of the day.

The program for that evening was intended as a homage to his Leipzig hosts and included Mendelssohn's Piano Concerto in D minor op. 40, three of Hiller's Etudes, Schumann's *Carnaval* in its entirety, and to close, Liszt had chosen the *Hexameron*, in its arrangement with orchestra.[41]

The performance itself, with which Liszt had hoped to cap his Leipzig visit, turned out to be something less than a complete success. As Schumann pointed out, "No man is a god, and Liszt visibly showed the strain of the past two weeks,"[42] a sentiment that was corroborated by the reviewer for the *All-*

---

38 *Ibid.*, p. 417 (23 March 1840): "Le Concert que Mendelssohn m'a donné hier a magnifiquement réussi.... Vous voyez par là quelle est ma position en Allemagne!"

39 *Neue Zeitschrift für Musik* 12 (April 1840), 118. Repr. in Robert Schumann, *Music and Musicians*, trans. F. R. Ritter, 8th edn. (London, n.d.), p. 151. See also *AmZ* 42 (1840), col. 197.

40 Litzmann, *Clara Schumann*, vol. I, pp. 419–20. Clara left Berlin on Saturday evening, 28 March, arriving in Leipzig a day earlier than Schumann had expected her.

41 *Ibid.*, p. 420. See also Raabe, *Liszts Leben*, pp. 270–71.

42 Schumann, *Music and Musicians*, p. 153.

gemeine musikalische Zeitung: "Herr Liszt did not play the Concerto very well, in fact, not satisfactorily even in a technical regard. The entire performance betrayed a certain unfamiliarity with the whole affair, and we cannot do otherwise than to express our regret about it publicly."[43] (Although the legend has persisted that Liszt sight-read the Mendelssohn Concerto at this concert, he had in fact taken the score with him to Dresden the previous Wednesday and had given a private performance of it there on Thursday.[44]) Despite Liszt's failure to bring off his final concert entirely as he had hoped, at least the marathon was over, and the next evening he left Leipzig for Paris. Everyone, but most of all Mendelssohn, heaved a sigh of relief.

It had been an exhausting and draining two weeks, and although Mendelssohn had publicly maintained the stance and persona of the perfect host, his personal thoughts about Liszt, even as a performer, were rapidly changing. As he confessed to his mother in a letter written on the day of Liszt's final performance, it had all been a "mad adventure":

> Today is Liszt's last concert.... Then Thursday is the performance of Hiller's oratorio, and then I hope we'll finally have some peace and quiet again. The turmoil of the past week has simply been too great. Liszt has again given me personally much pleasure; I consider him to be a superb artist. That he plays the best of all of them is beyond doubt, yet Thalberg, with his composure and restraint, is more perfect than a mere virtuoso, and that is the yardstick by which one must measure Liszt as well, since his compositions stand below his playing. ... Liszt has a certain suppleness and versatility in his fingers, as well as a thoroughly musical feeling, which may nowhere find its equal. (I pray you, however, dear Mother – I tell you! – to communicate this opinion to absolutely *no* friends, neither verbally nor in writing, and least of all to mention it to La Pereia, who could not keep it quiet, and then the next thing I know, I would see it in print. Consequently, tell *no one*.) In short, I have seen no musician whose musical sensitivity, like Liszt's, courses straight into his fingertips and then flows directly out from there. And with this immediacy and his enormous technique and skill, he would leave all others far behind him, if it were not that his own ideas always predominate in whatever he is playing, and at least up to now these seem to have been denied him by nature. Thus in this respect most other virtuosos can be said to be his equal, if not, in fact, his superior. – That he, moreover, *alone*, with Thalberg stands in the very top category of all living

---

43 *AmZ* 42 (1840), col. 298: "Herr Liszt hat das Concert nicht gut, ja nicht einmal in technischer Hinsicht befriedigend gespielt; die ganze Leistung verrieth eine ziemliche Unbekanntschaft mit der Sache, und wir können nicht umhin, unser Bedauern hierüber öffentlich auszusprechen."

44 *Letters of Franz Liszt*, ed. [Ida Marie Lipsius] La Mara and trans. C. Bache (London, 1894), vol. I. p. 42n. In a letter to Schumann Carl K[rägen?] writes (from Dresden), "He [Liszt] played me the glorious Mendelssohn Concerto."

pianists, and that the rest of them, neither Henselt, nor Döhler, nor whoever they may be, can be placed in the same class, is beyond question as far as I am concerned.

Unfortunately, the way Liszt behaves *vis-à-vis* his public does not please me. He has repeatedly gotten himself mixed-up in newspaper stories and has also written articles, and in a word, he has taken too much notice of a multitude of small matters and neglected the more important ones, such as the arrangements for his concerts, etc., etc. Whether it be on that account, or for other reasons, Thalberg was far better received by our local audiences, and Liszt has made almost more enemies than friends here. Beyond that, the whole contentiousness between him and our townspeople is like listening to two people harangue, both of whom are wrong, and whom you are tempted to interrupt at every word: the philistines, who are mostly concerned with the high prices and who resent it when a clever fellow knows how to make a go of it, and who grumble accordingly – as far as I'm concerned, you can have the lot of them. And Liszt, who takes along ridiculous business managers on his trips, who turn everyone against him, and who then writes newspaper articles – certainly [Liszt] himself is not irreproachable. Tonight he is playing my D minor Concerto; I'll write you about it in my next letter, but as I said, do not mention any of this to *any one* . . . .[45]

45 NYPL, No. 436 (30 March 1840). "Heute ist Liszts letztes Concert zum Besten des Instituts für alte und kranke Musiker, Donnerstag ist die Aufführung von Hillers Oratorium, und dann hoffe ich soll endlich einmal wieder Ruhe und Musse eintreten. Das Hin und Her der letzten Wochen war zu groß. Liszt hat mir persönlich wieder viel Freude gemacht; ich halte ihn für einen vortrefflichen Künstler. Daß er von allen am meisten spielt, ist gar kein Zweifel, doch ist Thalberg mit seiner Gelassenheit und Beschränkung vollkommener als eigentlicher Virtuose genommen, und das ist doch der Maßstab den man auch Liszt anlegen muß, da seine Compositionen unter seinem Spiele stehen, und eben auch nur auf Virtuosität berechnet sind. Eine gewiße Gelenkigkeit, und Verschiedenartigkeit der Finger, und ein durch und durch musikalisches Gefühl hat Liszt, das wohl nirgend seines Gleichen finden möchte. (Ich bitte Dich aber, liebe Mutter, sage Dich! [sic] dies Urtheil, durchaus *keinem* Freunde mitzutheilen, weder mündlich noch schriftlich, und allerwenigsten der Pereia, die es nicht würde verschweigen können, und wo ichs nächstens gedrückt sehe, also *keinem*). Mit einem Wort, ich habe keinen Musiker gesehen, dem so wie dem Liszt die musikalische Empfindung bis in die Fingerspitzen liefe und sich da unmittelbar ausströmte, und bei dieser Unmittelbarkeit und enormen Technik und Übung würde er alle Anderen weit hinter sich zurücklassen, wenn eigene Gedanken nicht bei alledem die Hauptsache wären, und die ihm von der Natur, wenigstens bis jetzt, wie versagt scheinen, so daß in dieser Hinsicht die meisten anderen Virtuosen ihm gleich, oder gar über ihn zu stellen sind. – Daß er übrigens mit Thalberg *allein* die erste Classe unter den jetzigen Clavierspielern einnimmt, und daß diese dort weder Henselt, noch Döhler, noch wie sie alle heißen, genannt werden können, ist mir ganz unbezweifelt. Leider ist die Art, wie sich Liszt gegen das Publikum verhält nicht die, die mir wohlgefällt; er hat sich abermals auch hier in Zeitungs-Geschichten eingelassen, Artikel geschrieben und mit einem Wort viel zu viel Notiz von einer Menge kleiner Sachen genommen, und größeren z.B. das Arrangement seiner Concerte, etc., etc. darüber vergessen. Sei es deswegen, oder aus einem anderen Grunde, aber beim hiesigen Publikum hat Thalberg bei weitem mehr gefallen, und Liszt hat sich fast mehr Feinde als Freunde hier gemacht. Es ist übrigens die ganze Streitigkeit zwischen ihm und den Hiesigen wieder so, als ob man zwei Leute peroriren hört, die beide Unrecht haben, und dann

Clearly, the gulf between Mendelssohn's public and private opinions of Liszt was widening, and equally clear, his concern lest his private views should become known – particularly at a time when the echoes of the Liszt–Thalberg "duel" were still reverberating throughout Europe. But beyond strictly professional matters, Mendelssohn's tone of impatience and annoyance with Liszt, Cohen, and their various antics underlies the entire letter.

Despite the cordial hospitality that Mendelssohn had shown Liszt throughout his visit in Leipzig, by the time he left, Liszt had evidently worn his welcome thin. Yet even after he had left Leipzig, the series of gaffes, *faux pas*, and *contretemps* that had attended his stay in Leipzig continued to haunt him. Barely a week after Liszt's departure Mendelssohn himself was packing to leave for Berlin and discovered to his consternation that several pieces of his clothing were missing, including his vest and a monogrammed black silk scarf. After searching in vain for the items, both at home and at Liszt's hotel, Mendelssohn concluded that Liszt must inadvertently have taken them. And as fate, of course, would have it, Liszt's servant, Ferco, had indeed packed them up along with Liszt's other clothes and shipped everything off to Paris. A matter of perhaps minor significance, but exemplary none the less, of how Liszt, even *in absentia*, continued to be a source of frustration and annoyance for Mendelssohn.

The incident of the purloined scarf served to generate the only exchange of letters between the two men that has survived, and although it reveals little about their professional views, each letter reveals characteristically the personality of its author and serves to underscore their sharply divergent natures.

Mendelssohn's letter is both warm and cordial, but essentially formal; he addresses Liszt as "Lieber Freund," and details his efforts to retrieve his vest and scarf.[46] Liszt, in reply, however, addresses Mendelssohn as "Mon cher Felix," and is seemingly oblivious to the inconvenience that, even indirectly,

man immer ins Wort fallen möchte: die Philister, denen es am meisten um die theuren Preise, und darum zu thun ist, daß es einem tüchtigen Kerl deshalb raisoniren – die können mir gar gestohlen werden, und Liszt, der sich alberne Geschäftsführer mit auf Reisen nimmt, die alle Menschen gegen sich aufbringen, und der dann Zeitungsartikel schreibt, ist auch nicht vorwurfsfrei: Heute Abend spielt er unter anderen mein d-moll Concert; über alles das schreibe ich Dir nächstens, aber wie gesagt – *keinem* theile es mit."

The printed version of this letter (*Briefe*, pp. 410–12) has been heavily edited and is, in fact, a conflation of at least two, possibly three or even four letters: a letter to his mother, NYPL No. 437 (30 March 1840); a letter to his sister, Rebecka, NYPL No. 436 (same date); evidently also an unpublished letter – from Mendelssohn to his sister, Fanny (7 April 1840), cited by Eric Werner in *Mendelssohn: Leben und Werk in neuer Sicht* (Zurich, 1980), p. 336 and p. 572, n. 16 – that I have been unable to trace; and finally, a possible fourth unidentified letter, which constitutes the final printed paragraph (p. 412). The two letters of 30 March 1840 have been fused by the editors, who have also added transitional words and phrases in order to produce a matrix.

46 *Briefe hervorragender Zeitgenossen an Franz Liszt*, ed. [Ida Marie Lipsius] La Mara (Leipzig, 1895), vol. I, pp. 15–16 (5 April 1840).

he has caused Mendelssohn and impervious to the wrangles he had caused with the Leipzig press. The tone is airy and informal: "What a victory, my dear Felix, for the *malicious Leipzig press!* 'M. Liszt has departed our city, fraudulently carrying off the vests and scarves of his best friends! Isn't it deplorable that artists, who ought at least to respect their profession (in default of talent and character), place themselves on the same level as thieves, etc., etc.,' You can imagine the joy that such an article would have caused. I, however, have resisted and have not sent such a communiqué to the *Eisenbahn* or any other weekly." (It was the critic for the *Eisenbahn* who had so offended Liszt with his review of his first Leipzig concert.[47])

Liszt goes on to tell Mendelssohn that he has just "transcribed and *disarranged* in my fashion" ("transcrites et *dérangés* à ma manière") several of Mendelssohn's songs and proposes to dedicate them to Cécile. Finally, Liszt takes the opportunity to recommend a singer he has just met – one Elise List – and he asks Mendelssohn to do what he can for her when she comes to Leipzig. And almost parenthetically, he assures Mendelssohn that his vest and scarf will be returned forthwith.

After so many mishaps anything involving Mendelssohn and Liszt might now seem destined for disaster. And so it was, even with Liszt's transcription of the various songs that he had mentioned in his letter. He had arranged to have them published simultaneously by Beale in London, Richaut in Paris, and Breitkopf & Härtel in Leipzig. The latter firm, however, rushed them into print precipitately, which cost Liszt both his English and French copyright benefits.[48]

Slightly more than a year and a half passed before Liszt returned to Leipzig, and when he did, he was greeted with the kind of enthusiasm that he was accustomed to elsewhere. The Leipzigers had forgotten their pique and now received him with open arms. On 6 December 1841 he performed in concert at the Gewandhaus, at which works by Schumann and himself were presented.[49] At the same concert he and Clara Schumann performed the original duet version of the *Hexameron*, and the whole affair was a great success. By that time, however, Mendelssohn had moved to Berlin and was safely out of reach.

Only for the moment, however, since Liszt travelled directly from Leipzig

47 Bodleian Library, Oxford, Ms. M.D.M. d. 38 (No. 226). Unpublished letter [April 1840].
48 La Mara, *Letters*, No. 31, p. 51, from Liszt in London to Breitkopf & Härtel in Leipzig, 7 May 1841. For a discussion of these piano arrangements see *AmZ* 43 (1841), col. 148. The manuscript of Liszt's arrangement of "Neue Liebe," the only surviving autograph of this set, was recently (October 1990) offered for sale by J. & J. Lubrano, antiquarian music dealer in Sheffield, Massachusetts.
49 Litzmann, *Clara Schumann*, vol. II, pp. 38–9.

to Berlin, where, as he wrote to Marie, he set off immediately to visit Meyerbeer, Mendelssohn, and Spontini.

This was Liszt's first visit to Berlin, and in the course of his ten-week stay
there he literally took the city by storm. Alan Walker notes that it was during
this winter of 1842 when "Lisztomania" began in earnest.[50]

As might be expected, Mendelssohn did not count himself among those
infatuated with Liszt's musicianship. Quite the contrary, Mendelssohn now
no longer saw in Liszt the urbane and genial colleague he had earlier, however
grudgingly, liked, and his distaste for Liszt's playing had hardened sharply. In
an unusually trenchant letter to Ferdinand David, Mendelssohn wrote from
Berlin,

> Even Liszt doesn't please me here half so much as he did elsewhere. He has
> forfeited a large degree of my respect for him through the ridiculous pranks that
> he plays, not only on the public, ... but rather on the music itself. He has played
> here works by Beethoven, Bach, Handel, and Weber so wretchedly and
> unsatisfactorily, so impurely and so unknowledgeably, that I would have heard
> them played by mediocre performers with more pleasure: here six measures
> added in, there seven omitted; here he plays false harmonies, and then later these
> are cancelled out by others. Then he makes a horrible *fortissimo* out of the softest
> passages, and goodness knows what other kinds of dreadful mischief. That may
> be all well and good for the public at large, but not for me, and that it was good
> enough for Liszt himself, that lowers my respect for him by a very great deal. At
> the same time my respect for him was so great, that there is still a lot left.[51]

Superficially, at least, Mendelssohn and Liszt remained on cordial personal
terms, though an element of tension seems almost perceptible. Only four days
before Mendelssohn had written to David, Liszt had apparently asked Mendelssohn to lend him his piano temporarily. In his one paragraph reply
Mendelssohn's tone is both professional and correct, but no more than that; he
explains that his need for the instrument prevents his complying with Liszt's

50 Walker, *Franz Liszt*, vol. I, p. 371.
51 Julius Eckhardt, *Ferdinand David und die Familie Mendelssohn-Bartholdy* (Leipzig, 1888),
p. 164. "Sogar Liszt gefällt mir hier nicht halb so sehr, wie an anderen Orten, er hat ein großes
Stück meiner Hochachtung durch die albernen Possen eingebüßt, die er nicht nur mit dem
Publicum (das schadete nichts), sondern mit der Musik selbst treibt. Beethovensche, Bachsche,
Händelsche und Webersche Sachen hat er hier so erbärmlich mangelhaft, so unrein und so
kenntnislos gespielt, daß ich sie von mittelmäßigen Spielern mit mehr Vergnügen gehört hätte;
da waren 6 Tacte zugesetzt, dort 7 ausgelassen, hier falsche Harmonien genommen und dann
später durch andre falsche ins Gleiche gebracht, dort aus den leisesten Stellen ein gräßliches
Fortissimo gemacht, und was weiß ich noch all den traurigen Unfug. Wohl ists gut genug für die
Leute gewesen, aber für mich nicht, und daß es für Liszt selbst gut genug war, das mindert eben
meine Hochachtung um ein ganzes Stück. Indeß war sie so groß, daß doch noch immer genug
übrig bleibt." (5 February 1842.)

request. Beyond their earlier exchange regarding Mendelssohn's vest and scarf, this is the only other extant piece of correspondence between the two.[52]

Liszt's Berlin stay was one of the most successful of his entire career, and it was only natural that he should plan a return visit. Thus he came back to Berlin at the end of 1842, just one year later. Again he arrived at Christmas time, and again, as he wrote to Marie on 23 December, both Meyerbeer and Mendelssohn were in town, if not there on hand to welcome him: "On arriving here I find more than twenty letters on my table; Meyerbeer and Mendelssohn are here. Everyone is awaiting me in an almost ridiculous fashion."[53]

Liszt's mention of Mendelssohn is problematic on two counts: in the first place, Mendelssohn's mother had just died on 12 December, and as his letters to his brother Paul reveal, he was in deep mourning, unable to concentrate on his work, and in no mood to see anyone, let alone Liszt.[54]

Second, Mendelssohn was not even in Berlin at the time. On 22 and 23 December Mendelssohn wrote two letters to his brother, both from Leipzig. Certainly, Mendelssohn had had to be in Berlin for his mother's funeral, but the likelihood that he would have sought out Liszt at such a time seems remote. In any case, Mendelssohn was fully occupied in Leipzig through most of the winter of 1843; the Conservatory was about to open its doors, and there was a multitude of other pressing demands on his time and energies.

After the winter of 1841/2 there seems to have been little or no further personal contact between Mendelssohn and Liszt. Clearly, as Mendelssohn's letter to David indicates, the grounds for further collegiality were being fast eroded. Eric Werner cites an unpublished letter from Mendelssohn to his sister Rebecka, written the following year, "Liszt's servile adulation of the hereditary nobility seemed to Felix 'utterly wretched and unworthy',"[55] which suggests that by then Mendelssohn had distanced himself even further from Liszt.

The extent to which Liszt was aware of Mendelssohn's growing estrangement is uncertain, but as he continued to mature as a composer, the greater the gulf that he perceived between Mendelssohn and himself. Although he continued to perform Mendelssohn's music in public – he had played the *Capriccio* in F sharp minor op. 5 in his latest Berlin tour – the evidence indicates that he felt a growing alienation toward Mendelssohn's music, which

52 La Mara, *Briefe*, vol. II, No. 27, p. 38.

53 d'Agoult, *Correspondance*, vol. II, p. 246. "En arrivant ici, je trouve plus de vingt lettres sur ma table, Meyerbeer et Mendelssohn sont ici. Tout le monde m'attend d'une manière presque ridicule."

54 NYPL, No. 609 (23 December 1842), to his brother Paul from Leipzig.

55 Werner, *Mendelssohn: Leben und Werk*, p. 410, to Rebecka, 23 December 1843. This letter is not among the family letters in the NYPL, and I have not been able otherwise to confirm it. "Liszts servile Anbetung des Geburtsadels vollends erschien Felix 'jämmerlich und nichtswürdig.'"

he came increasingly to regard as epitomizing the conservatism of Leipzig. "Leipzigerismus" and "Leipzigerisch" were terms he used derogatorily to connote the style and manner of the Leipzig school and the Leipzig Conservatory, for both of which Mendelssohn stood as the nominal head. None the less, seven years after Mendelssohn's death, in 1854, Liszt wrote an extraordinary encomium of Mendelssohn's music to *A Midsummer Night's Dream*.[56] Otherwise, Liszt had gradually developed serious reservations about the conservatism of Mendelssohn's music and felt that one should approach it with a certain degree of caution. In a letter to Franz Brendel, written in 1854, Liszt expressed his fears about the direction young Anton Rubinstein's musical career was taking, "I don't want to preach to him – he may sow his wild oats and fish deeper in the Mendelssohn waters, . . . but I am certain that sooner or later he will give up the apparent and the formalistic for the organically Real, if he doesn't want to stand still."[57]

The critical literature has taken very little specific notice of the relationship between Mendelssohn and Liszt, and even when it has, it has not generally been marked by balance or impartiality. In Eleanor Perényi's vivid biography of Liszt her sympathies for him are so strong and so visceral that they cloud her historical perception as well as her judgment. Liszt consistently assumes heroic proportions, and invariably at the expense of any who failed fully to appreciate him.[58] Alan Walker suggests that it was Mendelssohn who was responsible for whatever estrangement that may have developed between him and Liszt, "One by one his early acquaintances either abandoned him or turned against him."[59] Walker's list includes not only Mendelssohn, but Berlioz, Chopin, Hiller, Heine, Schlesinger, Wagner, Schumann, Joachim, and von Bülow, all of whom allegedly turned their backs on Liszt for little or no apparent reason.[60]

Critics of the Mendelssohn persuasion, on the other hand, criticize Liszt for his flamboyant manner and dress,[61] his womanizing,[62] even his "wildly temperamental pounding at the keys."[63]

---

56 Franz Liszt, *Gesammelte Schriften* (Leipzig, 1881), vol. III: *Dramaturgische Blätter: Essays*, trans. L. Ramann, vol. V, pp. 37–47.

57 La Mara, *Letters*, Vol. I, No. 127, p. 219.   58 Perényi, *Liszt*, p. 210 *et passim*.

59 Walker, *Franz Liszt*, vol. I, p. 189.   60 *Ibid.*, vol. II, p. 12.

61 Herbert Kupferberg, *Felix Mendelssohn: His Life, His Family, His Music* (New York, 1972), p. 101 *et passim*.

62 Eric Werner (*Mendelssohn* [London, 1963], p. 303) speaks obliquely of Liszt's "escapades"; Schima Kaufmann (*Mendelssohn* [New York, 1934], p. 106) alludes to Liszt's "warts as numerous as his future illegitimate offspring," and even Perényi acknowledges Liszt's "mixing himself up with a flaming whore like Lola Montez" (*Liszt*, p. 210).

63 Heinrich Eduard Jacob, *Felix Mendelssohn and His Time*, trans. R. and C. Winston (Englewood Cliffs, NJ, 1963), p. 191.

Such criticism, of whatever persuasion, leaves the central issue – which involves the reasons for the fundamental ambivalence in their relationship – largely unexplored. On close examination, however, the reasons for that ambivalence emerge relatively clearly. In their personal, as well as in their professional orientations Mendelssohn and Liszt were a classic combination of oil and water. In virtually every way: their family background, their social station, their education, their goals, their lifestyles, their perception of the public, their attitudes toward money, and so forth. Almost everything militated against their ever becoming anything more than the most casual friends. Given their radically different characters and outlooks, it is not entirely reasonable to assert that Mendelssohn abandoned or turned his back on Liszt. The two were simply never destined to be close. As Mendelssohn once remarked to Schumann, Liszt "seemed forever to vacillate between scandal and apotheosis." The observation is more than a snide comment: it reveals Mendelssohn's perception of the essential difference between himself and Liszt. For Mendelssohn, whose life was governed by discipline, order, and stability, Liszt marched to a different drummer, and one to whom these qualities seemed all but irrelevant. From a broader perspective, however, Mendelssohn and Liszt were separated by aesthetic, moral, cultural, and artistic differences which were ultimately irreconcilable. Temperamentally, they represented the two sides of the coin of creativity: in Thomas Mann's "Death in Venice" Aschenbach and Tadzio reflect essentially the same Nietzschean dichotomy that we find between Felix Mendelssohn, the Apollonian, and Franz Liszt, the Dionysian.

6 1848, anti-Semitism, and the Mendelssohn reception

DONALD MINTZ

IN MEMORY OF ELLIOTT W. GALKIN

The popular view that the revolutions of 1848 produced few far-reaching and lasting changes in European society has been widely accepted by musicology, usually, one supposes, quite unconsciously. By so doing, musicology has tended to underestimate the extent of the changes in music and musical life around mid-century and probably to misunderstand them somewhat as well. A look at the Mendelssohn reception in Germany at this time and at the many currents that contributed to it may act as a partial corrective to the conventional wisdom.

Of course, it is not unusual for composers' reputations to sink, sometimes quite sharply, at or shortly after their deaths. If nothing else, the number of new compositions that can be brought to performance or print by their artistic executors is necessarily limited; that in itself is enough to divert attention from them. Moreover, times change, and what was once new is thought to be old hat.

So in one sense, the decline of Mendelssohn's reputation after 1847 is in no way surprising. Nor, really, is the fact that in progressive circles at least, his reputation was in decline some years before his death. But in Mendelssohn's case, there are a number of additional occurrences and circumstances, some highly special and others not, that give us a particular window into important aspects of the nineteenth century's thought.

It may be useful to approach the subject somewhat indirectly by looking briefly at some more recent attitudes toward the composer, attitudes that

A different form of this essay was read – or rather talked around – at the Hartt Music History Forum of the Hartt School of Music, University of Hartford on 29 October 1990. My thanks to Profs. Myron Schwager and Imanuel Willheim for the invitation to speak and to their students for listening.

126

suggest something about the enormous swings his reputation has taken in the almost 150 years since his death; we shall begin then by briefly tracing backwards the path of some of these attitudes.

In 1974, there appeared a volume bearing the title *Das Problem Mendelssohn* and containing the proceedings of a symposium held in Berlin in November 1972.[1] What concerns us here is mostly Carl Dahlhaus' introduction. It begins by remarking that "it would doubtless be a gross exaggeration to speak of a Mendelssohn renaissance (and hence an example of the bad style that Mendelssohn so hated). But the fact that almost simultaneously there have appeared two sets of recordings of the youthful symphonies is more than a coincidence. And similarly striking is the increase in scholarly interest in Mendelssohn, an interest of which this book is to be seen as a document."

The problems that Dahlhaus saw in his introduction had to do with the use of terms like "classicistic," "romantic," and "neo-romantic." He touched on problems having to do with the quality of the music – or the lack of it – only somewhat indirectly by pointing out that the three terms in question often conceal value judgments. And he ended by remarking that one of the results of the symposium was to suggest the need for a careful reexamination of the music about which there circulated (and still circulates) a fair amount of ill-founded opinion. (A book like Friedhelm Krummacher's *Mendelssohn – der Komponist*[2] is clearly a response to that call for careful reexamination.)

Dahlhaus did not say that one of the reasons for the upswing in Mendelssohn scholarship in Germany was simply German guilt, the scholarship itself being a sort of artistic *Wiedergutmachung*. Mendelssohn's music of course had been banned by the Nazis because, although Mendelssohn was not only a Protestant but an uncommonly devout one for his time and place, he was a Jew by Hitler's Nüremberg laws. Anti-Semitism affected the Mendelssohn reception in the twentieth century (to put it very politely indeed), and it did so in the nineteenth as well.

We shall return to the theme of anti-Semitism in due course.[3] First, we need to deal with questions of taste, changes of taste, and so on, questions already adumbrated by Dahlhaus' three terms. The 1911 edition of the *Encyclopaedia Britannica* yields a remarkable example of these changes. The main article, carried over from earlier editions as the reference to Mendelssohn as being

---

1 Carl Dahlhaus, *Das Problem Mendelssohn*, Studien zur Musikgeschichte des 19. Jahrhunderts, No. 41 (Regensburg, 1974).

2 Friedhelm Krummacher, *Mendelssohn – der Komponist: Studien zur Kammermusik für Streicher* (Munich, 1978).

3 On Mendelssohn and anti-Semitism, mostly during his lifetime, see especially Eric Werner, *Mendelssohn: a New Image of the Composer and His Age*, trans. Dika Newlin (London, 1963), pp. 28–43, 230ff, 282f, 265f, 507f; the last deals with Wagner.

"among the great composers of the century" makes clear, is by W. S. Rockstro, himself an acquaintance of the composer. It reads in part:

> Mendelssohn's title to a place among the great composers of the century is incontestable. His style, though differing little in technical arrangement from that of his classical predecessors, is characterized by a vein of melody peculiarly his own, and easily distinguishable by those who have studied his works, not only from the genuine effusions of contemporary writers, but from the most successful of the servile imitations with which, even during his lifetime, the music-shops were deluged. In less judicious hands the rigid symmetry of his phrasing, might, perhaps, have palled upon the ear; but under his skillful management it serves only to impart an additional charm to thoughts which derive their chief beauty from the evident spontaneity of their conception. In this, as in all other matters of a purely technical character, he regarded the accepted laws of art as the medium by which he might most certainly attain the end dictated by the inspiration of his genius. Though caring nothing for rules, except as means for producing a good effect, he scarcely ever violated them, and was never weary of impressing their value upon the minds of his pupils. His method of counterpoint was modelled in close accordance with that practiced by Sebastian Bach. This he used in combination with an elastic development of the sonata-form, similar to that engrafted by Beethoven upon the lines laid down by Haydn. The principles involved in this arrangement were strictly conservative; yet they enabled him, at the very outset of his career, to invent a new style no less original than that of Schubert or Weber, and no less remarkable as the embodiment of canons already consecrated by classical authority than as a special manifestation of individual genius. It is thus that Mendelssohn stands before us at the same time as champion of conservatism and an apostle of progress; and it is chiefly by virtue of these two apparently incongruous though really compatible phases of his artistic character that his influence and example availed for so many years, to hold in check the violence of reactionary opinion which injudicious partisanship afterwards fanned into revolutionary fury.
>
> Concerning Mendelssohn's private character there have never been two opinions. As a man of the world he was more than ordinarily accomplished – brilliant in conversation, and in his lighter moments overflowing with sparkling humour and ready pleasantry, loyal and unselfish in the more serious business of life, and never weary of working for the general good. As a friend he was unvaryingly kind, sympathetic and true. His earnestness as a Christian needs no stronger testimony than that afforded by his own delineation of the character of St. Paul; but it is not too much to say that his heart and life were pure as those of a little child.[4]

---

4 W. S. Rockstro, "Mendelssohn," *The Encyclopaedia Britannica*, 11th edn. (Cambridge, 1911), vol. XVIII, p. 124.

To this account are appended a few paragraphs by Sir Donald F. Tovey, apparently with the intention of bringing things up to date:

> This article has the unique value of being the record of an eminent musical scholar who was an actual pupil of Mendelssohn. No change of reputation can alter the value of such a record of a man whom even his contemporaries knew to be greater than his works. Mendelssohn's aristocratic horror of self-advertisement unfitted him for triumph in a period of revolution; he died, most inopportunely, when his own powers, like Handel's at the same age, were being wasted on pseudo-classical forms; the new art was not yet ripe; and in the early Wagner-Liszt reign of terror his was the first reputation to be assassinated. That of the too modest and gentle "Romantic" pioneer Schumann soon followed; but as being more embarrassing to irreverence and conceit, it remains a subject of controversy. Meanwhile, Mendelssohn's reputation, except as the composer of a few inexplicably beautiful and original orchestral pieces, has vanished. . . .[5]

Rockstro's attempt to characterize Mendelssohn as both a conservative and a progressive, if not quite a radical, seems at first glance – and at second and third, too – to make little sense despite the talk of "engrafting" and the like. Yet he may well have understood better than is generally understood today the way in which in many works, the concert overtures for instance, Mendelssohn created drastically new structures whose connection to the past is nevertheless evident at every turn.[6]

Tovey's contribution is more enigmatic. What does he mean by a "period of revolution"? Most of Mendelssohn's life was in fact lived in a period of intense reaction. The frequent revolutions of those years, or more accurately those in the heart of Europe, were relatively small-bore affairs and essentially unsuccessful, though the Revolution of 1830 in France (which in any case is not in the heart of Europe) is in part an exception, while Belgium's winning independence was a genuine victory. Of course Mendelssohn died before the revolutions of 1848, and his entire adult life was lived during the *Vormärz*, the period between Napoleon's downfall and the consequent establishment of Metternich's system of reaction on the one hand and those revolutions on the other. Though in Germany the revolutions of 1848 likewise did not lead to lasting success, the very term "Vormärz" suggests how thoroughly they were considered to have constituted a major caesura in German life. This sense of caesura will eventually become one of our major themes.

On the other hand, revolution in a less literal sense is certainly the mark of the period. What is involved is nothing less than the coming of industrial-

---

5 Donald F. Tovey, "Mendelssohn," *The Encyclopaedia Britannica*, 11th edn. (Cambridge, 1911), XVIII, p. 124.
6 See my forthcoming "About some of Mendelssohn's sonata form movements."

ization to Europe. (It was well under way in England quite a bit earlier.) The significance of this for present purposes is two-fold: first, the rate of change objectively speaking was enormous; second, its subjective effect on people was likewise enormous but also incalculable. This, after all, was the period of the railroad. What that means is that distance – distance between places and distance within large cities – which for all of human history had been subjectively measured by muscle (by how far one could walk, how far a horse could walk) came at one stroke to be measured by machine. When that happened, the world changed, perhaps more than it does when confronted by computers, information explosions, space shuttles, and all the rest of the technological paraphernalia of the late twentieth century.[7]

Tovey's remark about Handel's "pseudo-classical forms" refers, one supposes, to Handel's Italian operas, though the chronology is a little loose. What Mendelssohn's "pseudo-classical forms" might have been is less clear. Does Tovey mean symphonies, string quartets? He was an admirer of the concert overtures, as the quotation suggests; perhaps he opposed them to the symphonies, concertos, and quartets. Certainly, if the concert overtures are viewed as forerunners of the symphonic poem, this interpretation makes sense. The reference to the "early Wagner-Liszt reign of terror" needs no interpretation, though it needs to be brought into contact with political events. The "reign of terror" of course was not carried on only in the name of artistic (or of political) progress; it was also carried on as a piece of calculated anti-Semitism, a fact Tovey does not mention. The assassination of Schumann's reputation is a fascinating topic, but exploration of it lies beyond our present purpose. In any case, it is interesting to observe that Tovey seems to imply that Mendelssohn might have made significant changes in style had he lived longer. If so, Tovey here (as in so many other contexts) anticipated modern views by quite a few years.[8]

Of course, neither Rockstro nor Tovey had the slightest interest in the relation of Mendelssohn – or of any other composer – to that composer's own time. They were interested only in the composer's relation to their own present time. Moreover, as they looked back, they saw the past as the precursor of its future in a manner which, though they apparently took it for

---

7 For a remarkable account of pre-industrial life and of this psychological change, see Laurie Lee, *Cider with Rosie: a Boyhood in the West of England* (London, 1959). Modernization came so late to Lee's part of Gloucestershire that his early twentieth-century experiences can easily stand for what most of Europe had gone through much earlier.

8 Apparently Georg Knepler was the first to deal with this during the period after World War II. See his *Musikgeschichte des 19. Jahrhunderts. II: Österreich – Deutschland* (Berlin, 1961), pp. 761–70, a section significantly titled "Versuch einer Einschätzung des Mendelssohnschen Werkes."

granted, is in fact quite peculiar. The main aspect of this peculiarity is its implication that the way in which the present has developed out of the past is the way in which the present *must* have developed out of the past. There is no recognition that a *logical* development (which is to say a development that can be explained as logical in a logical way) does not have to be at the same time a *necessary* development.[9] Because this attitude of mind tends to cause history to be viewed as both linear and teleological, it obscures the rich texture of the past.

The nineteenth-century view of "domestic music" is one of those largely ignored attitudes of the past that comes into play in questions of Mendelssohn's reputation. In a review of a BBC performance by Kathleen Long that appeared in *Musical Opinion* in November 1947, Richard Walthew said that the inclusion on the program of some of the *Songs without Words* "is perhaps rather surprising since these pieces are domestic music. . . . Social conditions and habits have altered so greatly since Mendelssohn's day," he remarked, "that one cannot expect such music to regain the popularity it once enjoyed. . . . But it will always have its admirers." The BBC, he continued, had called our attention to music "alien to our modern ways of thought and expression."[10]

This is a far cry indeed from the reception Schumann gave to the second group of the *Songs without Words* op. 30: "Who has not once sat at dusk at the keyboard – to say the pianoforte seems too high-toned – and in the middle of improvising unconsciously added a sung melody? Now if one could by chance combine the accompaniment with the melody in the hands alone and if one just happens to be a Mendelssohn, there thereby arise the most beautiful songs without words."[11] Schumann seems to assume that these pieces were domestic music, but he ascribed to that category no qualitative significance one way or the other. In short, function was one thing and quality was another, and the two did not necessarily have anything to do with one another. To Walthew, on the other hand, the category of domestic music is inherently suspicious, and if, as one surmises, he viewed the *Songs without Words* as sentimental, he probably connected that undesirable characteristic with the music's function, a connection that Schumann would not have made.

Mendelssohn is generally (and largely correctly) represented as a composer who was enormously successful in his own time. There were, of course, reservations in many circles. If one pages through Schumann's reviews of

9 For a marvelous explanation of this line of thought, see Stephen Jay Gould, *This Wonderful Life: the Burgess Shale and the Nature of History* (New York, 1989).

10 *Musical Opinion* 71 (1947), p. 47.

11 Robert Schumann, *Gesammelte Schriften über Musik und Musiker*, ed. Martin Kreisig (Leipzig, 1914), vol. I, p. 98. Originally in the *Neue Zeitschrift für Musik* 2 (1835), 202.

Mendelssohn's music, for instance, one sometimes finds muted notes of disapproval as well as whole-hearted admiration and approval for the best works. Schumann's objections, when he expressed them, were based on what he took to be questions of quality, sometimes phrased as questions about originality.[12] Principled opposition, however, came from many sources and had many different bases. One can get a fairly good idea of two very important aspects of it by looking at what Heinrich Heine had to say about Mendelssohn.

To begin with, it must be noted that Heine had a personal reason to detest Mendelssohn – or, more accurately, wrongly thought he had such a reason. In the summer of 1825, Heine, then twenty-seven years old, converted from Judaism to Christianity. It was entirely a business proposition, for he had completed law school and needed to escape the very real disabilities he would have had to face as a Jewish lawyer. Clearly, he was disturbed by his own act and remained so for his entire life. Now Heine somehow took it into his head that Mendelssohn, while not a convert under analogous circumstances, had at least reached the age of reason when he adopted Christianity. Consequently his hatred and scorn of what he took to be Mendelssohn's hypocritical Christianizing were enormous – one is almost tempted to say boundless. (It seems never to have occurred to Heine that Mendelssohn might actually have been a sincerely believing Christian.)

In fact, Mendelssohn's father had had Felix baptized in 1816 at the age of seven – the precocious Mendelssohn may well have been more reasonable than most at that age, but he was certainly not in a position to make independent decisions about such matters – and while he remained aware and proud of his Jewish heritage, there is no indication that he was ever other than a sincere and deeply believing Protestant.

One sees the ferocity of which Heine was capable from a stanza from his *Deutschland, ein Wintermärchen* of 1844. In a series of stanzas, Heine narrated the history of the Mendelssohns in a sort of parody of Genesis. The stanza about Felix runs something like this: "With Leah, Abraham / Begat a little boy named Felix. / He's a big deal in Christianity, / And has made it to Kapellmeister."[13] (The Kapellmeister reference is presumably to Mendelssohn's position in Berlin, not to his position in Leipzig. In Berlin, he may well have become a court Jew in Heine's soured view.)

While Heine had his own special reasons for doubting the sincerity of

12 For a discussion of this topic, see Leon Plantinga, "Schumann's critical reaction to Mendelssohn," in *Mendelssohn and Schumann: Essays on Their Music and Its Context*, ed. Jon Finson and R. Larry Todd (Durham, NC, 1984), pp. 11–19.

13 Caput XVI, verses 21–4: "Der Abraham hatte mit Leah erzeugt / Ein Bübchen, Felix heißt er, / Er hatte es weit im Christentum, / Ist schon Kapellmeister."

Mendelssohn's Christianity, something rather like his doubts, but without their bitterness and self-hate, may have been in the minds of Gentiles as well as of Jews and converted Jews. Why else would Rockstro have remarked on "his [Mendelssohn's] earnestness as a Christian"?[14]

For all the individual peculiarities of his position, Heine's views of art and artists are representative of an important vein of opinion. The professional version was often more finely differentiated and certainly more technically grounded, but Heine represented not only a large part – perhaps the largest part – of the cultivated public, but also expressed basic views that many musicians also held.

In the forty-third number of his *Lutetia*, dated "Paris, in the middle of April, 1842" and originally written for the *Allgemeine Zeitung* of Augsburg,[15] Heine described a religious procession he had seen in Sète, a town south of Montpellier, during the previous summer, a procession that moved him deeply and that he says was "the most naive expression of the deepest thought." It is precisely the childishness of the form of this manifestation, he added, that kept its content from being annihilated in his mind or from annihilating itself. The context eventually makes clear that Good Friday was the occasion despite Heine's saying that the event took place during the summer. He continued:

> This content is of such monstrous, sorrowful power and nobility that it towers above and destroys the pathetic-grandiose and extended means of representation. Accordingly, the greatest artists in music as in painting have sought to decorate the overwhelming horrors of the Passion with as many flowers as possible and to ameliorate its bloody seriousness with playful tenderness – and this is what Rossini did when he composed his "Stabat Mater."
>
> This last, Rossini's "Stabat Mater," was the outstanding work of those worth noting during the season. Discussion of it is still on the agenda, and it is precisely the sharp criticisms from the north German point of view that have been made against the great master that demonstrate the originality and depth of his genius. The handling of the material is too secular, too sensuous, too playful for the sacred stuff, it is too light, too pleasant, too entertaining – these are the complaints sighed by several heavy, boring petty critics who, if they are not deliberately simulating an exaggerated spirituality, nevertheless torment themselves with a very limited, very wrong concept of sacred music. Musicians, like painters, are dominated by a wholly incorrect view of the handling of Christian

---

14 Remarks about Mendelssohn's Jewish ancestry occur so frequently in the nineteenth- and early twentieth-century literature that one almost comes to take them quite for granted.

15 Summaries and translations are taken from the text in Heinrich Heine, *Sämtliche Schriften*, vol. V, ed. Klaus Briegleb. *Lutetia: Berichte über Politik, Kunst und Volksleben*, ed. Karl Heinz Stahl (Munich, 1974), pp. 396–400.

material. The painters believe that the truly Christian must be represented with subtly thin contours and as sorrowfully and colorlessly as possible. In this connection, Overbeck's drawing is their ideal. In order to counter this illusion by an example, I call attention to the holy pictures of the Spanish school. ... External dryness and paleness are not the marks of the artistically truly Christian; what is, rather, is a certain almost excessive enthusiasm which can be acquired neither by baptism nor by study either in music or in painting. Accordingly, I find the "Stabat" by Rossini more truly Christian than "St. Paul," the oratorio by Felix Mendelssohn-Bartholdy that is praised by Rossini's opponents as a model of Christianity.

Heaven forfend that I should wish to speak ill of so worthy a master as the author of "St. Paul." Still less would I want it to enter the heads of the subscribers to this paper that I wish to cavil about the Christianity of the aforementioned oratorio because Felix Mendelssohn-Bartholdy is by birth a Jew. But I cannot avoid indicating that at the age at which Herr Mendelssohn adopted Christianity – he was baptized in his thirteenth year – Rossini had already left it and had plunged into the secularity of the operatic world. Now when he has left opera and dreams about his youthful Catholic memories, back to the times when he sang in the Pesaro Cathedral as a chorister or functioned as an acolyte during Mass, now when the old organ tones rise again in his memory and he grasps his pen to write a "Stabat," he does not need to begin to construct the spirit of Christianity through learning. Still less does he need slavishly to copy Handel or Sebastian Bach. He needs only to call forth to his spirit the sounds of earliest childhood and lo! as solemnly, as deeply sorrowing as these sounds resound, as powerfully as they sigh and bleed, expressing the most power-ful, so do they also retain something childlike and remind me of the children's representation of the Passion in Sète.

Heine went on in this vein for a bit and then said, "I need say nothing about the first, exemplary performance; it is enough to say that the Italians sang." After a few sentences, he turned again to Mendelssohn:

In the same series of concerts we heard the "St. Paul" of Herr Felix Men-delssohn-Bartholdy who by this propinquity drew our attention to him and himself called forth the comparison with Rossini. In the view of the great public, this comparison in no way came out to the advantage of our young countryman. It is as if one compared the Apennines with the Templower Hill in Berlin. But that does not mean that the Templower Hill is thereby less worthy, for it wins the respect of the great masses because it bears a cross on its crest. "Under this sign ye shall prevail." But not in France, the land of unbelief, where Herr Mendelssohn has always had fiascoes.[16] He was the sacrificial lamb of the

16 Not surprisingly, this is overstated. For a fascinating discussion of Mendelssohn's five months in Paris from November 1831 to April 1832, see Adolphe Jullien, "Mendelssohn à Paris," in his *Airs variés: Histoire, critique, biographies musicales* (Paris, 1877), pp. 65–156. For a

season while Rossini was its lion whose growl continues to resound. The word is that Herr Felix Mendelssohn will soon personally come to Paris. One thing is certain, that through considerable effort as a representative and by diplomatic efforts, Herr Leon Pillet has induced Herr Scribe to prepare a libretto that Herr Mendelssohn is to compose for the opera.

Of course, Mendelssohn never set a libretto by Scribe.
Heine concluded his article with this send-off:

> With regard to talent, I find a great similarity between Herr Felix Mendelssohn and Mme. Rachel Felix, the tragedienne. Both possess a large, strict and very serious solemnity, a decided, almost passionate attachment to classical models, the finest, most intelligent ability to calculate, and finally a vast deficiency of naivete. But in art is there such a thing as brilliant originality without naivete? Up to now, no case of this has appeared.

Heine returned to Mendelssohn in a report written shortly thereafter (Paris, 25 April 1844).[17] He began with high praise for Berlioz. He then reported on the failure of Mendelssohn's "Scottish" Symphony and of his choruses for *Antigone*. He continues:

> Mendelssohn always offers us the occasion to consider the highest problems of aesthetics, that is, he always brings up the great question: What is the difference between art and falsehood? In the case of this master, we admire especially his great talent for form, for stylistics, his talent for making the most extra-ordinary his own, his charmingly beautiful writing, his tenderly filling horns, and his serious – I might almost say passionate – indifference. If we look for a parallel phenomenon in a sister art we shall find it in literature and it is called Ludwig Tieck. This master too knew how to reproduce the most advantageous qualities, whether in writing or in declaiming, and he even understood how to manufacture the naive; yet he never produced anything that moved the masses and remained lively in their hearts. The more talented Mendelssohn would more likely succeed in creating something lasting, but not on the territory where truth and passion are demanded at the very outset, namely on the stage. Tieck, too, in spite of his most intense wishes never brought off a real dramatic contribution.

Heine's dislike of Mendelssohn *qua* Mendelssohn – and what on earth is meant by "his ... passionate indifference"? – is one thing; Heine's aesthetic position, symbolized by his remark about the "North German school," is another. One could scarcely ask for a more trenchant statement of the

general survey of Mendelssohn's reputation in France, see Jean de Solliers, "Zur Mendelssohn-Rezeption in Frankreich," *Beiträge zur Musikwissenschaft* 15/3 (1973), 209–12.

17 *Lutetia. Anhang: Musikalische Saison von 1844 – Erster Bericht*, pp. 528–37.

"Italo-French" attitude at a time when the musical world was divided into "two cultures,"[18] two cultures that met only rarely. To Schumann, enthusiasm for Rossini was almost a moral failing. But to the partisans of Rossini and a bit later of Meyerbeer and Halévy as well as of younger Italians like Donizetti and Bellini, the music of the opposing camp was stiff, long-winded, excessively solemn and fundamentally boring. Historiography needs to bear in mind the implacable hostility between these two camps.[19]

While in word and most deeds, Mendelssohn belongs where Heine put him, in the "North German camp," there is one aspect of his production that is not entirely in keeping with the attitudes of the Leipzig cohort: Mendelssohn was probably the last of the major masters to write a great deal of music designed to satisfy the needs of the day. In this sense, then, if one believes in art for its own sake, Mendelssohn can easily be seen as having taken a large step back from the position Beethoven, at least in his last years, had come to occupy and which Schumann largely espoused. In writing music for male choruses and mixed choruses with and without simple accompaniment, Mendelssohn supplied the modest amateur choral groups of the day. The more ambitious religious music, the oratorios and psalm settings for chorus and orchestra, were meant for the large, sometimes huge (and presumably not so modest) amateur choral groups of the day. The first half of the nineteenth century, after all, was the high time of these often immense choruses and of their music festivals. Their needs were looked after by Mendelssohn and Handel (though the latter, of course, was unaware of his nineteenth-century role) and, beyond them, almost entirely by composers whose names (to say nothing of whose music) are known today only to specialists. Toward the end of his life, Mendelssohn even went so far as to write music for the Protestant services in Prussia, though the role and the nature of that music was drastically restricted by the *Kirchenagende* then in force.

Of course, Mendelssohn's own time was aware of this practical aspect of his production, but evaluations of it differed widely. For instance, Ernst Kossack, writing Mendelssohn's death notice for the *Neue Berliner Musikzeitung* on 10 November 1847,[20] ranked the *Midsummer Night's Dream* music, *Antigone*, St.

---

18 The phrase is Raphael Georg Kiesewetter's and comes from his *Geschichte der europäisch-abendländischen oder unsrer heutigen Musik* (1834) as quoted and enlarged upon by Carl Dahlhaus in his *Die Musik des 19. Jahrhunderts*, Neues Handbuch der Musikgeschichte, vol. VI (Wiesbaden, 1980), pp. 7–13.

19 Most general writing in English tends to adopt an attitude that is in effect Schumann's. One of the many merits of Dahlhaus' *Die Musik des 19. Jahrhunderts* is thorough discussion of this pitfall. On ideology, hidden and not so hidden, in general writing about music, see especially Leo Treitler, "The present as history," in his *Music and the Historical Imagination* (Cambridge, MA, 1989), pp. 95–156.

20 *Neue Berliner Musikzeitung* 1/45 (1847), 369–72.

Paul, and *Elijah* as Mendelssohn's greatest works. The first two of these (with the exception of the *Midsummer Night's Dream* Overture) were written at the command of the king for performance in the royal theater in Berlin, and the *Antigone* music is part of the strange movement to revive classical Greek forms in modern garb.

The two oratorios, though doubtless written from the heart, had a rather large and obvious market waiting for them. (One needs to bear in mind that Mendelssohn was very much in demand as a conductor of choral festivals.) Now interestingly enough, Kossack began his enumeration of the secondary works with those purely instrumental compositions which are all that have survived in the modern repertory from Mendelssohn's production. For Kossack, as for many people even at mid-century, opera remained not only the musical genre with the greatest popularity but also the highest musical genre. Kossack said that at his death Mendelssohn had only just begun to work on "the highest art form, the great tragic opera."[21] In this respect, Kossack agreed with Heine; for a moment the two cultures met.

Eduard Krüger, an opponent of Mendelssohn in his last days, naturally took a different view, though he took it in the same periodical.[22] Reviewing the *Three Psalms*, posthumously published as op. 78, Krüger said that to many people, Mendelssohn seems the highest manifestation of music. But not to him. Mendelssohn's constant concern with religious music was an error, an error of the sort great geniuses do not make. There is no reviving religious music. "The sacred cannot be re-won," wrote Krüger, "until our lives are transformed." More is needed than "the doubly reflected reflection of speculative scholasticism," he said, and toward the end of the review, the adjective "rabbinical" appears. Krüger thus accounted for the "error" on what he apparently wanted to be taken as high ground (a bit of insinuated anti-Semitism of course not lowering it any); either the issue of *Gebrauchsmusik* did not occur to him or was deliberately raised to this intellectually more elevated plane. Krüger also said he had often tried to show how "the soft virginal spirit of our Mendelssohn" could not reach the high road and how heroic shapes were inaccessible to him. This is proved by *St. Paul* and *Elijah*. "Their fame lasted an hour; praise for them was linked to the beloved singers then performing them and died with those singers."[23]

Around mid-century, the German musical press was obviously – and often rather uneasily – on the lookout for something new. On the one hand, the

---

21 The reference is to the unfinished *Loreley*.

22 *Neue Berliner Musikzeitung* 4/1 (2 Jan 1850), 3–5.

23 A strong rejoinder to Krüger's view of the impossibility of religious music appeared three weeks later: Wilhelm Wauer, "Felix Mendelssohn-Bartholdy und Dr. Eduard Krüger," *NBMz* 4/4 (23 Jan 1850), 25–7. According to Wauer, a pure and strong spirit can transcend his times.

notion of the standard repertory had been partly established (and not least because of Mendelssohn's activities); on the other, programs were still dominated by contemporary music and the masterpieces of the past could not replace it. For all that, *Historismus* was well established and the displays of learning it required were found everywhere.

Progressive reviewers tended to be dissatisfied with much of the new music not because it was new but because it continued in the old ways. There was, however, no clarity – indeed, before the dissemination of Wagner's theories scarcely an idea – about what the times required. Doubtless, this situation helps to explain the extraordinary position Wagner suddenly came to occupy at mid-century. He published *Das Kunstwerk der Zukunft* in 1849 and *Oper und Drama* in 1851. The musical press was immediately full of discussion of Wagnerian theory (including an absolutely splendid summary of it produced for the *Neue Berliner Musikzeitung* by Julius Schäffer).[24] As it happens, however, Wagner had not yet written much to demonstrate the practicality – or even what one might call the sounding expression – of his theories. There seems to have been general agreement that *Tannhaüser* of 1845 was but a step in the right direction. *Lohengrin*, first produced in 1850, was received with more enthusiasm both for itself and for its relation to Wagnerian theory. But the first performance was in Weimar, and it took some time for the work to become generally known.

The enormous growth of the musical press at this time was dominated by a relatively new type of musician: the musical intellectual. People like Eduard Krüger, Otto Lange, Franz Brendel and others often had doctoral degrees in subjects like classical philology and were frequently employed as professors of those subjects. Almost without exception, they had been musically trained, apparently quite thoroughly, and some became at least part-time professional musicians as adults. They were therefore *au courant* with the intellectual subjects of the day and as unlike earlier generations of book-writing musical craftsmen – the Leopold Mozarts, the Quantzes – as possible. With their control of a considerable part of the musical press, Wagner understandably generated a great deal of enthusiasm perhaps based as much on his theoretical positions as on his music. (Berlioz, Mendelssohn, and Schumann of course represent the first generation of composers with university educations. Though none of the three went through an entire course and became a proper graduate, all were clearly intellectuals, professional intellectuals one might almost say.)

24 "Über Richard Wagner's *Lohengrin* mit Bezug auf sein Schrift: 'Oper und Drama,' *NBMz* 6/20 (12 May 1852), 153–5; 6/21 (19 May 1852), 161–3; 6/22 (26 May 1852), 169–71; 6/25 (16 June 1852), 193–6; 6/26 (23 June 1852), 201–4.

Not surprisingly, views of Mendelssohn around this time were often conditioned by what the reviewer took to be modern. To the more old-fashioned, Mendelssohn continued to count as such for some few years after his death. In the *Neue Berliner Musikzeitung*, Lange reviewed a piano four-hands arrangement of the String Quintet op. 87 and called Mendelssohn one of the "most valuable and original representatives of the modern direction."[25] In the same paper some ten months later, G. A. Keferstein dealt with several disparate works, the music to *Oedipus in Kolonos*, the recitatives and choruses from the unfinished oratorio *Christus*, and the finale from the unfinished opera *Loreley*. Keferstein said that for some ten or twelve years he had been calling attention to the fact that Mendelssohn had been overrated. He added that nevertheless he wanted to recognize "the excellent services of a man who in everything in art that a fortunate talent can learn and achieve through iron diligence stands honorably beside the best of recent times." (Notice how similar this is to Heine's view, though the starting points may have been quite different.) But Keferstein praised the *Loreley* scene highly. He could not make friends with the *Oedipus* music, with music he rightly said is in "this new, unique genre," and he thought that for the *Christus* fragments Mendelssohn had put the text together arbitrarily and without inner organic necessity just as he had for *St. Paul*. Keferstein concluded by saying that Mendelssohn's achievements as pianist, organist, and conductor would not be forgotten and that "his overtures will be newly heard with heightened interest." He added that a great deal can be learned from the study of Mendelssohn's works whatever posterity's final judgment would be.

Despite the generally high level of reviewing at this time, there are certain signs of obtuseness here. Keferstein never seemed to consider that posthumous works are necessarily works which the composer did not publish and that unfinished works were necessarily just that – unfinished. He went about his task quite as if he were dealing with publications authorized by the composer, publications which accordingly may be assumed to represent his last and best thoughts on the matter at hand. Keferstein clearly grasped that the *Oedipus* music belonged to a new and strange genre, but how he could tell anything about the *Christus* libretto from the tiny fragment published is hard to see. Most important, he anticipated an interesting development, namely the recognition in some circles that Mendelssohn's major contribution lay not so much in the religious music, so popular in his own day and occupying so large a part of his production, or in the experimental theater music, but in the instrumental music and particularly the concert overtures.

25 *NBMz* 5/15 (9 April 1851), 114.

For the progressives, of course, there was a bit of an ideological agenda concealed in this admiration. Mendelssohn's concert overtures occupied a relatively honorable position in part because they were viewed as worthy forerunners of more modern developments, particularly of the symphonic poems of Liszt. Of course, Keferstein could not have known this when he wrote; what is doubly interesting is that he seems to have sensed the direction things were taking.

We need to pause momentarily to consider these experimental stage works: the music to Sophocles' *Antigone* op. 55, completed in October 1841, and published during the composer's lifetime; the music to Racine's *Athalie* op. 74, completed in 1845 and published posthumously, and the music to Sophocles' *Oedipus in Kolonos* op. 93, composed in 1845 and published post-humously. (The *Midsummer Night's Dream* music belongs to the series, all the pieces having been written for the royal Prussian theater in Potsdam at the king's command, but its character is entirely different.) What was involved here was an attempt to create a kind of modernized version of ancient Greek drama (and in one case, of Racine's vision of that drama). One of the principal instigators of this (besides the king, Frederick William IV) was Ludwig Tieck; Heine's reference to him in connection with Mendelssohn was a well-aimed shot, not just a more or less random comparison.

While there was no attempt to revive the ancient drama in a genuinely authentic form, there was a distinct effort to work out a modernized version of it. Thus Mendelssohn's choruses for *Antigone* and *Oedipus* are for male voices but employ a full modern orchestra; they scrupulously observe the distinction among strophe and antistrophe, but of course they make use of modern harmony. August Böckh, a professor of philology at the University of Berlin and an advisor to this somewhat curious project, wrote a simple and direct statement of its goals and methods for the *Preußische Staatszeitung* which fortunately was reprinted by the *Allgemeine musikalische Zeitung* for 24 November 1841 (Jahrgang 43, No. 47).

In 1852, Wilhelm Wauer returned to the subject of the *Oedipus* music in the pages of the *Neue Berliner Musikzeitung*.[26] The occasion, one supposes, was receipt of an advance copy of the published score which officially appeared in May of that year. Wauer, one of Mendelssohn's consistent defenders, said that "not only does the music not run counter to the inner character of the poetry but completely and admirably corresponds to it." He added that there was no question of attempting to revive Greek music, but rather of "creating music corresponding as closely as possible to the impression made on our spirits by

---

26 *NBMz* 6/6 (4 Feb 1852), 44–6.

the antique work of poetry." (This is entirely in line with Böckh's remarks.) *Antigone*, he continued, has had a great success. "The sublime, energetic declamation, the often shattering harmonies, the unique handling of the melodic element – all these together exert by their novelty a powerful enchantment, and in the end one comes to the general view that except for a few missteps that given the nature of the undertaking were unavoidable, Mendelssohn has created in the music to *Antigone* a work that alone would suffice to ensure him an honored place on the ladder of musical fame."

Let us now look at a few reviews from the *Allgemeine musikalische Zeitung* of Leipzig, bearing in mind that it was widely and properly viewed as the organ of conservative – not to say reactionary – opinion and that Schumann had founded the *Neue Zeitschrift für Musik* in direct opposition to it. In 1842, Carl Ferdinand Becker called the *Ninety-fifth Psalm* for chorus and orchestra op. 46, "a work by a truly talented and thoroughly cultivated artist, by a master whose name is firmly entrenched in the annals of the history of art and extends far beyond Germany's borders. A work by a coryphaeus of art like Mendelssohn-Bartholdy," he continued, "can be observed but never criticized."[27]

An anonymous review of the Symphony No. 2, the "symphony-cantata" *Lobgesang* op. 52, in the same paper during the same year remarked that it was unusual for a composer of Mendelssohn's reputation to write "church music" (a phrase that must be put in quotation marks, since the *Lobgesang* is church music only in a very broad sense even though its first performance took place in St. Thomas's in Leipzig). The writer defended choral fugues as arising naturally from polyphonic writing rather than artificially through imitation of the old masters and also said that Mendelssohn freed his music from the primarily harmonic thinking of the present day. He also maintained that church music must be viewed as essentially lyric.[28]

One more example from the same periodical, this time about a major orchestral work: A. K., writing about the "Scottish" Symphony, said that Mendelssohn excelled in the instrumental genre. This reviewer observed something that has escaped some modern critics, namely that the main theme of the first movement is derived from that movement's introduction and that the coda to the last movement is also so derived.[29]

There was fighting in Berlin on Saturday and Sunday, 18 and 19 March 1848, and it is positively thrilling to read the lead article in the *Neue Berliner Musikzeitung* for the following Wednesday, 22 March. It begins in ecstasy and

27 *AmZ* 44/1 (5 Jan 1842), cols. 1–7; 44/2 (12 Jan 1842), cols. 33–7.
28 *AmZ* 44/9 (9 March 1842), cols. 205–9.
29 *AmZ* 46/9 (28 Feb 1844), cols. 341–2.

proceeds almost to incoherence. The writer, Otto Lange, was convinced that a new age was dawning, a new age in which everything would be different and, of course, better. The emphasis was on freedom, political freedom (including, of course, press freedom) and it was taken as certain that this freedom would also lead to entirely new things in art.[30] (There was, of course, no notion that opposition to the old order and great hopes for freedom under the new do not make politics and that social and economic change cannot occur without politics.)

On 21 March the *Neue Zeitschrift für Musik* carried an "open letter" to the editors from Ernst Gottschald saying that "the latest lofty events have wrenched our German fatherland into a movement whose aim and ultimate goal pushes toward a new ordering of our social arrangement. This aim and goal is nothing other than an understanding and development of our nationhood on the basis of freedom."[31] Though talk about "our German fatherland" was far from new, there is no doubt that the events of March 1848 gave it enormous impetus. At first, German nationalism was a part of liberalism, though very unpleasant and illiberal overtones quickly manifested themselves.

The *Neue Zeitschrift für Musik* celebrated the occasion in a more formal way with a leader by its editor, Franz Brendel, beginning on 15 April 1848.[32] Brendel's article has a title suggesting the sometimes pretentious intellectualizing that was his trademark: "The Events of the Present and Their Influence on Questions of the Musical Press." In this great cry of freedom, Brendel remarked that "the nation will be spiritually strengthened by freedom of the press. From the newly attained good, from the enormous progress within a few weeks, I hope for and anticipate the most blessed consequences for music as well as for the musical press which here has been the exclusive topic."

Not quite the exclusive topic. For in the same part of this essay, Brendel undertook to defend Eduard Krüger's attack on *Elijah* which had appeared in

30 One needs at least the opening (and in German) to savor it: "Ein ruhmvoller Kampf ist bei uns in diesen Tagen gekämpft, Freiheiten sind errungen worden, durch welche nicht nur die Materiellen, sondern auch die geistigen Interessen Deutschlands mit Riesenschritten einer glücklichen Lösung entgegengehen. Berlin ist seit Jahrzehnten der Thronsitz deutscher Intelligenz, deutscher Wissenschaft und Kunst gewesen. Am 18. und 19. März sind seine Straßen und Wohnstätten mit Blut getränket worden, der Bürger hat die einige, aber auch zugleich die Freiheit der Wissenschaft und der Kunst erringen helfen. Wenn jene ihm am nächsten liegt, nimmt er doch Antheil an diesen. Führt ihm nach blutigem Kampf der Sieg zum ruhigen Genuß des Errungenen, so wird die freie Wissenschaft ihn zu sich heranziehen und ihn auf practischen Gebieten förderlich sein. Und die Kunst! Auch sie kann sich nur unter dem Banner der Freiheit zu höchster Blüthe entfalten. Der Boden, dem sie entsprießt, auf dem sie sich nach allen Richtungen hinausbreitet muß unumschränkt sein, damit sie überall Wurzel fasse und jedes Lebensgebiet mit ihrem mannigfaltigen Zauber durchdringe."

31 *NZfM* 28/24 (21 March 1848), 141–2.

32 *NZfM* 28/31 (15 April 1848), 181–84; 28/33 (22 April 1848), 193–6; 29/19 (2 Sept 1848), 101–5.

Nos. 45, 47, and 49 of volume 27 of the *Neue Zeitschrift* during December 1847 and had been sufficiently unpleasant for the editor to have appended a note saying that the review had been written and accepted for publication prior to Mendelssohn's death. Krüger had violently attacked the text of the oratorio as being unclear about developing its dramatic situations (a criticism with which many people would agree). He had also attacked the musical characterization saying that it is impossible to tell whether one was listening to angel or prophet, prophet or king, queen or widow, whether the choruses were Baal priests or the populace, and so on.

But in Nos. 1 and 2 for 1 January and 4 January 1846, Krüger had also had the highest praise for the violin concerto in an article that also discussed the organ sonatas. "Enough," he wrote about the concerto, "it is a blessing that Mendelssohn has said and done what is right – this is the best way of teaching others the right. A work in which the newest techniques are used as the means to higher things, as a bridge to insights that are beyond all techniques, that is a work for which the world should give joyful thanks." In short, Krüger was making a distinction between the religious works to which he ascribed relatively little value and the major instrumental works which he placed on a much higher plane; this is a judgment held by many today.

In later installments of his essay, Brendel avowedly moved beyond questions of the musical press and turned his attention to general musical questions. "The majority of musicians," he wrote, "has until now paid too little attention to the concerns of the nation and accordingly most musicians lack a well-defined view of the political events of the day." He pointed out that music, needing financial support, tended to be close to princes and to the upper classes. "A circumstance unique to music," he continued, "increased the indifference to outward events in musical spheres. With their sounds, musicians turn toward the generality of all who are sensitive to the art. Music is a world language while poetry is initially constrained within national borders. This has had the consequence that musicians have too much lost sight of the national basis, that they have yielded to a totally false international citizenship whose central point is indifference to all nationality. At home everywhere they must often lose interest in their fatherland and with the polished manners that develop, they deprive themselves at the same time of every characteristic individuality."

This came from a man who prided himself on his knowledge of the history of the art and who eventually was to write a well-regarded historical survey![33]

---

33 Franz Brendel, *Geschichte der Musik in Italien, Deutschland und Frankreich: 22 Vorlesungen gehalten zu Leipzig* (Leipzig, 1852). A number of subsequent editions, the more recent ones somewhat expanded, were issued.

Could Brendel really have imagined that the well-known international citizen and composer of Italian operas, Wolfgang A. Mozart, had deprived himself "of every characteristic individuality"? (He of course would have said that this was exactly what had happened to that well-known Italo-French master, Giacomo Meyerbeer.) But that a moment's reflection would have informed Brendel that he was writing nonsense and that he nevertheless went ahead says a great deal about the force with which these patriotic sentiments over-whelmed the minds of progressive German advocates of freedom at mid-century.

Eventually, Brendel arrived at a vital point about what he took to be the future of music. "I anticipate," he wrote, "that art will develop a new content from the general advance." He added that he thought that because of the importance of form in music, the question of content was often slighted. "Unaware of the importance of content, he [the composer] takes with the formal shell he has borrowed from the older masters likewise their content and is happy to repeat what has long since been said better. In such times and under such conditions, the question about content accordingly becomes much more important and attains a completely other significance. For here it is a question of directing express attention to what is otherwise assumed to be a given."[34] The longing for the new has been with us for quite some time and "the moment has come for musicians to reveal new treasures of content."

Obviously, not everyone agreed with that. Indeed, most likely relatively few did, for in the second half of the century the split between progressive artists and a relatively conservative public grew into a deep and wide chasm. But the people who agreed with Brendel were likely to be the influential creative artists and their supporters, at least until the time a few years later when the rise of Brahms gave the aesthetically relatively conservative party a master who could demonstrate how much vitality was left in the structures the progressives wished to consign to the rubbish heap.

It was possible to be reasonably specific (at least in a theoretical sort of way) about what this newness was to be. "Modern music," Brendel wrote in 1850, "shows a decisive striving for definiteness in expression and the greatest possible sharpness of characterization even in purely instrumental music. The common striving is to represent definite, palpable poetic states of soul, and to realize this goal are employed all available depictions of every sort, and painting. One needs only to recollect Mendelssohn's overtures to find con-firmation of this."[35]

34 In the first issue of the *Neue Zeitschrift für Musik* for 1852, Brendel formally acknowledged Wagner as the musician for the times and dedicated the paper to his support.
35 "Einige Worte über Malerei in der Tonkunst," *NZfM* 32/47 (11 June 1850), 241–4.

That is the definitive statement of the value Mendelssohn was to have to the next few generations of progressives, that is for those of them for whom he was to have any value at all. Tastes and interests had turned toward the issues of expression and characterization as the second half of the century understood them. For these tastes, much of Mendelssohn's music was simply irrelevant. Despite the growth of the historical repertory, this irrelevance was fatal. Earlier music that survived, Beethoven's in the first instance, survived largely by virtue of being reinterpreted so as to suit the concerns of the day. But it was difficult, perhaps impossible, to reinterpret music in genres that were becoming obsolescent, and in any case, there was no motive for attempting to do so; the religious choral works that are so large a part of Mendelssohn's output were thus doomed to near extinction.

Everyone knows that we continue to reinterpret today; this is nothing more than the dull truism that every generation makes of the masterpieces of the past what it needs to make of them. But for an age of historicism, the second half of the nineteenth century carried out this process in a particularly narrow and even violent way. In so doing, it rejected some recent and splendid music largely because that music did not fit largely theoretical preconceptions. Schumann's *Faust* music is a good example, rejected by the Wagnerians because it was insufficiently Wagnerian and damned by everyone else because it was too Wagnerian. Today, it continues in the obscurity to which it was relegated by partisans whose conflicts today have historical but not aesthetic significance.[36]

There has been an omission in the previous enumeration of Wagner's musical and theoretical works around 1850: "Das Judenthum in der Musik," published under the pseudonym K. Freigedank in Brendel's *Neue Zeitschrift für Musik* on 3 September and 9 September 1850.[37] In a later essay, "Aufklärung über das Judenthum in der Musik,"[38] Wagner ascribed all his difficulties following on the publication of "Das Judenthum" to the vendetta launched against him by Jewry in retaliation for this work. He said, and this is no doubt true, that the real author of the piece was quickly suspected. Indeed, he denied really having tried to conceal himself.

It soon becomes clear as one pages through the *Neue Zeitschrift* that the article had not come to Brendel over the transom; he was perfectly aware of its author. Indeed, he was about to make Wagner one of the paper's chief

36 On the reception of the Faust music, see my "Schumann as an interpreter of Goethe's Faust," *Journal of the American Musicological Society* 14/2 (1961), 235–56.

37 *NZfM* 33 (3 and 9 Sept 1850), 101–7 and 109–12. Wagner reprinted the essay as a pamphlet under his own name in 1869. The 1869 text can be found in *Richard Wagners Gesammelte Schriften*, ed. Julius Kapp, vol. XIII, "Der Polemiker" (Leipzig, n.d.) pp. 7–29.

38 *Richard Wagners Gesammelte Schriften*, vol. XIII, pp. 29–51.

contributors and accordingly also its chief theoretician. Brendel appended a footnote to the essay saying it was by one of our leading composers, suggesting that not everyone would agree with it, and also saying that it could not have been published earlier because of press censorship. Freedom, as Daniel Schorr has remarked, includes the freedom to hate. Despite the apparent disclaimer, Brendel's praise for what he considers the essay's objective argumentation makes clear that he was in fact largely in favor of its content.

Wagner began by discussing what he said was the natural revulsion against the Jew felt by all European peoples, particularly, of course, by Germans. He said that all European tongues are foreign to Jews and that Jews cannot speak of their feelings, lacking the speech knowledge to do so. It follows that Jews cannot sing. Jews have never had their own art, and when Jews imitate our art it is as if we heard a Goethe poem "read in Jewish jargon." Just as in this jargon, words and constructions are thrown about with amazing lack of expressiveness, so the Jewish musician throws together the most varied forms and styles of the old masters. Piled on top of one another, we meet the most varied confused chaos of formal characteristics scooped out from all schools. Jews, having no passion, can have no art.

The prime exemplar of all this is, of course, Mendelssohn. Bach's speech is largely formal whereas Beethoven's is human. Therefore Mendelssohn chose to imitate Bach. "The deliquescence and chaotic artlessness of our musical styles have, if not been caused by Mendelssohn, been brought to their highest point by his efforts to express an unclear, almost nugatory content in the most interesting and startling way." But of course our artists and our society have permitted this to happen. "So long as the specific musical art had a genuine organic need of life within it, that is up to the time of Mozart and Beethoven, there was no Jewish composer. No one to whom the living organism was a totally foreign element could take part in its development." Only when the organism is dead do "extreme elements" get power over it. The spirit of art can only be found in life.

There is more in this mode directed against Meyerbeer who is not mentioned by name though everyone discussing the article proceeded quite as if he had been. Heine and Ludwig Börne are, like Mendelssohn, attacked by name. At the time the essay was published, Mendelssohn and Börne were safely dead and Heine was an invalid in Paris. However, Meyerbeer, who by the way had brought out Wagner's *Rienzi* in Berlin, was alive and enjoying the protection of the Prussian court. For all that Wagner's essay created a storm, the serious attacks on it in the German musical press are less numerous than one might have expected. To his credit, Brendel carried one such response in the *Neue Zeitschrift* for 15 October 1850, Eduard Bernsdorf's "K. Freigedank und das

Judenthum in der Musik."[39] The main point is that the corruptions "Freige-dank" ascribed to the Jews are in fact those of the times, times in which all of us, Jews included, necessarily participate. There is no evidence that Jews are the cause. Bernsdorf set down a string of names of major Jewish actors by way of countering the argument that Jews cannot speak and said that "Freigedank" talked about Mendelssohn the composer without in any way demonstrating that what he was saying was necessarily the result of Mendelssohn's ancestral Judaism. "What he ['Freigedank'] says about Meyerbeer," maintained Berns-dorf, "is in many respects true, but not because Meyerbeer is a Jew but because Meyerbeer is a man of the nineteenth century."

The *Neue Zeitschrift* carried another "reply" – if that is the word – a work by Eduard Krüger bearing the title "Judenthümliches."[40] Krüger begins by suggesting that the Jews can get away with their various artistic sins and crimes because we have declined so. "Freigedank" failed to say this. (In fact, he had said just that.) About Mendelssohn Krüger says, "He was no Beethoven, but then neither is Schumann." Mendelssohn's religious music, however, is as "Freigedank" says it is. Nevertheless, Mendelssohn was personally attractive and should be honored for his services to music as a conductor.

"Today," said Krüger, "there is much talk of hostility to Jews and of friendship for them, and both views are ascribed to various political parties. But it is not possible for our newly liberated age to distinguish between persons and things? The [Jewish] people are as a whole alien to us and will remain so until they cease to be independent; the individual [Jew] on the other hand can be highly worthy of respect. Just as there can be honest Frenchmen and roguish Germans without the basic character of either nation being changed thereby, so also can one find Jews of spiritual depth and breadth that would shame many non-Jews. And when one reminds baptized Jews of their Semitic origin, one should not forget the reshaping contact with a richer life in which blood and goods have been crossed and exchanged."

One can understand that the orthodox Jew was a strange figure to Krüger in a time and place neither really accustomed to strange figures nor noted for multi-cultural sophistication. But one also observes the remark that quite clearly makes honesty a normal German characteristic and dishonesty a normal French one. From our vantage point, it is not hard to see a very great deal of what made the first half of our century so horrible in this episode of Wagner's little essay and the responses to it.

Johann Christian Lobe took a different tack, one that was not only more humane but – wonder of wonders in this quagmire of solemnly pernicious

39 *NZfM* 33 (15 Oct 1850), 165–8.   40 *NZfM* 33 (1 Oct 1850), 145–7.

nonsense – witty. This essay, he says, is not a pseudonymous work at all but rather a product of a great satirist who has created a fictitious character, namely K. Freigedank, and made this character the author of the tract. This is proved by the brilliant way in which the author exposed the gross errors of logic characteristic of this species of diatribe. Further proof, if any be needed, is supplied by the fact that the putative author undertook to assault the two most profound composers of the time.[41]

We have seen that what was viewed (or perhaps only hoped for) as an enormous caesura in European history, namely the revolutions of 1848, created a situation in which vast artistic change was anticipated with the corollary that the art of the first half of the century would sharply decline in validity and usefulness for the new present. If we add this to a general sense of compositional malaise following the death of Beethoven – to have read Schumann is to appreciate how real and how disturbing this was – one can easily appreciate how unstable the reputations of the composers of the first half of the century necessarily were.

In Mendelssohn's case we need to add to these general considerations the fact that much of his work was in media and genres whose utility either rapidly declined or moved to the fringes of progressive musical life as the century moved on. Because this is so, the Mendelssohn reception mirrors the conflicts and trends at mid-century: questions about the future and utility of the established musical genres to be sure, but also about the nature and direction of religion and its role in life. And behind varying views about this matter there are great complexes of social attitudes for which the religious argument is in part a surrogate. To this mix we need to add German and general European anti-Semitism, a sentiment that grew to a movement and culminated in the Holocaust. Mendelssohn's reputation was tossed about by these currents and counter-currents, perhaps more than that of any of his significant contemporaries, and so it is not surprising that his reputation declined so rapidly in the eyes of the advanced public soon after his death. If we consider the quality of some of his music and its continued popularity, it is also not surprising that occasional reexaminations of it have resulted in the composer's real, if hitherto temporary, rehabilitation. Though the motivation for much of the scholarly cottage industry that is currently being made of Mendelssohn is not entirely disinterested, there is no doubt that it has made a considerable contribution to the recent rise in the esteem in which he is held.

41 Johann Christian Lobe, "Das Judenthum in der Musik," in his *Consonanzen und Dissonanzen: Gesammelte Schriften aus älterer und neuerer Zeit* (Leipzig, 1869), pp. 1–17.

7 Marxian programmatic music: a stage in Mendelssohn's musical development[1]

JUDITH SILBER BALLAN

Any attempt to determine the precise extent of Adolf Bernhard Marx's influence on Mendelssohn, or Mendelssohn's on Marx, is hampered by the fact that their friendship came to an ugly and spiteful end eight years before Mendelssohn's death. For the rest of his life, Marx made no secret of his conviction that Mendelssohn was a "talent," but no genius.[2] And when writing his memoirs, Marx took great pains to distance himself from Mendelssohn's achievements. There are works, however, on which Marx did not wish to deny his influence, notably the Overture to *A Midsummer Night's Dream*, a work which Marx – even after their rupture – continued to consider a work of genius.[3] Mendelssohn wrote or conceived the bulk of his programmatic music during his friendship with Marx. Of this output, three works – the Overture to *A Midsummer Night's Dream*, the "Reformation" Symphony, and the *Calm Sea and Prosperous Voyage* Overture – were composed between 1826 and 1830, the period during which their friendship was close and intense.[4]

I OVERTURE TO *A MIDSUMMER NIGHT'S DREAM*: A LINK TO MARX'S PROGRAMMATIC THEORY

Marx first became acquainted with the Mendelssohn family in 1824 and 1825, when Felix was fifteen. By early 1825, Marx was fully integrated into their

1 Shorter versions of this article were read at the 54th Annual Meeting of the American Musicological Society, Baltimore, November 1988, and at a Mendelssohn Symposium held at Amherst College on 2 December 1989. I would like to thank Harry Ballan and Marian Smith who contributed greatly to the many versions of this article, and Laurence Dreyfus for immeasurable assistance in its earliest incarnation.

2 See for example A. B. Marx, *Ludwig van Beethoven: Leben und Schaffen*, 2nd edn. (Berlin, 1863), vol. II, p. 293.

3 A. B. Marx, *Erinnerungen aus meinem Leben* (Berlin, 1865), vol. II, pp. 231–3.

4 The friendship ruptured permanently in 1839. See Therese Marx, *Adolf Bernhard Marx' Verhältniß zu Felix Mendelssohn-Bartholdy in Bezug auf Eduard Devrient's Darstellung* (Leipzig, 1869), p. 22.

private circle.[5] The letters to and from members of the family contain the constant references and greetings to him that are accorded only the most intimate members of their group. Marx's identity within that group as the great critic and expounder of Beethoven was often referred to with good-humored irony. Fanny, for example, responding to Felix's negative impressions of the salon scene in Paris, writes to her brother:

> This much seems clear: your talent for fickleness develops brilliantly in Paris. My boy, your letters consist of nothing but criticism – Marx will be happy with you.[6]

By all accounts, Mendelssohn was thoroughly taken with Marx's ideas. Fourteen years Mendelssohn's senior, Marx was a brilliant conversationalist whose ideas about music were bold and idealistic. He spoke with moral urgency about the development of music and of the composer's duty to further that great tradition begun by Haydn, Mozart, and Beethoven, a tradition, which – in his view, and in the view of many composers of his generation – stood enfeebled by triviality and threatened by philistinism. This fervent appeal inspired Mendelssohn, who, especially during these early years, deplored the fashionable composers' neglect and the audiences' ignorance of Bach and Beethoven, and tended to moral outrage at the superficiality of current musical tastes.[7]

When, in 1826, Mendelssohn composed his Overture to *A Midsummer Night's Dream* he was completely under Marx's sway. According to Marx's memoirs as well as those of his principal detractor, Eduard Devrient, Marx's influence on the ultimate shape of the work was decisive. Mendelssohn had written only the exposition of the overture when Marx recommended a radical rethinking of the work. According to his own memoirs, Marx found that:

> The introductory chords and the dance of the elves were just as we know them. Then, alas, there followed the overture proper – a merry, delightfully vivacious, altogether pleasant and lovely piece – but I was unable to associate it with *A Midsummer Night's Dream*. As a faithful friend, I felt in duty bound to tell the

---

5 Mendelssohn's father may have had misgivings about Marx, considering him the sort who could only criticize and not himself produce anything. See Eduard Devrient, *My Recollections of Felix Mendelssohn Bartholdy and His Letters to Me*, trans. Natalia Macfarren (orig. 1869; rep. New York, 1972); see also Eric Werner, *Mendelssohn: a New Image of the Composer and His Age*, trans. Dika Newlin (New York, 1963; rep. 1978), p. 73. Marx's widow later disputed this, stating that the elder Mendelssohn often thanked Marx for the influence he had exerted over Mendelssohn. Therese Marx, *Adolf Bernhard Marx' Verhältniß*, p. 18.

6 Fanny to Felix, Berlin, 25 April 1825; see *The Letters of Fanny Hensel to Felix Mendelssohn*, ed. and trans. Marcia Citron (New York, 1987), p. 12.

7 See for example his letters from Paris in 1825 and Vienna in 1830.

composer frankly what I thought. He was concerned, provoked, even hurt, and ran away without saying good-bye. I had to put up with it as best I could and avoided his house for a few days; the more so since his mother and Fanny had received me, immediately after our clash, cooly, almost with enmity. . . .[8]

A few days later, when Mendelssohn asked for help in rewriting the overture, Marx recalls:

I did not fail him; [on the contrary, I] hurried to his assistance and pointed out that such an overture must reflect faithfully and completely the drama of which it was to be the prologue. Enthusiastically and with absolute devotion he took up the work again. Only the allusion to the lovers' wanderings in the first motif (E, D♯, D, C♯) could be salvaged from the original version; everything else had to be rewritten . . . "'Tis too mad, too absurd," he shouted when I insisted on his saving a place for the jesters and even for Bottom's ardent braying. But he followed my advice, and the overture took the form we know now. Mother and sister were conciliated by the composer's creative enthusiasm. The father even declared at the first performance in his house that the overture was in fact rather my work than Felix's! There is, of course, no foundation for such a statement. . . . The original idea and execution belonged to Felix; counsel alone was my duty and my part.[9]

That Marx recounts Herr Mendelssohn's remark – even with protestation – reveals a certain reluctance to deny his paternity of the work. Marx was a genius, though a frustrated one, and a talented but uninspired composer. Here he had found a young composer who could translate his ideas into music. His success in influencing Mendelssohn during these years, and the vicarious fulfillment that this success produced, go a long way to explaining their later acrimony and falling-out.

Eduard Devrient, court singer and close friend of Mendelssohn who during these years struggled with Marx unsuccessfully for influence over Mendelssohn, confirmed Marx's story later when he recalled, not without some lingering resentment: "Marx had an influence over Felix which no one ever again had. There is no doubt Marx had a share in the astonishing impetus to Felix's development seen in the *Midsummer Night's Dream*, and he rightly boasts of having overturned the first sketch of his piece and having advocated a more thoroughly characteristic treament; in this he propagandized for his system."[10]

8 A. B. Marx, *Erinnerungen*, vol. II, p. 231; translation from Eric Werner, *Mendelssohn: a New Image*, pp. 87–8. The early draft of the overture is discussed further in R. Larry Todd, "The Instrumental Music of Felix Mendelssohn-Bartholdy: Selected Studies Based on Primary Sources" (diss., Yale Univ., 1979), pp. 417–27.

9 A. B. Marx, *Erinnerungen*, vol. II, pp. 232–3.

10 Devrient, *Recollections*, p. 35 (translation emended slightly); see *Meine Erinnerungen an Felix Mendelssohn-Bartholdy und seine Briefe an mich* (Leipzig, 1869), pp. 38–9.

Devrient's pointed reference to Marx's "system" indicates a link between Mendelssohn's work and Marx's contemporaneous work as a systematic music theorist. Known today primarily for his explication of musical form, in his early years as a professional music theorist and journalist, Marx concentrated his efforts on the explication of music's content, creating a highly developed theory of programmatic music.

In 1824, as he approached the age of thirty, Marx abandoned his legal career to found and edit a new musical journal, Berlin's own *Allgemeine musikalische Zeitung*, intended as a rejoinder to the journal of the same name published in Leipzig. His efforts won him a doctorate from the University of Marburg in 1828, and, by some accounts on Mendelssohn's recommendation, a professorship at the University of Berlin in 1830.[11]

In his work as journalist and scholar, Marx aimed primarily to convince the public of Beethoven's greatness; he would not tolerate the attitude that Beethoven's later works were somehow less understandable than his earlier works or than those of Mozart and Haydn. Marx intended not only to make Beethoven understandable to all who listened, but also to influence the current generation of composers to follow Beethoven's path. This devotion to Beethoven, of course, struck a sympathetic chord in Mendelssohn. But Marx also had a theory about "characteristic" music, one which he believed held the key to understanding Beethoven's works. The championing of this theory, along with the championing of Beethoven, were the twin goals of his journal.

Between 1824 and 1826, Marx produced a stream of articles and reviews expounding characteristic music. All music since Mozart's symphonies, he claimed, had at its core an extra-musical idea, a *Grundidee* (or *Grundgedanke*) which – though not completely expressible in words – is quite specific, and which serves as the program of the work. In his feature article on "The Symphony and Beethoven's Contribution to this Genre," Marx proposed that, with Beethoven, the symphony had reached a stage of development where the *Grundidee* of a work was no longer a feeling or several feelings, but rather "a series of psychological states represented with great psychological accuracy."[12] The towering example of this, Beethoven's Fifth Symphony, depicted, according to Marx, "the struggle of a powerful being against an almost overpowering fate."[13] Marx notes the "unyielding battle" of the

11 Eric Werner points out that all accounts of Mendelssohn's intervention on Marx's behalf stem from Devrient's memoirs. There appears to be no corroboration. Werner, *Mendelssohn: a New Image*, p. 160.

12 Marx, "Etwas über die Symphonie und Beethovens Leistungen in diesem Fache," *BAmZ* 1/20 (19 May 1824), 174: "eine Folge von Seelenzuständen mit tiefer psychologischer Wahrheit darlegend."

13 *Ibid.*: "Es ist das Ringen eines kräftigen Wesens gegen ein fast übermächtiges Geschick..."

opening measures, and the "painful lament of a deeply wounded though not weakened spirit" of the second theme.[14] After considering each movement, he reaches the end of the finale, in which "every note celebrates the most magnificent victory of the spirit."[15]

Beethoven's other contributions were two-fold: to capture the stimulus of the external world – as in the "Pastoral" Symphony and *Wellington's Victory* – and to become more and more sensitive to the individual character, meaning, and abilities of the different orchestral instruments until "they came before him as fully delineated personalities."[16] In the "Eroica" Symphony all three contributions come together: "psychological development, combined with a series of external states, represented through the thoroughly dramatic activity of the orchestra-creating instruments."[17] Though Marx conceded that an inscription on a piece of music was essential to prepare the listener for the content,[18] in the "Eroica," Marx believed it was "not necessary to see the title in order to know that a hero is celebrated here."[19] After guiding the reader through the first movement's broad narrative outlines, Marx proclaimed: "the entire movement reveals to us the splendid picture of a hero's life – as well as the painful lament of much loss."[20]

Marx's assessment of Beethoven's explicitly programmatic works is intriguing, not least of all because Marx was one of the many musicians of this period who found Beethoven's *Wellington's Victory*, the occasional work also known under the name "Battle" Symphony, a great work. The contribution of this symphony, according to Marx, was to render in tone the external world around him – other people, nature, and most important *events*. Marx finds especially praiseworthy the narrative power of its musical allegory. Noting that Beethoven had used a characteristic theme to represent each of the

14 *Ibid.*: "Harter Kampf in den abgerissenen Schlägen des ersten Allegro ... schmerzvolle Klage eines tief verwundeten und doch nicht geschwächten Gemüthes in dem Seitensatze dazu. ..."

15 *Ibid.*: "Und nun endlich der erhabenste Hymnus [the opening measures of the last movement] der ... in jeder Note den herrlichsten Sieg des Geistes feiert."

16 *Ibid.*, 175: "Sie traten in voller fest gezeichneten Persönlichkeit vor ihn und das Orchester wurde ihm ein belebter, in dramatischer Thätigkeit begriffener Chor."

17 *Ibid.*, 174: "Nun alles sich vereinigte – psychologische Entwicklung, geknüpft an eine Folge äusserer Zustände, dargestellt in einer durchaus dramatischen Thätigkeit der das Orchester bildenden Instrumente."

18 See for example his extended discussion of the necessity of characteristic titles in *Ludwig van Beethoven*, pp. 257–8, stating that the title is important as the first clue (*Fingerzeig*) to the content of the artwork. But real content must follow, he insists. When it does, as for instance in the "Pastoral" and the "Eroica," it is then not possible, Marx says, to exchange titles.

19 *Ibid.*, p. 175: "Es bedarf nicht erst der Bemerkung auf dem Titel, um zu wissen, dass hier ein Held gefeiert wird."

20 *Ibid.*: "Dieser ganze Satz zeigt uns das gelungene Bild eines Heldenlebens – auch die schmerzliche Klage um manchen Verlust."

combatants, "Rule Britannia" for the English, and "Malbrouck s'en va-t-en guerre" for the French, Marx exclaims that "no one could doubt which nations had faced off against each other."[21]

This distinction was crucial for Marx because he deeply believed that the entire chronicle of the squaring off of the French and British armies and the defeat of the French was expressed *in the music*. One required no more than a characteristic title to set all these connections in motion. "After the battle has been waged," Marx continues:

> when the French march returns in the foreign key of F sharp minor (having appeared first in the bright key of C major), and returns *piano*, moving haltingly, as it were disorderly, and interrupted by the feverish tremolo of the strings, and by the empty, exhausted lamenting E in the horns, then no one can doubt the outcome of the battle.[22]

II THE "REFORMATION" SYMPHONY: A PROGRAMMATIC NARRATIVE

The idea that the symphonic genre could be put to use to tell a story – the narrative of a historical event – was explored in Mendelssohn's "Reformation" Symphony, a work, at the time he wrote it, completely unlike his only other full-scale symphony, that in C minor (op. 11), from 1824. In this new work Mendelssohn would try his hand at the kind of Marxian programmatic music that embodied a narrative – specifically, a narrative that could be fully understood without any verbal suggestions other than the title.

Just as Beethoven's work has musical tags for the English and French, "battle-like" music that surges and subsides, and the French theme emerging ripped and torn, so does Mendelssohn's "Reformation" Symphony use specific narrative devices. At the very opening is the imitative four-voice polyphony, reminiscent of the music of the so-called "Palestrina school," that musicians of Mendelssohn's time commonly associated with Catholicism.[23] At

21 *Ibid.*: "Die stehenden Volksgesänge z.B. in Beethovens Schlacht ... lassen niemandem Zweifel übrig, welche Nationen hier einander gegenüber stehen."

22 *Ibid.*: "Und wenn nach geschlagener Schlacht der französische Marsch Malborough u.s.w. in dem ganz fremden Fis-moll (vorher hatte er das helle, frische C-dur) wiederkehrt, piano, mit stockender Bewegung, gleichsam in Unordnung gebracht, unterbrochen von dem fieberhaften tremolo der Saiteninstrumente, von dem hohlen, ganz erschöpft klagenden E des Hornes – so kann niemand über den Ausgang der Schlacht ungewiss bleiben."

23 See for example A. F. J. Thibaut, *Über Reinheit der Tonkunst* (Heidelberg, 1824); expanded in 1826 and translated by W. H. Gladstone as *On Purity of Musical Art* (London, 1877), p. 24. In urging the adoption by Protestants of the music of Palestrina, Lotti, and others, Thibaut wrote: "No doubt such an adoption of old Catholic music might be an offense to some of our straitlaced church wardens. But if we gave in to them, our intercourse with the muses would be limited

the end is the chorale "Ein' feste Burg ist unser Gott," most clearly associated with Luther and Lutheranism. The first movement, in D minor, with its agitated string writing, martial fanfares and battle cries, presents, in the words of one nineteenth-century reviewer, "a portrayal of struggling and grappling."[24] Another called it a "powerful spiritual battle."[25] The last movement, in D major, with its *quasi* "victory march" second theme, ends with the chorale in triumphant jubilation.[26]

Accepting the broad outline of a narrative suggested by the title, and interpreting the details provided by the music, one may say that the work depicts, in order, the Catholic Church, a struggle, and then the victorious emergence of the Protestants. The inner movements do not unequivocally contribute to the narrative. Yet the parts of the symphony that *do* narrate, do exactly what Marx had so appreciated in Beethoven's work: they present an unmistakable historical event – in this case, the Protestant Reformation – without the use of words.[27]

III   *MEERESSTILLE UND GLÜCKLICHE FAHRT (CALM SEA AND PROSPEROUS VOYAGE)*: THE WORDLESS UNION OF TEXT AND MUSIC

As part of his proselytizing efforts, Marx wrote extensively to prepare his readers for the first Berlin performances of Beethoven's Ninth Symphony in 1826. For Marx, as for many of his contemporaries, this symphony represented the ultimate union of instrumental music and speech. Yet within two years, Beethoven's work had been replaced, in Marx's mind, by Mendelssohn's *Calm Sea and Prosperous Voyage* Overture. Mendelssohn was very much involved in the early performances of Beethoven's Ninth; in fact, the first

indeed; and, at this rate, all the old masterpieces of Gothic architecture and painting must fall under the Protestant ban, as being the productions of Catholic coreligionists."

24 H. Eiters, Review, *Leipziger Allgemeine musikalische Zeitung* 3/44 (28 October 1868), 350: "Der doppelte Charakter einer angestrengten Kraft und unbefriedigter Unruhe, der in dem Thema liegt, bestimmt den ganzen ersten Satz, [der] mit dem Bilde des Kämpfens und Ringens bezeichnet werden kann."

25 *Neue Zeitschrift für Musik* 64/46 (6 Nov 1868), 394: "Nach dem bedeutenden ersten Satze, der uns gewaltige Geisteskämpfe vorführt, folgt. . . ."

26 *Ibid.*: "Der Kampf aber spinnt sich weiter bis zum triumphierenden Siegesjubel am Schlusse."

27 For further discussion of the programmatic aspects of this work see the author's "Mendelssohn and the *Reformation* Symphony: a Critical and Historical Study" (diss., Yale Univ., 1987), pp. 99–125, 148–204.

Berlin performance appears to have been a public rendition with piano and voices, for which Mendelssohn played the orchestral part from full score.[28]

In a review spanning several months, Marx introduced the symphony to his readers.[29] After directing the reader through the first three movements, Marx pauses to summarize, as if in imitation of Beethoven's form: "Each of its movements," he writes:

> brought considerable satisfaction; each demanded, however, even more. A person can give his whole soul over to nature, and nevertheless will ultimately be pierced with a longing for human beings. At this point [the end of the third movement], the mass of instruments is fully under control, each is penetrated by its own life, each reiterates what the artist discovered in his deepest soul: and now, through their sounding together, he powerfully breaks out into human expression, and upward into song.[30]

In February 1827 the Ninth Symphony had an important première in Stettin under the baton of Carl Loewe. Mendelssohn's *Midsummer Night's Dream* received its public première on the same program.[31] While in Stettin Mendelssohn was excited by the enthusiasm Beethoven's symphony had generated. He found, too, that Marx's style of programmatic interpretation had been well received – though perhaps not in a way that Marx would have welcomed. In an unpublished letter that reveals awareness of and perhaps also anxiety about the open-endedness of "programmatic interpretations," Mendelssohn writes:

> All of Stettin is topsy turvy about the Beethoven symphony. O Marx! Marx! What a disaster he has created. Here they find his view of the symphony entirely wrong. So, for example, city councillor Schafer says "It is every gradation of joy. The first movement is the joy of men and youths – " "And the spirits of hell," interrupts Treasurer Mayer. "No," Koelpin says, "the scherzo is the spirits of hell." "Wrong," says Registrar Gebhard, "the scherzo is childish joy. When the drum plays, that's the boy turning a somersault, and not until the

28 Wulf Konold, *Felix Mendelssohn Bartholdy und seine Zeit* (Regensburg, 1984), pp. 20–21 (citing a notice that appeared the following day in the *Vossische Zeitung*, 13 November 1826, which stated in part, "Herr Felix Mendelssohn Bartholdy trug die Sinfonie am Pianoforte vor").

29 Marx, "Recension: Symphonie mit Schlusschor über Schillers Ode an die Freude," *BAmZ* 3/47 (22 Nov 1826), 373; 4/11 (14 March 1827), 83; 4/16 (18 April 1827), 124.

30 Marx, *BAmZ* 3/47 (22 Nov 1826), 376: "Jeder ihrer Sätze brachte hohe Befriedigung, bedingte aber noch höhere. Der Mensch kann seine ganze Seele auf die ihn umgebende Natur übertragen, sie sich gleichsam menschlich beseelen – und dennoch dringt zuletzt das Verlangen nach dem Menschen unabweislich auf ihn ein. Die Instrumentenmasse ist beherrscht, Jedes mit seinem eigenen Leben durchdrungen, Jedes tönt wieder, was der Künstler in innerster Seele empfunden; und nun reisst er sich gewaltsam durch ihren Zusammenklang zu Menschenaus-druck, zum Gesang empor."

31 Mendelssohn, who played first violin in the Beethoven, also performed a two-piano concerto with Loewe. See the review of the concert, *BAmZ* 4/11 (14 March 1827), 83.

trio does he learn to walk." "In the last vocal movement is an immense lamenta-
tion!" says the blond government councillor Werth. "No, jubilation." "No,
bravado."
If father were here ... – I shudder at the thought.[32]

If this letter betrays some anxiety or even skepticism about Marx's enterprise, Mendelssohn none the less remained a close friend and ardent supporter.
Marx's views had already won him many detractors; yet, as we learn in a letter
from London in 1829, Mendelssohn was clearly not among them:

> I can hardly wait for the time when he [Marx] will come out with his big works
> and put to shame all the dogs and cats who are barking and miaowing at him
> now. For it is infuriating the way the rabble line up against the single musician
> they have among them, and the more certain and settled my belief in his
> musicianship, the more I wish that everyone recognized it.[33]

Mendelssohn's overture *Calm Sea and Prosperous Voyage* appeared in 1828,
only a few years after Beethoven's cantata setting for chorus and orchestra of
the same pair of Goethe poems. That Mendelssohn would so directly challenge a setting by Beethoven with one of his own suggests an uncharacter-
istically critical attitude toward Beethoven's work. What is more, such an
attitude coincides with Marx's own. Marx's 1824 review of Beethoven's
version is one of the rare occasions that Marx not only criticizes a work by
Beethoven, but criticizes extensively Beethoven's fundamental compositional
decisions.[34]

Marx praised the way Beethoven had captured the *Grundidee* of the first
poem – the horrifying stillness of a motionless sea. Yet he found the choice of
genre and medium ultimately fatal. In particular, the human presence of a
chorus was for him a drawback in expressing the poem. "Anyone who truly
experiences the poem," Marx says, "can do so only in utter isolation.

32 Unpublished letter, Mendelssohn to his family, Stettin, 19 February 1827 (New York
Public Library): "Ganz Stettin geht auf dem Kopfe über die Beethovensche Symphonie. O
Marx! Marx! Welch Unglück richtet der an ... Hier findet man seine Ansicht von der
Symphonie ganz falsch. So sagt z.B. Stadtrath Schafer 'Es ist die Freude durch all[e] Grada-
zionen. Im ersten Satze freuen sich Männer u. Jünglinge –' 'und Höllengeister' fällt Rendant
Mayer ihm in das Wort. 'Nein' sagt Kölpin 'das Scherzo sind die Höllengeister.' 'Gefehlt,' sagt
Registrator Gebhard, 'das Scherzo ist kindische Freude. Wenn die Pauke kommt so schlägt der
Knabe einen Purzelbaum, u. im Trio lernt er erst gehen.' 'Im letzten Gesangstück ist doch ein
unendlicher Jammer!' sagt der blonde Reg. Rath Werth. 'Nein Jubel.' 'Nein Übermuth.' Wenn
Vater hier wäre, mich graut vor dem Gedanken."
33 Letter, Mendelssohn to Droysen, London, 3 November 1829, in *Ein tief gegründet Herz:
Der Briefwechsel Felix Mendelssohn-Bartholdys mit Johann Gustav Droysen*, ed. Carl Wehmer
(Heidelberg, 1959), p. 30.
34 Marx, "Recension: Meeresstille und glückliche Fahrt, Gedichte von J. W. von Göthe. In
Musik gesetzt ... von Ludwig van Beethoven. 112tes Werk," *BAmZ* 1/46 (17 Nov 1824), 391–6.

Beethoven has us facing a chorus – and the poem falls apart."[35] Marx may mean that the human voice itself has too human a presence. But more likely, his criticism is linked to the stagecraft of concert performances, which requires one literally to look at eighty or more faces while trying to imagine total aloneness. Thus it is not so much a musical criticism as a dramatic criticism, one that might not matter in the disembodied world of recorded sound.

For Marx, Beethoven's setting is unsatisfactory in other ways as well. Yet he avoids tying too much blame to his favorite composer by noting that the static quality of the poem may be inherently unsettable in music. For example, he finds a weakness in Beethoven's having a recapitulation of the music and text of the opening, after he has already offered his spine-tingling setting of the word "Weite," from the line "in der ungeheuern Weite," which, for Marx, captures the very soul of the poem. Marx writes:

> After this horrifying outcry can the poet's idea really allow for the return of the
> portrayal of stillness, the complete reprise that we find in Beethoven? For the
> sake of musical roundedness it was perhaps desirable, but all the more does it
> expose this poem's intrinsic incompatibility with music.[36]

Four years after Marx's review, Mendelssohn began setting the poems himself, avoiding Beethoven's fatal flaw by omitting human voices. Whether or not Marx suggested the idea, and whether or not Mendelssohn saw himself as correcting the conceptual errors of Beethoven's setting are open and suggestive questions. What is clear is that since writing his critique of Beethoven's setting Marx had come to know Felix Mendelssohn, and had seen, in the *Midsummer Night's Dream*, what the young composer could do with his musical suggestions. In 1828, Marx now believed he had found the person who could set this unsettable poetry to music.

In May 1828, well before Mendelssohn had completed his *Calm Sea*, Marx published his most extensive treatment of the subject of programmatic music. In a historical and polemical monograph entitled *Ueber Malerei in der Tonkunst* Marx addressed himself to the controversy in philosophical circles over whether music could and ought to represent things outside music.[37] Marx

35 *Ibid.*, 395: "Jeder, der das Gedicht empfinden will, kann es nur in diesem Alleinsein. Bei Beethoven steht uns ein Chor von Menschen gegenüber – und das Gedicht ist in sich selbst zerfallen."

36 *Ibid.*, 396: "Und kann die Idee des Dichters nach jenem furchtbaren Aufschrei eine Rückkehr der ruhigen Beschreibung, eine vollständige Reprise wie wir [sie] in Beethoven finden, zulassen? Für die musikalische Abrundung war sie vielleicht wünschenswerth, aber um so mehr erhellt [sie] die Unverträglichkeit dieses Gedichtes mit Musik."

37 The controversy spawned contributions from Wendt, Urban, and Gottfried Weber among musicians; Friedrich Schlegel, Trahndorf, K. F. Krause, and F. K. Griepenkerl, among writers on aesthetics in general. See Walter Serauky, *Die musikalische Nachahmungsästhetik im*

believed that the question itself was invalid; after all, every great composer (among whom Marx included Mendelssohn, Bach, Handel, Mozart, Gluck, and Beethoven) was known to have represented extramusical content in music, and furthermore, to have done so in works that are among their most significant.[38] Marx thus could imagine only two alternatives:

> Either all of the most important composers in their best periods, in their most superb works of the most staggering spiritual intensity, have all in this one regard committed a terrible folly – or you [critics] still have not understood them in this one regard.[39]

In this broadly historical account, Marx claimed that instrumental music headed inexorably toward programmatic music. Programmatic music was the logical consequence of a process of "rehumanization," in which instrumental music "strives to embrace the word."[40] Instrumental music, Marx suggests, began by imitating vocal models, but soon became entirely taken over by instrumental "play." Then, in the hands of the masters, a process of rehumanizing instrumental music began. "Haydn poured into it the joys of the human breast, Mozart [gave it] its sensitivity."[41] Beethoven, as we have seen, made a spectacular return to the company of human voices in the last movement of the Ninth Symphony. While in 1824, at the time of his review of the work, the Ninth Symphony was for Marx the ultimate synthesis of instrumental music and word, in 1828 he believed that the idea of rehumanizing instrumental music could be taken yet one step further: by expressing ideas as profound as those of Schiller's Ode to Joy, *without resort to actual words*. Capping his lengthy discussion, Marx exclaims: "And one of [Beethoven's] followers, Felix Mendelssohn Bartholdy, has brought this idea to perfection, expressing *Calm Sea and Prosperous Voyage* without using Goethe's words."[42]

Marx published these comments in early May. A letter from Fanny dated 18 June shows that Mendelssohn's work was still not complete in mid-June:

Zeitraum von 1700 bis 1850 (Westfalen, 1929), pp. 302–6; and Leon Plantinga, *Schumann as Critic* (New Haven, 1967), pp. 114–29.

38 *Ueber Malerei in der Tonkunst, ein Maigruß an die Kunstphilosophen* (Berlin, 1828), p. 23.

39 *Ibid.*, p. 24: "entweder haben alle bedeutendsten Künstler in ihrer besten Periode, in ihren herrlichsten Werken, neben der bewundernswerthen Geistensfülle, alle in einem Punkte eine Thorheit begangen – oder du hast sie nur in einem Punkte noch nicht verstanden."

40 Robin Wallace, *Beethoven and His Critics* (Cambridge, 1987), p. 56.

41 Marx, *Ueber Malerei in der Tonkunst*, p. 59: "Haydn gießt die Freude der Menschenbrust, Mozart ihre Empfindseligkeit in sie."

42 *Ibid.*, pp. 59–60: "Beethoven verläßt die Menschengesellschaft, um in der Natur und mit ihr allein zu leben. ... Klingt aus seinem Instrumentenhymnus an die Freude schmerzliche Sehnsucht nach Menschengesellschaft heraus, die er in i[r]discher Allvergöttlichung verloren, so hat er in seinem Lied der Meereswogen dem Dichter noch nicht zu entsagen gewagt. Und einer seiner Schüler, Felix Mendelssohn Bartholdy, hat diese Idee vollendet, der Meeresstille und glückliche Fahrt ohne Göthe's Worte aussprach."

"Felix is writing a great instrumental piece, *Meeresstille und glückliche Fahrt*, after Goethe's poem. . . . He has tried to avoid an overture with introduction and has made the whole thing into two separate tableaux."[43] The timing suggests at the least that Marx was privy to the compositional unfolding of Mendelssohn's work. It would not be surprising for Marx to want to mention an as-yet-unrealized work which he hoped would embody his highest musical ideals. That the work was certainly not yet completed did not restrain him in his praise. Marx did not discuss Mendelssohn's piece in *any* detail, and it may be that the details were not yet worked out at this time. But even if in May 1828 Mendelssohn's achievement was still entirely in the future, it is noteworthy that in May Marx was sure that he had found a composer who would translate his ideas about music into musical sound. One might conclude that Mendelssohn wrote the overture with Marx's aspirations in mind.

Is it too strong a statement to say that at least three of Mendelssohn's works – the Overture to *A Midsummer Night's Dream*, "Reformation" Symphony, and *Calm Sea and Prosperous Voyage* Overture – are unthinkable without Marx? Contemporaries who saw Marx's influence as deleterious did not hesitate to say so. To Ludwig Rellstab, who attended the première of the "Reformation" Symphony in 1832, the symphony's first movement bespoke a Marxian influence that he could scarcely abide:

> We do not intend this as a reproof of the composer, since it can never be the aim of music to represent sensuously an event that belongs almost exclusively to the world of pure thought. To music is opened only the world of the feelings, and in this world music does without, and should do without, any more explicit or precise designations. . . . Never has an endeavor seemed more wrong-headed than that which the *Musikalische Zeitung* of Herr Marx espoused: that is, to trace a specific course of *intelligible* thoughts in every piece of music, thereby reading things into a piece and out of a piece that are entirely foreign to it. We simply think that Herr Mendelssohn has let himself be too strongly influenced by this notion.[44]

---

43 Fanny Mendelssohn Bartholdy to Karl Klingemann, 18 June 1828, in Sebastian Hensel, *The Mendelssohn Family (1729–1847) from Letters and Journals*, 2nd edn. (New York, 1882), p. 161; translation emended slightly, based on *Die Familie Mendelssohn, 1729–1847. Nach Briefen und Tagebüchern*, 2nd edn. (Berlin, 1880).

44 Ludwig Rellstab, *Iris im Gebiete der Tonkunst*, 3/47 (23 Nov 1832), 187–88: "Wir wollen dies dem Komponisten nicht zum Vorwurf machen, denn es kann niemals die Aufgabe der Musik seyn, eine Begebenheit die der reinen Welt des Gedankens fast allein angehört, auf sinnliche Weise darzustellen. Ihr ist nur die Welt der Gefühle geöffnet, und in dieser wieder entbehrt sie und soll sie aller bestimmteren, näheren Bezeichnungen entbehren. . . . Niemals ist uns ein Bestreben verkehrter erschienen, als das welches die musikalische Zeitung des Herrn Marx hatte, in jedem Musikstück einen bestimmten Gang *verständiger* Gedanken nachweisen zu

We have noted, as Rellstab correctly surmised, that Mendelssohn began his very intense involvement with programmatic music under the influence of Marx's ideas. Between 1826 and 1830, the period of their closest friendship, Mendelssohn not only composed the three works already discussed, but conceived the *Hebrides* Overture and the "Scottish" Symphony as well; his "Italian" Symphony was not far in the future. The question of influence is always difficult, and is no less so here where close friendship ended in bitterest animosity. In 1833 their friendship began to wane, in part because Mendelssohn, appalled at Marx's mediocre compositional efforts, could find no tactful way except avoidance to keep from expressing his critical judgments.[45] Marx not only eagerly sought Mendelssohn's criticism, but hoped as well that Mendelssohn would promote his works. When, in 1839, Marx asked Mendelssohn outright to perform his oratorio, *Moses*, and Mendelssohn refused, the breach was complete. In an act of catharsis, Marx threw the bundle of letters he had received from Mendelssohn into the river, robbing future historians of vital documents which would undoubtedly have illuminated the relationship and Marx's influence.[46]

We shall never know as much as we might about Marx's influence on Mendelssohn, nor about Mendelssohn's on Marx. Perhaps this is how the principals would have wanted it. If intense influence is a difficult topic for the historian, it is infinitely more difficult still for the persons directly engaged in it. One is reminded of the words of Oscar Wilde: "But to influence a person is to give him one's own soul. . . . he becomes an echo of someone else's music, an actor of a part not written for him."[47] If their acrimonious falling-out saved Mendelssohn and Marx from so extreme a fate, perhaps we should be grateful. But let us not overlook the fact that their relationship and mutual influence provided the context from which emerged a legacy rich in masterpieces; and for this, too, we are grateful.

wollen, und so immer etwas Fremdes hinein oder heraus zu lesen. Allein, wir glauben daß Herr Mendelssohn sich zu stark durch diese Ansicht habe influiren lassen. . . ."

45 See Mendelssohn to Schubring (15 July 1834): "And his compositions, some of which he has now published, displeased me, to my distress, so greatly that I have lost confidence in his talent." In *Felix Mendelssohn: a Life in Letters*, ed. Rudolf Elvers, trans. Craig Tomlinson (New York, 1986), p. 199.

46 According to Marx's widow, Marx explained his act as preventing him from, in a weak moment, indulging in a sentimental desire to publish the correspondence. Therese Marx, *Adolf Bernhard Marx' Verhältniß*, pp. 23–4.

47 Oscar Wilde, *The Picture of Dorian Gray* (London, 1890).

8 *Me voilà perruqué*: Mendelssohn's Six Preludes and Fugues op. 35 reconsidered

R. LARRY TODD

You also write me that I should set myself up as an evangelist and instruct Onslow and Reicha ... how to love Sebastian Bach. I'm already doing that, as far as it goes. But just think, dear child, that the people here take Sebastian Bach to be a powdered wig properly stuffed with learning [*eine recht mit Gelehrsamkeit ausgestopfte Perücke*]![1]

Today I have sent my six preludes and fugues off to the press. They will be little played, I fear; nevertheless I would be pleased if you would look them through, if something in them pleased you, and if you would tell me that and also whatever does not. Also the organ fugues should be printed next month, *me voilà peruque* [*sic*].[2]

The monument for old Sebastian Bach is wonderfully pretty.... The several pillars, little columns, and scrollwork, especially the *bas* reliefs and the old, splendid wig-adorned countenance [*Perückengesicht*] shone freely in the sunlight, and gave me great joy. With its many decorative ornaments the whole really brought to mind the old Sebastian.[3]

---

1 "Du schreibst mir auch, ich soll mich zum Bekehrer aufwerfen und Onslow und Reicha ... Sebastian Bach lieben lehren. Das tu' ich schon ohne das, so weit es geht. Aber bedenke, liebes Kind, daß die Leute hier ... Sebastian Bach für eine recht mit Gelehrsamkeit ausgestopfte Perücke halten!" Letter from Mendelssohn to his family in Berlin (Paris, 20 April 1825), after the original in the New York Public Library. Portions of the letter were unreliably transcribed in *Die Familie Mendelssohn 1729 bis 1847: nach Briefe und Tagebüchern*, ed. Sebastian Hensel (Berlin, 1879; 15th edn., 1911), vol. I, p. 174.

2 "Ich habe heute meine sechs Präludien und Fugen in die Druckerei geschickt, sie werden wenig gespielt werden, fürchte ich, dennoch möchte ich gern, Du sähest sie Dir seiner Zeit mal durch und es gefiele Dir etwas darin und Du sagtest es mir sammt dem vorkommenden Gegentheil. Auch die Orgelfugen sollen nächsten Monat gedruckt werden, *me voilà peruque*." Letter from Mendelssohn to Ferdinand Hiller (Leipzig, 10 January 1837), in Ferdinand Hiller, *Felix Mendelssohn Bartholdy: Briefe und Erinnerungen* (Cologne, 1874), p. 71.

3 "Das Denkmal für den alten Sebastian Bach ist wunderhübsch geworden.... die vielen Säulen und Säulchen und Schnörkel, vor allem die Basreliefs und das alte prächtige Perückengesicht prangten frei im Sonnenschein, und machten mir große Freude. Das Ganze mit seinen vielen zierlichen Verzierungen erinnert wirklich an den alten Sebastian." Letter from Mendelssohn to his mother, Lea (Leipzig, 11 December 1842), in Felix Mendelssohn, *Briefe aus den Jahren 1833 bis 1847*, ed. P. and C. Mendelssohn Bartholdy (Leipzig, 1875), pp. 365–7.

The image of the wig-adorned contrapuntist professing dry, fugal erudition evidently challenged, if not haunted, Mendelssohn throughout his career, as the three passages gathered above from three decades of his correspondence suggest. The first dates from Mendelssohn's Parisian sojourn of 1825. When the sixteen-year-old performed two Bach preludes for Frédéric Kalkbrenner, an unidentified member of the audience claimed to detect a conspicuous resemblance with a duet from an opera of Pierre-Alexandre Monsigny, and this maladroitness elicited Mendelssohn's exasperated response, "everything before my eyes turned green and blue."[4] One can well imagine young Mendelssohn's bewilderment at the Bach–Monsigny comparison, for by 1825 Mendelssohn was an accomplished contrapuntist in his own right, and much of his skill in part writing was due surely to his emulation of Bach's music, not to ostensible French models. Indeed, by 1827 Mendelssohn had published his first academic fugue in the Bachian manner as the fifth piece of the *Sieben Charakterstücke* op. 7. This sturdy exercise in A major impressed as a rather arduous effort teeming with learned techniques, a feature not lost on one anonymous reviewer, who described it, somewhat uncharitably, in the pages of the *Berliner allgemeine musikalische Zeitung* as the work of an overly zealous pupil who wished "to display publicly how diligently he has studied, how he has mastered his material through counterpoint."[5]

In the following decade Mendelssohn incorporated fugues into several compositions. The fugato in the slow movement of the String Quartet op. 13 (1827, published 1830), the fugue in the cantata *Aus tiefer Noth* op. 23 no. 1 (1830, published 1832), the chorale fugue in the overture to *St. Paul* (premièred in Düsseldorf on 22 May 1836), and the fusion of fugal and sonata principles in the finales of the Octet op. 20 (1825, published in parts in 1833) and the String Quintet in A major op. 18 (1826, published in 1833) are five noteworthy examples. Then, in 1836 and 1837, Mendelssohn turned his attention to the fugue in a more systematic fashion, focussing his efforts on two collections of preludes and fugues, one for piano (Six Preludes and Fugues op. 35), and one for organ (Three Preludes and Fugues op. 37). Sending the recently completed piano collection to Ferdinand Hiller in January 1837, he

---

4 "Mir wurde grün und blau vor den Augen." Letter of 20 April 1825, New York Public Library, in Hensel, *Die Familie Mendelssohn*, vol. I, p. 175.

5 "No. 5 gives us a so-called master fugue, inversion of the subject, augmentation, diminution, stretto – in short, it seems as if the composer wishes to display publicly how diligently he has studied, how he has mastered his material through counterpoint." ("No. 5 giebt uns eine sogenannte Meisterfuge, Umkehrung des Thema, Vergrösserung, Verkleinerung, Engführung, kurz, es scheint, als habe der Componist hiermit öffentlich belegen wollen, wie fleißig er studirt habe, wie er den Stoff durch seinen Contrapunct beherrsche.") *Allgemeine musikalische Zeitung* 30 (1828), 63.

predicted that it would have a poor reception, and in our second extract again alluded to the metaphor of obsolete erudition: *me voilà perruqué*.

Another intense period of fugal composition followed in 1844 and 1845, when Mendelssohn undertook to assemble and compose what became the Six Organ Sonatas op. 65, several of which included full-fledged fugues. The turn to organ music was no doubt spurred by Mendelssohn's continuing study of Bach, which took two new directions during the 1840s. First, in 1845 the English firm of Coventry began to release Mendelssohn's editions of Bach's organ works based on chorales. In reading proof for his edition Mendelssohn discovered that Coventry had mistakenly added at the foot of each page "Bach's Fugues," and on 17 December 1844 he objected in a letter to the publisher, almost as if to distance himself from that strict contrapuntal genre: "Why is Bach's name always connected with Fugues? He has had more to do with Psalm-Tunes than with Fugues, . . ."[6] Second, four years before, Mendelssohn had undertaken to raise funds for a new Bach monument to be placed near the Thomaskirche in Leipzig. The inaugural benefit concert, given by Mendelssohn on 6 August 1840 in the Thomaskirche, was devoted to Bach's organ works, including two fugues (BWV 543 and 552) and Mendelssohn's own fugal improvisation on the chorale "O Haupt voll Blut und Wunden," into which, according to Robert Schumann, he introduced Bach's name as a motif. The whole performance, Schumann declared, could be printed as a perfected work of art.[7] Two more Bach concerts followed on Palm Sunday 1841 and on 23 April 1843; the latter fell on the very day the statue was unveiled. Writing to his mother a few months before the ceremony, Mendelssohn described in our third extract the monument and its ornamental detail, all reminiscent of "old Sebastian," and invoked once again the image of the wig-clad Kapellmeister, now no symbol of obsolescent counterpoint, but of sunlit splendor. With the successful completion of the monument, Mendelssohn not only gave renewed impetus to the nineteenth-century Bach revival, but reaffirmed a crucial part of his own identity as a composer.

6 Letter in English from Mendelssohn to Charles Coventry (Frankfurt am Main, 17 December 1844), after the autograph in the Margaret Deneke Mendelssohn Collection at the Bodleian Library, Oxford, Shelfmark d. 55. The letter originally appeared in Elise Polko, *Reminiscences of Felix Mendelssohn-Bartholdy*, trans. Lady Wallace (London, 1869), p. 329. Concerning Mendelssohn's editions of Bach, see Rudolf Elvers, "Verzeichnis der von Felix Mendelssohn Bartholdy herausgegebenen Werke Johann Sebastian Bachs," *Gestalt und Glaube: Festschrift für Oskar Söhngen* (Witten, 1960), pp. 145–9.

7 *Neue Zeitschrift für Musik* 13 (1840), 56. An incomplete draft for an organ composition on "O Haupt voll Blut und Wunden," quite possibly based on Mendelssohn's improvisation, survives in the M. Deneke Mendelssohn Collection at the Bodleian Library, shelfmark b. 5., f. 130r. (For a transcription, see the edition of Mendelssohn's 1830 chorale cantata, *O Haupt voll Blut und Wunden*, ed. R. L. Todd [Madison, 1980], pp. 59–60.) A valuable study of Mendels-

To be sure, Mendelssohn was not alone during the 1830s and 1840s in seeking to renew his art through the intensive study of Bachian counterpoint. Chopin turned again and again to the *Well-Tempered Clavier* for inspiration, and if he eschewed the writing of academic fugues, signs of a certain contrapuntal quickening of his music are nevertheless detectable, for example in the late Nocturne in E major op. 62 no. 2, or the *Polonaise-Fantaisie* op. 61 (both published in 1846). Franz Liszt, settling in Weimar in 1848 to devote himself to serious composition, produced his two most substantial fugues for organ, the Fantasy and Fugue on the pseudo-chorale "Ad nos, ad salutarem undam" from Meyerbeer's *Le prophète* (1850) and the Prelude and Fugue on BACH (1855), during a period which also saw work on his own edition of Bach's organ music.[8] In Leipzig, Mendelssohn was joined by Robert and Clara Schumann, who undertook intensive self-administered courses in counterpoint, the fruits of which were later gathered into three fugal collections: Robert Schumann's Six Fugues on BACH for organ op. 60 (1845, published 1846) and the Four Fugues for pedal piano op. 72 (1845, published 1850), and Clara Schumann's Three Preludes and Fugues for piano op. 16 (1845, published 1846). Aware that for many the fugue was a "not very marketable commodity" ("ein wenig gangbarer Artikel"), Robert Schumann strove to produce not arid fugal forms ("trockene Formfugen") but expressive compositions which he termed "character pieces, but in the strict style" ("Charakterstücke nur in strenger Form").[9]

Now what separated Mendelssohn from these contemporaries was his special, and continuing, preoccupation with Bachian counterpoint. If he did not always, as Emanuel Bach had claimed of his father, shake fugal intricacies out of his sleeves, he rarely missed an opportunity to explore contrapuntal textures and combinations in his compositions. Perhaps the most compelling evidence is Mendelssohn's seemingly instinctive turn to counterpoint in unexpected contexts: the quasi-canonic passage in the *Lied ohne Worte* op. 30 no. 4, with its subtle reversal of the *dux* and *comes* (see Ex. 8.1), or the full-fledged canons in the *Reiterlied* for piano (1844) and the orchestral March op. 108 for the Nazarene painter Peter Cornelius (1841), or the combination of prime and inverted thematic forms in the *Capriccio* op. 5 for piano (1825), for example. Imitative, canonic, or fugal passages adorn his compositions, investing them with a characteristic richness and complexity of part writing, a

sohn's 1840 organ concert is in Matthias Pape, *Mendelssohns Leipziger Orgelkonzert 1840* (Wiesbaden, 1988).

8 See my "Liszt, Fantasy and Fugue for Organ on 'Ad nos, ad salutarem undam,'" *19th Century Music* 4 (1981), 250–61.

9 Letter of 19 November 1849 to the publisher André; cited in Siegmar Keil, *Untersuchungen zur Fugentechnik in Robert Schumanns Instrumentalschaffen* (Hamburg, 1973), pp. 65–6.

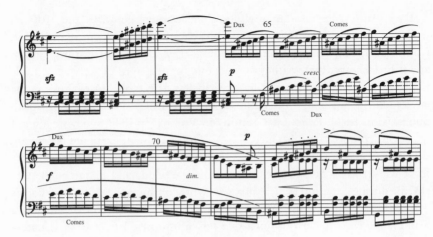

Ex. 8.1:   Mendelssohn, *Lied ohne Worte* op. 30 no. 4

quality which, as Mendelssohn confided to J. C. Lobe, could be attributed in part to his training under Carl Friedrich Zelter: "I love the finely crafted, worked-out voices and polyphonic composition, perhaps especially stimulated by my early contrapuntal studies with Zelter and by my study of Bach; purely homophonic writing pleases me less."[10]

The Six Preludes and Fugues op. 35 are one significant – but, in the Mendelssohn literature, relatively little considered – manifestation of this preference. In the present study, we shall endeavor to reconstruct the outlines of their evolution from independent fugues into a cyclical collection of preludes and fugues, and to consider in further detail the historical position and significance of the first, the Prelude and Fugue in E minor.

I

The historian endeavoring to chronicle Mendelssohn's compositional process is usually facilitated by an abundance of his meticulously dated manuscripts and by detailed references in his correspondence. In the case of op. 35, some special problems arise: not all the primary sources have survived; those that have are scattered in a variety of archives, where they appear in a variety of versions; and, finally, the compositional evolution of the opus spanned a

10 "Ich liebe die fein ausgearbeiteten Stimmen, den polyphonen Satz, wozu die kontrapunktischen Studien in früher Zeit bei Zelter und das Studium Bachs vorzüglich mitgewirkt haben mögen; die blos homophone Satzweise gefällt mir weniger." J. C. Lobe, "Gespräche mit Felix Mendelssohn," *Die Gartenlaube* 1/5 (1865), 290.

Table 8.1. *Mendelssohn, Six Preludes and Fugues op. 35: a Chronology*

Date	Manuscript	Letter, Review	Source
16 June 1827	Fugue, e (op. 35 no. 1)		Christies, 10 May 1977
21 December 1832	Fugue, b (op. 35 no. 3)		Berlin, DSB MN 23
30 July 1834	*Fughetta*, D (version of op. 35 no. 2 for organ)		DSB MN 29
3 December 1834	Fugue, f. (op. 35 no. 5)		DSB MN 28
	Fugue, A♭ (op. 35 no. 4, incomplete)		
6 January 1835	Fugue, A♭ (op. 35 no. 4)		DSB MN 28
11 January 1835	Fugue, D (op. 35 no. 2), arr. as organ duet for Thomas Attwood		Berlin, SPK MA Ms. 6
11 January 1835		Thomas Attwood *Etudes and Fugues*	Washington
10 April 1835		Breitkopf & Härtel *Etudes und Fugen*	Elvers, *Briefe*, 45
27 September 1835		Breitkopf & Härtel *Etudes & Fugues*	Elvers, *Briefe*, 47
30 December 1835	Fugue, f (op. 35 no. 5) for Clara Wieck		Dresden, Sächs. Landesbib. Ms. Mus. Schu. 193
8 April 1836		Carl Czerny to FMB, *Die Schule des Fugenspiels*	Oxford, Bodleian GB V, 63
c. June 1836?	Etude, e (early version of Prelude op. 35, no. 1)		Tokyo, Musashino Academia Musicae

Table 8.1. (Cont.)

Date	Manuscript	Letter, Review	Source
10 June 1836		Breitkopf & Härtel *Etuden und Fugen*	Elvers, *Briefe*, 50
2 July 1836		Simrock *Etuden und Fugen*	Elvers, *Briefe*, 205
7 October 1836	*Praeludium*, Ab (early version of Prelude op. 35 no. 4)		Oxford, Bodleian, M. Deneke Mendelssohn b. 1 (Horsley Papers)
12 October 1836	*Praeludium*, b (Prelude op. 104a no. 2)		Berlin, DSB MN 28
19 November 1836	Prelude, f (op. 35 no. 5)		DSB MN 28
27 November 1836	Allegro, D (Prelude op. 104a no. 3)		DSB MN 28
4 December 1836	Fugue, Bb (op. 35 no. 6)	Klingemann *Fugen und Präludien*	DSB MN 28 Klingemann, 208
6 December 1836	Prelude, D (op. 35 no. 2)		DSB MN 28
8 December 1836	Prelude, b (op. 35 no. 3)		DSB MN 28
9 December 1836		Lea Mendelssohn Bartholdy, *Präludien und Fugen*	New York
	Praeludium, Bb (Prelude op. 104a no. 1)		DSB MN 28
3 January 1837	Prelude, Bb (op. 35 no. 6)	Breitkopf & Härtel	DSB MN 28
10 January 1837	Completed manuscript of op. 35	Review of op. 35 by G. W. Fink	Elvers, *Briefe*, 56; Krause, 77
13 September 1837			*AmZ* 39 (1837), 597–9
27 October 1837		Review of op. 35 by Robert Schumann	*NZfM* 7 (1837), 135–6

Table 8.1 (*Cont.*)

Sources

AmZ	*Allgemeine musikalische Zeitung*
Berlin DSB	Deutsche Staatsbibliothek, Mendelssohn *Nachlaß*
Berlin SPK	Stiftung Preussischer Kulturbesitz, Mendelssohn Archiv
Christie's	Christie, Manson & Woods, *Fine Musical Instruments and Important Musical Manuscripts* (London, 10 May 1977), No. 28
Dresden	Sächische Landesbibliothek
Elvers	Felix Mendelssohn Bartholdy, *Briefe an deutsche Verleger*, ed. Rudolf Elvers (Berlin, 1968)
Klingemann	Karl Klingemann, ed., *Felix Mendelssohn-Bartholdys Briefwechsel mit Legationsrat Karl Klingemann* (Essen, 1909)
Krause	Peter Krause, ed., *Felix Mendelssohn Bartholdy – Autographen, Erstausgaben, Frühdrucke* (Leipzig, 1972)
New York	New York Public Library
NZfM	*Neue Zeitschrift für Musik*
Oxford	Bodleian Library, M. Deneke Mendelssohn Collection
Tokyo	Musashino Academia Musicae
Washington	Library of Congress

In addition to the dated sources for op. 35 listed in Table 8.1, several undated manuscripts survive: op. 35 no. 1, Prelude (DSB MN 23), Fugue (Vienna, Gesellschaft der Musikfreunde and Leipzig, Musikbibliothek [copy by Eduard Rietz]; op. 35 no. 3, Prelude (DSB MN 23), Fugue (J. A. Stargardt auction catalogue, Marburg, June 1962); op. 35 no. 4, Prelude (DSB MN 23 and Leipzig, Staatsarchiv [copy with autograph corrections]), and Fugue (DSB MN 19, sketch).

particularly complicated course of some ten years, from 1827 to 1837. For convenience, the chronology of the opus is summarized in Table 8.1.

In brief, the collection began as a series of independent fugues, the first of which was composed in 1827. Evidently early in 1835 Mendelssohn conceived the idea of a cycle of six fugues, joined not to preludes but to etudes. At some point, probably by October 1836, he decided to label his collection preludes and fugues. The final piece composed for the opus, the Prelude in B flat major op. 35 no. 6, was dated on 3 January 1837. One week later, Mendelssohn sent his finished manuscript to Breitkopf & Härtel, and the work appeared later that year.[11] The reviews by G. W. Fink and Robert Schumann appeared in September and October 1837.

Most, if not all, of the individual pieces in op. 35 underwent extensive revision; many of the fugues, perhaps all, took shape in different versions before gaining Mendelssohn's *imprimatur*. The issue of devising suitable etudes or preludes for the prefatory pieces proved especially troublesome. As we shall propose in the following chronology, as many as four preludes (in D major, B minor, F minor, and B flat major), possibly intended to be coupled with the four fugues op. 35 nos. 2, 3, 5, and 6, were rejected by Mendelssohn and replaced by fresh preludes; three of the rejected preludes were eventually published posthumously as op. 104a, with no reference to their earlier association with op. 35.

The history of op. 35 begins in 1827, with two piano fugues in E minor which Mendelssohn completed on 16 June. One of these ultimately came to serve as the first fugue of op. 35.[12] The other E minor fugue from 1827, passed over for inclusion in op. 35, was withheld by Mendelssohn until 1842, when it appeared in the album *Notre temps*, issued by Schott, with its own E minor prelude, composed by Mendelssohn on 13 July 1841.[13] The two fugal subjects from 1827 are cut from the same mold: they display particularly angular contours and feature dissonant leaps – the tritone in the one, the seventh and tritone in the other (see Ex. 8.2).

11 For the correspondence relating to the publication of op. 35, see Felix Mendelssohn Bartholdy, *Briefe an deutsche Verleger*, ed. Rudolf Elvers (Berlin, 1968), *passim*. The manuscript Mendelssohn sent to Breitkopf & Härtel has not survived intact. It may have been prepared by a copyist under the composer's supervision. The archives of Breitkopf & Härtel (now in Leipzig, Staatsarchiv) included a manuscript copy of the Prelude in A flat major op. 35 no. 4, which evidently served as part of the *Stichvorlage*. See *Felix Mendelssohn Bartholdy–Autographen, Erstausgaben, Frühdrucke*, ed. P. Krause (Leipzig, 1972), p. 77; and Wilhelm Hitzig, *Katalog des Archivs von Breitkopf & Härtel Leipzig* (Leipzig, 1925), p. 12.

12 The autograph of this version was sold at auction by Christie's of London on 10 May 1977. For a brief description, see the catalogue of Christie, Manson & Woods Ltd., *Fine Musical Instruments and Important Musical Manuscripts* (London, 10 May 1977), No. 28, p. 15.

13 *Notre temps* (Mainz, 1842). Manuscripts of the prelude (autograph) and fugue (copy) are in the *Mendelssohn Nachlaß*, vol. 35 (Kraków, Biblioteca Jagiellońska) and vol. 42 (formerly Berlin, Deutsche Staatsbibliothek, now lost).

Ex. 8.2:   Mendelssohn, Subjects of Fugue in E minor op. 35 no. 1 and Fugue in E minor
(both 16 June 1827)

Ex. 8.3:   Mendelssohn, Fugue in B minor op. 35 no. 3

On 21 December 1832, Mendelssohn completed a version of the second
fugue destined for op. 35, that in B minor op. 35 no. 3, a mirror-inversion
fugue based on an elaborate, pseudo-Baroque subject (see Ex. 8.3).[14] We then
encounter a gap in our chronology for more than a year, until June 1834,
when Mendelssohn wrote from Düsseldorf to his sister Fanny to request that
she send him the two E minor fugues.[15] But at this point there was still no
consideration of a cyclical series of fugues. Indeed, the next fugue composed
for op. 35, no. 2 in D major, originally was conceived as an organ fugue, not a
piano fugue, and may have been intended by Mendelssohn for inclusion in the
cycle of three organ preludes and fugues op. 37. An autograph copy of op. 35
no. 2, labelled "Fughetta," appears with Mendelssohn's manuscript of the
organ fugue in C minor op. 37 no. 1, dated 30 July 1834.[16] What is more, on
11 January 1835, Mendelssohn completed an arrangement of op. 35 no. 2 as an
organ duet, which he sent as a present to Thomas Attwood, the former pupil
of Mozart.[17] Mendelssohn had met Attwood during the first English sojourn
of 1829, and in fact would dedicate to Attwood the three organ preludes and

14 Berlin, Deutsche Staatsbibliothek, *Mendelssohn Nachlaß*, vol. 23.

15 See *The Letters of Fanny Hensel to Felix Mendelssohn*, ed. and trans. Marcia J. Citron
(Stuyvesant, 1987), p. 147.

16 Berlin, Deutsche Staatsbibliothek, *Mendelssohn Nachlaß*, vol. 29, p. 120.

17 Berlin, Stiftung Preußischer Kulturbesitz, Mendelssohn Archiv Ms. 6. For an edition of
the organ versions of the D major fugue, see Felix Mendelssohn Bartholdy, *Complete Organ
Works*, ed. Wm. A. Little (London, 1989), vol. I, pp. 8–11, 20–25.

Ex. 8.4:   Mendelssohn, Fugue in D major op. 35 no. 2; J. S. Bach, Fugue in D major, *Well-Tempered Clavier*, Book I

fugues op. 37. Exactly when Mendelssohn determined to reassign the D major fugue to the op. 35 piano cycle is unclear. In any event, in its piano or organ incarnation, this fugue reveals a particular debt to Bach: with its rising triadic motion decorated by the neighboring sixth scale degree, Mendelssohn's subject suggests a simplified rendition of the more florid subject found in the D major fugue of the *Well-Tempered Clavier*, Book I (see Ex. 8.4).

At the end of 1834 Mendelssohn created two more fugues. On 3 December he finished the first version of the Fugue in F minor op. 35 no. 5, and on its final page he began to notate the Fugue in A flat major op. 35 no. 4; a second version of the latter fugue was finished on 6 January 1835.[18] The chronological proximity of these two fugues and their close tonal relationship suggest, perhaps, that Mendelssohn was now beginning to think of developing a series of fugues according to a systematic tonal plan – and indeed, these two fugues ultimately occupied the fourth and fifth positions in op. 35. Stylistically, however, the two fugues are dissimilar: if the F minor fugue, with its disjunct head motif and strongly chiselled diminished seventh, suggests a baroque ancestry, the A flat major fugue, with its rising sequential fourths – A♭–D♭, B♭–E♭, and C–F – and rhythmic acceleration, point to the finale of Beethoven's Piano Sonata in A flat major op. 110 as a model (see Ex. 8.5).

By early January 1835 Mendelssohn determined to complete a collection of "6 Etüden und Fugen," which he planned to offer to Breitkopf & Härtel.[19] Several references to this title occur in his correspondence from 1835 and 1836. On 11 January 1835, to Thomas Attwood: "There is a favour I wanted to ask

18 Berlin, Deutsche Staatsbibliothek, *Mendelssohn Nachlaß* vol. 28, pp. 287–90, 295–7, 299.
19 Letter of 16 January 1835, in Mendelssohn, *Briefe an deutsche Verleger*, p. 42.

Ex. 8.5: Mendelssohn, Fugue in F minor op. 35 no. 5 and Fugue in A flat major op. 35 no. 4

from you; I am about to publish some etudes and fugues, and as I think some of them better than other things which I composed I wished you would allow me to dedicate them to you."[20] On 10 April 1835, to Breitkopf & Härtel: the etudes and fugues are not finished but will be sent as soon as they are ready; on 27 September 1835, to the same: Mendelssohn sets as his price for the etudes and fugues, the Three Caprices op. 33, the piano score and parts to the *Overture to the Fair Melusine* op. 32, and the Six Songs op. 34 an honorarium of 60 Louis; on 10 June 1836, to the same: the etudes and fugues will be sent at the beginning of August; and finally on 2 July 1836, to the firm Simrock, about to publish *St Paul*: Mendelssohn requests that Simrock write to Breitkopf & Härtel to inquire which opus number will be assigned to the etudes and fugues.[21]

Between January 1835 and July 1836 Mendelssohn thus was planning a cycle of fugues joined to a cycle of etudes, presumably with individual fugues paired to individual etudes; the idea of preludes and fugues had still not yet materialized. Notwithstanding the references in the correspondence, however, Mendelssohn apparently made little real progress on the cycle during these eighteen months, for few primary sources for op. 35 from this period are traceable. First of all, dated etudes which may have belonged to the "Etudes and Fugues" appear not to have survived, with, perhaps, one or two exceptions. A study in F minor, finished on 13 March 1836,[22] conceivably could have been composed to be joined to the fugue op. 35 no. 5, although Mendelssohn eventually released the study in the *Méthode des méthodes de piano* of Moscheles and Fétis, which appeared in Paris around 1840.[23] On 9 June 1836, Mendelssohn did finish an etude-like Presto in B flat minor, and it is plausible that this work, posthumously published in 1868 as the Etude op.

20 Letter of 11 January 1835, to Thomas Attwood. Library of Congress, Washington, DC.
21 See *Briefe an deutsche Verleger*, pp. 45, 47, 50, 205.
22 Berlin, Deutsche Staatsbibliothek, *Mendelssohn Nachlaß* vol. 28.
23 Paris: M. Schlesinger, 1840; rep. Geneva, 1973.

104b no. 1, was intended for op. 35.[24] On the other hand, there is no evidence that Mendelssohn ever composed or intended to compose a corresponding fugue in B flat minor. Second, the only piano fugue from the eighteen-month period is the second version of the F minor Fugue op. 35 no. 5, which Mendelssohn completed on 30 December 1835 as a present for Clara Wieck.[25] Apart from this revision, the only other pertinent item in our chronology from this time is a request Mendelssohn made on 30 June 1836, when he asked Conrad Schleinitz to return a manuscript of the B minor Fugue op. 35 no. 3 (identified in Mendelssohn's letter to Schleinitz by a thematic incipit), which Mendelssohn had given his friend earlier that year.[26] In sum, the chronology suggests this scenario: between January 1835 and July 1836 Mendelssohn contemplated a collection of six etudes and fugues but made relatively little progress on the etudes. Of the six fugues, at least drafts of nos. 1 through 5 were available by July 1836.

II

The final stages of the creation of op. 35 unfolded between October 1836 and early January 1837. What remained were the decisions to convert the cycle into a group of preludes and fugues, to compose the preludes, and, finally, to compose the remaining fugue, no. 6 in B flat major. When the conversion from etudes and fugues to preludes and fugues occurred is difficult to establish. In two letters of 4 and 9 December 1836, to Karl Klingemann and his mother, Lea, Mendelssohn referred to the cycle as preludes and fugues. Furthermore, he provided that title when, on 10 January 1837, he sent his final prepared manuscript – which, now lost, must have served as the *Stichvorlage* – to Breitkopf & Härtel.[27] But we are probably justified in moving the conversion to a few months earlier, for in October 1836, Mendelssohn began to compose a series of preludes, most of which he clearly designated as such in his autographs with the term "Praeludium."

Thus, on 7 October 1836 Mendelssohn finished the Prelude in A flat major op. 35 no. 4; on 19 November the Prelude in F minor op. 35 no. 5; on 6

---

24 Berlin, Deutsche Staatsbibliothek, *Mendelssohn Nachlaß* vol. 20.

25 Dresden, Sächsische Landesbibliothek, Ms. Mus. Schu. 193.

26 Letter of 30 June 1836 to Conrad Schleinitz, in Felix Mendelssohn, *A Life in Letters*, ed. Rudolf Elvers, trans. Craig Tomlinson (New York, 1986), p. 226.

27 Letter of 4 December 1836 to Karl Klingemann, in *Felix Mendelssohn-Bartholdys Briefwechsel mit Legationsrat Karl Klingemann in London*, ed. K. Klingemann (Essen, 1909), p. 208; letter of 9 December 1836 to Lea Mendelssohn Bartholdy, New York Public Library: "Auch jetzt haben sich wieder die Geschäfte u. meine Arbeit gedrängt, da ich die 6 Präludien u. Fugen noch vor meiner Abreise zu den Verlegern schicken will ..."; letter of 10 January 1837 to Breitkopf & Härtel, in *Briefe an deutsche Verleger*, p. 56.

December the Prelude in D major op. 35 no. 2; on 8 December the Prelude in B minor op. 35 no. 3; and on 3 January 1837, the Prelude in B flat major op. 35 no. 6. The sixth and final fugue, in B flat major, was finished on 27 November 1836.[28] During this time, too, Mendelssohn composed at least three other preludes which were likely intended for use in op. 35 but then rejected. The three have specific dates that in each case preceded the dates of composition for the corresponding preludes that were ultimately accepted into op. 35. The rejected pieces include a "Praeludium" in B minor, finished on 12 October 1836 and posthumously published in 1868 as the Prelude op. 104a no. 2; a prelude-like Allegro in D major, finished on 27 November 1836 and published as the Prelude op. 104a no. 3; and a "Praeludium" in B flat major, finished on 9 December 1836 and published as op. 104a no. 1.[29]

The three posthumously published preludes exhibit thematic and harmonic features which link them to the three fugues in D major, B minor, and B flat major, op. 35 nos 2, 3, and 6 – musical evidence which supports the notion that these preludes were intended for the cycle of preludes and fugues. The subject of the D major Fugue, for example, describes a triadic ascent on scale degrees 1, 3, and 5 (D–F♯–A) supported by scale degree 6 (B) as upper neighbor to 5 (see Ex. 8.4). The "Prelude" in D major op. 104a no. 3 begins with a stepwise thematic ascent in the soprano from scale degree 3 to 6 followed by descending step to degree 5 (F♯–G–A–B–A). And the cascading sixteenth-note figuration in the accompaniment of op. 104a no. 3 seems

Ex. 8.6:   Mendelssohn, Prelude in D major op. 104a no. 3

28 Oxford, Bodleian Library, M. Deneke Mendelssohn b. 1, f. 13 (from the Horsley family); and Berlin, Deutsche Staatsbibliothek, *Mendelssohn Nachlaß*, vol. 28, pp. 285–6, 291–2, 293, 317–18, and 321–4, respectively.
29 Berlin, Deutsche Staatsbibliothek, *Mendelssohn Nachlaß*, vol. 28, pp. 315–16, 307–9, and 303–5, respectively.

Ex. 8.7: Mendelssohn, Fugue in D major op. 35 no. 2 and Prelude in D major op. 104a no. 3

related to the fugal subject as well: the descending figure B–A–G–F♯, embedded in the accompaniment, is made particularly conspicuous by the skip to the B (see Ex. 8.6). Further on in op. 104a no. 3, we encounter two other passages with possible links to the fugue op. 35 no. 2. The middle section of the prelude reaches the key of the submediant B minor (a tonal reference to the prominence of scale degree 6 in the opening measures of the prelude). Mendelssohn arranges this tonal goal to overlap with the return of the opening material in the tonic (here the pitches D and F♯ act as common tones between I and vi); exactly the same procedure obtains in the fugue (see Ex. 8.7). Finally, in the concluding measures of op. 104a no. 3 Mendelssohn turns to the subdominant G major; again, the subdominant is emphasized in the closing passage of the fugue.[30]

The subject of the B minor Fugue op. 35 no. 3 (see Ex. 8.3) describes a decorated, ascending stepwise line from scale degree 1 to 6, B–C♯–D–E–F♯–G, which then falls through degrees 5, 4, and 3 (F♯–E–D). The first measure of

30 In the fugue Mendelssohn touches on both the major and minor forms of the subdominant, as he in fact does in the closing measures of the Prelude in D major op. 35 no. 2.

Ex. 8.8: Mendelssohn, Fugue in B minor op. 35 no. 3 and Prelude in B minor op. 104a no. 2

the Prelude in B minor op. 104a no. 2 contains a similar melodic contour in the rushing accompaniment of its bass line. The closing measures of the fugue are interrupted by an arpeggiated flourish on a diminished-seventh harmony; in the parallel passage of op. 104a no. 2, the same interruption is made even more emphatic (see Ex. 8.8).

Finally, in the case of the Prelude in B flat major op. 104a no. 1 we may

177

Ex. 8.9: Mendelssohn, Fugue in B flat major op. 35 no. 6 and Prelude in B flat major op. 104a no. 1

establish musical links to the Fugue in B flat major op. 35 no. 6 by noting in each the prominent rising scale-like line: in the Prelude, B♭–C–D (half notes, mm. 3–4), D–E♭–F (half notes, mm. 7–8), G and A (mm. 10, 12); in the fugue, the same rising line is incorporated in the head motif of the subject, measures 1–2 (see Ex. 8.9). In addition, the closing measures of the prelude contain a unison passage not unlike that near the close of the fugue (see Ex. 8.10): both passages feature descending arpeggiations of the tonic harmony

178

Ex. 8.10: Mendelssohn, Fugue in B flat major op. 35 no. 6 and Prelude in B flat major op. 104a no. 1

from the third scale degree, D; in both, the motion from D to B flat is traversed via the passing tone C.

These thematic and harmonic links indicate that from the start Mendelssohn was concerned about the coherence of the paired preludes and fugues. To incorporate specific references between preludes and fugues, after all, was to follow a procedure thoroughly explored by J. S. Bach in the *Well-Tempered Clavier*. But what about the coherence of the cycle as a whole? Unlike Robert Schumann's Six Fugues on BACH op. 60, in which all six fugues are derived from the musical symbol of Bach's name, the six fugues of Mendelssohn's op. 35 do not themselves share specific material. From a different perspective, however, that of tonal organization, op. 35 does show clear evidence of Mendelssohn's concern for the unity of the entire composition. To begin with, he arranged the cycle in an alternating series of minor and major tonalities (e–D–b–A♭–f–B♭), a procedure he also applied in the six *Lieder ohne Worte* op. 30, which had appeared two years earlier, in 1835

179

(E♭–b♭–E–b–D–f♯); in the Three Caprices op. 33, which had appeared in 1836 (a–E–b♭); and in the Three Preludes and Fugues for organ op. 37, which appeared later in 1837 (c–G–d).[31] But in op. 35, Mendelssohn went even further, to produce a nearly symmetrical scheme of tonalities. In this case, the alternating minor/major tonalities are comprised of three sharp keys followed by three flat keys. In addition, the four internal keys, nos. 2 through 5, D–b–A♭–f, describe a descending chain of minor-third-related tonalities (nos. 3 and 4 are related enharmonically). Finally, the two halves of the scheme are related by a series of tritone transpositions – e–B♭, D–A♭, and b–F – a feature which again underscores the essential symmetry of the tonal plan.

The musical evidence thus supports the thesis that Mendelssohn viewed op. 35 as a tonally unified cycle, that he forged a cohesive opus by carefully selecting and reordering what had been essentially an unrelated series of fugues, and that he ensured a high level of coherence in the cycle through the use of specific thematic and harmonic references between individual, paired preludes and fugues.

The issue of why Mendelssohn changed his conception of op. 35 from etudes and fugues to preludes and fugues still remains, however, unanswered. Of course, the title "preludes and fugues" would have invoked the *Well-Tempered Clavier*, and perhaps would have acknowledged Mendelssohn's debt to Bach more honestly than the title "etudes and fugues." Indeed, in reviewing op. 35 Robert Schumann observed, "these fugues have much of Sebastian and might deceive the sharp-sighted reviewer, were it not for the melody, the finer bloom, which we recognize as modern; and here and there those little touches peculiar to Mendelssohn, which identify him among a hundred other composers."[32] In addition, the title "preludes" would have reflected more accurately the introductory nature of those six pieces than the title "etudes," and perhaps would have alerted the listener more clearly to connections between paired preludes and fugues.

We may discover, perhaps, another explanation for the change in title of op. 35 in a non-Mendelssohn source, a separate cycle of preludes and fugues that appeared in 1836 with a dedication to Mendelssohn: Carl Czerny's *Schule des Fugenspiels* op. 400 (*The School of Playing Fugues*), published in Vienna by Diabelli around March 1836 (see Plate 8.1; the half-title page, not shown, has

---

31 The first volume of the *Lieder ohne Worte* op. 19 also has three minor keys and three major keys (E–a–A–A–f♯ –g), but does not maintain the strict alternation of modality.

32 *Neue Zeitschrift für Musik* 7 (1837), 135. Robert Schumann, *On Music and Musicians*, ed. Konrad Wolff, trans. P. Rosenfeld (New York, 1946), p. 215.

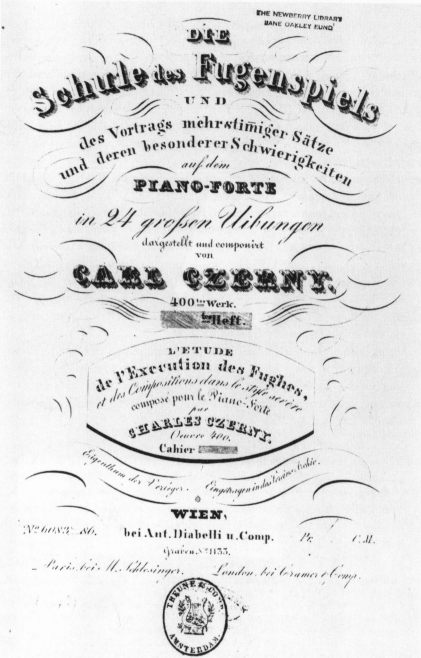

8.1.   Carl Czerny, *Die Schule des Fugenspiels* (Vienna: Ant. Diabelli, 1836); Chicago, The Newberry Library.

the inscription "Dem Herrn Musikdirector Felix Mendelssohn-Bartholdy aus freundschaftlicher Achtung zugeeignet vom Verfasser").[33] This work consists of twelve fugues introduced by twelve preludes (Czerny uses the Italian "Preludio"), though the full title of the collection underscores that this particular Czerny school, in fact, was conceived as a series of exercises: *und / des Vortrags mehrstimmiger Sätze / und deren besonderer Schwierigkeiten / auf dem / Piano-Forte / in 24 großen Uibungen* (*and of Performing Polyphonic Compositions and of Their Particular Difficulties on the Pianoforte in 24 Grand Exercises*; the French subtitle reads *L'Etude / de l'Execution des Fughes, / et des Compositions dans le style sévère*). In his foreword Czerny explained that op. 400 represented the "conclusion of a complete collection of practical and systematically progressive exercises and studies for all types and forms of playing the fortepiano";[34] it was, actually, the fifth opus in a series that included *Die Schule der Geläufigkeit* (*The School of Velocity*) op. 299, *Die Schule des Legato und Staccato* (*The School of Legato and Staccato*) op. 335, *Die Schule der Verzierungen* (*The School of Ornamentation*) op. 355, and *Die Schule zur besonderen Ausbildung der linken Hand* (*The School for the Particular Development of the Left Hand*) op. 399. For Czerny, in short, the mastery of playing fugues required one more series of specialized studies, of etudes in the strict style.

Mendelssohn most likely received his presentation copy of Czerny's *Fugenspiels* in April 1836. On 8 April Czerny wrote a letter to Mendelssohn, which, although it did not mention op. 400 by name, almost certainly was meant to accompany an exemplar copy of the new work. We provide a complete translation here (see also Plate 8.2).[35]

> Esteemed Sir and friend,
>
> Excuse the freedom that I take in inscribing to you the enclosed little work as a small token of my high esteem, to which I above all feel myself drawn, since I have essayed here a genre which, as I know, is especially esteemed by yourself, and which has also always been for me the most attractive. In that I have laid claim to your indulgence for this little work, the intention of which is chiefly to

---

33 Czerny's work was announced in a Viennese periodical on 12 March 1836. See A. Weinmann, *Beiträge zur Geschichte des Alt-Wiener Musikverlages*, Reihe, 2, Folge 24, *Verlagsverzeichnis Anton Diabelli & Co. (1824 bis 1840)* (Vienna, 1985), pp. 376–8.

34 Czerny, *Die Schule des Fugenspiels*, "Vorwort" ("Das gegenwärtige Werk macht den Beschluß der ganzen Sammlung der praktischen und systematisch nacheinanderfolgenden Übungen und Studien über alle Arten und Formen des *Fortepianospiels* ...").

35 Bodleian Library, Oxford, M. Deneke Mendelssohn Collection, Green Books, vol. V, item 63; Mendelssohn's copy of the Czerny is preserved in Berlin, Stiftung Preußischer Kulturbesitz, Mendelssohn Archiv. See the *Catalogue of Mendelssohn's Papers in the Bodleian Library, Oxford*, ed. P. Ward Jones (Tutzing, 1989), vol. III, p. 299.

8.2. Carl Czerny, Autograph letter to Mendelssohn, Vienna, 8 April 1836; M. Deneke Mendelssohn Collection, Green Books V, No. 63, Bodleian Library, Oxford.

promote the mechanics of performances in this genre, I bid you accept the assurances of the warmest respect, with which I sign, Herr Music Director,

> Your most humble,
> Carl Czerny[36]

Mendelssohn had met Czerny in Vienna in August 1830, and perhaps on that occasion had discussed ideas about fugal writing, though in a letter dated 22 August 1830 to his sister Rebecka, Mendelssohn seemed to have been particularly impressed by Czerny's unrelenting industriousness: "Czerny is like a tradesman on his day off, and says he is composing a lot now, for it brings in more than giving lessons."[37] Evidently the two never met again, though they did develop a special professional relationship: the ever diligent Czerny made piano-duet arrangements of several of Mendelssohn's works, including one for the Overture to *Die schöne Melusine* op. 32, which Czerny had sent to Mendelssohn in March 1836 (just one month before the inscription of Czerny's *Fugenspiels*), and which was judged by Mendelssohn to be excellent.[38]

By April 1836, when he received Czerny's *Fugenspiels*, Mendelssohn was still contemplating for op. 35 a cycle of etudes and fugues; as we have seen above, the decision to retitle the opus "Preludes and Fugues" was evidently taken by October 1836. With the dedication of Czerny's op. 400 to Mendelssohn the possibility arises that Czerny's work could have influenced Mendelssohn to adopt the new title of Preludes and Fugues for the cycle. After all, Czerny's opus, though described in his "Vorwort" as a series of specialized studies, was arranged in paired preludes and fugues. What is more, in Czerny's *Fugenspiels* Mendelssohn would have found distinctly baroque fugal subjects whose chromaticism was redolent of Bach (e.g., Fugue no. 10, with its embedded descending chromatic line of the fourth and prominent diminished-seventh leap; see Ex. 8.11) and fugal intricacies reminiscent of the master

---

36 "Geehrter Herr u. Freund, / Entschuldigen Sie die Freyheit, die ich mir nehme, / Ihnen beykommendes Werkchen als einen, obwohl / geringen Beweis meiner Werthschätzung zuzu = / eignen, wozu ich mich vorzüglich dadurch hingezogen / fühlte, daß ich mich hier in einer Gattung / versuchte, die Ihnen, wie ich weiß, vorzügs = / weise werth ist, und die auch mir stets die / anziehendste war. Indem ich für dieses Werkchen, / dessen Tendenz vorzüglich die Beförderung des / Mechanismus im Vortrage dieses *Genre* ist, Ihre / gütige Nachsicht in Anspruch nehme, bitte ich, / die Versicherung der aufmuthigsten Hochachtung / zu genehmigen, mit welcher ich mich zeichne / Herr Musikdirektor / Dero ergebenster / Carl Czerny / Wien den 8ten April 1836."

37 The original of this letter is in the New York Public Library. The translation cited here is from Felix Mendelssohn, *A Life in Letters*, p. 132.

38 Letter of 8 March 1836 from Mendelssohn to Breitkopf & Härtel, in *Briefe an deutsche Verleger*, p. 48. Other Mendelssohn works arranged by Czerny included the *Variations concertantes* op. 17 and the *Lieder ohne Worte* op. 38.

Ex. 8.11: Czerny, *Schule des Fugenspiels* op. 400, *Fuga X* in E minor

Ex. 8.12: Czerny, *Schule des Fugenspiels* op. 400, *Preludio* and *Fuga V* in D major

as well (e.g., the use of mirror inversion and stretto in Fugue no. 1 in C major). Second, in the *Fugenspiels* Mendelssohn would have discovered paired preludes and fugues with thematic links (most overtly in the Prelude and Fugue no. 5 in D major; see Ex. 8.12). And finally, Mendelssohn would have found in the *Fugenspiels* a cycle of preludes and fugues, organized, to be sure, not tonally, but by increasingly complex levels of part writing in the fugues, with two fugues *a 2* (nos. 1–2), four fugues *a 3* (nos. 3–6), and six fugues *a 4* (nos. 7–12). Conceivably, the appearance of Czerny's *Werkchen*, an especially industrious – and, we might add, wig-adorned – example of the nineteenth-century Bach revival, could have spurred Mendelssohn to take up once again and to finish his own homage to Bach.

III

Having traced the compositional history of op. 35, we may now consider one final question about the original conception of etudes and fugues. Simply asked, did vestiges of the etudes survive in the final version of op. 35, or did Mendelssohn abandon altogether the etude concept when he composed the bulk of his preludes in October, November, and December 1836? To begin with, at least two preludes from op. 35 can certainly be described as *etüdenhaft*. No. 2 in D major (6 December 1836) challenges the pianist with a turning

Prestissimo staccato

Ex. 8.13:   Mendelssohn, Prelude in B minor op. 35 no. 3

sixteenth-note line in the inner part which runs unabated throughout the entire piece. No 3 in B minor (8 December 1836) is clearly an arpeggiation study in staccato articulation – indeed, a study not unlike Czerny's more ponderous *Preludio* no. 12, also in B minor, which features detached, arpeggiated chords (see Ex. 8.13).

Of Mendelssohn's six preludes, one in particular – the first, in E minor – stands out for its etude-like qualities. This prelude arouses our suspicions further, for it represents Mendelssohn's response to a contemporary pianistic device made popular by virtuosi during the 1830s, a device Robert Schumann described in the issue of the *Neue Zeitschrift für Musik* that appeared on 11 August 1837: "Many of our young fantasia and etude composers have become infatuated with a texture, commonly used earlier, that has now reappeared in conjunction with the rich new effects of the modern piano. One just gives a passably broad melody to some voice, and surrounds it with all sorts of arpeggios and artful figurations in the same harmony."[39] In a typical version of this procedure, often referred to as the three-hand technique, a cantabile melody is placed in the middle register of the piano, where it is executed primarily by alternating the thumbs, and supported by some sort of bass line and treble arpeggiations.

According to François-Joseph Fétis, Sigismond Thalberg was the originator of this device, though in Hector Berlioz's view, Thalberg borrowed and adapted it from the English harp virtuoso Elias Parish-Alvars.[40] We may find some support for Berlioz's claim, perhaps, in an account of the piano teacher of Thalberg and close friend of Mendelssohn, Ignaz Moscheles, who noted about Thalberg in 1836, "I find his introduction of harp effects on the piano quite original. ... His theme, which lies in the middle part, is brought out clearly in relief with an accompaniment of complicated arpeggios which

39 *NZfM* 7 (1837), 47, trans. in Leon Plantinga, *Schumann as Critic* (New Haven, 1967), p. 213.

40 F.-J. Fétis, *Biographie universelle des musiciens*, 2nd edn. (Paris, 1875), vol. VIII, p. 208; *The Memoirs of Hector Berlioz*, trans. David Cairns (New York, 1975), pp. 304–5. Parish-Alvars concertized in Leipzig in 1842, when Mendelssohn would have had an opportunity to hear him.

remind me of a harp. The audience is amazed."[41] Whatever its origins, the three-hand device was quickly embraced by all manner of pianists during the 1830s as a remarkable technical innovation; among those pianists, of course, was Franz Liszt, who engaged and, by most accounts, prevailed over Thalberg in the celebrated piano duel held at the Parisian residence of Princess Belgiojoso on 31 March 1837, not quite three months after Mendelssohn completed his op. 35. Thalberg's pianism and compositions were vigorously disputed in the French music periodicals of 1836 and 1837, where Fétis, a steadfast apologist for Thalberg, rebutted in a protracted journalistic duel a series of attacks made by Liszt.[42] Though Mendelssohn did not visit Paris during these years, he did have access to the Leipzig *Allgemeine musikalische Zeitung*, which ran reports and articles about the Fétis–Liszt controversy,[43] and he would have known Schumann's reviews of Thalberg's music in the *Neue Zeitschrift für Musik*.[44] As early as 1830 Mendelssohn had met Thalberg in Vienna,[45] by November 1836 he was reviewing a composition *à la* Thalberg by his sister Fanny Hensel,[46] in 1840 he welcomed Thalberg to Leipzig,[47] and in 1844 he thanked Breitkopf & Härtel for the receipt of "the unbelievable Thalbergian thirty-second notes" ("die unglaublichen Thalbergschen Zweiunddreißigstel"), a copy of Thalberg's latest fashionable operatic fantasy.[48]

Probably influenced by Thalberg's pianism and innovative textures, Mendelssohn found himself especially drawn to the three-hand technique and used it in a variety of piano works, including the Prelude in E minor op. 35 no. 1. His first datable experiment with the device occurred in the Etude in B flat minor op. 104b no. 1 (see Ex. 8.14), finished on 9 June 1836[49] (as we have suggested above, this work may have been intended for op. 35). A second

41 Ignaz Moscheles, *Recent Music and Musicians*, ed. Charlotte Moscheles, trans. A.D. Coleridge (New York, 1873, rep. 1970), p. 229.

42 It now appears that Liszt's articles against Thalberg in fact were from the pen of his mistress Marie d'Agoult. See Alan Walker, *Franz Liszt: the Virtuoso Years 1811–1847* (New York, 1983), p. 236, n. 10.

43 See *AmZ* 39 (1837), cols. 106–9, 329–38.

44 See Plantinga, *Schumann as Critic*, pp. 207ff.

45 Letter of 22 August 1830 to his sister Rebecka, in Felix Mendelssohn, *A Life in Letters*, pp. 131–2.

46 Letter of 16 November 1836 from Fanny to Felix, in *The Letters of Fanny Hensel to Felix Mendelssohn*, p. 217. The composition, in C minor, is unidentified. A later piano piece by Hensel, "September" from the cycle *Das Jahr* (1841), is a further example of the three-hand technique; it was published as Hensel's op. 2 no. 2 in 1846.

47 See Mendelssohn's letter to his mother, 30 March 1840, in *Briefe aus den Jahren 1833 bis 1847*, pp. 233–5. A corrected text is presented in Professor Little's study in this volume, p. 118–19.

48 Letter of 16 March 1844 to Breitkopf & Härtel, in Mendelssohn, *Briefe an deutsche Verleger*, p. 144. The fantasy was either Thalberg's op. 50, on themes from Donizetti's *Lucretia Borgia*, or op. 51, on themes from Rossini's *Semiramide*; copies of each were in Mendelssohn's library. See Peter Ward Jones, *Catalogue of the Mendelssohn Papers*, vol. III, p. 296.

49 See note 24.

Ex. 8.14:   Mendelssohn, Etude in B flat minor op. 104b no. 1

application followed in the Piano Concerto No. 2 in D minor op. 40, finished on 5 August 1837 and premièred by Mendelssohn shortly thereafter at the Birmingham Music Festival. In the second theme of the first movement, Mendelssohn designed arpeggio passages in which, as Moscheles put it, "the melody seems to push its way."[50] Mendelssohn tested the device further in the *Serenade und Allegro giojoso* op. 43 of 1838; the thirteenth variation of the *Variations sérieuses* op. 54, finished on 4 June 1841;[51] the first variation of the Variations in B flat major op. 83 of 1841; and the Prelude in E minor composed on 13 July 1841 and published in the 1842 album *Notre temps*. This last work conveniently brings us back to the Prelude in E minor op. 35 no. 1, for, as we have seen, it was appended to Mendelssohn's other E minor fugue that had been finished on 16 June 1827. Perhaps not by coincidence did Mendelssohn add to his two E minor fugues from 1827 two etude-like preludes inspired by the three-hand technique.

No dated autograph survives for the E minor prelude op. 35 no. 1, though a little-known, undated autograph enables us to establish that the piece was indeed part of Mendelssohn's conception of a cycle of etudes and fugues. In the archives of the Musashino Academia Musicae in Tokyo is an autograph version of the prelude bearing Mendelssohn's title "Etude" (see plate 8.3).[52]

50 *Letters of Felix Mendelssohn to Ignaz and Charlotte Moscheles*, trans. and ed. F. Moscheles (Boston, 1888), p. 168.

51 Kraków, Biblioteca Jagiellońska, *Mendelssohn Nachlaß*, vol. 35.

52 A second, undated copy of the prelude is in vol. 23 of the *Mendelssohn Nachlaß*, Berlin, Deutsche Staatsbibliothek.

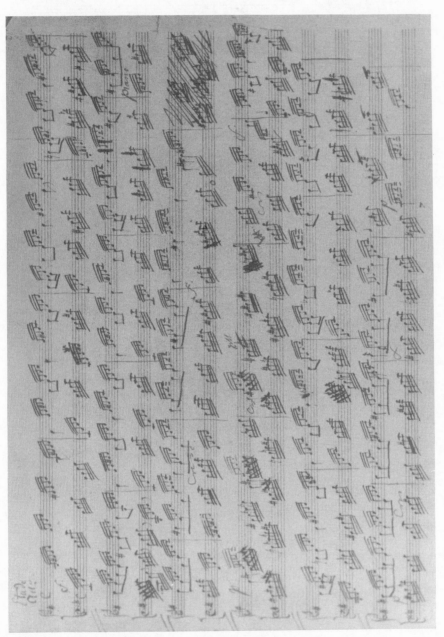

8.3. Mendelssohn, Autograph first page of "Etude" version of the Prelude in E minor op. 35 no. 1; Tokyo, Musashino Academia Musicae.

Ex. 8.15: Mendelssohn, Prelude in E minor op. 35 no. 1, (a) final version and (b) "Etude" version, Tokyo, Musashino Academia Musicae

Cursory examination of the manuscript reveals that it was the original composing manuscript of the piece. First of all, Mendelssohn included in the upper right-hand corner the initials "H.D.m." ("Hilf Du mir"), an invocation he habitually notated when beginning work on a new composition. Second, the Tokyo version contains several minor discrepancies from the final version. Thus, as Example 8.15 shows, Mendelssohn originally employed arpeggiations with a compass more restricted than that of those in the printed version; what is more, certain corrections entered by Mendelssohn further on in the Tokyo manuscript effectively incorporated readings that agree with the final version.

From the title "Etude," we can propose that the Tokyo version was composed between January 1835 and October 1836, when Mendelssohn

Fugue

Prelude

Ex. 8.16:   Mendelssohn, Prelude and Fugue in E minor op. 35 no. 1, reductions

visualized op. 35 as a cycle of etudes and fugues. If we assume that the etude's use of the three-hand technique was a response to Mendelssohn's study of Thalberg, we might tentatively assign the Tokyo version to circa June 1836, when Mendelssohn composed his Thalbergian Etude in B flat minor op. 104b no. 1, his first datable work to use the three-hand technique.

For all his interest in Thalberg's celebrated special effects (for Mendelssohn a rare concession to innovative pianistic devices), Mendelssohn nevertheless did not allow the claims of virtuosity to take precedence over fundamental concerns of thematic integrity and coherence in his E minor Etude/Prelude. We have here a composition that is thematically related to the subject of the E minor Fugue of op. 35 no. 1, and these similarities, which underscore the introductory, preparatory nature of the etude, perhaps help to explain Mendelssohn's subsequent reinterpretation of the etude as a prelude. Example 8.16 compares the opening theme of the prelude with the fugal subject (see also Ex. 8.2); as the following analysis demonstrates, the key to understanding the prelude lies in the fugal subject.

We are faced with an especially disjunct, dissonant fugal subject. The initial leap of the third (E–G) soon expands via a diminished triad to the tritone (D♯–F♯–A). Though the D sharp appears not to resolve, its implied resolution, to the E, is placed in parentheses in the analysis. As the A resolves to the G sharp, a new tritone (G♯–D) is introduced in overlapping fashion above,[53] with the G sharp proceeding to an implied A. As the D resolves to the C, the fourth C–F appears in a correspondingly higher register and gives way

53 An example, in Schenkerian terminology, of the *Übergreifung*.

to a stepwise descent, embedded into which is a second appearance of the tritone D♯–A. The real answer on the dominant that follows then introduces two additional overlapping tritones (A♯–C♯–E and D♯–A). As the reduction in Example 8.16 shows, the series of disjunct leaps suggests that the subject is a type of compound melody that now states, now implies voices in different registers and, furthermore, that beneath the surface of the subject there operates an underlying principle of registral transfer.[54] Thus it is possible to extract from the subject a chromatic line descending from the tonic to dominant scale degrees, with the final arrival on the dominant corresponding to the beginning of the answer: E–D♯–D♮–C–B.

Analysis of the E minor Prelude reveals some noteworthy similarities to the fugal subject. The prelude begins with the same third, E–G, though the skip is now filled in with a passing tone. When the pitch A is reached, Mendelssohn harmonizes it with a diminished-seventh sonority that features the tritone D♯–A. The rhythmic pattern in the second measure of the quarter and two eighths recalls the eighth and two sixteenths used for the same pitches in the first measure of the fugal subject. And the skip to the C in a higher register, and its resolution by step to B, recalls a similar overlapping effect in the fugue. Finally, the descending chromatic line – E–D♯–D♮–C–B – dispersed in the fugal subject in different registers, now appears in a direct linear fashion in the prelude, and in a full chromatic descent – E–D♯–D♮–C♯–C♮–B. In just this way, then, Mendelssohn related his etude/prelude of circa 1836 to his fugue of 1827, and, as we shall now see, in attempting to relate the two, he may have provided a clue that bears on our interpretation of the fugue.

IV

As an avid student of Bachian counterpoint Mendelssohn composed fugues during the 1820s throughout his period of apprenticeship under Carl Friedrich Zelter, and at first glance we might judge the E minor Fugue op. 35 no. 1 to be one more example of the influence of his traditional training in Berlin, a conservative bastion where Sebastian Bach's music was held in especially high regard. But a little-known nineteenth-century memoir of Mendelssohn reveals that the immediate inspiration for the fugue may not have been the creation of another contrapuntal exercise, but a tragic event in Mendelssohn's life, the prolonged illness and death of his friend August Hanstein. We owe this interpretation to the pastor Julius Schubring (1806–89), who later assisted

---

54 Mendelssohn utilized a similar procedure in crafting the D minor theme of his *Variations sérieuses* op. 54. See my "Piano Music Reformed: the Case of Felix Mendelssohn Bartholdy," *Nineteenth-Century Piano Music*, ed. R. L. Todd (New York, 1990), pp. 205–6.

Mendelssohn in preparing the libretti for the oratorios *St. Paul* and *Elijah*.[55]
Armed with a letter of introduction from none other than the poet Wilhelm
Müller, Schubring arrived in 1825 in Berlin to study theology at the university under Schleiermacher; he soon became a frequent guest in the Mendelssohn household. In 1866 Schubring published his reminiscences of Mendelssohn, and here he divulged the special meaning of the E minor Fugue op. 35
no. 1:

> When I recollect, however, with what a serious religious feeling he pursued his
> art, the exercise of it always being, as it were, a sacred duty; how the first page of
> every one of his compositions bears impressed on it the initial letter of a prayer;
> how he devoted the time, as he watched through the night by the bed of his
> dying friend, Hanstein, to marking in the first fugue, composed here, of the six
> he afterwards published – in E minor – the progress of the disease as it gradually
> destroyed the sufferer, until he made it culminate in the choral[e] of release in E
> major, . . . this was why his music possessed such a magic charm.[56]

Schubring's account thus suggests that the fugue was meant to convey a
specific program, that Mendelssohn's contrapuntal prowess displayed within
the work was intended not so much a homage to Bach but an exploration of
fugal procedures as expressive agents. Little analysis is required to show that the

Ex. 8.17: Mendelssohn, Fugue in E minor op. 35 no. 1

55 Much of the Mendelssohn–Schubring *Briefwechsel* was brought out by Schubring's son as
the *Briefwechsel zwischen Felix Mendelssohn Bartholdy und Julius Schubring*, ed. J. Schubring
(Leipzig, 1892; rep. Wiesbaden, 1973).
56 Julius Schubring, "Reminiscences of Felix Mendelssohn-Bartholdy," *Musical World* 31 (12
May 1866). Translated from the original German text which appeared in *Daheim* 2 (1866), 373.

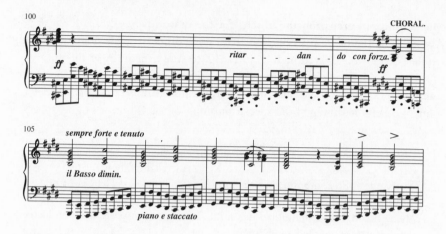

Ex. 8.18:   Mendelssohn, Fugue in E minor op. 35 no. 1

course of the fugue corroborates Schubring's account. In the opening exposition, we indeed encounter Mendelssohn's most dissonant musical language,
featuring, as we have seen, the tritone as a melodic and harmonic interval.
Beginning in measure 29, and following in measure 39, Mendelssohn calls for
a series of accelerandos to increase the rhythmic and dramatic pace of the
composition. Meanwhile, a contrapuntal intensification is achieved in measure
41, where, exactly at the moment of a dissonant, deceptive cadence on the
submediant of the dominant, Mendelssohn introduces the mirror-inverted
form of the subject (see Ex. 8.17). In measure 58 a third and final accelerando
to *Allegro con fuoco* is indicated, and here Mendelssohn establishes sixteenth-
note motion as an additional rhythmic intensification. In measure 73, at a
dramatic, and deceptive, *fortissimo* arrival on the submediant C major – a
counterpart to the deceptive cadence on G major in measure 41 – Mendelssohn reverts to the prime form of the subject. A culminating pedal-point
passage then builds up to the final climax: a tense octave passage with a series
of forceful diminished-seventh sonorities; the last of these diminished sevenths
disintegrates into an arpeggiated octave passage which proceeds directly into
the E major "chorale of release," marked "Più lento, maestoso."
    The chorale, a freely composed melody, unfolds in five strains against a
walking bass line in octaves. The turn from minor to major has the effect of
resolving the dissonant language of the fugue proper; indeed, one can see how
the stepwise motion of the bass effectively smoothes out the disjunct leaps of
the subject (see Ex. 8.18). In the closing section of the composition, marked
"Andante come prima," Mendelssohn brings back the subject, but now in the

major mode; the final cadence offers the ultimate resolution of the character-istic tritone A–D♯, which has so permeated the fugue.

Schubring's programmatic interpretation of the fugue encourages additional lines of inquiry and speculation. First of all, are we entitled to consider a programmatic interpretation of the E minor prelude? As we have seen, the prelude is linked to the fugue thematically and harmonically through similar applications of the tritone; what is more, the prelude displays complete statements of the descending chromatic fourth, a figure implied in the compound structure of the fugal subject. Since the Baroque period, of course, the descending fourth had been used as a topical symbol of the lament, and it is not at all implausible to suppose that the figure, implicit in the fugal subject, carried an expressive purpose which Mendelssohn sought to make explicit in the prelude.

Second, the extraordinary use of the culminating, freely composed chorale in the fugue invites further discussion. Of course, Mendelssohn employed well-known chorale melodies in a variety of choral and instrumental works.[57] But to create new, untexted chorale melodies and to incorporate them in instrumental contexts was a somewhat unusual procedure. Already as a student under Zelter, Mendelssohn had composed chorale melodies which he harmonized and set to the devotional poetry of the eighteenth-century poet Christian Fürchtegott Gellert.[58] And Mendelssohn knew intimately, of course, the extraordinary use of a textless chorale-like melody in the *Heiliger Dankgesang* movement of Beethoven's String Quartet in A minor op. 132. More important for our consideration, however, Mendelssohn devised new, and textless, chorale melodies in two works he composed after the E minor Fugue. The slow movement of the Cello Sonata in D major op. 58 (1843) alternates between chorale-like strains and recitative-like passages. And in the finale of the Piano Trio in C minor op. 66 (1846), we find a chorale introduced as the second theme. Whether or not these experiments carried specific programmatic connotations is not clear, though, in light of Schubring's claims for the E minor Fugue, the possibility should not be ruled out.[59]

---

57 As, for example, in the series of chorale cantatas composed between 1827 and 1832 (*Christe, Du Lamm Gottes, Jesu, meine Freude, Wer nur den lieben Gott läßt walten, O Haupt voll Blut und Wunden, Vom Himmel hoch, Wir glauben all an einen Gott*, and *Ach Gott vom Himmel sieh' darein*), the "Reformation" Symphony op. 107, the oratorios *St. Paul, Elijah*, and *Christus*, and the Organ Sonatas op. 65.

58 See my *Mendelssohn's Musical Education* (Cambridge, 1983), pp. 36–9.

59 The technique of utilizing freshly composed chorales can be traced in other nineteenth-century works. For example, Meyerbeer composed a pseudo-chorale melody for the chant of the three Anabaptists in *Le prophète* (1849), "Ad nos, ad salutarem undam." The overture of Wagner's *Die Meistersinger* gives way, of course, to a chorale. New chorale melodies were used by Adolf

Ex. 8.19:   Mendelssohn, Fugue in G major op. 37 no. 2

Third, the remarkable plan of the E minor fugue – based essentially on the principle of *Steigerung* – and its presentation and resolution of intensely dissonant melodic, harmonic, and tonal elements, was not without significance for Mendelssohn's later work. The fugal subject alone, marked by prominent tritones, is related to the subjects of two organ fugues by Mendelssohn. In the Fugue in G major op. 37 no. 2 (see Ex. 8.19), we find a compound melodic line that unfolds a series of three consecutive tritones. More striking is a comparison of the E Minor Fugue with the first movement of the Third Organ Sonata from op. 65 (1845). Following a majestic exordium in A major,

Ex. 8.20:   Mendelssohn, Organ Sonata in A major op. 65 no. 3

Henselt in his Piano Concerto in F minor op. 16, and by César Franck in his *Prélude, choral et fugue* (1884).

196

Ex. 8.21:   Mendelssohn, Overture to *Elijah* op. 70

Mendelssohn proceeds with a dissonant fugue in A minor, and its subject (see Ex. 8.20) strikingly brings to mind that of op. 35 no. 1: beginning with a step, it expands to a tritone, which, after a rhythmic variant, gives way to an eighth-note line that contains two tritones.

Several other details of the A minor organ fugue prompt additional comparisons with op. 35 no. 1. As the opening four-part exposition is completed, Mendelssohn introduces the chorale "Aus tiefer Noth," placed, appropriately enough, in the pedals.[60] The chorale proceeds strain by strain, contraposed against the ongoing fugue that provides a kind of connective tissue; the fugue is, in fact, an example of the chorale fugue. After the third strain of "Aus tiefer Noth," Mendelssohn specifies a gradual accelerando, coordinated with a fresh subject in sixteenth notes that marks a distinct rhythmic intensification. The fugue culminates in a pedal passage built upon a broken arpeggiation of a diminished-seventh sonority, in which the interval D–G♯, the original tritone of the subject, is displayed prominently. This pedal passage then yields to the return of the opening section in A major, and in the final cadence we hear the ultimate resolution of the tritone. Several features in the design and construction of the organ fugue – the subject and its marked tritones, the introduction of the chorale, the accelerando, the pedal passage, and the conclusion in the major mode – are clearly reminiscent of procedures first explored by Mendelssohn in op. 35 no. 1.

Finally, the E minor Fugue op. 35 no. 1 may have been recalled by Mendelssohn when he composed the overture to *Elijah*, where we find a fugue that has strong ties as well to the A minor organ fugue from op. 65 no. 3. Indeed, as Example 8.21 illustrates, the opening of the fugue in *Elijah*, with its step expanding to a tritone, seems directly modeled on the subject of the organ fugue. Now the use of the tritone in *Elijah* has, of course, a clear programmatic purpose, for in the celebrated introductory recitative that precedes the fugue, a series of three stark, overlapping tritones graphically symbolizes the pronouncement of the Lord that "There shall not be dew nor rain these years, but according to my word" (see Ex. 8.22). As in the op. 35 no. 1, then, a fugue with prominent tritones is used expressively to suggest struggle – a struggle

---

60 Earlier Mendelssohn had explored the use of this particular chorale melody in a fugal context in the cantata "Aus tiefer Noth" op. 23 no. 1, composed in Italy in 1830.

Ex. 8.22:   Mendelssohn, *Elijah*, Introduction

depicted in Mendelssohn's most dissonant language, that based on the interval of the tritone.

A few additional details further link the opening of *Elijah* with the E minor Fugue op. 35 no. 1. There is, of course, the introduction of mirror inversion to intensify the part writing (mm. 42ff.); in *Elijah*, Mendelssohn goes one step further by combining the prime and inverted forms (mm. 57ff.), yet another level of intensification. Then there is the dramatic deceptive cadence on the submediant (mm. 66–7) and pedal point (mm. 74ff.). And finally, in the choral fugue that follows ("The harvest now is over, the summer days are gone"), there is a fresh fugal subject that incorporates a clear reference to the descending chromatic fourth, emblem of the lament (see Ex. 8.23).

V

Was Mendelssohn a wig-adorned contrapuntist? To be sure, his fugues "have much of Sebastian," as Schumann admitted. Ever the perceptive critic, however, Schumann went on to observe that Mendelssohn had written his op. 35 not for mere "pastime, but rather to call the attention of pianoforte players once more to this masterly old form and to accustom them to it again. That he has chosen the right means for succeeding in this – avoiding all useless imitations and small artificialities, allowing the melody of the cantilena to predominate while holding fast to the Bach form – is very much like him."[61] To twentieth-century ears all too familiar with the intricacies of Bach's music, Mendelssohn's fugal style does seem at times perilously close to Bach; indeed,

The har- vest now is o - ver, the sum- mer days are gone,   and yet no power cometh to help us

Ex. 8.23:   Mendelssohn, *Elijah*, No. 1, "The harvest now is over"

61 Schumann, *On Music and Musicians*, p. 215.

for Berlioz, Mendelssohn was "still, it must be said, a little too fond of the dead."[62] But in Schumann's view – and Schumann was surely one nineteenth-century composer who prized originality – Mendelssohn was no slavish imitator. Rather, he had found an appropriate middle course: in the op. 35, the essence of Bach's counterpoint was presented in a garb still suitably modern enough for audiences of the 1830s. Perhaps we should not be surprised, then, that both Robert and Clara Schumann found inspiration in Mendelssohn's piano and organ fugues of 1837.[63]

We should remember, too, that in these fugues Mendelssohn was responding not only to Bachian counterpoint but to the expressive programmatic potential of the genre. The use of the fugue as a topic for struggle was an approach shared by several, though dissimilar, nineteenth-century composers; witness the finale of Berlioz's *Symphonie fantastique*, the opening of his *Roméo et Juliette*, the Mephistopheles movement of Liszt's *Faust* Symphony or Liszt's Fantasy and Fugue on "Ad nos, ad salutarem undam." Throughout his career, of course, Mendelssohn remained characteristically aloof from programmatic interpretations of his instrumental works. Nevertheless, we should not interpret his reticence to discuss such issues necessarily as a denial of their validity. Schubring's suggestion about the inspiration behind the E minor Fugue reminds us that Mendelssohn, wigified Bachian contrapuntist that he may have been, was also a child of the nineteenth century, and of nineteenth-century aesthetics.

---

62 *The Memoirs of Hector Berlioz*, p. 294.

63 On Robert Schumann's response to Mendelssohn's fugues, see Keil, *Untersuchungen zur Fugentechnik*, pp. 52–4 and the literature cited there. The three fugues of Clara Schumann's op. 16 have subjects similar to those in Mendelssohn's op. 35 nos. 5, 4 and op. 37 no. 2; the second fugue of Robert Schumann's op. 72, in D minor, has a subject similar to that of Mendelssohn's op. 37 no. 3, also in D minor.

9 Mendelssohn's letters to Eduard Devrient: filling in some gaps

J. RIGBIE TURNER

Mendelssohn's letters to his friend Eduard Devrient have long been a rich source of information about the composer's life.[1] Of the fifty-five known letters from Mendelssohn to Devrient, twenty are found today in The Pierpont Morgan Library, New York, and fourteen in the Library of Congress, Washington. Of the twenty-one remaining letters most are known only from the quotations from them in the *Erinnerungen*, or from citations in auction catalogues.[2] Devrient did not publish all of Mendelssohn's letters in his *Erinnerungen*, and not all of those he did include were published completely. The purpose of this article – which deals only with the thirty-four letters in the Morgan Library and the Library of Congress – is to publish the letters, or sections of letters, that Devrient omitted. (Devrient's letters to Mendelssohn, which were not examined in preparing this article, are bound in the so-called Green Books, now in the Bodleian Library, Oxford.[3]) Although it cannot be said with certainty whether any of the omitted material has previously appeared in print, probably most of the material presented here appears for the first time. This is not a critical edition of the letters: the many places where Devrient's reading differs only slightly from Mendelssohn's originals – that is, where Devrient's version does not significantly misrepresent what Mendelssohn wrote – are not noted.

From the beginning Mendelssohn has been ill-served by his editors, and critics were quick to point out the deficiencies in the early editions of the letters. In 1865, George Grove wrote to E. M. Oakeley, a master at Clifton

1 Eduard Devrient, *Meine Erinnerungen an Felix Mendelssohn-Bartholdy und seine Briefe an mich* (Leipzig, 1869) [hereafter *Erinnerungen*]; and, in English as *My Recollections of Felix Mendelssohn-Bartholdy, and His Letters to Me*, trans. Natalia Macfarren (London, 1869; New York, 1972) [hereafter *Recollections*].

2 I am grateful to Rudolf Elvers for this information.

3 See, further, *Catalogue of the Mendelssohn Papers in the Bodleian Library, Oxford*, vol. I: *Correspondence of Felix Mendelssohn and Others*, ed. Margaret Crum (Tutzing, 1980).

College, reproaching the editors (Paul Mendelssohn-Bartholdy and Carl Mendelssohn-Bartholdy) of the composer's letters, which had recently been translated into English:[4]

> The editors of Mendelssohn's Letters ... have suppressed *all mention* of many of the most prominent of his contemporaries and the dearest of his friends. It is hardly credible that the names of Jenny Lind, Joachim, Sterndale Bennett, J. W. Davison, Robert Schumann, and Clara Wieck, with whom he was in the closest intimacy and constant correspondence, should either not be found at all in either of the volumes or else only be mentioned in some such terms as "the Schumanns are here," "Bennett has just arrived," and so on. What the motive for this exclusion is, I do not know. I can only observe one fact: that Mendelssohn had a very high opinion of all these persons, and that therefore if he had mentioned them, it would always be in terms of praise. Now very few of the letters printed contain praise of his contemporaries; blame of Meyerbeer and Auber and others is occasionally to be found, but praise of anybody rarely if ever. This seems to have been one guiding principle in selecting the letters, and it is a very reprehensible one, because it not only suppresses Mendelssohn's good opinion of the various persons, but also leads one to believe that he was jealous of his rivals – which is the reverse of the truth. Quantities of letters exist *full of praise* of Jenny Lind, Joachim, Schumann, &c.[5]

Philipp Spitta, writing some years later, faulted the editors of two books containing letters of Mendelssohn to Ferdinand David and to Ignaz and Charlotte Moscheles. He found especially objectionable their practice of conflating two or more letters into one, with little or no indication to the reader that more than one letter was involved, that omissions had been made, or that freely invented connecting passages had been added. As an example, he cites a letter from Mendelssohn to David of thirty-two lines: the first twelve lines are taken from the middle of a letter dated 21 October 1841; the next seven lines come from a letter of 23 September (that is, an *earlier* letter), with two alterations in construction [*Konstruktionsänderungen*] and an omission; then come five lines from the letter of 21 October, "und der Rest scheint ein freies Potpourri nach Mendelssohn'schen Motiven zu sein."[6] Spitta concludes that "the owners of Mendelssohn's surviving letters have the right to publish them or not. But they do not have the right to mutilate them, to cut them up and patch them together in a new order. A new, thoroughly revised edition of

---

4 *Letters from Italy and Switzerland*, trans. Lady Wallace (London, 1862) and *Letters, 1833–1847*, trans. Lady Wallace (London, 1863).

5 Charles L. Graves, *The Life and Letters of Sir George Grove* (London, 1903), pp. 128–9.

6 Philipp Spitta, review of *Ferdinand David und die Familie Mendelssohn Bartholdy*, ed. Julius Eckardt, and *Briefe von Felix Mendelssohn Bartholdy an Ignaz und Charlotte Moscheles*, ed. Felix Moscheles, *Vierteljahrsschrift für Musikwissenschaft* 5 (1889), 221–2.

the two-volume collection of letters is urgently needed. In its present form it has lost all credibility."[7]

Similar obstacles obtain in Sebastian Hensel's book on the Mendelssohn family,[8] a singularly unreliable edition, as a comparison with the original letters at the New York Public Library shows, and in Ferdinand Hiller's book of letters and recollections.[9] Until we have trustworthy texts for these letters, scholarship remains, to some extent, at the mercy of nineteenth-century editions and editorial methods. Clearly, much new information about Mendelssohn and his times is to be gained from accurate publications of the letters. Compared with the willful omissions and the mutilations cited by Grove and Spitta, Devrient's sins are venial indeed. True, Devrient did leave out passages critical of Mendelssohn's contemporaries, but one senses that he did so as much to safeguard their reputation as to sanitize Mendelssohn's. And nowhere (so far as I have found) did Devrient engage in the cut-and-paste practices denounced by Spitta. But Devrient has left us with an incomplete and biased redaction of Mendelssohn's letters – a state of affairs all too common in editions of many musicians' letters, not only Mendelssohn's, and it is hoped that the present article may be taken as but one example of the fundamental type of research that still remains to be done for one of the central figures of nineteenth-century musical life.[10] It need hardly be pointed out that only when we have complete and accurate editions of these letters can we hope to have complete and accurate translations of them. Macfarren's translation of the *Erinnerungen* leaves something to be desired, aside from the dated locutions and all but useless index; while it generally conveys Mendelssohn's sense, it too often misses his individuality, his idiosyncrasy, his special turn of phrase – in short, precisely those attributes that we recall from a memorable correspondent.

The reasons for Devrient's omissions for the most part are readily surmised. Mendelssohn was often more critical of his musical and artistic contemporaries than the *Erinnerungen* suggest, and even though he had died more than twenty years before the book appeared, some of the targets of Mendelssohn's acerbic remarks were still living. For example, Devrient's gloss on Mendelssohn's

7 *Ibid.*, 222.
8 Sebastian Hensel, *Die Familie Mendelssohn 1729–1847, nach Briefen und Tagebüchern*, 3 vols. (Berlin, 1879).
9 Ferdinand Hiller, *Felix Mendelssohn-Bartholdy: Briefe und Erinnerungen* (Cologne, 1874).
10 Three recent books are the result of just such a scholarly approach to the letters of Mendelssohn and his family: Felix Mendelssohn Bartholdy, *Briefe an deutsche Verleger*, ed. Rudolf Elvers (Berlin, 1968); Felix Mendelssohn Bartholdy, *Briefe*, ed. Rudolf Elvers (Frankfurt, 1984); and *The Letters of Fanny Hensel to Felix Mendelssohn*, ed. and trans. Marcia J. Citron (Stuyvesant, 1987).

early opinion of Wilhelm Taubert[11] barely hints at Mendelssohn's lengthy criticism of the young composer and his songs (see Letter 7). But Taubert was still alive, and Devrient understandably chose to leave out this candid passage. Several letters (nos. 11, 14, and 15) mention singers – most of them long forgotten – who, if they were still alive, might have taken umbrage at Mendelssohn's casual references to them. Letter 16 conveys an unflattering portrait of a young art student. A passage in Letter 19, in which Mendelssohn offers some Bach cantatas and motets to "meinen guten Stuttgartern," is unexceptionable; perhaps Devrient considered Mendelssohn's suggestion that the works might prove too coarse-grained and bristly for the people of Stuttgart an unnecessary slight on them. Other letters (for example nos. 20, 22, 23, 28, 30, 32, and 33), of a social or business nature, could easily be omitted from the *Erinnerungen* without loss of continuity or substance. In addition to softening the composer's more outspoken opinions, Devrient frequently omits personal names altogether, although in many places it is not clear to readers today why Devrient chose to alter the wording of Mendelssohn's letters.

According to the *Erinnerungen*, Devrient and Mendelssohn first met in January 1822; Mendelssohn was twelve years old, Devrient twenty. Devrient had studied singing and thorough-bass with Zelter (who taught Mendelssohn composition) at the Berlin Singakademie. From the early 1820s Devrient was a leading baritone at the Royal Opera, where he sang until 1831, when, owing to overwork, he lost his voice. He later concentrated on producing and acting, but left his most prominent mark as a librettist and as a theater reformer and historian; his major publication, the five-volume *Geschichte der deutschen Schauspielkunst* (Leipzig, 1848–74), remains a fundamental reference work on the history of German theater.

The *Erinnerungen* begin with an affectionate portrait of the young Mendelssohn that vividly conveys his genial (if frequently changeable) temperament and immense musical gifts. Early in their friendship Devrient became convinced that Mendelssohn's true calling lay in dramatic music, and he wrote a libretto based on an episode from Tasso's *Gerusalemme liberata*. The text remained unused, the first of many attempts at collaborating on an opera – all unsuccessful, as the *Erinnerungen* (and some of the letters that follow) show. Devrient could be sharply critical of Mendelssohn's works, and he astutely criticized the ill-fated *Hochzeit des Camacho*, Mendelssohn's opera based on episodes from *Don Quixote*, which was premièred in Berlin on 29 April 1827 but soon withdrawn. He thought that by ushering in the Don's every speech

---

11 *Erinnerungen*, pp. 139–40; *Recollections*, p. 141.

with an imposing flourish of trumpets, Mendelssohn had entirely missed Cervantes' irony in portraying his hero's comical knight-errantry. The composer maintained that "the knight of the rueful countenance believed himself to be a genuine hero"; Devrient pointed out that "Cervantes himself everywhere places the grotesqueness of antiquated chivalry in the strongest light; I urged that the composer might safely follow the poet, and that no actor would think of personating the old knight as a veritable hero, but always as the vainglorious boaster; and how was this universal interpretation of character to be reconciled with the grandiose instrumentation of Felix?"[12] It is indeed to be regretted that a writer of such evident musical and dramatic intuition was unable to produce a libretto that was to Mendelssohn's liking. But Devrient's judgment – or just his memory? – was not without fault. In the overture to *A Midsummer Night's Dream* (1826), Devrient wrote, Mendelssohn "throws off scholastic fetters and stands forth in native strength. ... The Mendelssohn we possess and cherish, dates from this composition."[13] But he has overlooked the Octet op. 20, composed the previous year, which must be counted among the most astonishing creations of musical precocity.

In 1827 Devrient wrote *Hans Heiling* for Mendelssohn; he did not set the libretto and Devrient later revised it for Heinrich Marschner. First performed in 1833, it was Marschner's most important opera, and one of the major German Romantic operas before Wagner's. In addition to *Heiling*, Devrient proposed (and Mendelssohn rejected) the legend of Blue-Beard; *Drosselbart* and *Bisamapfel*, two German folk tales; an original work about two friends whose separation and reconciliation take place in Germany, the Italian Carnival, and the Swiss Alps; Kohlhaas;[14] Andreas Hofer;[15] and finally an episode from the *Bauernkrieg* (for more on the *Bauernkrieg*, see Letter 30).[16] One other subject progressed further: the *Loreley*, a collaboration with Emanuel Geibel. Mendelssohn set two numbers in 1847, and might well have completed the opera had he not died the same year. "There is a Hamlet-like tragedy about Mendelssohn's operatic destiny," wrote Devrient. "During eighteen years he could not make up his mind firmly to adopt any subject and work it out, because he wanted perfection; and when at last he overcame his scruples and

12 *Recollections*, p. 27.   13 *Ibid.*, p. 31.

14 Presumably based on Heinrich von Kleist's novella *Michael Kohlhaas* (1810).

15 The Tyrolese patriot (1767–1810). His story was the subject of Karl Immermann's most successful dramatic work, *Das Trauerspiel in Tyrol* (1828), later revised and retitled *Andreas Hofer* (1834). For more on Immermann and Mendelssohn, see note 56.

16 Konrad Huschke, "Vom Freundschaftsbund Mendelssohns mit Eduard Devrient," *Neue Musikzeitschrift* 1 (1947), 360.

determined upon a poem, though far from what it should have been, he sank with his fragment into the grave."[17]

Devrient also played a central role in Mendelssohn's historic revival of the *St. Matthew Passion* in 1829. Mendelssohn first heard parts of Bach's work in Zelter's classes, and, at about the same time, with Devrient at Zelter's special Friday meetings of select members of the Berlin Singakademie, which Zelter had directed since 1800. "Here we used to sing what Zelter called the 'bristly pieces' of Sebastian Bach," wrote Devrient, "who was at that time generally considered an unintelligible musical arithmetician, with an astonishing facility in writing fugues. . . ."[18] Eduard Rietz, Mendelssohn's violin teacher and close friend, made a copy of the Passion, which was presented to the composer on Christmas Day 1823. (Rietz and his brother, Julius, copied out the parts for the 1829 performance, at which Eduard served as concert master.)

In the winter of 1827 Mendelssohn assembled "a small and trusty choir" that began to learn the Passion piece by piece. As they contemplated a performance of the complete work, both Mendelssohn and Devrient (who "longed more and more to sing the part of Christ in public") were acutely aware of the difficulties they faced: the work itself, which in its day posed unprecedented technical demands; the public, whose reception of such a huge, utterly unfamiliar work was still in doubt; and Zelter himself, who, though he revered Bach's music, was fiercely protective of his own efforts to promote his works, harbored outspoken reservations about the Passion project, and init- ially offered little encouragement to Mendelssohn and Devrient. When they finally confronted Zelter and outlined their plans, he retorted: "That one should have the patience to listen to all this! I can tell you that very different people have had to give up doing this very thing, and do you think that a couple of young donkeys like you will be able to accomplish it?"[19] Despite this skeptical outburst, Zelter soon gave Mendelssohn and Devrient per- mission to pursue the venture, and preparations for the performance began in earnest. The now-celebrated concert took place on 11 March 1829; Mendels- sohn conducted from the piano, Devrient sang the role of Christ and Heinrich

---

17 *Recollections*, p. 294.   18 *Ibid.*, p. 13.

19 *Ibid.*, p. 53 – a rather free translation of: "'Das soll man nun geduldig anhören! Haben sich's ganz andere Leute müssen vergehen lassen diese Arbeit zu unternehmen, und da kommt nun so ein Paar Rotznasen daher, denen alles das Kinderspiel ist'" (*Erinnerungen*, p. 57). Zelter's "Rotznasen," which Macfarren translates as "donkeys," is, literally (and crudely), "snot-noses," or, more politely, "brats." Georg Schünemann cautions us not to take Devrient's *Erinnerungen* literally on this point. "Zelter's objections concerned the question of the arrangement [of the *St. Matthew Passion*]. Since both [Mendelssohn and Devrient] could rely on Zelter himself to conduct a performance, he had no reason to oppose one. On the contrary: he assisted with all his strength." Georg Schünemann, *Die Singakademie zu Berlin, 1791–1941* (Regensburg, 1941), pp. 53–4.

Stümer the Evangelist; other parts were taken by Anna Milder-Hauptmann, Pauline Schätzel,[20] Auguste Türrschmiedt (also listed as Türrschmidt and Thürrschmidt), Karl Adam Bader, J. E. Busolt, and Weppler. There was a second performance ten days later and, on 17 April, a third, conducted by Zelter, of which Mendelssohn's sister Fanny Hensel has left a critical (and not wholly disinterested) account.[21] "This was the decisive turning-point in Bach's reputation," observes Nicholas Temperley, "for it swiftly transformed the [Bach] revival from a cult of intellectuals into a popular movement."[22]

On 26 December 1829, Devrient sang in *Die Heimkehr aus der Fremde*, a *Singspiel* that Mendelssohn wrote to celebrate his parents' silver wedding anniversary. (Other parts were taken by the composer's younger sister, Rebecka, and his brother-in-law, Wilhelm Hensel, for whom Mendelssohn wrote a part requiring him to sing on only one note.) Their published correspondence dates from the same year, although three earlier letters are known. (Devrient's first surviving letter to Mendelssohn is dated 22 February 1829.) When the correspondence opens, Mendelssohn was on his first trip to London.

The following information is given for the letters: the place and date of writing; the location of the original (the Morgan Library, hereafter NYpm, or the Library of Congress, hereafter Wc);[23] where the published letter appears in the *Erinnerungen* and in the *Recollections*; the page and line where the omitted or revised passage would occur in the *Erinnerungen*; the emended reading; and the translation of the passage or letter,[24] with a reference to the page and line where the omitted passage would be found in the *Recollections*. In several places the opening or closing words of the translation do not correspond exactly to the German text, but have instead been rendered so as to connect smoothly with Macfarren's text in the *Recollections*. No substantive differences were found between the original and published versions of Letters 9, 12, 25, 26, and 27.

[1]

London, 19 May 1829; original in NYpm. *Erinnerungen*, pp. 77–80; *Recollections*, pp. 73–7.
Erinnerungen, p. 80, lines 6–7:

20 For more on Schätzel, see note 47.
21 See Citron, *The Letters of Fanny Hensel to Felix Mendelssohn*, pp. 25–6.
22 Nicholas Temperley, "Bach Revival," *The New Grove Dictionary of Music and Musicians*, ed. Stanley Sadie, 20 vols. (London, 1980), vol. I, p. 884.
23 I express my thanks to those institutions for granting permission to publish their letters.
24 Reading Mendelssohn's famously elegant handwriting, which Eduard Hanslick compared to that of his "musikalischen Gegenpols" Richard Wagner, posed few problems; translating his

for Donizetti
read Donzelli
Recollections, p. 76, line 10:
  This is tentatively corrected in a footnote. The reference is, of course, to the Italian tenor Domenico Donzelli (1790–1873).
Erinnerungen, p. 80, lines 11–12:
  after Du solltest sie sehen! *insert*:
  Bauer hat mir durch seinen Brief an Mühlenfels, der ihm nächstens antwortet, den größten Gefallen gethan. M. ist ein herrlicher Mensch, den ich trotz der kurzen Zeit unsrer Bekanntschaft sehr lieb gewonnen habe.
Recollections, p. 76, line 16, after "You should see her!"
  Baur[25] has done me the greatest favor by his letter to Mühlenfels,[26] who will answer him at once. Mühlenfels is a wonderful human being of whom I have become very fond in spite of our short acquaintance.

[2]

London, 17 June 1829; original in NYpm; Devrient has misdated the letter 19 June. *Erinnerungen*, pp. 81–5; *Recollections*, pp. 78–83.
Erinnerungen, p. 84, line 18:
  for die Meeresstille für
  read die Meeresstille, deren Worte Mühlenfels trefflich übersetzt hat, für
Recollections, p. 82, line 5:
  Calm Sea [and Prosperous Voyage], the words of which Mühlenfels has translated admirably

[3]

London, 29 October 1829; original in Wc. *Erinnerungen*, pp. 87–90; *Recollections*, pp. 84–8.
Erinnerungen, p. 89, lines 19–20:
  for aber vergleicht man doch ein englisches Musikfest mit einem deutschen

---

(to Anglo-American ears) occasionally unwieldy sentences posed rather more. For her invaluable help with both tasks, I should like to thank Dr. Ruth Kraemer.

25 The theologian Albert Baur (1803–66), a friend of Mendelssohn's. For these brief identifying notes, I have drawn freely on several sources; in addition to standard reference works, I have used the Index of Names in Citron, *The Letters of Fanny Hensel to Felix Mendelssohn*; Crum, *Correspondence of Felix Mendelssohn and Others*; Elvers, *Briefe*; and *Giacomo Meyerbeer: Briefwechsel und Tagebücher*, ed. Heinz and Gudrun Becker, 4 vols. (Berlin, 1960–85).
26 The lawyer Ludwig von Mühlenfels (1798–1861), a friend of Mendelssohn's.

read aber vergleicht man doch ein englisches Musikfest mit solch lum-
pigem deutschen

Recollections, p. 87, lines 8–10:

but the difference between a musical festival here and such a shabby one
in Germany

Erinnerungen, p. 89, line 25–p. 90, line 1:

for gar zu sehr. Denke ich an die Musiker in Berlin, Devrient, so wird mir
grimmig und gallig zu Muthe. Es sind Jammerfürsten und dabei alle
solche Gefühlsmenschen

read gar zu sehr; es sind Jammerfürsten, voll Eitelkeit, Unwissenheit,
Rohheit, u. Leerheit. Denke ich an die Musiker in Berlin, Devrient, so
wird mir grimmig u. gallig zu Muthe. Sie haben nicht einmal die
Eigenschaft, die ich von meinem Schuster fordere, sie sind nicht einmal
ehrbar u. dabey alle solche Gefühlsmenschen

Recollections, p. 87, lines 14–17:

altogether. They are pitiful wretches, all vanity, ignorance, crudeness,
and dullness. Devrient, when I think of the musicians in Berlin I am
furious and bitter. They don't even have the character that I demand of
my shoemaker; they are not even honest, with all their sentimentality

[4]

Vienna, 5 September 1830, and Kloster Lilienfeld, Steiermark, 2 October
1830; original in NYpm. *Erinnerungen*, pp. 105–11; *Recollections*, pp. 103–11.

Erinnerungen, p. 109, lines 13–14:

for einem bekannten Berliner zu begegnen.

read auf einmal Herrn Henoch aus Berlin zu begegnen.

Recollections, p. 108, lines 13–14:

suddently to meet Mr. Henoch[27] from Berlin.

Erinnerungen, p. 109, lines 18–20:

for wie Du weißt, und so muß ich Dir sagen, daß mir die Münchener
Maler gar wenig gefallen haben, denn es fehlt ihnen das Erste

read wie du wohl weißt, u. da muss ich dann auch sowohl den Förster als
den Maler Hermann in München bei Dir verklagen, die beiden Leute
haben mir gar zu wenig gefallen. Erstlich ihre Malereien nicht, denn die
sind so künstlich = einfach, u. so schwächlich = colossal, u. so mesquin =
großartig, u. so geziert = rekelhaft; zweitens sie selbst nicht, denn sie sind
wie ihre Malereien, u. suchen Deutschland in der Tracht, u. tragen das

27 Unidentified.

Grosse immer fort im Munde, u. suchen das Eigenthümliche in kurzen Röcken, langen Haaren, u. einem nackten Halse, u. sprechen so viel von der Herzlichkeit; dann ihre Ansichten nicht, denn es fehlt ihnen das erste

Recollections, p. 108, lines 18–20:

as you may know, and so I must indict not only Förster[28] but also the painter Hermann[29] in Munich. They both pleased me all too little: first, their paintings, because they are so artificially simple, so feebly colossal, so shabbily grandiose, so primly loutish; second, the men themselves, because they are like their paintings, they try in their costumes to be German, always have grand things to say, seek the characteristic feature in short coats, long hair, a bare neck, and talk so much of cordiality; I dislike even their opinions, for they lack the first quality

[5]

Milan, 13 July 1831; original in NYpm. *Erinnerungen*, pp. 112–22; *Recollections*, pp. 111–22.

Erinnerungen, p. 118, lines 24–5:

for denn solch ein Kerl, wie ich einen angetroffen habe

read denn solch ein Kerl, wie Herr Teschner, den ich hier angetroffen habe

Recollections, p. 118, lines 22–3:

for such a fellow, like Mr. Teschner,[30] whom I met here

Erinnerungen, p. 119, lines 6–8:

for Aber höre nur solche italienisch Gebildeten an, wie die so *gar keine* Methode haben,

read Aber höre nur eine Italiänische Dilettantinn, oder Mlle. Carl! Wie sie so *gar keine* Methode haben!

Recollections, p. 119, lines 7–9:

Could you but hear an Italian dilettante, or Miss Carl![31] How devoid of any method they are!

[6]

Lucerne, 27 August 1831; original in NYpm. *Erinnerungen*, pp. 122–31; *Recollections*, pp. 122–32.

Erinnerungen, p. 127, lines 8–9:

28 Ernst Förster (1800–1885), the German history painter, lithographer, and writer on art.
29 Carl Heinrich Hermann (1802–80), the German painter.
30 Gustav Wilhelm Teschner (1800–1883), the German singer, teacher, and music editor.
31 Henriette Carl (1805–90), the German soprano.

for was Du von Deinen Versen Anderes wolltest; ist es von innen heraus
read was Du von Deinen Versen anderes wolltest, u. warum Du nicht
begreifst, daß die platten, schönen Verse Deines Bekannten nicht zur
Oper paßen; ist es von innen heraus

Recollections, p. 128, lines 6–7:
what you wanted altered in your verses, and why you do not understand
that your friend's dull, pretty verses are not fit for opera. If they have
sprung from within

Erinnerungen, p. 128, line 16:
for ein Buch,
read ein Buch von Hotho,

Recollections, p. 129, line 19:
a book by Hotho;[32]

Erinnerungen, p. 130, lines 16–17:
for das Ding liegt gut für Dich. – Deinen Opernplan
read das Ding liegt gut für Dich, doch schreibe mir einmal, ob Du das
hohe F nehmen kannst, nicht ausgehalten, sondern nur ein Viertel lang; es
kommt am Ende drin vor. Deinen Opernplan

Recollections, p. 131, lines 22–3:
it lies well for you, but write and tell me if you can take the high F, not
sustained but only a quarter note; it occurs at the end. Your plot for a
libretto

[7]

Paris, 5 January 1832; original in NYpm. *Erinnerungen*, pp. 132–4; *Recollections*, pp. 133–5. (See Plate 9.1)

Erinnerungen, p. 133, the last 5 lines:
for Dich. Das fühlte ich recht lebhaft, als ich aus Rom einen Brief
nachgeschickt bekam und ich auf dem Brief den Mai las und wie Du so
freundlich besorgt um mich warst und dem Grafen Redern mich und
meine Compositionen lobtest, und wie Du von Garten und Wärme
read Dich.

Wenn ich Dir nun sage, wie es gekommen, so ist es möglich, daß Du es
mir erst gar übel nimmst, und es ist vielleicht nicht Recht, daß ich Dir es
so gerade heraus sage; verschweigen habe ich es gewollt, aber halb sagen
geht nicht und so muß es denn heraus. Mir hat nämlich Taubert's
mitgeschickte Musik zu Deinen Worten sämtlich nicht gefallen, und

---

32 Heinrich Gustav Hotho (1802–73), a writer on aesthetics and art history.

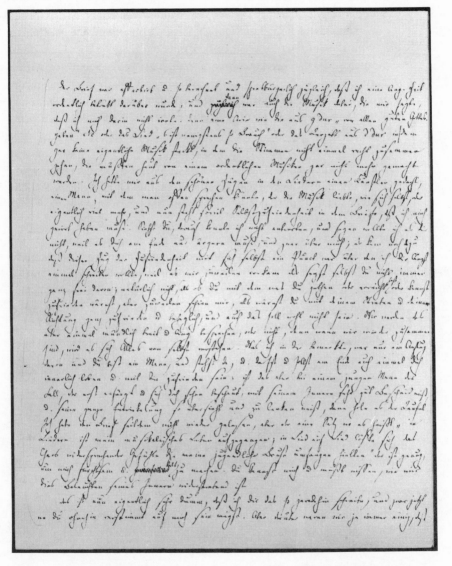

9.1:   Letter from Mendelssohn to Eduard Devrient, 5 January 1832, The Pierpont Morgan
Library, New York

das wäre noch nichts sehr schlimmes, aber der Brief, den er dazu schrieb
an Deine Zeilen heran, war so, daß er mich der ich für ihn gewiß
eingenommen war, mit kaltem Wasser übergoß u. es mir unmöglich
machte, ihm ein Wort darauf zu antworten. Der Brief war affectirt u.
so berechnet und spies[s]bürgerlich zugleich, daß ich eine lange Zeit

ordentlich betrübt darüber wurde, und dann war auch die Musik dabei, die mir sagte, daß ich mich darin nicht irrte. Denn eine Arie wie die aus g dur "von allen guten Gottesgaben" etc oder das Lied "[e]s ist wenigstens so Brauch" oder das Terzett aus d dur in dem gar keine eigentliche Musik steckt, in dem die Stimmen nicht einmal recht zusammen gehen, die müßten heut von einem ordentlichen Musiker gar nicht mehr gemacht werden. Ich hatte mir aus den schönen Zügen in den Liedern einen Künstler gedacht, einen Mann, mit dem man offen sprechen könnte, der die Musik liebte, wie sich selbst, oder eigentlich viel mehr, und nun steht soviel Selbstzufriedenheit in dem Briefe, daß ich mich geirrt haben muß. Siehst Du, darauf konnte ich nicht antworten, und sagen wollte ich es Dir nicht, weil es Dich am Ende nur ärgern muß, und zwar über mich; es kam noch dazu daß dieser Zug der Zufriedenheit mit sich selbst ein Punct war über den ich Dir längst einmal schreiben wollte, weil es mir zuweilen vorkam als seyst selbst Du nicht immer ganz frei davon; natürlich nicht, als ob Du mit dem was Du gethan oder erreicht hast oder kannst zufrieden wärest, aber zuweilen schien mir, als wärest Du mit Deinem Streben u. Deiner Richtung ganz zufrieden u. behaglich, und auch das soll wohl nicht sein. Wir werden das aber einmal mündlich breit u. lang besprechen, oder nicht, denn wenn wir wieder zusammen sind, wird es sich Alles von selbst verstehen. Was ich in Dir bemerkte, war nur ein Anflug davon und Du bist ein Mann, und stehst da, u. darfst u. sollst am Ende auch einmal Dich innerlich loben u. mit Dir zufrieden sein: ist das aber bei einem jungen Mann der Fall, der erst anfängt u. sich doch schon beschaut, mit seinem Innern sehr gut Bescheid weiß, u. seine ganze Entwickelung [sic] so übersieht und zu lenken weiß, dann hole es der Teufel. Ich habe den Brief seitdem nicht wieder gelesen, aber der eine Satz wo es heißt "in Liedern ist mein musikalisches Leben aufgegangen; in Lied auf Lied löste sich das Chaos widersprechender Gefühle die meine jugendliche Brust umfangen hielten" der ist genug, um mich furchtsam u. kalt zu machen. Du kennst mich u. mußt wissen, wie mir dies Beleuchten seines Innern widerstrebend ist.

Das ist nun eigentlich sehr dumm, daß ich Dir das so geradehin schreibe, und zwar jetzt wo Du ohnehin verstimmt auf mich sein magst. Aber darüber waren wir ja immer einig, daß man nur vor allen Dingen aufrichtig gegen einander sey, das Übrige werde sich dann schon leicht finden. Ich bin es nun gewesen, sey Du es ebenso sehr, u. sage mir gerade heraus, wenn Du mir böse darüber bist, laß aber nichts zurück, damit Du mir nicht brummst, und schreibe mir von allen Dingen gleich, wenn auch nur zwei Worte. Das muß ich aber noch hinzusetzen, daß Alles vorige nur von den Briefen u. dem Geschriebnen gilt; wenn T. und ich uns einmal kennen lernen dann werde ich so unterfangen mit ihm sein, als wäre das alles nicht geschehen, und werde mich doppelt freuen, wenn ich ihm Unrecht gethan. Bis dahin nur weiß ich ihm nichts zu sagen, denn predigen darf ich nicht, kann es auch nicht, u. die Wahrheit nicht sagen, geht noch weniger. So sage mir also nicht, daß ich ein Vorurtheil habe, denn ich habe es wirklich nicht, sage mir nur ob Du mir trotz alledem noch gut und mein alter Freund bist. Das ist die Hauptsache. – Ich hätte Dir das Alles nicht geschrieben, und hätte vielleicht lieber still geschwiegen bis auf mündlich Wiedersehen, da bekam ich aus Rom einen Brief geschickt, den Du an mich im Mai geschrieben hattest, und den Dr. Röstel erstlich mit nach Italien nahm, als ich schon fort war, u. dann nach Paris schickte, als ich noch nicht da war. Wie ich auf dem Brief den Mai las, und wie Du so freundlich besorgt für mich warst und dem Grafen Redern mich u. meine Compositionen lobtest, der darauf meinte, ich werde ja seinen Bruder in Neapel sprechen, und wie Du von Garten und Wärme

Recollections, pp. 135, lines 1–6:

you.

If I tell you now how it happened, it's possible that you may think quite ill of me, and perhaps it's wrong to speak to you so openly; I would have preferred to remain silent, but it won't do to mince words and so I must speak my mind. Taubert's[33] setting of your texts did not please me at all; that would not in itself be very bad, but the letter that he wrote about your texts had the effect of pouring cold water over me – I, who had such a high opinion of him – and made it impossible for me to give him one word in reply. The letter was so affected, so calculated and narrow-minded, that for a long time I was truly depressed about it; but then there was the music as well, which told me that I was not mistaken. For an aria like that in G major, "Von allen guten Gottesgaben," or the song "Es ist wenigstens so Brauch," or the trio in D major in which there is absolutely no real music, in which the voices do not even once go together properly; these simply are no longer composed by any true musician today. On account of the beautiful lines of the songs I had imagined an artist, a man with whom one could speak openly, who loved music as he did himself (actually much more), and now the letter displays so much self-satisfaction that I must have been wrong. So you see, I wasn't able to answer it and I didn't want to tell you, for in the end it must only annoy you, and for my sake at that.

33 Wilhelm Taubert (1811–91), the German conductor, composer, and pianist.

It also happened that this trait of self-satisfaction was a point about which I long wished to write to you, because it occurred to me at times that you yourself are not always entirely free of it – naturally not, as if you were satisfied with what you have done, or were able to do or achieve – but occasionally it seemed to me as though you were quite content and comfortable with your striving and aim, and that really should not be. But we shall speak of this at length in person sometime – or perhaps not, since when we're together again it will all go without saying. I only observed a hint of it in you, and you are a man and you stand there and you should and ought to praise yourself inwardly and be content with yourself. But when that happens in a young man who is just beginning, yet already fully acquainted with his inner self, and thus surveys his whole development and knows how to guide it, then the devil take it. I have not reread the letter since then, but a sentence like "my musical life is wrapped up in my songs; in song after song is released the chaos of contradictory emotions that enveloped my youthful breast" – that is enough to make me apprehensive and cold. You know me and must realize how repugnant his soul-baring is to me.

It's really very unwise of me to write so rashly to you about this, especially at a time when, moreover, you may well be cross with me. But on this we always agreed, that people be candid with each other; after that, the rest is easy. Now it has been me, you must be equally candid and tell me frankly if you are angry with me about it, but hold nothing back, so that you don't grumble at me, and write at once about everything, if only two words. I must add, however, that the foregoing is intended only for letters and the written word; once Taubert and I become acquainted I shall try to behave towards him as though none of this had happened, and shall be doubly happy if I am proved wrong about him. Until then I don't know what to say to him, for I have no right to preach (and am unable to do so anyhow), and not to tell the truth is even worse. So, do not tell me that I am prejudiced, for I truly am not; just tell me if, despite everything, you still care for me and are my old friend: that is the most important thing.

I should not have written all this to you, and perhaps should have said nothing until we meet again in person, when I received from Rome a letter you wrote me in May that Dr. Röstel[34] took with him to Rome, after I had left, and then sent to Paris, where I had not yet arrived. [I felt this so much when] I read the date "May" on the letter in which you

---

34 Unidentified.

expressed such friendly anxiety about me, and praised me and my compositions to Count Redern,[35] who then thought that I would of course speak with his brother in Naples; in which you speak of the garden, of heat

Erinnerungen, p. 134, line 11:

after brauchen., *add*:

Heut aber daran nichts, dann vor allen Dingen erwarte ich Deine Antwort.

Über die Sache selbst schreibe mir gar nicht, das führt nicht weiter, sondern schreibe mir nur, ob Du es machen willst u. kannst, wie ich, sie von jetzt an ganz vergessen und liegen lassen, u. weiter schreiben u. leben, als wäre sie nicht vorgefallen. Taubert selbst sage auf keinen Fall hieran, ich bitte ausdrücklich darum, es möchte unsre Bekanntschaft ganz verderben; ob Du ihm diesen Brief verschweigen willst, oder sagen ich ließe ihm für die Sendung vielmal danken, überlasse ich Dir.

Recollections, p. 135, line 16:

act. No more about this today, for first of all I await your reply.

Don't write me anything at all about the matter itself – that leads nowhere – but just tell me if from now on you, like me, are willing and able to forget it completely, put it aside, and continue to write and live as though it had never happened. May I expressly ask that under no circumstances you say anything about it to Taubert; that would utterly spoil our acquaintance. Whether you wish to withhold this letter from him, or to convey my thanks for what he sent, I leave to your discretion.

Writing to Taubert from Lucerne, on 27 August 1831, Mendelssohn avoids criticizing the songs with exquisite courtesy, and tactfully withholds comment until he sees Taubert's next works. He thanks Taubert for "the pleasure your songs gave me in Milan," and continues:

It is quite as fitting that people should be presented to each other through the medium of music paper as by a third person in society. . . . Your songs have pronounced your name clearly and plainly; they also disclose what you think and what you are; that you love music, and wish to make progress; thus I perhaps know you better than if we had met frequently. . . . Your songs . . . gave me especial pleasure, because I could gather from them that you must be a genuine musician. . . . The most agreeable part [of Taubert's letter] however is your promise to send me something to Munich. . . . I will then tell you my honest opinion. . . . I am very eager to see those recent works that you have promised me, for I do not doubt

---

35 Count Wilhelm Friedrich von Redern (1802–83), director of the royal opera house in Berlin. The world première of Heinrich Marschner's *Hans Heiling* was given there in 1833.

that I shall be much gratified by them, and many things that are only foreshadowed in the former songs will probably become manifest and distinct in them. I can therefore say nothing today of the impression your songs have made on me, because possibly any suggestion or question will already be answered in what you are about to send.[36]

Three years later, after a performance of Taubert's opera *Die Zigeuner*, Mendelssohn thanked Taubert for the pleasure this music gave him, adding that "it pleased me far more and made a clearer, fairer impression, and it again became quite obvious to me, as it once did in Milan, that you must, and will, compose very beautiful things."[37] In 1844, Mendelssohn dedicated his hymn "Hear My Prayer" to Taubert.

[8]

Paris, 10 March 1832; original in Wc. *Erinnerungen*, pp. 134–7; *Recollections*, pp. 136–8.

Erinnerungen, p. 136, between the paragraphs, insert:

Es müßen aber auch ein Paar Worte an Sie hinein, liebe Mde. Devrient, denn Schelle bekommen, u. dazu stillschweigen, habe ich niemals gekonnt, und dann immer eine Schelle bekommen, wegen meiner Antwort. Nun kann ich gar nicht leugnen, daß ich das letzte hier gerade gern möchte, also replicir ich frischweg, und sage, daß Sie mir ganz entsetzlich Unrecht gethan. Wenn ich Ihren Brief lese, so halte ich mich für einen mistrauischen, ganz grämlichen Kerl, dem nichts recht zu machen ist, und der mit Vorurtheilen gespickt ist. Und doch habe ich geschrieben, u. wiederhole es jetzt, daß ich bei meiner Rückkunft Taubert kennen lernen will und mich so darauf freue, als hätte ich nichts von ihm gespielt u. gelesen, u. daß Alles dies nicht die geringste Spur zurücklassen soll und darf, so bald ich ihn anders sehe, u. daß mich's nicht einmal furchtsam macht, sondern daß ich im Gegentheil weil er Eduards Freund ist, die allerbeste Erwartung von seiner Person u. seinem Treiben habe. Aber solange ich die nicht anders kenne, solange bleibt mir der vorige Eindruck vorherrschend, das können Sie nicht mistrauisch nennen, denn Musik ist mir doch einmal eine bestimmtere Sprache, als

36 Felix Mendelssohn, *Letters*, ed. G. Selden-Goth (New York, 1945) pp. 164–5. The autograph is in NYpm.

37 "Sie hat mir ungleich besser gefallen und einen klareren schöneren Eindruck gemacht, und es ist mir wieder wie damals in Mailand recht deutlich geworden wie Sie sehr schöne Sachen componiren müssen und componiren werden." Mendelssohn to Taubert, 24 September 1834, in Ernst Wolff, "Sechs unveröffentlichte Briefe Felix Mendelssohn Bartholdys an Wilhelm Taubert," *Die Musik* 8 (1908–9), 165–6.

Worte u. Briefe. Ich kann mir es übrigens wohl denken, daß ich Ihnen damit einigermaßen wie eine Nachteule vorkomme, da sie [sic] gewiß meine Widerlegung in den Händen oder vielmehr in den Ohren haben, aber bedenken Sie nun auch, daß es mit mir nicht so ist, und daß Sie mich am Ende doch kennen, also gebe ich es zurück, und sage seien Sie auch nicht mistrauisch gegen mich, denken Sie nicht schlimmer u. nicht eulenhafter von mir, als ich bin, u. glauben Sie nicht aber gar, ich habe mich verändert, u. sey ein Griesgram. Quod non.

Recollections, p. 137, between the paragraphs:

I must include a few words for you, dear Mme. Devrient, for I could never remain silent after receiving a box on the ears – and then still receive the same thing because of my answer. I can by no means deny that in this instance I would quite prefer the latter, and so respond without hesitation by saying that you have done me a terrible injustice. On reading your letter I see myself as a mistrustful, peevish fellow who can never be pleased and who is filled with prejudice. I have, however, written – and I repeat it here – that when I return I want to meet Taubert, and I look forward as though I had never played and read anything by him, and that, if I find him to be otherwise, all of this should not and must not leave the slightest trace. This does not make me in the least apprehensive; on the contrary, because he is Eduard's friend I have the most favorable expectation regarding his personality and activities. But so long as I know nothing different, the previous impression will prevail; you cannot call that mistrustful, because to me music is still a more precise language than words and letters.[38] I can well imagine that I seem to you in a way like a screech owl, since you[39] clearly have my rebuttal in your hands (or, more likely, ears), but bear in mind that it's not that way with me, and that you do know me after all. And so I return it and ask you not to be mistrustful of me, not to think me worse and more owlish than I am, and by no means believe that I have changed and become a grouch. Quod non.

---

38 Ten years later, in his celebrated letter to Marc-André Souchay, Mendelssohn wrote of this uniquely expressive power of music: "People often complain that music is too ambiguous; that what they should think when they hear it is so unclear, whereas everyone understands words. With me it is exactly the reverse, ... The thoughts which are expressed to me by music that I love are not too indefinite to be put into words, but on the contrary, too *definite*." Letter of 15 October 1842. Mendelssohn, *Letters*, ed. G. Selden-Goth, pp. 313–14.

39 Mendelssohn's original reads *sie*, but it is not clear what the antecedent is; perhaps Mendelssohn meant to write *Sie*, referring to Mme. Devrient.

[9]

[Berlin], 10 July 1832; original in Wc. *Erinnerungen*, pp. 141–2; *Recollections*, pp. 142–3.

[10]

[Berlin, 4 September 1832];[40] original in NYpm; unpublished.

Lieber Eduard, Du hast gestern Abend vergessen, Deine Bemerkung zu machen, daß man es nicht besonders erwähne, daß die Beschlüsse "ohne Abstimmung" gefasst worden seien. Es könnte dies R. Gelegenheit geben zu glauben, die Versammlung sey überrascht worden, u. sich auf eine nächste Versammlung, u. die Stimmen der Abwesenden zu berufen; deshalb wäre es gut Du merktest es noch an, ich glaube es kommt zweimal darin vor. Mir fiel es gleich ein, als Du weg warst u. ich nahme mir vor, Dir davon zu schreiben. Schlaf wohl, denn hoffentlich bist Du noch im Bette, wenn dies ankommt.

Dienstag früh.

FMB.

Dear Eduard:

Last evening you forgot to point out that it should not be specifically mentioned that the resolutions were made "without voting." This could give R.[41] occasion to suppose that the committee was caught off guard and to call for a new meeting and the absentee votes. It would therefore be well if you made a note to that effect (I think it occurs twice). I thought of this only after you had left, and I made up my mind to write to you about it. Sleep well; hopefully you will still be in bed when this arrives.

Early Tuesday.

FMB.

40 The date has been added in another hand.

41 Carl Friedrich Rungenhagen (1778–1851), the German conductor, composer, and music director. Soon after Carl Friedrich Zelter died, on 15 May 1832, and his position as director of the Berlin Singakademie became vacant, Rungenhagen and Mendelssohn became the leading candidates to succeed him. A committee proposed that Rungenhagen and Mendelssohn share the directorship; this letter may refer to the meeting of the committee at which Mendelssohn formally accepted the proposal. Soon afterward Rungenhagen rejected it, considering himself to be Zelter's sole successor; on 22 January 1833, he was elected the new director. "The result," wrote Devrient, "doomed the Vocal Academy to a long course of mediocrity. ...." For Devrient's account of this bitter episode in Mendelssohn's life, see *Erinnerungen*, pp. 145–55, and *Recollections* pp. 145–56.

[11]

[Berlin], 13 October 1832; original in NYpm; unpublished.

Lieber Eduard

Schreib mir doch ob Du es delicat fändest, wenn die Hähnel in meinen Concerten sänge. Ich habe sie noch nicht gehört, weiß also nichts davon. Oder räthst Du zur Grünbaum, Lenz, Böttcher, Schuster, Schneider u. s. f. (Macht Alles den Kohl nich fett[.]) Und wie macht man es um mit diesen Damen bekannt zu werden? Geht man geradezu hin, und sagt: singt? Oder muß man zart sein?

Schreib mir eine Antwort auf langem, groben, gebrochnen Papier und fange an: Dem Musikus Felix MB wird hiemit erwiedert

13 Oct. 32.

Dein

Felix MB.

Dear Eduard:

Write and tell me if you would consider it ticklish if Hähnel[42] sings in my concerts.[43] I have not yet heard her and so know nothing about her. Or would you suggest Grünbaum,[44] Lenz,[45] Böttcher,[46] Schuster,[47]

---

42 Amalie Hähnel (or Haehnel, 1807–49), the Austrian mezzo-soprano.

43 Mendelssohn was planning three concerts at the Singakademie for the benefit of the *Orchesterwittwenfond*. On 15 November he conducted his "Reformation" Symphony op. 107, and overture to *A Midsummer Night's Dream* op. 21, and played his G minor Piano Concerto op. 25 and Beethoven's "Waldstein" Sonata; Eduard Mantius sang an aria from Gluck's *Iphigenia in Tauris*, and Lenz (see note 45), Mantius, Devrient, and Gustav Nauenburg sang Mozart's "Mandina amabile," K. 480, and "Dite almeno in che mancai," K. 479. On 1 December Mendelssohn conducted his overture *Meeresstille und glückliche Fahrt* op. 27; played his *Capriccio brillant* in B minor for piano and orchestra op. 22, Bach's D minor Concerto BWV 1052, and Beethoven's *Moonlight* Sonata, and conducted Ludwig Berger's Symphony in D minor; Anna Milder-Hauptmann and Mantius sang a duet from Gluck's *Armide*, and Lenz and Milder-Hauptmann sang a scene from his *Iphigenia in Aulis*. And on 10 January 1833 (in a concert originally planned for 20 December, but postponed because Devrient was ill) Mendelssohn conducted his *Hebrides* Overture op. 26, and played Beethoven's Fourth Piano Concerto op. 58; Lenz sang an aria that Weber composed for Cherubini's *Lodoïska*; Mendelssohn and Heinrich Bärmann played Weber's *Grand duo concertant* for clarinet and piano op. 48 (J. 204); and Mendelssohn conducted the première of his *Erste Walpurgisnacht* op. 60, with Mantius and two other soloists.

44 Therese Grünbaum (1791–1876), the Austrian soprano.

45 Bertha Lenz, the soprano.

46 Possibly Caecilie Bötticher (*d*. 1835), a soprano who made her operatic début in 1832, married in 1834, and died following childbirth the next year; see also Letter 14.

47 I can find no singer named Schuster who was active in Berlin at this time. Perhaps Mendelssohn had in mind Pauline Schätzel (1812–82), the German soprano, who, after four extremely successful years in both opera and oratorio – she sang in the 1829 *St. Matthew Passion* – retired from the stage in 1832 and devoted herself to oratorio performances.

Schneider,[48] etc. (All that won't help much.) And how does one make these ladies' acquaintance? Does one go straight to them and say, sing? Or must one be tactful?

Answer me on tall, rough, creased paper, and begin: In answer to the musician Felix MB...

13 October 1832

Yours,

Felix MB.

[12]

Düsseldorf, 30 September 1833; original in NYpm. *Erinnerungen*, pp. 159–63; *Recollections*, pp. 161–5.

[13]

Düsseldorf, 5 February 1834; original NYpm. *Erinnerungen*, pp. 164–74; *Recollections*, pp. 166–76.

Erinnerungen, p. 167, lines 6–7:

for darfst Du leben, oder nicht? Das ist wichtig in Berlin;

read darfst Du leben, oder nicht? Und wie hast Du es ohne Heinr. Beer im Sinne setzen können? Klatschte Mosson? Dies ist alles wichtig in Berlin;

Recollections, p. 169, lines 1–2:

Can you live or not? And how were you able to set it without Heinrich Beer[49] in mind? Did Mosson[50] gossip? All this is important in Berlin.

Erinnerungen, p. 167, lines 9–11:

for aber Plethi ist mir doch lieber, als Euere Theater = habitués

read aber Plethi ist mir doch noch lieber wie Mosson.

Recollections, p. 169, lines 4–5:

but I still prefer our motley public to Mosson.

Erinnerungen, p. 168, lines 6–7:

for gute Leute beim Handwerk zu wissen. Und dann mußt Du

read gute Leute beim Handwerk zu wissen. Und dann könnte es doch

---

48 Probably Maschinka Schneider (1815–82), the German soprano; in 1837 she married the violinist and composer Franz Schubert (1808–78).

49 Heinrich Beer (1794–1842), Giacomo Meyerbeer's brother; in 1818 he married Mendelssohn's cousin Betty Meyer.

50 It is unclear to whom this refers – presumably a relative of Meyerbeer who, in 1826, married his cousin Minna Mosson.

dem lieben Gott gefallen Spontini bei den Zähnen zu sich zu nehmen, und dann wärest Du weg davon. Und dann mußt Du

Recollections, p. 170, lines 2–3:

to keep good people in the trade. And then it could please God to take Spontini[51] to Himself by the teeth, and you would be free from there. Indeed, you must

Erinnerungen, p. 169, lines 7–10:

for weil er in Paris auch kein Glück gemacht hat. – Aber ich bitte Dich, was schreibst Du von Euren Bestellungen! Glaubst Du denn

read weil er in Paris auch kein Glück gemacht hat. Du findest diese Vorschläge nicht thunlich, u. hältst Dich wie Christus ans Practische. – aber ich bitte Dich, thut denn das Graf Redern? Glaubst Du

Recollections, p. 171, lines 9–11:

it would fail as it has done in Paris. You find these suggestions inconvenient, and may want, like Christ, to keep to the practical.[52] But I ask you: will Count Redern do it? Do you think

Erinnerungen, p. 169, lines 21–2:

for und sobald der "Sommernachtstraum" so besetzt ist, will ich Chöre dazu versprechen

read u. sobald mir das Redern so besetzt, will ich ihm meine Chöre versprechen

Recollections, p. 172, lines 1–3:

and as soon as Redern has filled the parts according to my suggestion, I am willing to promise the choruses

[14]

Düsseldorf, 4 July 1834; original in NYpm. *Erinnerungen*, pp. 175–7; *Recollections*, pp. 177–80.

Erinnerungen, p. 176, lines 21–2:

---

51 Gaspare Spontini (1774–1851), the Italian composer and conductor; at this time he was court composer and general music director in Berlin.

52 This curious expression occurs in an 1830 letter from Mendelssohn to Devrient: "ich mache es wie der Heiland und halte mich an's Praktische. ..." (*Erinnerungen*, p. 103). In a footnote, Devrient explains that he encountered the phrase in the prospectus "einer neuen Bibelübersetzung von Dinter," that its peculiarity appealed to him and Mendelssohn, and that thereafter they often used it between themselves. (As its title implies, Gustav Friedrich Dinter's *Die Bibel als Erbauungsbuch für Gebildete*, published between 1831 and 1833, is not a translation but a devotional book.) Macfarren's translation of the expression – "I shall do like a revered personage, and hold by the practical" (*Recollections*, p. 102) – could more accurately be rendered "I shall do like the Saviour, and keep to the practical," although the meaning is still not entirely clear.

for also giebt es Beschäftigung vollauf. – Nimm Dich doch der Sache ein wenig an

read also giebt es Beschäftigung vollauf. – Mit der Bötticher von der ich im vorigen Briefe schrieb, ist es wohl nichts? Sie kam mir immer etwas kalt u. unbildsam vor; schlägts aber fehl mit der Grosser u. die wäre zu haben, so wäre es auch gut. Überhaupt nimm Dich doch der Sache ein wenig an

Recollections, p. 179, lines 12–13:

so we shall have plenty of work to do. I suppose nothing will happen with Bötticher,[53] of whom I wrote in my previous letter? In any case, she seemed somewhat cold and inflexible; if nothing should come of Grosser,[54] and she were available, that would also be fine. Above all I hope you will take care of the matter

Erinnerungen, p. 177, lines 11–12:

between denkst. *and* Ein, *insert*:

Wahrscheinlich kreuzt sich dieser Brief mit einem von Dir, als Antwort auf meinen letzten u. die verlangte Partit. von Händel; aber es wäre mir lieb, wenn Du auf diesen hier so bald als möglich Antwort gäbst und mich vom Erfolg benachrichtigst.

Recollections, p. 180, between lines 6 and 7:

This letter will probably cross with one from you in answer to my last letter about the Handel score[55] I requested. But I would very much appreciate your sending an answer about this as soon as possible, and informing me of the outcome.

[15]

Düsseldorf, 2 August 1834; original in NYpm. *Erinnerungen*, pp. 178–80; *Recollections*, pp. 181–83.

Erinnerungen, p. 178, lines 8–9:

between Eduard! *and* Vor *insert*:

Da Du mir in Deinem letzten Briefe schriebst Du würdest auf einige Wochen von Berlin weggehen, ohne mir den Aufenthaltsort näher anzugeben, so habe ichs bis heute aufgeschoben Dir zu schreiben, da ich jetzt bald wieder zurück in Berlin denke.

Recollections, p. 181, between lines 5 and 6:

---

53 See note 46.   54 Henriette Grosser (*b.* 1818), the German singer.

55 Between 1833 and 1835, Mendelssohn made his own arrangements of five of Handel's oratorios. Several were first performed in Düsseldorf, where he had been engaged to conduct at the Lower Rhine Music Festival; he was eventually appointed city music director.

Since you wrote in your last letter that you would be away from Berlin for several weeks, without telling me of your precise whereabouts, I have delayed writing to you until today, as I now intend to return to Berlin soon.

Erinnerungen, p. 178, lines 17–18:

between mehr. *and* Daß *insert*:

Geht es doch mit den Menschen zu einander auch so. Nur hat mir u. Immermann es leid gethan, daß wir Deine Notiz wegen Mde. Höffert[?] u. ihres Mannes nicht benutzen konnten, indem gerade einige Tage vorher das Engagement für diese Löcher schon gemacht worden war. Dies ist mir umso mehr leid, da Du schreibst, daß auch Dir ein Dienst dadurch geleistet worden wäre; doch weißt Du, wie es mit Engagements steht, u. ich erlebe vielleicht noch, daß die vorher Engagirten ihr Engagement wieder mitten durchbrechen, u. dann soll nicht ein Tag vergehn, ohne daß ich Dir darüber schreibe, ich werde es nicht aus den Augen verlieren.

Recollections, p. 181, between lines 13 and 14:

Things between one person and another are indeed the same. Immermann[56] and I were sorry that we could not avail ourselves of your note about Mme Höffert[?][57] and her husband, since just a few days earlier the engagement for these openings had already been made. This is all the more regrettable, for you write that this would have rendered a service to you as well. But you know how it is with engagements, and it may yet turn out that those already engaged may still break their engagement in the middle of the run. In that event not one day will pass without my writing to you about it; I shall not lose sight of it.

Erinnerungen, p. 179, last line–p. 180, first line:

for Respect bewiesen? Doch habe ich viel zu reden

read Respect bewiesen? Freilich achte ich Gubitz und Häring – brrrr-rrr[?] – im ungekehrten Sinne hoch, und wo die Herren sind, da passe ich mich mein Lebenlang nicht hin, und nehme die Mütze ab, u. gehe sacht aus dem Weg – aber das ist es nicht. Doch habe ich viel zu reden

Recollections, p. 182, last line–p. 183, first line:

(certainly not as a man)? It's true that I highly respect (in the opposite

---

56 Karl Immermann (1796–1840), the German poet, dramatist, and novelist, with whom Mendelssohn was working to establish a theater in Düsseldorf; it was formally opened on 28 October 1834. Mendelssohn resigned soon thereafter.

57 Unidentified.

sense of the word) Gubitz[58] and Häring[59] (brrrrrrr[?]); where these men are, it ill becomes me to live my life, and I take off my cap and stay carefully out of their way – but that's not the case. I have much to say about it

[16]

Düsseldorf, 26 November 1834; original in Wc. *Erinnerungen*, pp. 181–3; *Recollections*, pp. 184–6.
Erinnerungen, p. 181, line 20:
> *before* Du wünschest, *insert*:
> Lieber Eduard Dank Dir für Deine lieben, guten Zeilen; Du mußt wohl schwere böse Tage gehabt haben, u. je weniger sich zu solchem Unglück aus der Ferne sagen läßt, um so lieber möchte ich bei Dir in der Zeit gewesen sein, aber auch wohl nicht um viel zu sagen, aber um doch einander näher zu sein. Was Du von Baur schreibst betrübt mich wirklich. Hat er dann den Dr. Kramer auch gefragt? Und was braucht er denn? Grüß ihn mir vielmal, wenn Du schreibst, und sag ihm ich würde ihm schreiben, sobald mein Paulus, der ins Stocken gerathen war u. diesen Frühling fertig sein soll, mich dazu kommen läßt.

Recollections, p. 184, three lines from the bottom, before "You end your letter":
> Dear Eduard:
> Thank you for your kind, good lines; you must surely have experienced difficult and bad days, and the less one comments on such a misfortune from afar, all the more I should have preferred to have been with you at the time, not so much to say a great deal, but rather to be nearer to one another. I am truly disturbed by what you write about Baur.[60] Did he then also ask Dr. Kramer?[61] What does he need? Send him my best greetings if you write, and tell him I shall write as soon as my *Paulus*,[62] which has come to a standstill and must be finished this spring, allows me the time.

Erinnerungen, p. 183, lines 7–8:
> *after* oder wo es ist", *add*:

---

58 Friedrich Wilhelm Gubitz (1786–1870), the German writer, publisher of the periodical *Der Gesellschafter*, and theater critic of the *Vossische Zeitung*.
59 Georg Wilhelm Häring (1798–1871), the German journalist and novelist.
60 See note 25.
61 Unidentified.
62 Mendelssohn's oratorio, completed the following April, and first performed a month later in Düsseldorf.

Hier ist einliegend ein Brief von Schadow an Hrn. HfR. Hof[f]mann, den ich Dich ihm zu geben bitte, leider aber sind die Nachrichten, die ich auf Deinen u. der Eltern Wunsch eingezogen, so ungünstig für den jungen Hoffmann, daß ich Dich bitten muß mich bei dem Vater zu entschuldigen wenn ich ihm nicht direct auf seine Fragen antworte, da von einem Fremden so etwas immer noch unangenehmer ist. Hildebran[t], der sonst eher zu gutmüthig, als das Gegentheil ist, spricht durchaus tadelnd von ihm, seinem Betragen, u. seiner Thätigkeit, er habe in jeder Beziehung schlecht gelebt, sey unfleißig auf der Akademie gewesen, habe nicht die Fortschritte gemacht die er hätte machen sollen, u. er wünsche daher ihn nicht wieder in seine Classe aufzunehmen. Schadow, der mir als ich zuerst davon sprach, im Allgemeinen nur sagte er müße erst mit Hildebr. sprechen, ehe er den Eltern schriebe, da er viel Ungünstiges gehört habe, der aber doch nicht ganz gegen sein Kommen zu sein schien, hat nach einer Besprechung mit Hild. seine Meinung geändert, will ihn nicht auf der Akademie als Schüler annehmen u. hat in dem Sinn an die Eltern geschrieben. Ich sehe also nichts was ich dem Vater sagen könnte, um diesen Brief weniger hart für ihn u. den Sohn zu machen, u. deshalb entschuldige mich bei ihm. Taubert heirathet, und bald wird der *kleine* Taubert wieder ein Concert spielen u.s.w. Das wäre alles schön u. gut, aber wenn doch nur irgend jemand in Deutschland jetzt hübsche Musik machte! Man wird ja meiner Treu zum Misanthrope! Auf meiner Herreise sah ich Spohr, u. der Mann gefiel mir mit seiner Kälte und Vornehmheit ganz ausnehmend, weil er doch arbeitet, u. es so gut macht, wie er kann, u. weil ihm seine eigne Musik doch wenigstens so recht aus Herzensgrunde gefällt, aber der ist auch schon alt und ein Honorazior, wo stecken die vielen jungen Musiker, die es doch offenbar in Deutschland geben muß? Wenn in Berlin einer auftaucht, so schreibe mir es umgehend, aber ich fürchte, dafür ist gesorgt u. weder Thrun [*sic*] noch Jähns noch andre junge Berliner machen den Kohl fetter. Na, never mind, muß also auch so gehen. Das Papier schließt. Lebewohl, Du Lieber, schreib mir bald wieder wenn Du kannst, sag mir wie Du lebst, ob Du die Novelle machst oder gemacht hast oder was sonst Neues, u. grüß die Deinigen.

Dein

Felix MB

Recollections, p. 186, six lines from the bottom:

or where you like.''

I enclose a letter from Schadow[63] to Hofrath Hoffmann,[64] which I ask you to give to him; unfortunately, the accounts that I have gathered at your request and that of the parents are so unfavorable regarding young Hoffmann that I must ask you to apologize to his father for my not answering his questions directly, since it is always even more unpleasant to hear such things from a stranger. Hildebrandt,[65] who otherwise is usually rather too good-natured than the contrary, speaks thoroughly disapprovingly of him, of his conduct and activity. He says that Hoffmann has in every respect led a poor life, has been lazy at the Academy, has not made the progress he should have, and that he therefore no longer wants Hoffmann in his class. When I first spoke about this with Schadow, he said, in general, only that he must first speak with Hildebrandt before writing to his parents, since he had heard many unfavorable things, and seemed not to be entirely against Hoffmann's coming. But after speaking with Hildebrandt he changed his mind, does not want to accept Hoffmann as a student at the Academy, and wrote to the parents to that effect. I therefore see nothing that I could say to the father to render the letter less severe for him and his son, and therefore make my excuses to him.

Taubert has married, and soon the *little* Taubert will be giving a concert, etc. That would all be well and good, but if only someone in Germany made lovely music today! This could truly make one a misanthrope! On my trip here I saw Spohr,[66] and the man, with his coolness and refinement, pleased me exceedingly, because he still works and does as well as he can, and because at least his own music still pleases him so profoundly. But he is also already old, and a local dignitary; where are the many young musicians hiding who clearly must exist in Germany? If one surfaces in Berlin, write to me at once, but I fear that's taken care of and neither Truhn[67] nor Jähns[68] nor other young Berliners will help much. Well, never mind, that's how it must be. The paper is full. Farewell, dear friend; write to me again soon if you can, tell me how you

63 Wilhelm von Schadow (1788–1862), the German painter and writer. Mendelssohn studied drawing with him in Düsseldorf.

64 Johann Gottfried Hoffmann (1765–1847), a senior government councillor and, from 1810, a university professor of political science in Berlin.

65 Theodor Hildebrandt (1804–74), the German painter, a student of Friedrich Wilhelm von Schadow's.

66 Louis Spohr (1784–1859), the German composer, violinist, and conductor.

67 Friedrich Hieronymus Truhn (1811–86), the German composer and writer on music; he briefly studied orchestration with Mendelssohn.

68 Friedrich Wilhelm Jähns (1809–88), the German scholar, singing teacher, and composer, best known today for his works on Carl Maria von Weber.

are, if you are writing or have written your novella or something else new, and greet your family.

Yours,

Felix MB

[17]

Berlin, 28 November 1835; original in Wc; unpublished.

Lieber Eduard

Erst gestern Mittag erhielt ich Deinen Brief vom 16ten Sept. nebst den Anlagen. Ich war überrascht den Operntext zu finden, u. wünsche Du mögest mir erlauben ihn mit nach Leipzig zurückzunehmen, um ihn dort zu lesen, da ich mich hier dazu noch nicht entschließen konnte, u. auch wirklich nicht im Stande wäre, etwas der Art recht aufzufassen. Glaubst Du, es werde zu lange damit werden, so will ich versuchen ihn morgen vorzunehmen, aber wie gesagt, ich fürchte es liegt mir jetzt zu fern.

Die Petition (deren Abfassung u. Zweck mir übrigens recht sehr gefällt) schicke ich Dir anbei zurück. Ich kann sie nicht unterschreiben, weil mein Name, als dramatischer Componist, zu wenig oder gar nicht bekannt, und von keinem Werthe für Eure Absicht ist.

Übermorgen früh werde ich abreisen und so Gott es will die Meinigen zu Weihnachten wieder besuchen.

Dein

Felix Mendelssohn Bartholdy

Berlin d. 28 Nov.

1835.

Dear Eduard:

I received your letter of 16 September, along with the enclosure, only midday yesterday. I was surprised to find the libretto and hope you will let me take it back to Leipzig in order to read it there, since I could not decide about it here, and would not really have been in a position to understand something of this sort. If you think that will take too long, I'll try to tackle the matter tomorrow – but, as I said, I'm afraid it's too far from my thoughts right now.

I return herewith the petition, the style and purpose of which please me enormously. I cannot sign it, because as a dramatic composer my name is too little known – or not known at all – and is of no value for your purpose.

I leave early the day after tomorrow and, God willing, shall again be with my family for Christmas.

Yours,
Felix Mendelssohn Bartholdy
Berlin, 28 November 1835.

[18]

Leipzig, 2 October 1839; original in NYpm. *Erinnerungen*, pp. 200–203; *Recollections*, pp. 205–8.
Erinnerungen, p. 203, lines 13–14:
for geschrieben. Nun
read geschrieben. – Ich erhielt vor einigen Tagen Deine Zeilen durch Hrn. Hartmann; er reist heut wieder ab, ich hab ihn mehremale bei mir gesehn u. Musik mit ihm gemacht, u. hätte ihn gern noch öfter gesehn, wenn das arge Treiben u. Drängen dieser 14 Tage mich nicht daran verhindert hätte. Nun
Recollections, p. 207, last two lines:
yet. Several days ago I received your letter through Mr. Hartmann,[69] who leaves today. I saw him here frequently and played music with him, and I would gladly have seen him more often had the frightful rush and pressures of these past two weeks not prevented it. Now,

[19]

Leipzig, 16 November 1840; original in Wc. *Erinnerungen*, pp. 205–7; *Recollections*, p. 210–12.
Erinnerungen, p. 207, lines 1–3:
for Viele! Lebe wohl
read Viele!
 Gern ließ ich Deinem Wunsch zu entsprechen, die Bachsche[n] Cantaten schreiben u. schickte sie Dir. Doch ehe ich das thue, will ich Dich darauf aufmerksam machen, daß gerade von den eingänglichsten u. herrlichsten, sechs gedruckt in Partitur, Clav. Auszug u. Stimmen zu haben sind. Bei Simrock in Bonn sind sie erschienen, von Marx herausgegeben. Bessere und zu dem bewußten Zweck passendere wüßte ich auch nicht zu verschaffen, u. jedenfalls wärs gut, sie probirten sich erst an den bekannten, gedruckten. Ich fürchte, ich fürchte, sie werden meinen guten Stuttgartern zu grobkörnig sein; u. feiner hat er sie einmal nicht gemacht. Liegt dies aber daran, daß sie Manuscriptsachen bekommen sollen, so will ich Dir gern etwas davon schicken; sag es mir nur. Wollen

---

69 Johan Peter Emilius Hartmann (1805–1900), the Danish composer and organist.

sie Sachen *a capella*, so sind die 6 Motetten, bei Breitkopf & Härtel hier gedruckt. Wie gesagt, ich fürchte, Du bekehrst sie nicht dazu; das Instrumentiren von Marcelloschen Psalmen durch Lindpaintner ist gar zu bedenklich, u. Bach gar zu borstig. Das spricht der unzufriedne polnische Graf wieder aus mir, wirst Du wieder sagen.

Lebwohl

Recollections, p. 212, lines 2–3:

much?

I would gladly comply with your wish to have the Bach cantatas copied and sent to you. But before doing so, I want to inform you that, just of the most accessible and most magnificent, six have been printed in full score, piano score, and parts, published by Simrock, in Bonn, edited by Marx.[70] I could not provide anything better or more suitable to the known purpose, and in any event it would be good if they first tried out those that are known and published. I fear, I fear they will prove too coarse-grained for my good people of Stuttgart – and Bach just never wrote them any finer. But if it is important for them to get the manuscripts I shall gladly send some; you have only to tell me. If they want *a cappella* works, the six motets have been published here by Breitkopf & Härtel. As I said, I fear you will not convert them; Lindpaintner's[71] orchestration of Marcello's Psalms[72] is much too delicate, and Bach entirely too bristly. "There speaks once more the discontented Polish count[73] in me," you will say again.

Good-bye

[20]

Berlin, 20 October 1841; original in Wc; unpublished.

Lieber Eduard   Deine Frau versprach mir neulich noch in dieser Woche einen Abend mit uns zuzubringen. Da frage ich denn ob Du und sie und Deine Schwägerinn u. Frl. Marie uns wohl morgen Donnerstag Abend die Freude Eures Besuchs schenken wolltet? Meine Frau vereinigt ihre Bitte mit der meinigen und wir hoffen auf Eure freundliche Zusage.

70 Adolf Bernhard Marx (1795–1866), the German music theorist, author, and composer.

71 Peter Josef von Lindpaintner (1791–1856), the German conductor and composer. When this letter was written, he was Kapellmeister of the royal orchestra at Stuttgart.

72 Benedetto Marcello (1686–1739), the Italian composer, writer, and theorist, whose *Estro poetico-armonico, parafrasi sopra li primi [secondi] venticinque salmi* was published in Venice between 1724 and 1726. Lindpaintner rescored a number of the *Psalms*, as well as Handel's *Judas Maccabaeus*.

73 According to Devrient, this nickname was given to Mendelssohn because of his discontentedness; see *Erinnerungen*, p. 179n, and *Recollections*, p. 182n.

Dein
Felix
Berlin 20. Oct.
1841

Hast Du im Theater zu thun, so kommst Du auf dem Heimwege wohl noch!

Dear Eduard:

Your wife recently promised to spend an evening with us this week. Would you, your wife, your sister-in-law, and Frl. Marie give us the pleasure of a visit on Thursday, tomorrow evening? My wife joins me in this request, and we look forward to your kind acceptance.

Yours,
Felix
Berlin, 20 October 1841

If you are occupied at the theater, then perhaps come by on your way home.

[21]

Leipzig, 28 June 1843; original in NYpm. *Erinnerungen*, pp. 232–6; *Recollections*, pp. 239–43.

Erinnerungen, p. 232, lines 20–21:

for bleiben. Aber ein oder zwei Tage sind

read bleiben. Wir besprächen dann alles mündlich hundertmal besser, als ich meinestheils irgend etwas *beschreiben* kann. Du triffst uns in den nächsten Wochen jedenfalls hier. Aber richte Dich auf mehr, als einen halben Tag ein! Einer oder zwei sind

Recollections, p. 240, lines 1–2:

can. We would then discuss everything in person a hundred times more profitably than I, for my part, could *describe* something. In any case, you'll find us here for the next few weeks – but be prepared for more than half a day! One or two days is

Erinnerungen, p. 232, last line–p. 233, first line:

for Wär's länger"!

Das Operngedicht

read wär's länger." Setz zu, soviel Du kannst! Und laß mich ein wenig vorher die bestimmte Zeit Deines Kommens wissen, damit ich mir die Tage recht frei halte.

Das Operngedicht

Recollections, p. 240, lines 6–7:

"were it but more." Stay on as long as you can! And let me know a little ahead of time just when you are coming so I may leave the days completely free.

Erinnerungen, p. 233, last two lines–p. 234, first line:

for Ueberzeugung. Zauberei und Wunderquellen machen das Opern-hafte ... nicht

read Überzeugung. Die Nymphe der Poesie, der Musik, der Baukunst &c., der Gott des Zephyr, die Mutter der Winde, Zauberei, Wunder-quellen &c. &c. – das alles macht das Opernhafte ... nicht

Recollections, p. 241, lines 4–6:

thinking. The nymph of poetry, of music, of architecture, etc., the god of the zephyr, the mother of the winds, magic, miraculous springs, etc., etc. – all of that is not sufficient to make a subject operatic.

Erinnerungen, p. 234, lines 14–15:

for als ein Gefallstück. Ich weiß wohl, daß das Gefallen hier

read als ein Gefallstück. Ich aber halte auch dabei das Gefallen für Nebensache, wenn nur ein gutes Werk da steht. Und das ist mit der Rücksicht auf Gefallen oder Nicht = Gefallen nun. u. nimmermehr zu Stande zu bringen. Ich weiß wohl, daß es hier

Recollections, p. 241, four lines from the bottom:

popular. Moreover, I consider popularity of secondary importance pro-vided that the work is a good one, and that is never achieved with an eye to popularity or unpopularity. I am aware that here it

Erinnerungen, p. 234, lines 19–23:

for machen zu lassen, und deshalb hoffe ich auch noch eine Oper zu schreiben, die ich mit gutem Gewissen und mit Freude schreiben kann, weil ich mich in meinen Grundgedanken nicht irre machen lassen. Ich sehe

read machen zu lassen, fehlt auch an solchen nicht, die das Publicum u. seinen Geschmack predigen, und deshalb hoffe ich auch in jenem Fache noch das Glück zu haben, ein Werk zu schreiben, das ich mit gutem Gewissen und mit Freude schreiben kann, weil ich weiß wie lange es dauerte bis man mich in diesen Fächern mit solchen Rücksichten in Ruh ließ, u. weil ich mich doch am Ende wohl dabei befinde, daß ich mich darin von Niemand irre machen lassen wollte. Ich sehe

Recollections, p. 242, lines 2–5:

external considerations – there is no lack of what the public and their taste preach – and I therefore hope that in that field I may somehow still have the good fortune to write a work with joy and good conscience, because I know how long it took until I was left in peace in these activities, with such considerations, and because, in the end, I shall feel good that in doing so I was not led astray by anyone. I see

Erinnerungen, p. 236, lines 10–11:

for Versprechens. Mündlich über das Alles.

read Versprechens daß ich übrigens mit dem Orchester u. dessen Corporationsgeiste das geringste Mitleid hätte, kann ich auch nicht sagen – aber mündlich, mündlich über das Alles

Recollections, p. 243, lines 4 and 5 from the bottom:

promise that, after all, I would have the least sympathy with the orchestra and its *esprit de corps*, I can also not say. More when we speak.

[22]

Leipzig, 31 July 1843: original in Wc; published, in part, in *Erinnerungen*, p. 237, lines 4–8; *Recollections*, p. 244, lines 15–19.

> Leipzig d. 31 July
> 1843.
> Lieber Freund
> Gleichzeitig mit Deinem lieben Brief erhielt ich einen von Berlin in meiner ewig = langen Anstellungsangelegenheitscorrespondenz, der mir viel Aerger verursachte, lange Schreibereien hervorrief, und das Ende vom Liede ist nun daß ich noch einmal zum König nach Berlin reisen soll und zwar übermorgen. Unter andern Annehmlichkeiten, um die mich diese Reise bringt ist auch der Besuch, den ich Dir in Dresden machen wollte; ich hoffe nur, daß ich darüber nicht auch den Deinigen in Leipzig versäumen werde. Montag den 7ten oder Dienstag spätestens denke ich wieder hier zurück zu sein. Halte ja Wort und bring einmal einen Tag bei uns zu. Ich hatte mir alles schon so schön zur Dresdner Fahrt zurecht gemacht, u. mich so darauf gefreut, und nun muß ich Zahna und Luckenwalde statt dessen zu sehen bekommen; schlimm genug. Darum verzeih auch das lange Schweigen auf Deinen Brief, grüß Frau u. Kinder und bleib gut und komme ja zu
> Deinem
> Felix MB

Dear Friend:

Just as I received your kind letter one arrived from Berlin in my never-ending correspondence about employment matters that annoyed me greatly, gave rise to endless writing, and the upshot is that once more I am to go to the king in Berlin, and in two days at that. Among other amenities of which this trip will also deprive me is the visit with you in Dresden that I had wished to make; I only hope that in so doing I will not miss yours in Leipzig. Monday the 7th or Tuesday at the latest I expect to be back here. Keep your word and spend a day with us. I had already prepared so splendidly for my Dresden trip, and so looked forward to it, and now instead of that I must see Zahna and Luckenwalde;[74] worse luck! So forgive also the long silence in reply to your letter, greet your wife and children, think well of me, and do come to

Your

Felix MB

Leipzig, 31 July 1843.

[23]

Berlin, 25 October 1844; original in Wc. *Erinnerungen*, pp. 245–7; *Recollections*, pp. 254–6.

Erinnerungen, p. 245, 4 lines from the bottom:

for Brief, zugleich

read Brief durch Dr. Josephson in Leipzig, zugleich

Recollections, p. 254, line 10:

letter through Dr. Josephson[75] in Leipzig, and then

Erinnerungen, p. 247, lines 6–7:

between mehr. – *and* Mit, *insert*:

Folgende Adresse hat mir Dein Schwager für Dich gegeben: Hr. Steinitz, 10 Berner Street, Commercial Road East, London. Nach der Art, wie er sie mir gab, und unsrer ganzen übrigen Unterredung schien mir es nicht nothwendig, Dir gleich davon zu schreiben. Entschuldige jetzt den Verzug.

Noch eine Bitte, die Du entschuldigen mußt. Man hat in Dresden, wie ich höre, jetzt die Antigone mehrere Mal aufgeführt, von Honorar ist aber nicht die Rede gewesen; Hr. v. Lüttichau ließ die Partitur damals in Leipzig abschreiben – eigentlich sogar ohne mein Vorwissen – es gab eine etwas piquirte Correspondenz darüber – indeß ist das alles längst wieder beigelegt, u. wir stehen wieder im schönsten Vernehmen. Nun möchte ich ihn aber nicht direct an die Sache erinnern u. mahnen, auch möchte

74 Two towns between Leipzig and Berlin.
75 Presumably Jacob Axel Josephson (1818–80), the Swedish composer and conductor, who in 1844 came to Leipzig, where he studied composition with Moritz Hauptmann and Niels Gade.

ich nicht, daß *Du* es thätest – aber vielleicht könntest Du durch jemand anders in Erfahrung bringen, wie das zusammenhängt, ob es eine bloße Vergeßlichkeit ist oder sonst einen andern Grund hat? Die Musik zum Sommernachtstraum ließen sie damals durch Hrn. v. Küstner besorgen, der in meinem Namen ein sehr anständiges Honorar (20 Fr. d'or) dafür ausbedingte; die Sache mit der Antigone wurde aber durch den jetzigen Minister v. Falkenstein betrieben, u. der hat jenen Punct wahrscheinlich übersehen. Wie gesagt, kannst Du *mit Behutsamkeit* etwas darüber erfahren, oder daran erinnern, so thu mirs zu Gefallen, u. schreib mirs in 2 Zeilen, oder sag mir *ob* u. *was* ich dazu thun kann, denn direct mahnen möchte ich natürlich nicht gern.

Was Werder mir unter dem Siegel der Verschwiegenheit von Wagner erzählt hat, war mir eigentlich nichts Neues.

Recollections, p. 255, between lines 5 and 6 from the bottom:

Your brother-in-law gave me the following address for you: Mr. Steinitz, 10 Berner Street, Commercial Road East, London. By the manner in which he gave it to me, and the way the rest of our discussion went, it did not seem urgent that I write to you about it immediately. Do forgive the delay.

Another request, which you must forgive. I hear that *Antigone*[76] has been given several times in Dresden, but the question of payment has not been raised. Mr. Lüttichau[77] had the score copied in Leipzig, and what's more without my knowledge (there was a rather heated correspondence about it); that's all long been settled in the meantime and we are again on the friendliest terms. Now, I do not want to remind him of the matter directly and to press him over it, nor would I wish that *you* did so, but perhaps you could find out from a third party about the connection: is it simply an oversight, or is there some other explanation? They once procured my music to *A Midsummer Night's Dream*[78] through Mr. von Küstner,[79] who insisted on a very generous payment for me (20 Fr. d'or); the matter of *Antigone*, however, was handled by the present Minister, von Falkenstein,[80] who has probably overlooked that point. As I said, if you can *with discretion* find out something about this, or remind someone

76 Mendelssohn's incidental music for Sophocles' play was completed on 10 October 1841 and first peformed, in Potsdam, a few weeks later.
77 August Freiherr von Lüttichau (1786–1863), the Intendant of the court theater in Dresden.
78 Mendelssohn's incidental music for Shakespeare's play was completed in 1843 and first performed in Potsdam, in October 1843.
79 Karl Theodor von Küstner (1784–1864), who, in 1842, had succeeded Count Redern (see note 35) as director of the royal opera.
80 Johann Paul Freiherr von Falkenstein (1801–82).

of it, do it for my sake and write me two lines, or tell me *if* I can do something about it, and *what*; naturally, I do not want to remind them directly.

What Werder[81] told me about Wagner under the seal of secrecy was really not new to me.

[24]

Frankfurt, 26 April 1845; original in NYpm. *Erinnerungen*, pp. 248–52; *Recollections*, pp. 257–61.

Erinnerungen, p. 252, line 10:

   for Schwägerin. Die

   read Schwägerinn. Deinen Brief an Gutzkow habe ich, wie Du sagtest, auf die Post gegeben, da ich ihn seit jenem Mittag bei Dir (den er drucken ließ) nicht wiedergesehen habe. Die

Recollections, p. 261, lines 6–7:

   sister-in-law. As you told me, I mailed your letter to Gutzkow,[82] as I have not seen him since that noontime with you (which he published). I

[25]

Bad Soden bei Frankfurt, 2 July 1845; original in NYpm. *Erinnerungen*, pp. 252–3; *Recollections*, pp. 261–2.

[26]

Leipzig, 15 September 1845; original in Wc. *Erinnerungen*, pp. 258–61; *Recollections*, pp. 267–69.

[27]

Leipzig, 11 December 1845; original in NYpm. *Erinnerungen*, pp. 261–3; *Recollections*, pp. 270–72.

[28]

Leipzig, 13 January 1846; original in Wc; unpublished.

81 Karl Werder (1806–93), the German aesthetician and dramatist. After the second performance of Wagner's *Fliegender Holländer* in Berlin, on 9 January 1844, he told Wagner that he had written "an unprecedented masterpiece ... that evoked new and undreamed-of hope for the future of German art." Richard Wagner, *My Life*, trans. Andrew Gray, ed. Mary Whittall (Cambridge, 1983), p. 265. Wagner had met Werder at Mendelssohn's home the day before.

82 Karl Gutzkow (1811–78), the German writer, who was considered one of the leaders of the *Junges Deutschland*, a movement Mendelssohn derided.

Lieber Eduard Kannst Du mir (für die Direction[s?] der Abonnement = Concerte) die Orchesterstimmen meiner Musik zum Sommernachtstraum für einige Wochen vom Dresdner Theater leihweise verschaffen? Wir brauchen die 4 Saiteninstrumentstimmen jede 3 mal *wo möglich* aber 4 mal. Kannst Du es so bitte ich Dich schick sie mir *umgehend*; wo nicht so sag mir in zwei Zeilen daß Du es *nicht* kannst, da der Copist dann in größter Eil dann schreiben muß indem ich sie von Berlin nicht erhalten kann, worauf ich gerechnet hatte. Verzeih die Bemühung und die eiligen Zeilen

Deinem

Felix MB

Leipzig d. 13 Jan.

1846

Dear Eduard,

Can you get on loan for me from the Dresden theater the orchestral parts for my music to *A Midsummer Night's Dream* for the management of the subscription concerts? Of the four string instruments we need three parts each and, *if possible*, four. If you can do so, please send them to me *immediately*; if you cannot, tell me in two lines, for the copyist must then write them out in the greatest haste since I cannot obtain them from Berlin as I had expected. Forgive the trouble and the hasty lines of

Your

Felix MB

Leipzig, 13 January 1846

[29]

Leipzig, 4 April 1846; original in NYpm; unpublished.

Lieber Eduard,

So eben habe ich einen Brief an Hrn. Vermeulen abgeschickt, wenn er dem widersteht so ist er ein "ausgepichter Wolf." Sobald ich von ihm Antwort erhalte theile ich sie Dir natürlich mit. Glück auf! Glück auf! Glück auf!

Dein

Felix Mendelssohn Bartholdy

Leipzig 4ten April

1846.

Dear Eduard,

I have just now sent a letter to Mr. Vermeulen;[83] if he resists it he is a

---

83 A. G. C. Vermeulen (1798–1872), secretary of the Association for the Promotion of the Art of Music, in Rotterdam.

sly wolf. I shall of course let you know his answer as soon as it arrives. Good luck! Good luck! Good luck!

Yours,

Felix Mendelssohn Bartholdy

Leipzig, 4 April 1846.

[30]

Leipzig, 27 April 1846; original in NYpm; unpublished.

Leipzig d. 27 April

1846

Lieber Eduard, Eine grosse Bitte heut. Kannst Du mir die *Partitur* meiner Antigone vom dortigen Theater leihen und umgehend hieher schicken? Bitte thu's, und sage mir zugleich mit 2 Worten, ob irgend eine Aufführung davon dort im Werke ist oder ob ich die Partitur nöthigenfalls einige Zeit behalten kann. Aber bitte thu mir *gleich* den Gefallen, denn es eilt damit. Es wäre mir lieber wenn Du Dich direct mit Lüttichau darüber besprächest, als mit Winkler (dem ich vorige Woche geschrieben u. die Stimmen v. Spohr remittirt habe) indeß wie Du willst. In jedem Fall antworte mir gleich 2 Zeilen; grüß alle die Deinigen u. sage mir wie sich die unzufriedenen Bauern befinden. Dein unzufriedener Polnischer Große

Felix MB.

Leipzig, 27 April 1846

Dear Eduard,

A big favor today: Can you borrow the score of my *Antigone* from the theater there[84] and send it to me immediately? Please do so and tell me in two words if any performance of it is planned there or whether, if need be, I can keep the score for a while. But oblige me at once, for I'm in a hurry. I would prefer it if you discussed this directly with Lüttichau, rather than with Winkler[85] (to whom I wrote last week and returned the Spohr parts); however, do as you please. In any case send me two words immediately. Greet your family and tell me how things stand with the discontented "Bauern."[86] Your discontented Polish grandee

Felix MB.

84 In Dresden.

85 Karl Gottlieb Theodor Winkler (1775–1856), the German writer, and vice-director of the court theater in Dresden. He was a close friend of Meyerbeer's and the guardian of Weber's children. Under the pseudonym Theodor Hell, he wrote the libretto for Weber's *Die drei Pintos* and translated, among other librettos, those of Weber's *Oberon* and Meyerbeer's *Robert le diable*.

86 Among the many opera projects that Devrient proposed to Mendelssohn over the years was one called *Der Bauernkrieg*, based on the German peasant's revolt of 1524; it was portrayed by Goethe in *Götz von Berlichingen* (1773) and by Gerhart Hauptmann in *Florian Geyer* (1896). Like all the others, it did not meet Mendelssohn's exacting requirements.

[31]

Leipzig, 9 May 1846; original in NYpm. *Erinnerungen*, pp. 267–71; *Recollections*, pp. 277–82.

This letter consists mostly of Mendelssohn's criticism of Devrient's libretto for their proposed opera on *Der Bauernkrieg*. Devrient's printed version of the letter varies in several places from Mendelssohn's original, but the differences are mostly small, awkward to incorporate and translate in context, and do not radically change the meaning of the letter as published.

[32]

Leipzig, 15 May 1846; original in Wc. *Erinnerungen*, pp. 274–5; *Recollections*, pp. 284–5. At the end of the letter Devrient writes: "Dies ist der letzte Brief, den ich von ihm empfangen habe" (*Erinnerungen*, p. 275). In fact, Mendelssohn wrote at least one more letter and one brief note to Devrient.

Erinnerungen, p. 274, line 3:

for Tausend Dank für Deinen Brief, aber

read Eben da ich die Partitur der Antigone an Dich adressiren u. fortschicken will mit dem besten Dank dazu, kommt Dein Brief. Habe tausend Dank dafür! Aber

Recollections, p. 284, line 11:

Just as I am about to send you the score of *Antigone* with my best thanks, your letter arrives. A thousand thanks for it! But

Erinnerungen, p. 275, add the following postscript:

Ich schicke die Partitur mit einer Morgen gefundenen Gelegenheit. Sollte sie übermorgen nicht richtig in Deine Hände gelangt sein, so laß michs ja [?] wissen.

Recollections, p. 285:

I shall send the score tomorrow when I'll have an opportunity. If it is not in your hands the day after, let me know.

[33]

Leipzig, 19 March 1847; original in Wc; unpublished.

Lieber Eduard,

Thust Du mir wohl den Gefallen mir den Clavier = Auszug meines Liederspiels, den Deine Frau hat, *stante pede* abschreiben zu lassen, so aber daß ich ihn bis *spätestens* den 3ten April hier habe. Ich werde nämlich wahrscheinlich an dem Tage nach England abreisen müssen, und habe Klingemann diese Abschrift versprochen. Bitte hilf mir sie halten,

u. höre ich nicht anders von Dir so darf ich wohl darauf rechnen sie zum 3ten hier zu haben? Die Rechnung leg bitte gleich bei. Tausend Grüße an alle die Deinigen von Deinem Schnupfen, Husten, Kreuz = u. Gliederweh, Kopf = u. Halsschmerzen, Ohren = u. Zahnreißen habenden, auch ganz grimmig wüthenden, aber dabei sehr vergnügten

Felix MB

Leipzig d. 19 März

1847.

P.S. Am Bequemsten wäre es wohl Du schicktest mir *umgehend* den Clav. Auszug selbst damit ich ihn von meinem hiesigen Copisten schreiben lasse, u. Dir dann vor meiner Abreise das M.S. zurückschicke. Du hast dann keine Mühe dort[? . . .].

Dear Eduard,

Would you please oblige me and have the piano score of my *Liederspiel*, which your wife has, copied immediately, so that I have it here by 3 April *at the latest*. I shall probably have to leave for England that day, and have promised this copy to Klingemann.[87] Please help me to keep my promise, and if I hear nothing to the contrary from you may I surely count on having it here on the 3rd? Please include the bill. A thousand greetings to your family from your sniffling, coughing, back-, limb-, head-, and throat-aching, ear- and tooth-pain-suffering, also quite fiercely angry, but for all that still very cheerful

Felix MB

Leipzig, 19 March 1847.

P.S. Perhaps it would be most convenient if you *immediately* sent me just the piano score so that my copyist here can make a copy; then I shall return the manuscript to you before I leave. This way you will have no trouble there [? . . . this sentence may be incomplete].

[34]

Leipzig, 5 April 1847; original in Wc; unpublished.

Mit bestem Dank und herzlichen Grüßen

Felix MB

Leipzig 5ten April 1847

With many thanks and warmest greetings,

Felix MB

Leipzig, 5 April 1847

87 Karl Klingemann (1798–1862), secretary of the Hanoverian embassy in London, and Mendelssohn's closest lifelong friend. The *Liederspiel* is *Die Heimkehr aus der Fremde* op. 89, for which Klingemann wrote the words; the autograph manuscript of the piano-vocal score, and a copyist's manuscript of the piano-vocal score corrected by Mendelssohn, are in NYpm.

10 Mendelssohn and his English publishers

PETER WARD JONES

In the course of his short life Felix Mendelssohn visited England no fewer than ten times.[1] For scenery and general tranquility he may have preferred Switzerland, but for a congenial social and political atmosphere, coupled with enthusiastic reception of his music, England was a clear favorite. Here too lived some of his closest friends, including Ignaz and Charlotte Moscheles, and Karl Klingemann, Secretary at the Hanoverian Legation. It is therefore hardly surprising that his contact with English music publishers extended from the time of his first visit in 1829 to the very end of his life. We are fortunate in the amount of surviving correspondence, which allows a very full picture of his major dealings with English publishers to emerge. This comprises not only letters to and from the firms concerned, but also frequent references to his publishing activities in the correspondence with Moscheles and Klingemann, both of whom often acted as go-betweens. In the majority of cases Mendelssohn was only disposing of the English copyright in works which were being simultaneously published in Germany or Austria, and usually in France as well. In this respect his dealings were very similar to those of Chopin. Occasionally, however, as with the Organ Sonatas op. 65, the impetus for compositions came from English publishers, or the works themselves might even be intended principally for English consumption, as with the *Te Deum* of the Morning and Evening Service. Copyright law in England during Mendelssohn's lifetime was in a state of flux, especially as regards the rights of foreigners.[2] At best, copyright in foreign works could only be claimed by an

This study is an extended and revised version of a paper given at the Conference on Nineteenth-Century Music held in Oxford in July 1988. Thanks are due to Novello & Co. for permission to quote from material in the firm's archives.

1 In 1829, 1832, 1833 (twice), 1837, 1840, 1842 (with his wife), 1844, 1846, and 1847.

2 Jeffrey Kallberg's dissertation "The Chopin Sources" (diss., Univ. of Chicago, 1982) provides an excellent summary of the prevailing legal position in England, France, and Germany. A resumé of this dissertation is offered by Kallberg's article "Chopin in the marketplace: aspects of

English publisher if the work was first published in England; at worst, all copyright protection for foreign works found itself under challenge on more than one occasion. As similar laws applied in other countries, simultaneous publication became the normal way of protecting copyright in a work with international sales potential, although the validity of this procedure was not tested in the English courts until 1848.[3]

Prior to Mendelssohn's first visit to England nine of his works had appeared in print (opp. 1–8 and 10), but only on the Continent. They were published by Adolph Martin Schlesinger or Friedrich Laue in Berlin, with certain works also being issued by Maurice Schlesinger in Paris. In 1829 they were therefore in the public domain in England, and could be reprinted at will by any English publisher without payment. In fact there was no rush to take advantage of this situation even after Mendelssohn had established his reputation in the country. Apart from a few individual songs from the op. 8 set, virtually the only one of these early works to be reissued in England before the 1840s was the *Capriccio* in F sharp minor for piano op. 5, originally published by the two Schlesinger firms in Berlin and Paris in 1825, and published in London by Clementi, Collard & Collard at the end of 1829. This was the first work of Mendelssohn to appear in England, and was followed between 1830 and 1832 by a series of new publications which Mendelssohn sold to Cramer, Addison & Beale. These comprised the piano works opp. 14, 15, and 16, the Variations for cello and piano op. 17, and piano duet arrangements of the C minor Symphony op. 11 and the *Midsummer Night's Dream* Overture op. 21, both of which had been great successes under the composer's direction at the Philharmonic Society's concerts during his first visit. The concerts were led by Franz Cramer, whose brother, Johann Baptist Cramer, headed the publishing firm, which may account for the business relationship. There is unfortunately only one letter from the composer to the firm from this period, but Mendelssohn seems to have transacted his business at least in part with Klingemann acting as intermediary.[4] In all Mendelssohn had commercial dealings with half a dozen English publishers, and inquiries from several more. Two firms, those of Novello and Ewer, were, however, between them responsible for the great majority of the English editions of his works, and it is on them that this study will concentrate.

The association with the house of Novello dates from the composer's

---

the international music publishing industry in the first half of the nineteenth century," *Notes* 39 (1982/3), 535–69, 795–824.

3 Cocks v. Purday. See Kallberg, "The Chopin Sources," p. 21.

4 See letters to Klingemann, 15 April and 6 August 1830, in *Felix Mendelssohn-Bartholdys Briefwechsel mit Legationsrat Karl Klingemann in London*, ed. Karl Klingemann (Essen, 1909), pp. 81–4. The letter to Cramer, 26 November 1829, is in the Library of Congress.

second visit to England in 1832, and the publication of the first book of *Lieder ohne Worte* op. 19. The accounts of its publication as usually given state that Novello was unwilling to bear the cost of publishing it on his own, and so it had to be issued at Mendelssohn's risk, with the composer being paid a royalty of two shillings a copy.[5] This, however, is somewhat misleading, and it seems worthwhile setting out the facts in greater detail. Mendelssohn had plans for publishing a set of *Lieder ohne Worte* (or *Romanzen* as he first thought of calling them) while still in Paris early in 1832 at the end of his Grand Tour. Although the compositions were not yet finished, he made agreements with Schlesinger in Paris and Simrock in Bonn for the French and German rights.[6] He then proceeded to London in April. We know from his correspondence with Simrock that Cramer, Addison & Beale were once more due to be the English publishers, but in the second half of June something went wrong, and the agreement with Cramer fell through.[7] The cause may perhaps have been an argument over errors in the piano duet arrangement of the *Midsummer Night's Dream* Overture, which Mendelssohn mentions in a letter to Klingemann.[8] It may on the other hand have been a disagreement over money. A note by Sir George Macfarren in the Philharmonic Society's program book of 21 June 1875 is interesting in this regard. Discussing the "Italian" Symphony, first performed under Mendelssohn at the Philharmonic's concert on 13 May 1833, Macfarren adds: "Having arranged it for the pianoforte, Mendelssohn offered this symphony to the firm of Cramer & Co. for publication, who declined it upon the ground that his works had not been profitable which they had already printed! Its publication thus delayed, was not again sought by Mendelssohn." Although documentary confirmation of Macfarren's statement is lacking, there is little reason to disbelieve it, and it corresponds to the general experience of English publishers with Mendelssohn's works in the 1830s, as will presently emerge. The Cramer firm did not cease business with Mendelssohn completely, but they subsequently only published two comparatively unimportant works (the *Scherzo à capriccio* and the piano duet arrangement of the Overture op. 24). Whatever the reason for Cramer's dropping out, Mendelssohn was left without an English publisher for the *Lieder ohne Worte* just as he was due to leave the country. At this point Ignaz

---

5 See for example *Letters of Felix Mendelssohn to Ignaz and Charlotte Moscheles*, ed. Felix Moscheles (London, 1888), p. 65.

6 Letters to Simrock, 23 January and 28 February 1832, in Felix Mendelssohn Bartholdy, *Briefe an deutsche Verleger*, ed. Rudolf Elvers (Berlin, 1968) [hereafter Elvers, *Briefe*], pp. 176–7. On the history of the composition of op. 19 see Christa Jost, *Mendelssohns Lieder ohne Worte* (Tutzing, 1988), pp. 28–34.

7 Letter to Simrock, 7 July 1832 (Elvers, *Briefe*, p. 179).

8 4 July 1832 (Klingemann, *Felix Mendelssohn-Bartholdys Briefwechsel*, p. 95).

Moscheles stepped in and offered to solve the problem for him. Mendelssohn and Vincent Novello had become acquainted with one another during his 1829 visit through their common enthusiasm for the organ and for Bach, and in 1832 Novello had persuaded Mendelssohn to undertake the composition of an English cathedral service.[9] (In the event this was to be a long time in coming to fruition, and Novello was not to publish it.) Moscheles now got Novello to take on the *Lieder ohne Worte*, but Novello, although willing to sell it, did not want to risk money on it. Moscheles therefore arranged and paid for the printing himself, being reimbursed by Mendelssohn's father in August.[10] He initialled each title page "I. M. for F. M." ("Ignaz Moscheles for Felix Mendelssohn") and delivered 150 copies to Novello for publication on 20 August under the title *Original Melodies for the Pianoforte*. It sold for four shillings of which the composer received half. To describe this, however, as a royalty in the conventional sense is a misnomer, for out of this sum Mendelssohn had to recoup his printing costs. The royalty system was, in any case, a development of the second half of the nineteenth century. Novello probably had nothing to do with the actual printing, and this would account for a curious error in the imprint, which reads "Published for the author by T. A. Novello." "T." should, of course, be "J.," for Joseph Alfred Novello, Vincent's son, in whose name the business was run. It is most unlikely that such a mistake would have slipped through unnoticed if the edition had been prepared "in house."

At the time of publication Mendelssohn wrote jokingly to Moscheles, "The work will certainly go through at least twenty editions, and with the proceeds I shall buy a house at No. 2 Chester Place [next door to the Moscheleses] and a seat in the House of Commons, and become a Radical by profession."[11] By June 1833 only forty-eight copies had been sold, netting Mendelssohn the princely sum of £4/16-![12] On reflection, however, the choice of Novello as selling agent was rather a strange one. The Novello firm, although it had its origins in the editions of sacred music that Vincent Novello compiled and published at his own expense from 1811 onwards, only became established as a proper business when set up in Frith Street in 1829 in his son's name. It was thus barely three years old when the *Original Melodies* appeared, and the firm's early publications were still basically of sacred music. It is therefore not surprising that the work failed to sell well with such an outlet, nor perhaps that the Novellos were reluctant to finance it. Apart from Cramer, Addison &

9 Letter of Mendelssohn to Vincent Novello, 22 August 1832 (British Library, Add. MS. 11750, f. 129).

10 Letter of Mendelssohn to Moscheles, 10 August 1832 (Moscheles, *Letters*, p. 29).

11 *Ibid.*

12 Moscheles, *Letters*, p. 65.

Beale, firms such as Chappell, Lonsdale, or Mori & Lavenu would have appeared more logical choices for piano music at this time. It cannot have helped either that the work, unusually for a Mendelssohn piece of this period, was not reviewed in *The Harmonicon*. Also the choice of title, *Original Melodies for the Pianoforte*, was perhaps not distinctive enough to provide healthy sales. Why Mendelssohn avoided the obvious term "Songs without Words" is unclear, but he continued to do so for the English editions of these works throughout his life. The French edition, published at the same time, was *Six romances sans paroles*,[13] whilst the German edition appeared as *Sechs Lieder ohne Worte*, although its publication was curiously delayed until well into 1833 – a strange, but untypical, failure of simultaneous publication in practice.[14] His original idea of "Romanzen" for the German title had, however, been dropped in favor of "Lieder" by July 1832.[15]

Having had a disappointing début with Novello's, Mendelssohn quite understandably looked elsewhere when it came to the publication of the second book of *Lieder ohne Worte* op. 30, in 1835. They were published by Mori & Lavenu under the title *Six Romances for the Piano Forte*. The firm was run by Nicholas Mori, who, like Franz Cramer, led the Philharmonic Society's orchestra at many of Mendelssohn's concerts. Mori had also begun publishing his works in 1832, with the *Capriccio brillant* op. 22, and the First Piano Concerto op. 25. Very little of the firm's correspondence with Mendelssohn has survived, so a detailed study of their business dealings is difficult. One letter from Mori, however, deserves quotation for the further evidence it offers as to Mendelssohn's marketability in the mid-1830s. In a letter of 27 December 1834 Mori expresses his anxiety over Mendelssohn's more technically demanding piano works:

> difficult music on the Continent is so much more valuable to a publisher there, it being more highly appreciated than in England. Here the difficult music is only purchased by a few professors who are able to combat with it in order to enhance their own talent. As the sale of this style of music is thus limited, I am thus prevented giving you such a price as your great talent ought to command. Having had a little experience with two or three works of your's, I am enabled to say what they have produced, and I give you my word of honor as a gentleman that your second Rondeau [the *Rondo brillant* op. 29] which Moscheles played at his last concert & which is so fine a composition, has not sold 100 copies – in fact were I not ashamed of the honor of the profession I could say that it has not sold more than 50. By-the-by several public performers have

13 Listed in *Bibliographie de la France* (8 September 1832).
14 See letter to Simrock, 2 June 1833 (Elvers, *Briefe*, p. 183). Listed in Hofmeister's *Musikalisch-literarischer Monatsbericht* for September/October 1833.
15 Letter to Simrock, 7 July 1832 (Elvers, *Briefe*, p. 179).

mentioned they would readily play it if it had an introduction, which would further the sale of it very much & this you could oblige me with, with very little trouble, when you have occasion to send to me – a couple of pages would be sufficient & I am of the opinion that it requires it.[16]

Mendelssohn did not oblige with an introduction, but Mori continued to buy his works, and in fact published just as many of his compositions during the 1830s as Novello, including piano duet arrangements of the *Hebrides* and *A Calm Sea and Prosperous Voyage* overtures, and the Preludes and Fugues for Piano op. 35. The composer, however, found Mori a rather odd fellow and eventually broke off his associations with the firm a few months before Mori's death in June 1839.[17]

Novello next appears on the Mendelssohn scene with *St. Paul* in 1836, when for the first time Mendelssohn deals with Alfred Novello rather than Vincent.[18] *St. Paul* was more in Novello's normal line of business, and they paid 30 guineas for the copyright. Although the sums often paid to Mendelssohn for his works may appear at first sight to be miserably small, there is no reason to suppose that they were not perfectly valid commercial rates for their time, particularly given the vulnerability of foreign copyrights. No English publisher made a fortune out of Mendelssohn's works during his lifetime; the real profits came posthumously with the evolution of the cheap music era. The evidence rather suggests that sales of his works were often distinctly sluggish before the 1840s. Alfred Novello, in negotiating prices, repeatedly comments on "the somewhat limited sale of these sorts of works" (in this case Psalm 42, op. 42).[19] Even *St. Paul* was no more than a steady seller. Novello notes in 1840 that "the English indeed I hope are beginning to understand it, which it is a work of some labor to make them do, anything that is good."[20] *St. Paul* also provides an interesting sidelight on the development of international cooperation in music publishing. The necessity of simultaneous publication meant that a mutually acceptable date had to be fixed. This was sometimes done in direct correspondence between the publishers concerned, but more commonly in Mendelssohn's case with the composer himself acting as intermediary. Not infrequently, too, the proofs of one publisher's edition would be used to engrave the plates in another country. The most striking

16 Letter in the "Green Books" (GB) of Mendelssohn's incoming correspondence in the Bodleian Library, Oxford (MSS. M. Deneke Mendelssohn b.4 and d.28–53). The letters are cited here by volume and item number within the set. This letter is GB III, 342.

17 Letter to Moscheles, 13 January 1839 (Moscheles, *Letters*, p. 178).

18 Michael Hurd in *Vincent Novello – and Company* (London, 1981), p. 40, states that Alfred initiated the contact with Mendelssohn, but it was clearly Vincent with whom he first corresponded. It is worth noting that Alfred was actually a year younger than Mendelssohn.

19 Letter of 6 March 1838 (GB VIII, 104).   20 Letter of 29 May 1840 (GB XI, 164).

development in the case of *St. Paul*, however, concerns the full score. Novello himself engraved only the vocal score and separate chorus parts, both having just the English words. Although the title page of the vocal score advertises the full score and orchestral parts as being on sale, the demand for these was met by simply importing the German Simrock edition. Simrock's own vocal score and chorus parts had only the German text, but for the full score he was prevailed upon to include both the German and English words. This no doubt suited Simrock well, since for comparatively little extra effort he was able to increase his sales potential. *St. Paul* appears to have been the first work to have been co-published in this way, although it was to become standard practice with the full scores of Mendelssohn's works, regardless of publisher.[21] The full scores were mostly sold in England as they stood, with perhaps the English publisher's stamp added to the title page, although there is at least one copy of the full score of the *Lobgesang* Symphony where Novello has substituted his English title page (as used for the vocal score) for the original German one.[22] On the sale of full scores in general, it is worth noting that despite the immense popularity of *Elijah* with English audiences, no English publisher has ever issued his own edition of the full score.

Following the publication of *St. Paul* Novello gradually assumed the role of Mendelssohn's principal English publisher, and began to put at the head of his title pages "Novello's Edition of the Works of Felix Mendelssohn Bartholdy." In 1837 he took the third book of *Lieder ohne Worte* op. 38, which had now become on the title page "the celebrated Lieder ohne Worte," notwithstanding the fact that only 114 copies of the first book had been sold in the four years up to 1836.[23] At the same time he finally bought the copyright of that first book.[24] Novello's, however, was by no means a prosperous firm in the 1830s. There is an interesting memorandum in the Novello archives which illustrates this. Late in 1837, in order to pay Mendelssohn the comparatively large sum of £42 he had agreed upon for the Second Piano Concerto op. 40 – he had faced competition from Mori – Alfred Novello borrowed £30 interest free from George Frederick Anderson. In return he granted Anderson's wife, the well-known pianist Lucy Anderson, the exclusive rights to perform it in England for the period of about six months prior to publication. Anderson

---

21 *St. Paul* was of course by no means the first score to be published with bilingual texts, which was quite common since the end of the eighteenth century, particularly for operatic works, but none was published as part of an arrangement with a foreign publisher. The nearest precedent is probably the full score of Haydn's *Creation*, which the composer published himself in 1800 with German and English texts, and, which was principally distributed in England by Longman, Clementi & Co., who in the same year published a vocal score with English text.

22 Bodleian Library (Tenbury Mus. c.129 (2)).   23 Moscheles, *Letters*, p. 66.

24 Memorandum of 9 September 1837 in the Novello archives. Reproduced in Moscheles, *Letters*, p. 67.

was then to be repaid as sales of the work allowed. Novello paid back £10 in 1841, but the remaining £20 not until 1849.[25] In his correspondence with Mendelssohn Alfred Novello constantly pleaded to have works as cheaply as possible "as the yet untaught taste of the English public does not allow me to give as good price as I could wish for such works."[26] What every publisher wanted from Mendelssohn, of course, was an opera. William Chappell offered him £300 for one in 1837, and Mendelssohn was tempted,[27] but as on so many other occasions it came to nothing for lack of agreement on a libretto. Novello's parsimoniousness was probably a contributory factor to the eventual rift between composer and publisher to which it is now time to turn attention.

Up to about 1838 Mendelssohn seems to have enjoyed a fairly good personal relationship with Alfred. Inviting him to the Lower Rhine Music Festival in Cologne in 1838, Mendelssohn tempts him by saying "We could have plenty of fun and still more Rhine wine."[28] But over the next two years Mendelssohn's enthusiasm for the Novello firm was to cool. One of his persistent complaints was that Novello was a poor correspondent – not a good thing to be with a composer as busy and as punctilious in letter writing as Mendelssohn. This went back as far as September 1836, when Mendelssohn writes: "I am extremely sorry not to have heard from you since your departure from The Hague, when you promised to let me have an answer to many questions, and some news of the performance of my oratorio, for which I waited all the time of my residence in Frankfurt, but in vain."[29] It clearly became more irritating as time went on. There was also the matter of Mendelssohn's dislike of Alfred's sister. Clara Novello had made a sensational singing début in Leipzig under Mendelssohn's baton in 1837, and the composer had written an enthusiastic account of her reception to Alfred.[30] The latter thereupon promptly incurred Mendelssohn's disapproval by producing lithographed facsimiles of this letter for distribution to his friends. It was also picked up by the English press, and Mendelssohn, having got to hear of it, rebuked Novello in a letter of December 1837 with the modest comment: "O God, I am not a fit person to write English letters for an English public – I pray why do you allow them to do so?"[31] Mendelssohn, while admiring her

25 Letter of Alfred Novello to George Anderson, 9 February 1849 (Staatsbibliothek Preussischer Kulturbesitz, Berlin, Autogr. I/202/5). Anderson's copy of the memorandum is in the same library (Autogr. I/202/6).

26 Letter of 26 June 1840 (GB XI, 215).

27 Letter to Klingemann, 17 Nov. 1837 (Klingemann, *Felix Mendelssohn-Bartholdys Briefwechsel*, p. 224).

28 12 February 1838 (Novello archives).   29 27 September 1836 (Novello archives).

30 18 November 1837 (lithographed copy in the Novello archives).

31 Letter postmarked 21 December 1837 (Novello archives).

singing, disliked Clara's snobbish and superior manner, as he confessed to Karl Klingemann in January 1838: "I have a certain inner antipathy to all her doings, which I can never explain, but which never leaves me."[32] Alfred continued to extol Clara's virtues and to send him news of her European triumphs. He also tried to persuade Mendelssohn to dedicate his setting of Psalm 42 to her.[33] Mendelssohn, however, refused to accede to this, and likewise never produced an apparently promised song for her, despite several promptings from Alfred.[34] It is probably fair to view Clara as a further mild irritant in his relationship with Alfred. More pertinent, perhaps, is what may be considered as Alfred's occasional insensitivity to Mendelssohn's status as a composer. The most obvious instance of this is to be found in a letter of 6 March 1838, when Alfred tried to get Mendelssohn to enter for the Dublin Antient Concerts choral prize. "I send you at the head of this letter two setts of words and the regulations for a prize competition, and think for many reasons it would be well for you to set them, and let me have them as soon as you can."[35] Mendelssohn replied diplomatically to the effect that he did *not* go in for prize competitions![36]

At the end of 1839 Mendelssohn offered Novello his new Piano Trio in D minor op. 49.[37] Novello was very tardy in replying to this letter, and when he did so it was to dismiss the offer rather casually: "I am sorry to decline the purchase of your trio which I suppose is for stringed instruments, but I fear such a work would command a very small sale amongst our ignorant public."[38] In the meantime Mendelssohn had heard through Raymund Härtel that a certain Edward Buxton, proprietor of Ewer & Co., had just visited him in Leipzig, and had expressed the wish to publish a Mendelssohn work.[39] Härtel obviously thought well of him, and so Mendelssohn immediately wrote offering him the Piano Trio for 10 guineas.[40] Buxton wrote back saying that he was "much flattered" and eagerly accepted the Trio.[41] Despite Novello's prediction, the work clearly sold well, for Buxton was soon asking

---

32 "Habe ich eine gewisse innere Abneigung gegen all ihr Tun und Lassen, das ich mir nicht immer erklären kann, das mich aber niemals verlässt." Letter of 9 January 1838 (Klingemann, *Felix Mendelssohn-Bartholdys Briefwechsel*, p. 227, partly translated in Wilfrid Blunt, *On Wings of Song* [London, 1974], p. 201).

33 Letter of 2 July 1838 (GB VIII, 3).

34 See letters of 12 February 1839 (GB X, 193), 9 April 1839 (GB IX, 114), and 28 October 1839 (GB X, 105).

35 GB VIII, 104.   36 Letter of 7(?) April 1838 (Novello archives).

37 See Mendelssohn's reminder in a letter of 21 January 1840 (Novello archives).

38 18 February 1840 (GB XI, 63).

39 See letters of Mendelssohn to Breitkopf & Härtel, 12 March 1840 (Elvers, *Briefe*, p. 105) and to Buxton, 25 February 1840 (Library of Congress).

40 25 February 1840 (Library of Congress).   41 6 March 1840 (GB XI, 79).

for another.[42] Thus was born Mendelssohn's association with Ewer & Co., to which we will return.

The indications in 1839 and 1840 are that Felix was becoming rather tired of Novello's constantly seeking for works on the cheap, and late in 1839 rebuked him when he tried to delay payment for Psalm 114 op. 51 until three months after publication.[43] The final cause of the rift between the two, however, was what may be termed the "*Lobgesang* affair." The *Lobgesang* (*Hymn of Praise*) was originally written for the Leipzig celebrations in the summer of 1840 of the 400th anniversary of the invention of printing. An English performance quickly followed under Mendelssohn's direction at the Birmingham Festival on 23 September, and Novello undertook to publish it. Over the winter months, however, the composer decided, as on so many other occasions, that it needed revision before publication. He requested Klingemann in a letter of 20 December to tell Novello to be sure to see that the copy of the full score and parts that he had did not leave his hands, as the new version would soon be with him.[44] Mendelssohn's reaction can therefore be imagined when he heard from Sophy Horsley, who was on a visit to Leipzig in March 1841, that the Philharmonic Society had just or was about to perform the *Lobgesang* – i.e. in its unrevised state from the material in Novello's possession. Writing to Klingemann he forbade such a performance in the strongest terms, and demanded that Novello give up his score to Klingemann.[45] It was in fact too late, as the performance had already taken place. His fury continued in the next letter: "You cannot believe how terribly angry such a performance makes me, since you do not know the new pieces. With them the whole thing becomes a totally different work, and comes so much nearer to my original conception and expresses it so much more clearly, that any repetition of the old version is for me a real injustice and insult."[46] He wanted to know if Klingemann had perhaps forgotten to pass on his request for Novello not to part with the score, or whether Novello had gone and done so regardless. If the latter were the case "then I will never exchange another word or letter

42 5 February 1841 (GB XIII, 57). Novello, however, seems to have been under the mistaken impression that it was a string trio, in which case his assessment may well have been justified.

43 Undated letter in the Novello archives.

44 Klingemann, *Felix Mendelssohn-Bartholdys Briefwechsel*, p. 255.

45 10 March 1841 (Klingemann, *Felix Mendelssohn-Bartholdys Briefwechsel*, p. 259). Klingemann evidently did not recover the score from Novello, for it remained in the Novello archives until recently. It was sold in London at the Phillips' sale on 14 June 1989, and is now in the Bodleian Library (MS. M. Deneke Mendelssohn c.93).

46 "Du glaubst nicht, wie mich eine solche Aufführung so schrecklich ärgern würde, weil Du die neuen Sachen nicht kennst. Das ganze Stück wird dadurch wirklich ein anderes, und kommt meiner ursprünglichen Idee so viel näher, drückt sie so ungleich deutlicher und besser aus, dass mir jede Wiederholung des alten, ein wahres Unrecht, eine wahre Beleidigung antut." 15 March 1841 (Klingemann, *Felix Mendelssohn-Bartholdys Briefwechsel*, p. 260).

with him."[47] The anger rumbled on for many months. Klingemann, it seems, may have forgotten to pass on Mendelssohn's message since he was ill at the time, but Novello knew perfectly well that revisions were on the way. The final outcome was that, although Novello did publish the *Lobgesang* in 1841 (in its revised form, of course), Mendelssohn sold him nothing more. The only work published by Novello after the *Lobgesang* was the setting of Psalm 95 op. 46 which the composer had sold him two years earlier, but which was not ready for publication until 1842.

Henceforth Ewer & Co. were to become Mendelssohn's main English publishers. In the middle of the "*Lobgesang* affair" the composer offered Buxton the fourth book of *Lieder ohne Worte* op. 53 and the Thomas Moore song "The Garland,"[48] which were quickly accepted. The way lay open for the warmest of relationships to develop between the two men over the remainder of Mendelssohn's lifetime. Buxton himself remains an elusive figure biographically. He was a wool broker, who had taken over the firm of Ewer out of love for music.[49] In his first letter to Mendelssohn on 6 March 1840 he remarks apropos the pricing of works: "As I am but a tyro in the publishing line, I am of course not acquainted with the value of such a work and therefore leave it entirely in your hands to demand a fair price for it." Saying he is keen to be offered further works, he adds "Altho' I may not *always* buy, as you are already aware that music is not my trade, but merely a hobby."[50] A note to Felix later that year, when the composer was in London, informs him that "I shall probably have to attend public wool sales every day this week" and that Felix was therefore unlikely to find him in.[51] Nevertheless, amateur publisher that he may have been, all the evidence points to him having run the Ewer firm in a sound commercial manner, even if not at great profit – there are occasional hints of cash flow problems in his correspondence with Mendelssohn. Buxton seems to have had a German background – his mother may well have been German – for although he and Mendelssohn almost always corresponded in English, Buxton could write fluent German (employing German script). William Bartholomew (Mendelssohn's chief English translator) notes in a letter to the composer in 1843 that Buxton was

---

47 "Dann will ich doch nie wieder ein Wort oder einen Brief mit ihm wechseln." *Ibid.*

48 Letters of Mendelssohn to Buxton, 2 May 1841 (Library of Congress) and 5 June 1841 (Bodleian Library, MS. M. Deneke Mendelssohn c.42, f.64).

49 On the evidence of the London Post Office directories Buxton was a partner in the firm of Buckler & Buxton, *c*.1837–40. By 1841 he was senior partner in Buxton & Slack, and from 1847 in business alone until 1858. Subsequently the firm became Buxton & Metcalfe (1858–66) and Buxton & Hunter (1866–75), before Buxton's son, Henry, who had been in the wool business on his own account since 1865, took over the firm as Henry Buxton & Co.

50 GB XI, 79.   51 28 September 1840 (GB XII, 229).

"more than half a German."[52] His wife, Therese (c. 1806–1900) was probably German, for she and the children spent quite some time in Leipzig in 1842 and 1843. This cultural bond may have helped cement the relationship between composer and publisher, for right from the earliest exchange of letters (before they had met in person) there is evident goodwill on both sides. It is perhaps not too fanciful to see Mendelssohn revealing himself here as his father's son – in the role of the banker Mendelssohn conducting business amicably with someone he feels instinctively he can trust. The contrast with Novello is marked not only in the promptness of his replies to Mendelssohn, but also in regard to negotiations over prices. Buxton never quibbled over the price Mendelssohn asked for his works, and a spirit of fairness on both sides is clear throughout their dealings. For the little song "The Garland" Mendelssohn said that Buxton could "pay for it *whatever* you like."[53] Buxton replied: "As the English taste is rather capricious and as you leave it to me to fix a price, I will for the present say £3. ... And if the sale of the song in any degree answers my expectation I shall be most happy to add a further sum."[54] What more could a composer wish for? Buxton was in fact to make such voluntary extra payments for works on at least two occasions (for *Die erste Walpurgis-nacht* and *Elijah*). He was soon keen to take everything that Mendelssohn had to offer, from the Second Cello Sonata to male voice part-songs and the incidental music to *Antigone*. From 1842 onwards only two works went to other English publishers, but as both are of particular interest, they merit a digression.

Mendelssohn's Six Songs op. 57, were published in England by Wessel & Stapleton in 1843. The music critic J. W. Davison, an acquaintance of the composer, made initial inquiries in the summer of 1842 on behalf of the firm as to whether he had works to sell them.[55] By December 1842 Mendelssohn had offered them the op. 57 songs, and Stapleton had accepted.[56] Davison's interest in the matter continued, since not only did he do the English translations, but the English edition was dedicated (ostensibly at Stapleton's suggestion) to Charlotte Dolby, with whom Davison was, as he confessed to Mendelssohn, madly in love.[57] The significance of the publication lies in the fact that it was the first complete set of Mendelssohn's songs to be published in England – the German Lied seems to have made little impression in the country before the 1840s. It was not long, however, before Buxton at Ewer's decided to publish a uniform edition of Mendelssohn's four previous sets of

52 18 July 1843 (GB XVIII, 26).
53 Letter of 5 June 1841 (Bodleian Library, MS. M. Deneke Mendelssohn c.42, f.64).
54 27 July 1841 (GB XIV, 17).   55 Letter of c.23 June 1842 (GB XV, 271).
56 9 December 1842 (GB XVI, 155).
57 Letter of 12 December 1842 (GB XVI, 160).

songs (opp. 8, 9, 19, and 47) with German and English words, which appeared in 1845 and 1846. Being non-copyright works of course, he did not have to pay anything for them. In 1843 Stapleton's partner, C. R. Wessel, wrote to Mendelssohn attempting to persuade him to do a deal for all his future compositions; he wanted to add the Mendelssohn stallion to the Chopin already in his stable.[58] Nothing came of it, however, and he obtained no further works. Perhaps Moscheles, whose low opinion of Wessel is known, may have warned his friend off.[59]

The other non-Ewer work, the six Organ Sonatas op. 65, was the result of a commission by Coventry & Hollier in 1844. Charles Coventry had been on friendly terms with Mendelssohn since at least 1836, when he sent the composer copies of his new edition of Bach organ works.[60] It was their common advocacy of Bach that was to lead to their business relationship. Early in 1844 Coventry reminded Mendelssohn that he had promised to send some correct copies of further Bach organ works which Coventry wanted to publish.[61] The eventual outcome was six books of Bach's chorale-based organ works, edited by Mendelssohn, as well as his violin and piano arrangement of the Chaconne, all issued from 1845 to 1847.[62] Coventry also suggested that Mendelssohn write some original pieces for organ, which, starting life as individual movements or "voluntaries" between July 1844 and January 1845, were refashioned (at Mendelssohn's suggestion) into the Six Sonatas before publication in September 1845. The interesting feature of this work from the publishing point of view is that Coventry published it initially by subscription, the only one of Mendelssohn's works ever to be so issued. The reason for this is made clear in Coventry's letter of 29 April 1845. Announcing his decision he adds: "I do so in consequence of there having been a doubt raised with regard to music copyright. It is said that a foreigner cannot maintain a copyright. Several actions between several of the music sellers have been brought."[63] Initial publication by subscription would hopefully ensure that Coventry covered his costs (including £60 to the composer) whatever the outcome of the copyright dispute. In the event foreign copyright survived this attack, but the Organ Sonatas provide an instructive example of the

58 31 May 1843 (GB XVII, 281).

59 Letter of Moscheles to Maurice Schlesinger, 2 November 1842 (Bibliothèque Nationale, Paris). Printed in Kallberg, "The Chopin Sources," pp. 133–5, and partially in Kallberg, "Chopin in the Marketplace," 565–6.

60 Inscribed copies in the Bodleian Library (Deneke 183).

61 8 February 1844 (GB XIX, 94).

62 See Rudolf Elvers, "Verzeichnis der von Felix Mendelssohn Bartholdy herausgegebenen Werke Johann Sebastian Bachs," Gestalt und Glaube: Festschrift für ... Oskar Söhngen zum 60. Geburtstag (Witten, 1960), pp. 145–9.

63 GB XXI, 159.

fragility of the publisher's situation at this time. An amusing sidelight on the Sonatas is offered by an extraordinary letter to Mendelssohn from the publisher Robert Cocks on 27 July 1844, shortly after he had begun work on the pieces for Coventry:

> A friend, one of our cathedral organists, has suggested the following work, and I proposed to him I would submit it to your opinion. If you think well of it, please to favor me with your terms for the copyright for England. i.e. A work of 12 pieces for pedal organs or rather organ with obligato pedals, to be thus composed. I will describe *one* piece.
>
> *Slow introduction* of one page.
>
> Second movement introducing solo stops of about 2 pages and to conclude with a *lively* fugue of about 3 pages. Accordingly the whole work would occupy about 72 pages.
>
> You may remember my name as a publisher and that I am appointed publisher to Her Majesty. Would you desire the above to be dedicated to H.R.H. the Prince Albert? Have you any more songs ready without words to offer me &c. &c.[64]

Mendelssohn's reply to this request for made-to-measure music is unfortunately not preserved!

Returning to Mendelssohn's association with Ewer, it is noticeable that the tone of Buxton's letters became more informal as the years progressed. He could urge Mendelssohn on to deliver promised wares, whilst still maintaining an underlying deference. Having in 1844 published the fifth book of *Lieder ohne Worte* op. 62 (by now they were clearly best sellers in contrast to ten years previously), Buxton asked for more on 14 January 1845: "Make me up another book – do it at once. I know you have got plenty ready. You need not be afraid of the people getting tired of them, they are the very things which have made you so many friends. Recollect that Shakespeare says in the instance: 'To be well done, 'twere well, 'twere done quickly'. So set about it at once."[65] And Buxton did get another book the same year! In December 1845 Buxton says he is expecting a parcel which he hopes will contain "a few more *trifles* of yours – a few more 2-part songs, a book of bass songs, a few single organ pieces (not above ¾ of a yard each), a bundle of pianoforte music, an overture or two, and a new symphony, or an old one dyed to look as good as new."[66] Mendelssohn replied in similar Shakespearean vein: "I wish I could send you all the manuscripts which you quote in your list; at the moment they are still – I do not know where – but if you have patience I hope to send you

---

64 GB XX, 35.   65 GB XXI, 27.

66 30 December 1845 (GB XXII, 328). It is possible that the reference to the organ pieces relates back to Cocks's request.

one after the other and to make the list complete. But when? That is the question."[67] Nevertheless Mendelssohn did keep Buxton well supplied with new works, and Ewer was even to publish in 1846–7 the long delayed settings of the Morning and Evening Canticles which Vincent Novello had requested in 1832.

Buxton's ultimate achievement was naturally the publication of *Elijah*, which Novello and others had also been keen to acquire. The story of its genesis and Buxton's role in it was well told by F. G. Edwards as long ago as 1896.[68] One small error in Edwards's account, that has been perpetuated by all successive ones, is worth correcting, and that is the price paid for the English copyright. Mendelssohn was unsure what sum to ask for, and tried to get Buxton to suggest a price: "I wish on such an occasion that neither you nor I should be the loser."[69] Buxton on his part was unable to name a price – he had not published an oratorio before, nor did he know its extent: "I am proud of being your Verleger and consequently leave it entirely in your hands. ... If after a twelve month I find you have put too low a price on the oratorio you may rely on it I will raise it."[70] The price is not discussed further in the subsequent correspondence, and it was probably settled verbally when they met in England at the time of the first performance in the summer of 1846. Edwards says that Mendelssohn sold the copyright for 250 guineas, and that immediately after his death Buxton sent a further £100 for it voluntarily to Mendelssohn's widow.[71] Later writers have followed this with minor variants, sometimes quoting £250 with or without mentioning the extra payment. A letter of 7 May 1847 from Buxton to Mendelssohn, giving notice of payment, clearly lists, however, the *Elijah* copyright sum as £157/10/-, i.e. 150 guineas.[72] With the posthumous voluntary extra £100 this makes a total of £257/10/-, which is precisely the sum quoted in an indenture of 1850 between Buxton and Cécile Mendelssohn, which lists and confirms the sale of all the copyrights sold to Buxton by the composer in his lifetime.[73] The 150 guineas for *Elijah* was still easily the highest sum paid by any English publisher for a Mendelssohn work. It is, however, also worth noting that at the same time he sent the 150 guineas, Buxton also sent 200 guineas from the Exeter Hall Committee as Mendelssohn's fee for conducting four performances of the work.

The delay between the first performance and publication of *Elijah* proved

---

67 15 January 1846 (Library of Congress).
68 F. G. Edwards, *The History of Mendelssohn's Oratorio "Elijah"* (London, 1896). See also Arntrud Kurzhals-Reuter, *Die Oratorien Felix Mendelssohn Bartholdys* (Tutzing, 1978).
69 22 April 1846 (Library of Congress).   70 27 April 1846 (Library of Congress).
71 Edwards, *Mendelssohn's "Elijah"*, pp. 131–2.   72 GB XXV, 261.
73 Novello archives.

an anxious time for Buxton. On 10 November 1846 he wrote to Mendelssohn: "There is moreover some danger in keeping the work too long out of print, as there is the possibility of some of the single pieces being copied out and getting into the hands of any of the music sellers here, who would be unprincipled enough to publish them before I could enroll my copyright, which I can only do when it is all in print. I know there are several looking out for it and who have expressed their determination to print the songs if they could get hold of them."[74] It was eventually published after considerable revision in June 1847, Mendelssohn proving as scrupulous a proof reader as ever, and Buxton as usual tolerating all his last-minute changes. *Elijah* was the last major work of Mendelssohn that Buxton was to publish before the composer's premature death in November of that year. It was, however, by no means the end of his association with his works, for Buxton was offered and accepted all the first batch of Mendelssohn's posthumously published works, comprising opp. 73–100, which appeared between 1848 and 1852. The cynic might be tempted to see in Buxton's voluntary extra *Elijah* payment to Cécile merely a sweetener to ensure that he was offered these posthumous works, but as has been seen, such a payment was entirely consistent with his intentions and practice during Mendelssohn's lifetime. It is also doubtful whether, at the time of the payment, Buxton would have had any idea of the extent of the unpublished works, or that their publication was contemplated.

It is interesting in conclusion to note the posthumous fate of Mendelssohn's English editions. Despite being so abruptly discarded by the composer in 1841, the Novello firm was ultimately to acquire a near monopoly of his works. By 1856 they had the rights to the Organ Sonatas (which had apparently passed to Robert Cocks after Charles Coventry ceased business in 1851), and over the following years they bought a number of the Ewer copyrights, including the Morning and Evening Canticles. Finally in 1867 they took over the Ewer firm completely (becoming Novello, Ewer & Co.), gaining *Elijah* and the remaining copyrights. By this time Buxton was no longer involved with the firm, having sold it to William Witt in about 1859. Whether Mendelssohn turned in his grave we shall never know!

74 GB XXIV, 130.

Index

Abraham, Lars Ulrich, 60
Abrams, M. H., 69n
d'Agoult, Marie, 110, 116f, 122, 187n
Anderson, G. F., 246
Anderson, Lucy, 246
Attwood, Thomas, 167, 171, 172
Auber, D. F. E., 201

Bach, C. P. E., 165
Bach, Johann Sebastian, 7, 32, 40, 43f, 57,
   57n, 83, 87, 91, 95, 96, 98, 99, 122, 128,
   134, 146, 150, 159, 162–6, 184, 185,
   192f, 198, 203, 229, 243, 252;
   "Chaconne" from Partita, d, vn solo,
   BWV 1004, 42n, 252; Concerto, d, hpd,
   BWV 1052, 219n; Concerto, d, 3 hpd,
   BWV 1063, 116; Goldberg Variations
   BWV 988, 57; Mass in B minor BWV
   232, 89; Organ Fugues, 164 (BWV 543,
   552); St. Matthew Passion BWV 244, 79;
   205, 219n; Well-Tempered Clavier, 165,
   179, 180
Bader, K. A., 206
Bärmann, Heinrich, 219n
Baillot, Pierre, 106
Bartholomew, W., 95, 96n, 100, 250
Bauer (Baur), Albert, 4, 10, 64, 207, 224
Beck, Hermann, 42n
Becker, C. F., 141
Beer, H., 220
Beethoven, Ludwig van, 33, 34, 35, 42n, 44,
   58n, 65, 70, 83, 91, 98, 111, 122, 128,
   136, 146, 147, 148, 149n, 152, 154, 155,
   156, 158, 159; Adelaide (Lied) op. 46, 37;
   An die ferne Geliebte op. 98, 54; Christus
   am Ölberge (Christ on the Mount of
   Olives) op. 85, 96; Coriolanus Overture
   op. 62, 37; Egmont op. 84 (incidental
   music), 37; Eroica Variations op. 35, 49;
   Fidelio op. 72, 37; Geshöpfen des
   Prometheus, Die, op. 43, 37; Meeresstille

und glückliche Fahrt op. 112, 157; Missa
   Solemnis op. 123, 89, 96; Piano Concerto
   No. 4, G, op. 58, 219n; Piano Concerto
   No. 5, E flat, op. 73 ("Emperor"), 33,
   89n; Piano Sonata No. 8, c, op. 13
   (Pathétique), 37; Piano sonata No. 14, c
   sharp, op. 27/2, 219n; Piano Sonata
   No. 21, C, op. 53 ("Waldstein"), 219n;
   Septet, E flat, op. 20, 37; String Quartet,
   f, op. 95 (Serioso), 39; String Quartet, a,
   op. 132, 195; Symphony No. 3, E flat,
   op. 55 ("Eroica"), 37, 153; Symphony
   No. 5, c, op. 67, 152; Symphony No. 6,
   F, op. 68 ("Pastoral"), 37, 113, 152;
   Symphony No. 9, d, op. 127, 37, 40,
   155, 156, 159; 32 Variations on an
   Original Theme, c, WoO 80, 44, 54, 58ff;
   33 Variations on a Waltz by Diabelli
   op. 120, 38, 39, 41; Wellingtons Sieg
   op. 91, 153
Bellini, V., 136
Bennett, W. Sterndale, 201
Berger, Ludwig, 219n
Berlioz, Hector, 81, 82, 124, 135, 138, 186;
   Harold en Italie, 78; Roméo et Juliette,
   199; Symphonie fantastique, 78, 199
Bernsdorf, E., 146
Bernstein, Michael A., 64, 66
Bigot, Marie, 106
Böckh, August [?], 140f
Börne, L., 146
Bötticher, Caecilie, 219, 222
Bortniansky, Dmitri, 7, 10, 14
Brahms, Johannes, 65
Brendel, Franz, 43, 124, 138, 142, 145
Brosche, Günter, 38n
Bülow, Hans von, 124
Bunsen, C. K. J. von, 2, 4, 10, 27, 30f, 32
Busolt, J. E., 206
Buxton, E., 91n, 248, 250, 253, 255
Buxton, Therese, 250

256

Cahn, Peter, 60
Carl, Henriette, 209
Cervantes, Miguel de, 203f
Chappell, W., 246
Cherubini, Luigi, 106ff, 219n
Chopin, Frédéric, 35, 110, 124, 165, 240, 252;
    Nocturne, E, *op. 62/2*, 165;
    Polonaise-Fantaisie op. 61, 165; Prelude, c
    sharp, *op. 45*, 37
Chorley, H. F., 80n
Citron, Marcia J., 202n
Cocks, R., 253, 255
Cohen, Hermann, 112f
Cooper, John Michael, 80
Cornelius, P., 165
Coventry, Charles, 97, 164, 252f, 255
Cramer, Franz, 241, 242, 244
Cramer, Johann Baptist, 241
Crum, Margaret, 200n
Czerny, Carl, 35, 37, 37n, 38, 108, 167, 180ff

Dahlhaus, Carl, 44, 93, 127, 136n
David, Ferdinand, 14, 16, 40, 42n, 122, 201
Davison, J. W., 201, 251
Devrient, Eduard, 79, 90n, 150, 151, 152,
    200–39
Devrient, Thérèse, 216, 217n
Diabelli, Anton, 38
Dinter, G. G., 221n
Dirichlet, Rebecka (*née* Mendelssohn), 20n,
    21, 42, 113, 115, 120, 123, 184
Döhler, Theodor, 35, 37, 118
Dolby, Charlotte, 251
Donizetti, G., 136, 187n, 207
Donzelli, Domenico, 207
Dostoyevski, F. M., 64
Dreyfus, Laurence, 149n
Droysen, J. G., 157n
Dyer, Richard, 78n

Eckermann, J. P., 68n
Edwards, F. G., 80n, 95, 96n, 254
Eichhorn, J. A. F., 2n, 3, 10, 30
Einbeck, J. D. C., 5
Elvers, Rudolf, 35n, 164n, 200n, 202n, 252n
Erard, S., 109

Falkenstein, J. P. F. von, 234
Fallersleben, Hoffmann von, 43
Felix, Rachel, 135
Fellinger, Imogen, 35
Fétis, F.-J., 173, 186, 187
Field, John, 92
Fink, G. W., 168, 170
Finscher, Ludwig, 33
Fischer, Kurt von, 39
Förster, E., 208f
Forchert, A., 95n

Friedländer, Max, 56
Friedrich Wilhelm IV (King of Prussia),
    1–15, 30, 32, 140, 232–3
Fuller-Maitland, J. A., 89n

Gade, Neils, 233n
Galkin, Elliott W., 126
Geibel, Emanuel, 204
Geiger, J. N., 35
Gellert, C. F., 195
Gluck, C. W. von, 159; *Armide*, 219n;
    Iphigénie en Tauride, 219n
Goethe, Johann Wolfgang von, 33, 64–79,
    90n, 145n, 146, 159, 160, 237n
Gould, Stephen Jay, 131
Gounod, Charles, 82
Grell, Eduard, 5, 10, 14n, 21n
Griepenkerl, F. K., 158n
Grosser, Henriette, 222
Großmann-Vendrey, S., 97
Grove, George (Sir), 100n, 200, 202
Grünbaum, Therese, 219
Gubitz, F. W., 223–4

Hähnel, Amalie, 219
Häring, G. W., 224
Härtel, R., 248
Halévy, J. F., 136
Handel, George Frederick, 32, 40, 42n, 57n,
    82, 84f, 87, 95, 96, 122, 129, 130, 134,
    136, 159, 222; *Judas Maccabeus*, 229n;
    Keyboard Suite No. 3, d, 58f; *Lessons for
    the Harpsichord* (1720), 44; *Messiah*, 14f,
    16, 17
Hanstein, Auguste, 192f, 195
Hardenberg, Friedrich von, 66
Hartmann, J. P. E., 228
Hauptmann, Gerhard, 237n
Hauptmann, Moritz, 23, 32, 233n
Hauser, R., 89n
Haydn, Franz Joseph, 58n, 82, 128, 150, 152;
    Schöpfung, Die, 246n
Heine, Heinrich, 39n, 43n, 124, 132–6, 138,
    146
Heitmann, J., 112
Hell, Helmut, 35n
Hell, Theodor (*see* Winkler, K. G. T.)
Henning, Carl, 6
Hensel, Fanny (*née* Mendelssohn), 20, 41,
    43n, 120n, 150, 159, 171, 187, 206
Hensel, Sebastian, 89n, 91n, 202
Hensel, Wilhelm, 206
Henselt, Adolph, 35, 37, 119, 195n
Hermann, C. H., 208f
Hildebrandt, T., 225–6
Hiller, Ferdinand, 21n, 57, 90n, 109, 113,
    114, 116, 117, 124, 163, 202
Hoffmann, E. T. A., 56f

Hoffmann, Hofrath, 225–6
Homer, 114
Horsley, Sophy, 249f
Hotho, H. G., 210
Humboldt, Wilhelm von, 66
Hummel, J. N., 107
Hurd, M., 245n
Huschke, K., 204n

Immermann, Karl, 204n, 222

Jähns, F. W., 225–6
Jaenecke, Joachim, 37n
Joachim, Joseph, 124, 201
Josephson, J. A., 233
Jost, Christa, 242n
Jullien, Adolphe, 134

Kalkbrenner, Frédéric, 35, 37, 38, 39, 106,
    107, 108, 163
Kallberg, J., 240n
Kapp, Reinhard, 42n
Katz, Jacob, 41
Kaufmann, Schima, 124n
Keferstein, G. A., 139
Keil, S., 165n
Kiesewetter, R. G., 136n
Kleist, Heinrich von, 204n
Klimt, Gustav, 37
Klingemann, Karl, 1n, 4, 33, 41, 91n, 160n,
    168, 174, 238–9, 240, 241, 248, 249f
Knepler, Georg, 92, 93, 130n
Konold, Wulf, 81n, 156n
Kossack, Ernst, 136
Kraus, K. F., 158n
Kreutzer, Conradin, 107
Krüger, Eduard, 137, 138, 142, 147
Krummacher, Friedhelm, 127
Küstner, K. T. von, 234
Kunt, Karl, 33
Kunze, Stefan, 57
Kurzhals-Reuter, A., 254n
Kutzkow, K., 235

Lange, O., 138, 139
Laue, F., 241
Lee, Laurie, 130n
Leibowitz, René, 33n
Lenz, Bertha, 219
Leseur, Jean Françoise, 106
Leupold, Ulrich, 7n
Lind, Jenny, 201
Lindpaintner, P. J., 229
Lipinsky, Gustav, 111
Liszt, Franz, 35, 37, 38, 41n, 82, 106–25, 129,
    130, 140; 165, 187; Don Sanché (opera),
    109; Fantasy and Fugue on "Ad nos
    salutarum undam," 165, 199; Faust

Symphony, 199; Großes Konzertstück
    über Mendelssohn's Lieder ohne Worte, 2,
    pf (R. 355), 111; Marcia funèbre [= pf
    transcription of Funeral March from
    Beethoven, "Eroica" Symphony], 37;
    Prelude and Fugue on B-A-C-H, 165
Little, Wm. A., 98, 187n
Lobe, J. C., 147, 166
Loewe, Carl, 23, 156
Long, Kathleen, 131
Lüttichow, A. F. von, 233–4
Luther, Martin, 7, 10, 23, 255

McFarland, Thomas, 66, 69n
Macfarren, G. A., 202, 206, 221n, 242
Mann, Thomas, 125
Mantius, Eduard, 219n
Marcello, B., 229
Marschner, Heinrich, 204, 215n
Martainville, A., 107
Marx, A. B., 1, 38, 149–61, 228–9
Marx, Therese, 149n, 150n, 161
Massow, Ludwig von, 2, 4n, 5, 6n, 10, 15n
Mechetti, Pietro, 33, 35, 37
Mellers, Wilfrid, 80n, 86f, 88, 89, 91n, 92,
    93, 95
Mendelssohn Bartholdy, Abraham, 79, 132,
    151, 243
Mendelssohn Bartholdy, Carl, 201
Mendelssohn Bartholdy, Cécile, 115, 121,
    229–30, 254, 255
Mendelssohn Bartholdy, Fanny (see Hensel,
    Fanny)
Mendelssohn Bartholdy, Felix
    Ach Gott vom Himmel sieh' darein (chorale
        cantata, 1832), 195n
    Andante, E, Str qu, op. 81/1, 49
    Antigone (incidental music) op. 55, 135,
        136, 140, 141, 233–4, 237, 238, 251
    Aus tiefer Noth op. 23/1, 163, 197n
    Capriccio, f sharp, pf, op. 5, 123, 165, 241
    Capriccio brillant, b, op. 22, 219n, 244
    Cello Sonata No. 2, D, op. 58, 195; 251
    Chorale harmonizations, 1843, ch, winds,
        17f
    Christe, Du Lamm Gottes (chorale cantata,
        1827), 195n
    Christus op. 97, 95; 139; 195n
    Ehre sei dem Vater (Gloria Patri, dbl ch,
        1844), 19
    Elijah op. 70, 43, 85f, 90n, 91, 94–7, 137,
        193, 195n, 197f, 250, 254f
    Erste Walpurgisnach, Die, op. 60, 44, 65, 67,
        76–9, 89n, 219n, 250
    Fantasia, e, on "The Last Rose of
        Summer," op. 15, 241
    Fugue, e, pf (1827), 170
    "Garland, The" (T. Moore, 1829), 250–55

Hear My Prayer (*Hör mein Bitten*; 1844–7), 91f, 94, 100–105

Hebriden, Die, op. 26, 91, 161, 219n, 245 (2 pf)

Heimkehr aus der Fremde, Die, op. 89, 206, 238–9

Herr, gedenke nicht unsrer Übeltaten op. 79 no. 4, 19

Herr Gott, dich loben wir (German *Te Deum*, 1843), 15, 17

Herr Gott, du bist unsrer Zuflucht op. 79 no. 2, 16, 18

Hochzeit des Camacho, Dir Op. 10, 203f

Jesu, meine Freude (chorale cantata, 1828), 195n

Lieder ohne Worte (*Songs without Words*), 43, 57, 65, 99; *op. 19b*, 180n, 242–4; *op. 30*, 131, 165, 179; *op. 38*, 184n, 246; *op. 62*, 253

Loreley op. 98, 139

March, D, orch, *op. 108*, 165

Meeresstille und glückliche Fahrt (Calm Sea and Prosperous Voyage) Overture *op. 27*, 65, 67, 68–76, 78, 116, 149, 155–60, 207, 219n, 245 (2 pf)

Octet op. 20, 163, 204

Oedipus at Colonus (incidental music) *op. 93*, 43, 139, 140

O Haupt voll Blut und Wunden (chorale cantata, 1830), 195n

Organ Sonatas *op. 65*, 43, 91, 94, 97–100, 143, 195n, 196f, 240, 252

Ouvertüre zum Märchen der schönen Melusine op. 32, 173, 184

Overture, C, wind insts, *op. 24*, 242

Paulus (St. Paul) op. 36, 16, 17, 83, 94, 95, 96, 116, 128, 134, 137, 163, 173, 193, 195n, 224, 245, 246

Piano concerto No. 1, g, *op. 25*, 109, 219n, 244

Piano Concerto No. 2, d, *op. 40*, 43, 117f, 246

Piano Trio No. 1, d, *op. 49*, 40, 67, 248f

Piano Trio No. 2, c, *op. 66*, 65, 67, 195

Piano Quartet, b, *op. 3*, 109

Psalm 42 ("Wie der Hirsch schreit") *op. 42*, 21, 116, 245

Psalm 91 ("Denn er hat seine Engeln befohlen," 1844), 31

Psalm 95 ("Kommt, lasst uns anbeten") *op. 46*, 21, 141

Psalm 98 ("Singet dem Herrn ein neues Lied") *op. 91*, 16, 17, 21, 27n

Reiterlied, d, pf (1844), 165

Rondo brillant, pf, *op. 29*, 244

Rondo capriccioso, E, *op. 14*, 241

Scherzo a capriccio, f sharp, pf (1835), 242

Seemanns Scheidelied (1831), 43

Serenade and Allegro giojoso op. 43, 188

Sieben Charakterstücke op. 7, 40

Six Preludes and Fugues, pf, *op. 35*, 98, 162–99, 245

Six Songs *op. 19a*, 251f

Six Songs *op. 34*, 173

Six Songs *op. 47*, 251f

Six Songs *op. 57*, 251

Sommernachtstraum, Ein (*Midsummer Night's Dream*) (overture), *op. 21*, 67, 83, 136f, 149, 150ff, 158, 160, 204, 219n, 221, 241, 242

Sommernachtstraum, Ein (*Midsummer Night's Dream*) (incidental music), *op. 61*, 11, 83, 124, 136f, 234–5, 236

String Quartet, E flat, *op. 12*, 91

String Quartet, a, *op. 13*, 163

String Quartet, E flat, *op. 44/3*, 91n

String Quartet, f, *op. 80*, 65

String Quintet No. 1, A, *op. 18*, 163

String Quintet No. 2, B flat, *op. 87*, 139

Symphony No. 1, c, *op. 11*, 241 (arr. pf duet)

Symphony No. 2, B flat, *op. 52* (*Lobgesang*), 141, 246, 249

Symphony No. 3, a, *op. 56* ("Scottish"), 65, 83, 91, 135, 141, 161

Symphony No. 4, A, *op. 90* ("Italian"), 79, 91, 161, 242

Symphony No. 5, d, *op. 107* ("Reformation"), 43, 149, 154–5, 160, 195n, 219n

Te Deum, Morning Service (1832), 240, 254

Three Caprices, pf, *op. 33*, 173, 180

Three Preludes and Fugues, org, *op. 37*, 163, 180, 196, 199n

Three Psalms *op. 78* [Ps. 2, 43, 22], 31n, 137; Psalm 2, 17, 21–7, 27n; Psalm 43, 19, 21; Psalm 22, 19, 26–9

Three Preludes, pf, *op. 104a*, 175, 177

Three Studies, pf, *op. 104b*, 174, 188, 191

To The Evening Service (Lord Have Mercy Upon Us; 1833), 92, 255

To The Morning Service, 254, 255

Trois Fantasies ou caprices op. 16

Twelve Songs *op. 8*, 241, 251f

Twelve Songs *op. 9*, 251f

Um unsrer Sünden op. 79 no. 6 (dbl ch, 1844), 19

Variations, E flat, pf, *op. 82*, 34, 49

Variations, B flat, pf, *op. 83a*, 34, 188

Variations concertantes, D, vcl, pf, *op. 17*, 184n, 241

Variations on "Marche bohémienne" from C. M. von Weber's *Preciosa* [composed with I. Moscheles, published as Moscheles's *op. 87b*], 41f

Variations sérieuses op. 54, 33–63, 188, 192n

Viola Sonata, c (1824), 59f
Vom Himmel hoch (chorale cantata, 1831), 195n
Wer nur den lieben Gott läßt walten (chorale cantata, 1829), 195n
Wir glauben all an einen Gott (chorale cantata, 1831), 195n
Mendelssohn Bartholdy, Lea, 118, 132, 168, 174
Mendelssohn Bartholdy, Paul, 6n, 15n, 21, 110, 201
Metternich, Karl, 37, 129
Metzger, H.-K., 81
Meyerbeer, Giaccomo, 21n, 107, 123, 126, 144, 146f, 195n, 201, 237n; *Prophète, Le*, 165; *Robert le diable*, 237n
Milder-Hauptmann, Anna, 206, 219n
Monsigny, P. A., 163
Moore, Thomas, 37n, 250
Mori, N., 244, 245, 246
Moscheles, Charlotte, 201, 240
Moscheles, Ignaz, 34, 35, 37, 38, 41, 106, 107, 110, 115, 173, 186, 188, 240, 242f, 252
Mozart, Leopold, 138
Mozart, Wolfgang Amadeus, 37, 58n, 83n, 107, 144, 150, 152, 159, 171; *Dite almeno in che mancai K. 479*, 219n; *Don Giovanni*, 42n; *Mandina amabile K. 480*, 219n
Mühlenfels, L. von, 207
Müller, Wilhelm, 193

Nauenburg, G., 219n
Naumann, Emil, 21, 21n
Neithardt, August, 5, 14n, 21n, 23
Neukomm, Sigismund, 106
Nicolai, Otto, 21n, 30
Nietzsche, Friedrich, 125
Novalis, *see* Hardenberg, Friedrich von
Novello, Clara, 247, 248
Novello, J. A., 243, 245, 246, 247, 248, 249
Novello, Vincent, 243, 244, 254

Oakeley, E. M., 200
Onslow, Georges, 92, 162
Overbeck, J. F., 134

Palestrina, G. P. da, 1, 4, 32, 154
Pape, Matthias, 165n
Parish-Alvars, E., 186
Pearce, C. W., 80n, 97n
Perényi, Eleanor, 111, 124
Pillet, Leon, 135
Plantinga, Leon, 132n, 159n
Poliakov, L., 79n

Quantz, J. J., 138

Raabe, Peter, 113
Radcliffe, Philip, 80n, 100n
Rajan, Tilottama, 69n
Ranft, P., 81n
Ranke, Leopold von, 10n
Redern, Wilhelm von (Count), 5, 15n, 23, 31, 213, 215, 221
Reger, Max, 98
Reicha, Antoine, 106, 108, 162
Reimer, E., 96
Reissiger, C. C., 21n
Rellstab, L., 160f
Rheinberger, Joseph, 98
Riehn, R., 81n
Rietz, Eduard, 109, 205
Rietz, Julius, 205
Robert, Frederike, 43n
Robinson, J. Bradford, 33
Robinson, Joseph, 100n
Rockstro, W. S., 128, 129, 133
Rode, Pierre, 106, 107
Rosen, Charles, 44
Rossini, Giacchino, 106, 107, 136, 187n; *Stabat Mater*, 133f
Rubinstein, Anton, 124
Rummenhöller, Peter, 58
Rungenhagen, C. F., 218n

Saint-Saëns, Camille, 82
Schadow, W. von, 225–6
Schäffer, J., 138
Schätzel, Pauline, 206
Schering, A., 82n
Scheumann, A. R., 5n
Schiller, Friedrich von, 68, 159
Schlegel, A. W., 66
Schlegel, F., 158n
Schleinitz, C., 174
Schlesinger, A. M., 124, 241
Schlesinger, Maurice, 241, 242, 252n
Schneider, Maschinka, 219, 220
Schoenberg, Arnold, 60
Scholes, Percy A., 89n
Schorr, Daniel, 146
Schubart, C. F. D., 42n
Schubert, Franz Peter, 70, 128; Symphony No. 9, C (Great), 91, 116
Schubring, Julius, 95n, 192, 193, 199
Schünemann, G., 205n
Schuhmacher, G., 81n
Schulze, Hans-Joachim, 5n
Schumann, Clara (*née* Wieck), 110, 114, 117, 121, 174, 199, 201; Three Preludes and Fugues, pf, *op. 16*, 165
Schumann, Robert, 42n, 43, 65, 78, 93, 96, 111, 113–19, 121, 124, 129, 130, 131, 136, 138, 141, 147, 148, 164, 170, 180, 186, 187, 198, 199, 201; *Carnaval op. 9*,

117; Four Fugues, pedal pf, *op. 72*, 165; *Paradies und die Peri op. 50*, 91; Six Fugues on B-A-C-H, org, *op. 60*, 165, 179; *Szenen aus Geothe's Faust*, 145
Scribe, A. E., 135
Shaw, George Bernard, 65, 80n, 82–6, 88, 89, 91n, 92, 93, 105
Simrock, N., 242, 246
Smith, A. Brent, 80n
Smith, Marian, 149n
Solliers, Jean de, 135n
Souchay, Marc-André, 39, 217
Spitta, Philipp, 201, 202
Spohr, Ludwig (Louis), 23, 40, 57n, 225–6, 237
Spontini, G., 221
Stratton, S. S., 80n, 100n
Strauss, F. A., 10, 20
Stümer, H., 206

Tasso, T., 203
Taubert, Wilhelm, 6, 21n, 35, 37, 100, 203, 210–17, 225–6
Temperley, Nicholas, 206
Teschner, G. W., 209
Thalberg, Sigismund, 35, 37, 118f, 120, 186, 187, 189
Thomas, Max, 5n
Tieck, Ludwig, 135, 140
Todd, R. Larry, 39, 54, 151n
Tovey, D. F., 64, 76, 129, 130
Treitler, Leo, 136n
Truhn, F. H., 225–6
Türrschmiedt, Auguste, 206

Vermeulen, A. G. C., 236

Wagner, Cosima, 41n
Wagner, Richard, 40, 79, 105, 124, 129, 130, 138, 145f, 195n, 204, 234–5; *Parsifal*, 89
Walker, Alan, 113n, 122
Walthew, Richard, 131
Ward Jones, Peter, 5n, 187n
Wauer, Wilhelm, 137n, 140
Weber, C. M. von, 41, 42n, 122, 128, 219n, 237n; *Drei Pintos, Die*, 237n; *Grand duo concertant*, cl, pf, *op. 48*, 219n; *Konzertstück*, f, pf, orch, *op. 79*, 117; *Oberon*, 237n
Weber, Gottfried, 158n
Weber, William, 88
Wendt, J. A., 157
Werder, K., 234–5
Werner, Eric, 20n, 44, 81n, 89n, 95, 100n, 123, 124n, 127n, 151n, 152n
Werner, Jack, 79n, 90n, 95
Werner, Rudolf, 20n, 100n
Wessel, C. R., 252
Westrup, J. A., 82n, 89n
Wieck, Friedrich, 113n
Wilde, Oscar, 161
Williams, Peter F., 97n
Winkler, K. G. T., 237
Wittmann, Franz Carl, 40
Wolff, E., 100n, 216n

Zacher, G., 97n
Zelter, Carl Friedrich, 7, 10, 166, 192, 195, 205, 218n